New Frontiers

New Frontiers

Law and Society in the Roman World

Edited by Paul J. du Plessis

EDINBURGH
University Press

Acknowledgement

The editor wishes to thank Mr Benedikt Forschner who assisted in the editing of this work.

First published in hardback in 2013
This paperback edition 2014

Edinburgh University Press Ltd
The Tun – Holyrood Road
12 (2f) Jackson's Entry
Edinburgh EH8 8PJ
www.euppublishing.com

Typeset in 10/12pt Goudy Old Style by
Servis Filmsetting Ltd, Stockport, Cheshire.

A CIP record for this book is available from the British Library

ISBN 978 0 7486 6817 5 (hardback)
ISBN 978 0 7486 6820 5 (paperback)
ISBN 978 0 7486 6818 2 (webready PDF)
ISBN 978 0 7486 6819 9 (epub)

Contents

Contributors

Jean-Jacques Aubert is Professor of Classical Philology and Ancient History at the University of Neuchâtel.

Cynthia J. Bannon is Associate Professor in the Department of Classical Studies, University of Indiana (Bloomington).

Paul J. du Plessis is Senior Lecturer in the School of Law, University of Edinburgh.

Jill Harries is Professor of Ancient History at the University of St Andrews.

Joseph A. Howley is Assistant Professor in Latin Literature in the Department of Classics at Columbia University.

Caroline Humfress is Professor in the Department of History, Classics and Archaeology at the University of London, Birkbeck.

Éva Jakab is Professor of Roman Law in the Faculty of Law, University of Szeged.

Dennis P. Kehoe is the Andrew W. Mellon Professor of Humanities at Tulane University, New Orleans.

Saskia T. Roselaar is a Teaching Fellow in the Department of Classics at Reading University.

Jan Willem Tellegen is Senior Lecturer Emeritus in Roman Law and Jurisprudence at the University of Utrecht.

Olga Tellegen-Couperus is Associate Professor in the School of Law, Tilburg University.

Philip Thomas is Professor Emeritus of Roman Law in the Faculty of Law, University of Pretoria.

Jakub Urbanik is Associate Professor in the Taubenschlag Foundation in the Faculty of Law and Administration, Warsaw University.

Abbreviations

§	paragraph
a	anno
ap	apud
B	Basilica
BCE	Before the Common Era
BGU	Berliner Griechische Urkunden
c	circa
C	Codex Iustinianus
CE	the Common Era
ch.	chapter
Coll	Collatio Legum Mosaicarum et Romanarum
Const	Constitutio
cos	Consul
CTh	Codex Theodosianus
D.	Digest
DNP	Der Neue Pauly
Ep.	Epistula
FIRA	Fontes Iuris Romani Anteiustiniani
fn.	footnote
FV	Fragmenta Vaticana
ILS	Inscriptiones Latinae Selectae
Inst	The Institutes of Justinian
Inst.Gai.	The Institutes of Gaius
ll.	lines
no.	number
Nov.	Novellae
P. (Pap.)	Papyrus
PL	Patrologia Latina
pr	principium; prooemium
Pr	Preface
Ps	Pseudo
PSI	Papiri della società Italiana
Reg.	Regulae
SC	Senatus Consultum
TPSulp	Tabulae Pompeianae Sulpiciorum

All abbreviated references to authors from classical antiquity and their works follow the standard conventions in Lewis and Short's Latin Dictionary. All abbreviated references to ostraka and papyri follow the standard conventions in these disciplines.

Chapter 1

Introduction

Paul J. du Plessis

In the introduction to *Law and Life of Rome* (1967), John Crook described the aim of his book as follows:

> This is not quite a book about Roman law, on which there already exist any number of excellent treatises. Neither is it quite a book about Roman social and economic life; that subject, too, is already illuminated by massive works of scholarship. It is a book about Roman law in its social context, an attempt to strengthen the bridge between two spheres of discourse about ancient Rome by using the institutions of the law to enlarge understanding of the society and bringing the evidence of the social and economic facts to bear on the rule of law.[1]

As an ancient historian with a keen interest in Roman law, Crook must have been aware that he was courting controversy with this statement which essentially called for a broadening of disciplinary horizons and greater collaboration between both 'spheres of discourse'. Not only did this approach expect historians to take greater account of Roman law, but it also expected legal scholars to look beyond the then prevailing dogmatic approach to the study of Roman law practised by most.[2] It was perhaps owing to an awareness of the complexity of what Crook was advocating, since the crossing of disciplinary boundaries is never easy, that he took great care to explain what he meant by a 'law and society' approach to the study of Roman law. While Crook was undoubtedly influenced by contemporary debates in jurisprudence regarding the relationship between law and society, he was also aware that these debates had limited use in the study of ancient Rome.[3] The study of Roman law could not be subjected to a sociological enquiry in the contemporary sense, since too much of the empirical data required for such an enquiry was lacking.[4] Furthermore, as Crook pointed out, controversies

---

[1] Crook (1967), p. 7.

[2] For perspectives on the dogmatic methodology, see Ernst and Jakab (2005), p. v; Tuori (2006), p. 13.

[3] See Crook (1967), p. 7. On the purpose of a 'law and society' methodology in modern legal scholarship, see Cotterrell (2006), p. 5.

[4] Crook (1967), p. 9. See also Cotterrell (2006), pp. 17, 54; and Travers (2010), pp. 5–6, 9, 19 for a summary of the prerequisites of the modern sociological study of law.

surrounding the meaning of concepts such as 'Roman society', 'Roman law' and the fact that both law and society change with time also complicate matters.[5] Nevertheless, Crook maintained that since some relationship between law and society existed, it was possible to provide a broader context for Roman law using elements of social and economic history.[6]

> [L]aw is certainly some reflection of society (usually of its more conservative aspects, because of the law's function as a guarantor of stability), and not only a reflection, but also in some degree an influence upon it (usually a brake, providing only cautiously and tardily the mechanisms to fulfil the changing desires of society as a whole, but sometimes an accelerator, a tool in the hands of a particular section of the community such as an intelligentsia for achieving new ends that people in general do not actively want but will not positively oppose).[7]

It is not the aim of this introduction to engage once more with the critics of Crook's approach as this debate has been comprehensively explored recently elsewhere.[8] Studies such as those by Cairns and du Plessis have shown that Alan Watson's view on 'law and society' in the Roman world, sometimes cited as being in opposition to that of Crook, is in fact complementary and that new insights can be achieved, provided that scholars are sufficiently sensitive to the methods, perspectives and legitimacy of the conclusions of the other 'sphere of discourse'.[9]

Since the ground rules for interdisciplinary collaboration have now been established, further exploration of the emergent field of research relating to 'law and society' in the Roman world has become possible. This is what this book seeks to do. It is designed to be read as an integrated whole. The chapters have been grouped into three larger themes and within these, individual chapters have been arranged in a specific order to form a cumulative picture.

The first theme explored in this book, 'perspectives on Roman legal thought', addresses issues of Roman juristic writing and its contexts. The chapter by Howley, which introduces this theme, examines the place of Roman juristic writing within the broader context of Roman society using the work of Aulus Gellius as his example. By investigating the way in which Gellius used juristic writing when compiling his own works, Howley provides a fascinating external perspective on the way in which these works were perceived and utilised by the Roman educated classes at large. In doing so, Howley demonstrates that Roman juristic writing formed part of the broader intellectual culture of the Roman world and was used by the elite for

---

[5] Crook (1967), pp. 9–10.
[6] Crook (1967), p. 7; see also Treggiari (2002), p. 47.
[7] Crook (1967), p. 7.
[8] See Watson in Cairns and du Plessis (2007), pp. 9–23.
[9] See Sirks (2002), pp. 169–79; Aubert (2002), pp. 183–6; Cairns and du Plessis (2007), pp. 3–8. On the dangers of interdisciplinarity with reference to modern socio-legal scholarship, see Cotterrell (2006), p. 18.

a variety of different purposes, apart from merely as juristic authority. The theme is continued by Tellegen-Couperus and Tellegen on the relationship between law and rhetoric. Their elegant chapter explores the extent to which Roman juristic thought as recorded in the works of the jurists was doctrinal and thus removed from the demands of legal practice dominated by orators trained in rhetoric. The authors argue that the prevailing orthodoxy whereby Roman juristic thought is said to be removed from legal practice in the courts based on rhetoric is incorrect and should be abandoned in favour of a more integrated assessment whereby Roman juristic thought and rhetoric are seen as two sides of the same coin. The last chapter on this theme is that of Harries who, using a controversial senatorial decree relating to slavery as an example, argues in favour of a greater appreciation of the context in which law was created and developed and the interest groups which drove the enactment of a law.

The second theme, 'interactions between legal theory and legal practice', explores Roman law as a working 'legal order'. This theme is introduced by a fascinating chapter by Humfress in which she challenges the prevailing view about the universal application of Roman law in the Roman Empire post 212 CE. Using elements of an anthropological approach, Humfress argues that the notion of an Empire-wide 'legal system' imposed from above by the Roman state onto its people should be rejected in favour of a more nuanced, pluralist understanding of Roman law as a number of interconnected 'legal orders' in terms of which individuals had access to different legal solutions based on status and affiliations to local communities. In reaching this con-clusion, Humfress advocates that research in this area should not merely focus on the perceived 'gap' between legal theory and legal practice, but on the motivations of individuals for choosing to use one legal solution over another and the manner in which this informs modern understanding about the concept of an Empire-wide 'Roman law'.[10] This challenge is reflected in the remaining chapters on this theme in which three authors explore the relationship between legal theory and legal practice in three different periods of Roman society. The first of these, by Roselaar, is devoted to the notion of *conubium* and the legal significance of this concept in the early Roman Republic. Through a re-examination of the sources, Roselaar shows that *conubium* was an instrument that the Roman state employed strategically to secure allegiances in order to gain political supremacy on the Italian main-land. The second chapter explores the legal world of the Sulpicii archive with a view to assessing the role of women in commercial transactions. This chapter challenges the accepted view that women, owing to various legal restrictions and social conventions in Roman society, did not engage in commerce directly, but relied instead on (mostly male) relatives or business

---

[10] Humfress's chapter also ties in with recent advances in 'law and society' research in relation to 'community'; see Cotterrell (2006), pp. 62–9.

agents. From Jakab's analysis of the sources, it becomes clear that women engaged far more actively and fully (albeit sometimes indirectly on account of their status) in Roman commercial transactions, and that some of the legal impediments which appear to have inhibited their participation in commerce could be circumvented. The last chapter in this theme, by Urbanik, investigates the use of 'classical' Roman law in sixth-century Byzantine legal practice. Using the contract of pledge as an example, Urbanik assesses whether the legal needs of society were met by the existing law, and highlights certain creative legal solutions to new problems.

The last theme explored in this book is 'economic realities and law'. Three chapters examine the interplay between law and economic considerations in the context of the Roman world. Kehoe uses a 'law and economics' approach to investigate the law of agency. He argues that in developing the Roman law of agency, the jurists and the Imperial bureaucracy were aware of and driven by the economic implications of law. The remaining two chapters explore related issues. Aubert focuses on the liability of slave agents for debts incurred in relation to their *peculium* and argues that the legal rules in this area of law cannot be fully understood without an appreciation of the economic realities in which commercial transactions by a slave operated. Bannon's account of fixtures and fittings in relation to the sale of property demonstrates that the jurists were aware of the commercial reality of such sales and factored these into their legal thought.

The final chapter by Thomas is meant to provoke further thoughts on interdisciplinarity. Thomas explores a topical theme in modern historical scholarship, namely plurality of perspective, which has yet to make a significant impact on traditional Roman-law scholarship.[11] He argues that it is possible to look at Roman legal texts from different angles to appreciate the full complexity of their different layers of meaning. In a certain sense, Thomas's chapter represents the very essence of the approach of this book. When read as a whole, the themes explored in this book demonstrate that it is possible, to paraphrase John Crook, to ask 'new questions about Roman law'.[12] These are the new frontiers of 'law and society' in the Roman world.

BIBLIOGRAPHY

Aubert, J.-J. and Sirks, A. J. B. (eds), *Speculum Iuris: Roman Law as a Reflection of Social and Economic Life in Antiquity* (2002).
Cairns, J. W. and du Plessis, P. J. (eds), *Beyond Dogmatics: Law and Society in the Roman World* (2007).
Cotterrell, R., *Law, Culture and Society* (2006).

[11] For the effect of post-modernism on 'law and society' scholarship, see Cotterrell (2006), pp. 19–20, 62, 66; Travers (2010), pp. 144–8; Southgate (2001), pp. 61–2, pp. 115–16, 158.
[12] Crook (1996), pp. 31–6.

Crook, J. A., 'Legal history and general history', *BICS*, 41, 1996, p. 31.

Crook, J. A., *Law and Life of Rome: 90 B.C.–A.D. 212* (1967).

Ernst, W. and Jakab, E. (eds), *Usus Antiquus Iuris Romani* (2005).

Sarat, A. (ed.), *The Blackwell Companion to Law and Society* (2004).

Southgate, B., *History: What and Why?* 2nd edn (2001).

Travers, M., *Understanding Law and Society* (2010).

Treggiari, S., *Roman Social History* (2002).

Tuori, K., *Ancient Roman Lawyers and Modern Legal Ideals* (2006).

Part I

Perspectives on Roman Legal Thought

Chapter 2

Why Read the Jurists? Aulus Gellius on Reading Across Disciplines

Joseph A. Howley

1. INTRODUCTION

Aulus Gellius, the Antonine chronicler of his own and others' reading, knew a thing or two about the hazards of misjudging the contents of a book.[1] Among the books he describes reading in his *Noctes Atticae* are many works of Republican and early Imperial jurists, preserving fragments of them for modernity.[2] It is often assumed that his reading was connected to his occasional service as a judge, despite his lack of interest in reconciling his reading of older material with his own contemporary legal situation.[3] If we consider the *Noctes* as simply the product of scholarly efforts, then we are left to conclude that he finds jurists' work an interesting source of facts for his project. But the *Noctes* is a literary work with its own strategies, and so we might ask: how does Gellius, one of the most involved narrators of reading in the Roman empire and the only non-jurist author to discuss in such depth the reading of jurists, represent that reading and its relationship to the intellectual life of a learned member of the elite?

What I offer here is a brief tour of that material. I am interested not in the legal content of Gellius's juristic reading, or even the jurists themselves, but rather how he describes and represents the reading of them; I thus am interested here to interpret and characterise narrative technique rather than analyse legal substance. I take the *Noctes* as a strongly protreptic text: understanding its narration of its author's reading as a careful and intentional programme of self-representation (rather than mere documentary fact), designed to emphasise and prompt reflection on certain elements of an intellectual lifestyle, will allow us to take its use of narrative, rhetoric, and juxtaposition as a valuable illustration of an imperial Roman who was thinking and talking about his own mind. In short, if we let it, the *Noctes* can begin to help us situate juristic literature along more 'mainstream' disciplines on the intellectual landscape – or at least elite bookshelves – of Antonine Rome.

---

[1] E.g. *Noctes Atticae* 9.4, 14.6, 18.6 (*Noctes Atticae* is hereafter abbreviated to *N.A.*).

[2] For a tally, see Holford-Strevens (2003), pp. 298–9, in the course of a discussion with different interests than mine here.

[3] The assumption implicit at Frier (1985), p. 205 fn. 35; but see Holford-Strevens (2003), p. 31.

Jurists feature regularly in a kind of narrative moment important to Gellius's project: he turns towards an authority figure. I will examine the various questions that Gellius turns to a jurist to answer, and the other authorities who are present when a jurist has something to offer. Gellius frames encounters with juristic literature as an important part of learning about the *mos maiorum* and the language of the ancient Romans, carefully integrating jurists into enquiries alongside other kinds of authoritative source. He emphasises the studiousness and curiosity of good juristic writers which lead them to provide accounts of customs and words that can supplement or even supplant those of more commonly-encountered writers of *antiquitates*.[4] As he excludes juristic reading from his judicial duties, he also emphasises the broad range of other kinds of knowledge and literature whose authority can speak to questions that arise from actual legal experience.

The effect is twofold: we are reminded that when we answer legal questions, it is important to be well read, but we are also encouraged to make jurists part of our wide reading, for purposes that go well beyond the legal. Juristic knowledge, for Gellius, is both culturally mainstream in its antiquarian methodology, and uniquely complementary to the other genres and modes of books and enquiry available to the curious Roman intellectual.

2. GELLIUS AND DISCIPLINARY KNOWLEDGE

Adopting the proper attitude towards disciplinary expertise and knowledge concerns Gellius greatly. For many kinds of knowledge, Gellius weaves into the *Noctes Atticae* autobiographical reflections on formative experiences with those disciplines: tales of learning that kind of knowledge and learning about the nature of the discipline's experts. For example, he realises that *grammatici* cannot be trusted with innocent and earnest questions because they are often too rude and ignorant.[5] He also offers glimpses of the various steps of learning about the nature of authority, finding the rare good experts but also identifying their limits.[6] This gives the reader a framework in which to understand the text's contents as having been encountered and excerpted by a judicious author: we have met the bad experts and the good ones, we have learned what Gellius thinks is the right way to approach a topic, and so we have more confidence in (or have more specific questions for) his own researches on that topic. There are high ethical stakes for an individual's intentional decision to self-educate in a realm that has its own experts.

Gellius does not ever clearly articulate the turn toward juristic self-

---

[4] On jurists and antiquarians, see Harries (2006), pp. 176–7.

[5] *N.A.* 6.17 is the *locus classicus*. For a full analysis, see Vardi (2001).

[6] There is more on this below, but consider, e.g., *N.A.* 18.5, where the beloved rhetorician Antonius Julianus speaks '*erudite . . . et adfabiliter*', but the words are revealed not to be his own (18.5.12).

education (with the exception of *Noctes* 20.10, discussed below). However, an interesting and rare articulation of why a learned Roman might study the law can be found in Cicero's *De Oratore*.[7] There, part of Crassus's case for the orator having mastery of the law (1.166 ff) is that it can be easily mastered even by an amateur (1.191–2) because its basic principles are part of everyday life and practice; and, moreover, the study of law is pleasant and stimulating because of the various kinds of interests it satisfies:

> [. . .] plurima est et in omni iure civili et in pontificum libris et in XII tabulis antiquitatis effigies, quod et verborum vetustas prisca cognoscitur et actionum genera quaedam maiorum consuetudinem vitamque declarant.[8] (*De Oratore* 1.193)

> [. . .] there is in all the civil law and in the pontiff's books and in the Twelve Tables an immense portrait of antiquity, as the ancient antiquity of words is mastered and certain kinds of legal formula reveal the customs and lifestyles of the *maiores*.

Political science, institutions of state, the Twelve Tables themselves – all this knowledge is yielded by study of law, of more value to those interested in ethics than 'all the libraries of philosophers' (1.193–5). By framing Roman law as a uniquely Roman cultural property, Crassus makes the study of law (and realisation of Roman superiority to Greece) a patriotic act that also brings pleasure through the pictures it paints of ancient *mores*.[9]

Gellius makes a turn toward medical self-education that seems to echo these terms in important ways. As a youth in Athens staying at the country villa of Herodes Atticus (when and where, he tells us in his Preface, he began composing the *Noctes*),[10] he was taken ill (*Noctes* 18.10). A doctor comes to check on him and, in the presence of Gellius's teacher Taurus and various learned friends, gauchely mishandles the terms for veins and arteries (18.10.4–5), earning a careful rebuke from the philosopher Taurus (18.10.5–7).[11] This sickbed experience leads Gellius later to an epiphany (18.10.8): that it is shameful (*turpe*) not to know even those things about one's body (such as taking a pulse) which Nature has made clear and self-evident (*in promptu . . . in propatulo*). So he hunts up medical books and with a taste (*attigi*) of them he learns various such things relevant to the human condition (*humanitatis usu non aliena*).

Learning a little medicine helps one understand one's body, but what is – to Gellius – the value of studying law? Here the problem of disciplinary

---

[7] Known to Gellius, *N.A.* 1.15.17, 4.8.8.

[8] I omit the disputed beginning of the sentence, a comparison to *Aeliana studia*, which refers either to early grammatical and antiquarian writing (by way of Varro's and Cicero's teacher L. Aelius Stilo Praeconinus, *Brutus*, pp. 205–7) or the early jurist Sextus Aelius Paetus Catus. For the controversy, see Leeman and Pinkster (1981), pp. 100–1.

[9] On the Twelve Tables as common Roman property, see Harries (2006), p. 171.

[10] *N.A.* Pr. 4.

[11] 18.10 also arrogates the intimacy and affection of Taurus seen in 12.5.

authority is central: as Crassus says, law not only touches on all aspects of life, but its practice can involve a variety of methodologies. Law's utility is in fact so ubiquitous that Gellius uses it to identify the limits of other disciplines' authority: so, in 12.13, Gellius recalls when as a young man, having been appointed *iudex*, he has a question about the terms of legal procedure and takes it to his preferred *grammaticus*, Sulpicius Apollinaris. This is the story of learning that a beloved teacher does not know everything, and that one's own questions may not be properly formed: Gellius recalls asking what he knows now to be a silly question about what it means that he must rule *intra Kalendas*.[12] Apollinaris demands to know why he has not taken a procedural question to the usual *periti studiosique iuris* (12.13.2). Gellius responds that he would consult a jurist for the interpretation of a law, but his question here is simply about a word (12.13.3–4). Apollinaris assents, but makes Gellius promise not to actually use this grammatical answer in his duty as *iudex*, seeing how language is as susceptible to the depradations of usage as law is to obsolescence (12.13.5). And when Apollinaris finally explains the word *intra*, Gellius reveals he has challenges prepared to counter this interpretation (12.13.17). Apollinaris responds with a smile and a counter-argument, enjoying the repartee.[13] Gellius here models the sort of sophisticated, friendly and well-informed conversation that one should aspire to have with a truly qualified *grammaticus*; but he also shows himself having found the actual limit to his teacher's knowledge in this matter:

> haec tunc Apollinaris scite acuteque dicere visus est. Set postea in libro M. Tullii epistularum ad Servium Sulpicium sic dictum esse invenimus [. . .] (12.13.20–1)

> At that time, Apollinaris seemed to have said these things knowledgeably and acutely. But later I found the word used thus in a book of *Letters of Marcus Tullius to Servius Sulpicius* [. . .]

Gellius is always keen to appeal to Cicero, and it is only fitting that he is reading Cicero's correspondence with a jurist friend.[14] But he is also making explicit to the reader his discovery of Apollinaris's limitations in this matter, and we might read it as Gellius's 'graduation' from his devotion to grammatical studies when he finds that his teacher (1) does not have all the answers and (2) cannot offer answers directly relevant to Gellius's professional needs. And this revelation about the apparently *scite acuteque* speech of the teacher comes as a result of later, independent reading on Gellius's part.[15]

The tension played out in this passage about the boundaries of utility and

---

[12] Holford-Strevens (2003), pp. 85–6, with fn. 30.

[13] 12.13.19: *Tunc Sulpicius Apollinaris renidens: 'non me hercule inargute' inquit 'nec incallide opposuisti hoc [. . .].'* Cf. Keulen (2009), p. 75.

[14] Gellius may know these letters well, given the general resemblance in premise between *N.A.* 2.21 and Cic. *Fam.* 4.5.

[15] As it does in *N.A.* 18.5.12.

relevance between different disciplines is inherent to the nature of ancient disciplinary thinking. Gellius establishes a clear rivalry between the experts with a natural claim to a question by virtue of their title (*iuris periti* versus *grammatici*), but also points out the possibility of reading begun for one reason yielding an answer relevant to something else entirely. One's private intellectual lifestyle is thus a place of active synthesis, in which wide reading and enquiry has unexpected rewards. And as Gellius turned to a *grammaticus* to help with the law, so he regularly finds that turning to the law helps with other things, including grammar.

A hallmark of Gellius's regular forays into 'archaic' and Republican literature is the frequent consultation of grammatical commentaries for assistance with the difficulties that old language presents.[16] He represents an instinctive turn toward such commentaries with questions arise in reading, but also regular disappointment with them: so in 17.6 a group encounters an obscure phrase in a speech by Cato and immediately calls for the obvious commentary (17.6.2: *libri statim quaesiti allatique sunt Verrii Flacci de obscuris Catonis*). But Gellius rejects Flaccus's answer and instead reports his own better one: so a story that relates a fact (the meaning of the phrase in question) also plays out a lesson about how such facts are found.

In a similar encounter, in *Noctes* 20.2, when the grammarian fails, it is not Gellius but the Republican jurist Ateius Capito who comes to the rescue. There, three words (*siticines, liticines, tubicines*) from a speech of Cato's prompt confusion (20.2.1). Caesellius Vindex's *Commentarii Lectionum Antiquarum* yields definitions of the latter two – *lituus*- and *tuba*-players, respectively – but Vindex, a regular target of Gellius, throws up his hands for the first.

> nos autem in Capitonis Atei Coniectaneis invenimus 'siticines' appellatos, qui apud sitos canere soliti essent, hoc est vita functos et sepultos, eosque habuisse proprium genus tubae, qua canerent, a ceterorum tubicinum differens. (20.2.3)

> However, I found, in the *Miscellanies* of Ateius Capito, that those are called *siticines* who customarily played in the presence of the 'stored' (*siti*), that is, the dead and entombed, and that they had a special kind of *tuba*, on which they played, differing from that of the rest of the *tubicines*.

Following Gellius's scepticism about *grammatici* to its margins, then, has taken us over into the land of the jurists. Reasoning simplistically has led Vindex to a dead end, but Capito brings knowledge of ancient custom to bear on the problem and finds the answer: the bad grammarian knows only how to disassemble and reassemble words, but the good jurist knows far more than law, a clear contrast between those who restrict themselves to

---

[16] On Gellius and archaism, see generally Marache (1952); Vessey (1994). For Gellius on archaism and obscurity, see 1.10, 11.7.

disciplinary boundaries and those who are truly learned (and happen to specialise or direct that learning toward a particular end). Jurisprudence, with its unique interests, has emerged to fill the cracks in another discipline's expertise, and the reading of juristic literature provides knowledge one might not otherwise come across. To the elite gentleman who spends his *otium* on intellectual efforts, the jurists would seem to have something to offer.

3. GELLIUS READS JURISTS

The main authoritative role which Gellius assigns to juristic authors (and legal primary texts) is not the answering of legal questions. My discussion here will focus on what kinds of questions the juristic texts seem to solve – that is, not why Gellius tells us he is reading them (for he rarely, if ever, does), but to what benefit of *having read them* he is drawing our attention by setting them in the context he does.

A jurist's analysis of a word may be cited as one among several competing explanations for Gellius. So *Noctes* 6.4 is a short piece on why captives for sale as slaves are said to be *sub corona*, and it opens with a citation of Caelius Sabinus on the use of headgear to distinguish slaves for sale; explaining which ones wear *pilleati* and which *sub corona* (6.4.1–3). 'However,' says Gellius, 'there is another reason', and he supplies a competing but unsourced theory (6.4.4). Then, as often, he passes judgment on the two, the evidence supporting Caelius's explanation being a rhetorical usage of the term by Cato in his work *de Re Militari* (6.4.5). Gellius combines juristic thought, common opinion, and archaic literary evidence to come to an authoritative answer. Similarly, Masurius Sabinus's etymology of *religiosus* (from his *Commentarii de Indigenis*) is just one of many pieces of evidence consulted in Gellius's lengthy exploration of that word, prompted by a line of verse quoted without citation by Nigidius Figulus (4.9.8–9). The jurist here is an effective antiquarian etymologist.[17]

The turn to authority with which Gellius is concerned is often based on assumptions about who will know what, and more often than not is explicitly depicted in part because it was misguided. So in 10.20 he attempts to answer a common question:

> quaeri audio, quid 'lex' sit, quid 'plebiscitum', quid 'rogatio', quid 'privilegium'. Ateius Capito, publici privatique iuris peritissimus, quid 'lex' esset, hisce verbis definivit: [. . .] (10.20.1–2)

> I hear it asked what a *lex* is, and what a *plebiscitum* is, and what a *rogatio* is, and what a *privilegium* is. Ateius Capito, a man most learned in public and private law, defines what a *lex* is with these very words: [. . .]

---

[17] For another comparison, see the anonymous *Commentarii ad Ius Pontificum Pertinentes* that offer an account of *bidentes* in 16.6.13.

This seems to sketch an assumption by Gellius that an answer would be found in this qualified juristic source. But if Capito's definition is true, then the various legislative documents that survive from the Republic are misnamed (10.20.3), which allows an excursus that requires Gellius to quote some Lucilius (10.20.4), after which we return to Capito and his rationale for *plebiscitum* (10.20.5–6) – and only then can Gellius explain, on his own authority, that it all comes down to *rogatio* because the people are *rogatur* their opinion (10.20.7). But, Gellius observes, the usage one encounters fails to respect any of this careful distinction (10.20.9).

> Sallustius quoque proprietatum in verbis retinentissimus consuetudini conces-
> sit et privilegium, quod de Cn. Pompei reditu ferebatur, 'legem' appellavit.
> (10.20.9–10)

> Even Sallust, the most observant of correctness in speech, yielded to custom and
> called the *privilegium* which was passed about the return of Cn. Pompey a *lex*.

There follows the relevant quotation from Sallust. Where does this whole discussion leave us? What is the answer to the question Gellius was hearing about the difference between the terms? This encounter with Capito's grammatical authority thus casts juristic reading, or rather the knowledge to be gained therefrom, as a kind of bonus to the usual literary canon of Republican speeches and histories. It is neither incorrect nor irrelevant; indeed, it is both exceptionally authoritative and off the beaten path.

Although juristic interest in language is an obvious element of their prac-
tice, Gellius makes a special effort to identify a jurist whose legal expertise is augmented by his researches into language. *Noctes* 13.10, which provides etymolgies of *soror* by Antistius Labeo and of *frater* by Nigidius Figulus, introduces the former thus:

> Labeo Antistius iuris quidem civilis disciplinam principali studio exercuit et con-
> sulentibus de iure publice responsitavit; set ceterarum quoque bonarum artium
> non expers fuit et in grammaticam sese atque dialecticam litterasque antiquiores
> altioresque penetraverat Latinarumque vocum origines rationesque percalluerat
> eaque praecipue scientia ad enodandos plerosque iuris laqueos utebatur. sunt
> adeo libri post mortem eius editi, qui posteriores inscribuntur, quorum librorum
> tres continui, tricesimus octavus et tricesimus nonus et quadragesimus, pleni sunt
> id genus rerum ad enarrandam et inlustrandam linguam Latinam conducentium.
> praeterea in libris, quos ad Praetoris edictum scripsit, multa posuit pariter lepide
> atque argute reperta. sicuti hoc est [. . .] (13.10.1)

> Antistius Labeo cultivated the discipline of the *ius civile* with especial zeal and
> gave *responsa* to those who consulted him about the *ius publicum*; but he was
> not without experience of indeed the rest of the fine arts, and he delved deeply
> into dialectic and older and more remote literature and became well versed in
> the origins and derivations of Latin words, and he applied this especially to the

unknotting of many tough points of law. Indeed, there are books of his published after his death, which are called *Posteriores*, of which three continuous volumes – the thirty-eight, thirty-ninth and fortieth – are full of that kind of material that tends to explain and shed light on the Latin language. And in addition to that, he has included in his books that he wrote *On The Praetorian Edict* many things he has figured out finely and cleverly. Such a one is this: [. . .]

In this passage – itself longer than both etymologies it introduces (13.10.3–4) – Gellius gives a clear rationale for the wide and careful reading of juristic literature, reminding the reader of the grammatical knowledge it can provide.[18] Gellius honours Labeo in that sphere by here giving him a sibling role to Nigidius Figulus, a scholar himself the equal of Varro.[19] Labeo was not only a legal expert, but made a special point of seeking grammatical knowledge he could apply productively to the law. Gellius explains that it is not only his obviously language-related works that have something to offer in this regard, but that indeed a grammatically learned jurist will leave traces of that learning in everything he writes. The best jurists, in Gellius's view, are learned in language too, and so authority on matters of grammar is not a matter of one's professed title (to the contrary, this is often the problem with his *grammatici*). It is instead a matter of what interests, learning and skills one has actually mastered, and grammar, we are reminded, falls into that category for a good (to Gellius) jurist. So, when we consider a word of the sort that everyone uses without knowing exactly what it means, we might quite sensibly turn to a jurist, even if we end up listening to Sulpicius Apollinaris cite Lucretius, Lucilius and Virgil for a fuller account of its *ratio*.[20] When a word is under examination, those who have read their jurists will have something extra to contribute.

Similarly, the jurists' necessary interest in the *mos maiorum* makes their generous intersection with 'antiquarianism' unsurprising. Gellius understands jurists to be a useful source of such knowledge about the customs and institutions of Romans and, as with grammar, he intentionally inserts them into the interrogation of such topics so as to highlight their utility in that regard.

Gellius cannot resist a good *exemplum*. He cherishes stories about impressive words and deeds, stories well told, and even competing versions of the same story.[21] In *Noctes* 4.20 Gellius has gathered three examples of the

---

[18] Intrinsic to the nature of their work and a common juristic activity; see, for example, the collected definitions at D.50.16.

[19] N.A. 4.9.1: *Nigidius Figulus, homo, ut ego arbitror, iuxta M. Varronem doctissimus [. . .]*. Cf. 19.14.

[20] N.A. 16.5 turns first to Gaius Aelius Gallus, *On the meaning of Words Which Pertain to the Ius Civile* for a meaning of *vestibulum* that accords with the choice *ratio* Gellius recalls hearing from Sulpicius Apollinaris.

[21] For example, 4.18 or 9.13. N.A. 10.27 offers two versions of a story we are likely to know from Liv. *Hist.* 21.18, that of the Roman emissary offering 'peace' or 'war' to the Carthaginian senate, but it also appears – ascribed to a different figure entirely – in Pomponius, D.1.2.2.37 (Pompon. 1 Enchirid.), attesting perhaps to its currency at the time of Gellius's writing.

traditional severity of the censors.[22] The first two are introduced without source, but Gellius admits at the end that he has taken them from a speech of Scipio (4.20.10). For the third, he turns to the first-century CE jurist Masurius Sabinus (4.20.11).[23] Here again he models explicitly the added wealth of knowledge that comes from reading not just the classic works of oratory but also volumes of juristic scholarship.

Thematic collections of material in juristic works can offer the backbone for a Gellian enquiry. The piece Gellius offers 'on old-time frugality, and on ancient sumptuary laws' (*cap.* 2.24) in fact uses the latter as a way of exploring the former; and the synthetic application of juristic reading to antiquarian enquiry is also framed by explicit gestures on Gellius's part to his own habits of reading and writing, emphasising the performance for his reader of an intellectual activity. Montaigne-like, he opens by asserting a premise about the *mos maiorum*, and then offers an example to support it:

> parsimonia apud veteres Romanos et victus atque cenarum tenuitas non domestica solum observatione ac disciplina, sed publica quoque animadversione legumque complurium sanctionibus custodita est. legi adeo nuper in Capitonis Atei coniectaneis senatus decretum vetus C. Fannio et M. Valerio Messala consulibus factum [. . .]. (2.24.1–2)

> Among the ancient Romans, frugality and simpleness of nourishment and meals was observed not only by domestic observation and discipline but also by public censure and the restrictions of many laws. In fact, I recently read in the *Miscellany* of Ateius Capito that in the consulships of Gaius Fannius and Marcus Valerius Messala an old decree of the Senate was made that [. . .]

Capito has cited senatorial decrees, and Gellius picks up this research technique, citing six more (2.24.3–14) which he may well have by way of Capito but which he re-articulates to suit his discussion, injecting a claim to additional autopsy research (2.24.12). He also intersperses snippets of verse from his usual stable of archaic poetic readings: Lucilius on the Fannian law in 2.24.4–6, with a pause to engage rival commentators on the poet, and Laevius and Lucilius both on the Licinian law in 2.24.8–10. Not until the end does Ateius Capito re-emerge.

> esse etiam dicit Capito Ateius edictum, divine Augusti an Tiberii Caesaris non satis commemini; quo edicto [. . .] (2.24.15)

> Ateius Capito also says that there is an edict, whether it was of the deified Augustus or the deified Tiberius, I don't rightly remember; by this edict [. . .]

Gellius creates a sense of collaboration with Capito, seeming to follow the general outline of his discussion but laying at least verbal claim to it and

---

[22] Cf. Holford-Strevens (2003), p. 315.
[23] Harries (2006), p. 88.

adding a by-now recognisable literary body of evidence to the legal. He also uses the device of incomplete recollection to direct the reader's attention to the text in question. Elsewhere, we are tantalised by the content of the story of Papirius Praetextatus to seek out Cato's rendering of it that so caught Gellius's eye (1.23.1–3), and to seek out the answer (which Gellius knows Aristotle will have) to a disagreement between Herodotus and Homer (13.7). *Noctes* 2.24 is, by the same token, both a use of juristic reading and a *depiction* of that reading and use. Gellius invites us into his compositional process to show how a jurist's discussion provides insight into the *mos maiorum* when combined with fashionably archaic literature, and leaves just enough unfinished to point the way to further enquiry.

Gellius hangs several discussions of Roman religious institutions on writers on pontifical law (not properly jurists, but operating analogously as far as the antiquarian aspects of their expertise go) as well as the occasional primary text, larding them often with these gestures of active research and judgment that foreground both the industry of his own approach and its viability as an option for his audience. *Noctes* 13.14 cites anonymous augural authors *de Auspicis* (13.14.1), M. Valerius Messala (13.14.5), and a juicy titbit of the recently-read grammarian 'Elys' (13.14.7: *praetermittendum non putavi, quod non pridem ego in Elydis, grammatici veteris, commentario offendi* [. . .])[24] for the nature and history of the *pomerium*, all of which is framed as a matter of long and current debate (13.14.4). Messala continues to be the source for the next few pieces, offering a lengthy and well-sourced explanation of the *magistratus minores* (13.15) and their relationship to the consul as regards the holding of *contiones* (13.16), and Gellius lets the jurist speak for him:

> quaeri igitur solet, qui sint magistratus minores. super hac re meis verbis nil opus fuit, quoniam liber M. Messalae auguris de auspiciis primus, cum hoc scriberemus, forte adfuit. (13.15.2–3)

> So, it is often asked who the *magistratus minores* are. On this subject there's no need for my words, since the first book of M. Messala the augur *On Auspices* happens to be right here as I am writing this.

In a similar vein, on the *flamen Dialis*, Gellius offers pointers to some primary sources and then relates material limited, he reminds us, by his own powers of recollection (10.15.2: *unde haec ferme sunt, quae commeminimus*). That collection of facts is capped with language from the praetor's edict (10.15.31) and Varro's *Divine Antiquities* (10.15.32). Meanwhile, *Noctes* 7.7, on Acca Larentia, gathers *antiqui annales* (7.7.1), the *lex Horatia* (7.7.2), the Twelve Tables (7.7.3), and historians (7.7.6: Valerias Antias, inter alios); Masurius Sabinus (7.7.8), who has the last word, is quoted verbatim at length, and –

---

[24] Holford-Strevens (2003), p. 163 observes something is wrong with Elys's name.

we are told – has consulted actual historians himself on the matter (*secutus quosdam historiae scriptores*).

Perhaps the best example of the way Gellius stages an active and productive enquiry to which jurists contribute is 1.12, on the taking (*cepi*) of vestal virgins. Gellius starts by citing various authors on the topic, 'of whom Antistius Labeo wrote most diligently' (1.12.1). Then Ateius Capito is invoked (1.12.8), and again Capito seems to bring with him legal primary texts (here, an uncited *lex Papia*). At 1.12.13 Gellius pivots around the word *cepi* and pursues that linguistic question, involving, in short order, Fabius Pictor (1.12.14), the autobiography of Sulla (1.12.16), and a *bon mot* of Cato (1.12.17), culminating in quotation from Labeo *ad XII Tabulas* (1.12.18–19).

Discussions of old civic procedure likewise involve juristic writing. Gellius in 15.27 epitomises a survey of kinds of *comitia* from Book 1 of Laelius Felix's *ad Q. Mucium*, which itself quotes Labeo. Varro's monologue on senate procedure is challenged by something Ateius Capito says that Tubero said (14.7.12–13); but Capito and Varro are found in 14.8 to join ranks *contra* Junius on the praefect of the Latin festival. Another discussion of senatorial procedure at the end of the Republic seems like it will turn to Tullius Tiro for Cicero's account second-hand, but Tiro is surpassed by Capito, who offers the same information alongside other material of interest (4.10.6–8).

Opinions on the civil law are persistently useful. Tackling the delineation between one day and the next, Gellius turns at first to Varro's *Human Antiquities*, considering Roman custom, Athenian custom, and what can be gleaned from the Roman taking of auspices at night (3.2.1–11). But Gellius then introduces, second-hand, an opinion of Q. Mucius concerning emancipation that allows Gellius to conclude Mucius's opinion about the question at hand (3.2.12–13). *Noctes* 4.3 and 4.4, on the history of divorce and betrothal in Italy, starts out with what is *memoriae traditum* (4.3.1) but then turns to Servius Sulpicius *de Dotibus*, on which both pieces depend heavily (the latter being confirmed in its account by Neratius *de Nuptiis*, 4.4.4).[25] Such writings also offer evidence of the general severity of the *veteres Romani*: *Noctes* 6.15 needs to relate Labeo's observation on the cruelty of old-time judgments (6.15.1) to contextualise Q. Mucius's opinion in Book 16 *de Iure Civili* that improper use of a loaned item constitutes theft (6.15.2). Ateius Capito, meanwhile, offers us in his *Commentarii de Iudiciis Publiciis* a juicy *exemplum* of the plebeian *aediles'* punishment of arrogant speech (10.16).

Juristic observations and facts are extricated thoroughly from whatever discussion they originally appeared in, and are interpreted and synthesised by Gellius with other material to yield observations about the *mos maiorum*.

---

[25] For this sort of enquiry, compare the not-quite-antiquarian discussion in 5.19 of adoption procedure, in which no jurist or indeed any authority is cited until 5.19.11. On Servius as antiquarian, see Harries (2006), p. 84, and on Gellius's use of Servius, see Harries (2006), pp. 85–90 (and on adoption, pp. 153–5).

Gellius demonstrates two ideas to his reader simultaneously: that he read juristic writing and it prompted a wider-ranging enquiry into some aspect of the *mos maiorum*, and that, pursuing an enquiry (for whatever reason) into some *mos maiorum*, Gellius turned to jurists and found they yielded thorough and learned material.

Perhaps the most interesting appearance of juristic reading in an anti-quarian or grammatical enquiry (and we should note that Gellius rarely distinguishes between the two except in refutation of the latter) comes on an occasion when it serves to elucidate a word the meaning of which is of critical programmatic importance to the *Noctes Atticae* itself. *Noctes* 4.1 is the much-discussed *penus* episode, a discussion of this word for provisions or a store of food that pits a philosopher against a grammarian. Favorinus casually exposes a boastful *grammaticus* who knows the various declensions and genders of the noun (4.1.1–4) but, when faced with a challenge to define it (4.1.5), sputters and flails about with examples but not definitions (4.7–14). Having shown up the man's intellectual limitations, Favorinus shares various competing definitions he has found in juristic reading (4.15–18). After an explanation of Favorinus's socratic mode (4.19), Gellius offers some further juristic writing (4.20–3) to emphasise that, indeed, jurists over the years have been unable to reach a consensus on the word's meaning.

The scene offers an important paradigm for the Gellian exposure of a fraudulent professor, focusing on the *grammaticus*'s rudeness and elucidat-ing the exact nature of his intellectual flaws.[26] There is the genital pun that is suspiciously aptly fitted to Favorinus's infamous sexual ambiguity.[27] And, perhaps most critically, there is its confrontation of the 'axial' term *penus*, which can only recall Gellius's own preface.[28] Near where our text of the Preface picks up, Gellius, describing his compositional method, explains that whenever he saw or heard something worthy of memory in either lan-guage, he made a note of it and stored these things up 'as a reinforcement to memory, like a certain *penus* of letters' (Pr. 2: *quasi quoddam litterarum penus recondebam*). The Preface goes on to emphasise that material in the *Noctes* is meant to be useful, a stimulation to further study, and also to invite careful scrutiny and reevaluation;[29] so in 4.1 we are in the presence of something critically important to Gellius's intellectual value set.

Favorinus's speech here is Gellius's; he too reads his Scaevola second-hand (4.1.16; cf. 3.2), and at the close of the speech Gellius immediately chimes in with more of the kinds of things Favorinus was quoting (4.1.20).[30]

---

[26] Holford-Strevens (2003), pp. 1213–14.
[27] Keulen (2009), pp. 87–94.
[28] Gunderson (2009), pp. 75–7.
[29] Pr. 14–18.
[30] For this, cf. 2.22.30, where Gellius refers to Favorinus's speech as his own, or 14.1, where the pretense of modestly reporting a Favorine speech cannot withstand Gellius's ambition for *aemulatio*.

It is not uncommon for Favorinus to serve as a Gellian mouthpiece.[31] Here he preaches the Gellian gospel of juristic reading for better Latinity and better *Romanitas*; he concludes thus his report of what he has 'heard' Scaevola used to say:

> 'haec ego,' inquit 'cum philosophiae me dedissem, non insuper tamen habui discere; quoniam civibus Romanis Latine loquentibus rem non suo vocabulo demonstrare non minus turpe est, quam hominem non suo nomine appellare'. (4.1.18)

> 'Although I am a philosopher,' he said, 'nevertheless I did not think it beneath me to learn these things; for it is no less shameful for a Latin-speaking Roman citizen to indicate something by a word that is not its proper name than to call a man by something other than his name'.

Favorinus attaches to proper speech the same ethical value (*turpe*) that Gellius attached to knowledge of readily apparent medical phenomena (see section 2 above), with the nationalistic twist of Cicero's Crassus.[32]

But as we zero in on a meaning of *penus*, we also explore an important programmatic aspect of the *Noctes*. We have been pointed at the idea that the *penus* contains goods and materials set aside for household use (4.1.17–13). This makes Gellius's claim that his work is a *penus* into a forceful confrontation of traditional fiscal language around knowledge; his predecessor and regular target for attack as a knowledge-glutton, Pliny the Elder, assigns *thesaurus* the analogous role in his own *Naturalis Historia*, and in spite of that term's long history as the name for a personal store of knowledge, Gellius, by offering the dynamic *penus* as contrast, renders the *thesaurus* a static hoard.[33] The *penus*, full of things useful and productive, placed there for a purpose, goes some way to making Gellius's unsystematic disorder an anti-encyclopedic claim for the idiosyncrasy and engagement of the intellectual lifestyle. And Favorinus's explanation of what he learned from the jurists – that there is no agreed-on definition of the word, even among such wise men – makes the stocking of a *penus* a process of constant re-evaluation. Does this belong? Does that?

The *penus* episode is a clear example of knowledge (the meaning of *penus*) being put into action (to prove a point about *grammatici*) in service of a programmatic argument about actionable knowledge; and in all of this, it relies heavily on juristic reading. Gellius has given juristic reading and what it can offer those with an interest in language a starring role in the *Noctes*'s

---

[31] For example, the moral of 11.7 about excessive archaism is also put forth, with more flair, by Favorinus in 1.10.

[32] Cf. Swain (2004), pp. 32–3.

[33] Plin. *H.N.* Pr. 17 (cf. 22). See especially *N.A.* 9.4 and 10.27 for (unfair) attacks on Pliny. Cic. *De Or.* 1.18 also invokes the *thesaurus* ideal, but cf. Quint. *Inst.* 10.1.2 for its negative side. On finance and wealth in Pliny, see Murphy (2003); Lao (2011).

treatment of authority as well as its self-awareness about intellectual activity and standards.

The kinds of questions Gellius invokes jurists to answer and the other kinds of sources to which he compares them situate them strongly in the interlinked realms of antiquarian and grammar. One juristic source can provide various facts and contribute to the examination of divergent topics, as the same volume of Masurius Sabinus has the last word in both the *penus* episode of 4.1 and the comparison of *morbus* and *vitium* in 4.2.[34] At *Noctes* 11.18, a survey of the punishment of theft throughout history, Gellius pauses in his (rare) exegesis of modern law to endorse a juristic work:[35]

> sed quod sit 'oblatum', quod 'conceptum' et pleraque alia ad eam rem ex egregiis veterum moribus accepta neque inutilia cognitu neque iniucunda, qui legere volet, inveniet Sabini librum, cui titulus est de furtis. in quo id quoque scriptum est, quod volgo inopinatum est [. . .] (11.18.12–13)

> But anyone who wants to read about what *oblatum* is, and what *conceptum* is, and many other things along these lines excerpted from the outstanding *mores* of the ancients, neither useless nor unpleasant to learn, will look up the book of Sabinus's which is titled *de Furtis*. Also written there is this thing, which is surprising to most people [. . .]

To set oneself and one's speech and one's learning apart from the *vulgus* is a recurring concern in the *Noctes*. The message from Gellius's use of juristic reading is clear: the best jurists have been diligent scholars of language and custom, and so to read their works is to learn things about those topics that might not be available elsewhere. The primary documents of Roman law are also documents of law and custom and so worthy of attention in their own right.[36] What one finds in reading about the history of the law, then, is clear depictions of the customs and language of the past.

4. GELLIUS CONSIDERS LEGAL QUESTIONS

Gellius shows himself reading jurists to learn about various topics, mostly antiquarian, but not to resolve specific legal questions. In a neat corollary, problems that do arise from discrete legal encounters are often answered with knowledge from these other spheres. The use of grammatical, philosophical and even antiquarian expertise to resolve legal questions illustrates Gellius's commitment to the diverse intellectual life and sheds some light on the place assigned to juristic learning.

We have seen that the kind of legal study that returns to the Twelve

[34] For the latter, cf. D.21.1.1–12 (Ulpian. 1 ad Ed. Aed. Cur.).
[35] But note Holford-Strevens (2003), p. 299, and Stevenson (2004), p. 154.
[36] Consider 15.13.11, 2.15, and especially 11.17.

Tables and their original language provides a useful frame of reference for the mastery of archaic language. Correspondingly, Gellius finds that the grammatical approach helps to elucidate technical language. Why is it called a *divinatio*? Gavius Bassus, *On the Origin of Words* tells us (2.4). How is *ususcapio* pronounced and formed? Reason by analogy to Cato's account of *pignoriscapio* (6.10). Does the future perfect in a law refer to the past or future? Not even the great jurists of the Republic could agree, as Nigidius Figulus will explain (17.7). And just think – in the courtroom as well as in the street, people use *superesse* to incorrectly refer to legal representation (1.22.1–2); advocates fail to speak *integre*, having not read their Varro, and so open themselves up to punning humiliation by a more learned judge (1.22.3–6). Courtroom speech should be informed by thorough grammatical knowledge.[37] So those whose *negotium* takes them into the courtroom would do well to spend their *otium* as Gellius does, walking in the evening and quietly reflecting on questions which seem minor but in fact have great significance for understanding of the Latin tongue (11.3.1), such as the meanings of *pro*.[38]

Rightly or not, Gellius often makes the turn to philosophy for questions that arise from law. This is not just because logical flaws should be avoided in argument (5.10, 9.15), but because legal rulings have ethical dimensions: among the initial essays that gesture to values integral to the whole project (*Noctes* 1.1's nod to Plutarch and the utility of knowledge; 1.2's paradigmatic fraud exposure) is 1.3, a lengthy survey of philosophical opinions from Chilo to Favorinus on ruling on the interests of a friend. Favorinus elucidates a law of Solon to explain the moral hazards of impartiality (2.12), and plays a starring role in a passage which suppresses the judicial utility of juristic handbooks: *Noctes* 14.2 paints the author as only initially emerging from curricular liberal education, at that tender age – *adulescens* – which in the *Noctes* is ignorant of nothing so much as its own ignorance.[39] Knowing only rhetoric and poetry, and having no juristic teacher, he seeks out writings on the duties of the judge (14.2.1). They teach him old laws, but fail to prepare him for the *inexplicabilis* ethical dilemmas a judge often encounters (14.2.3). Faced with one such, Gellius convenes a *consilium* of busy legal professionals who have no time for such considerations and advise him to simply

---

[37] Gellius's ascription of the mocking pun in 1.22 to an unspecified learned praetor may recall, for example, the speechifying 'mask' character for Lucian in his *Peregrinus*. For the difference grammar can make to those practising law, cf. also *N.A.* 7.6, where the grammarian Sulpicius Apollinaris invokes Homer to explain the sense of *praepes* in the context of discussing augural law with an urban prefect.

[38] For this, cf. Taurus's defense of the *captio* in 7.13, taken to heart by the Roman students at Athens in their expat Saturnalia games of 18.2 and 18.13. The question that seems small but has large significance is a defining programmatic concept for the *Noctes*. On recreational habits, see 10.25.

[39] See, for example, 9.15. Cf. Keulen (2009), p. 68 fn. 3.

rule on the available evidence (14.2.9).[40] He turns to Favorinus, who offers a lengthy disquisition on the subject (14.2.12–24).[41] Although Favorinus, unlike Sulpicius in 12.13, makes no warning about the inapplicability of his philosophical advice to a legal situation, Gellius realises that making the ethical judgment which Favorinus encourages would demand an *auctoritas* he lacks as a youth, and so he declares *non liquet* (14.2.25). Jurists feature here only for their unhelpfulness; what 14.2 illustrates to the reader is not just the many kinds of knowledge one should consider in a tricky legal situation, but also the way that each authority figure's status, profession and age will affect the practical utility of his knowledge. In rapid succession, young Gellius has found the practical limits of grammar and rhetoric, jurists, philosophy, and – most importantly – his own youthful intellectual ideals. If nothing else, this delineates clearly to readers the differences not only between different spheres of knowledge but between the private realm of learning and the public realm in which articulations of knowledge are also articulations of social power.[42]

Indeed, where actual legal questions arise, the turn to juristic knowledge is treated with no small amount of skepticism. The image in 14.2 of young Gellius called out of his studies and forced to reconcile what he knows with judicial duties complements that found in 13.13. In the preceding essay, 13.12, Gellius has been learning from the letters of Ateius Capito about his ideological rivalry with Antistius Labeo, manifested in his obstinate refusal of a summons by a tribune of the commons (13.12.1–4). Gellius appends a more expanded version of Labeo's opinion from Book 21 of Varro's *Divine Antiquities* (13.12.5–6), and then passes judgment himself on Labeo's obstinacy (13.12.7–9), laying the groundwork for the following essay.

Noctes 13.13 offers a valuable example of Gellius's portrayal of juristic authority:

> cum ex angulis secretisque librorum ac magistrorum in medium iam hominum et in lucem fori prodissem, quaesitum esse memini in plerisque Romae stationibus ius publice docentium aut respondentium, an quaestor populi Romani ad praetorem in ius vocari posset. id autem non ex otiosa quaestione agitabatur, sed usus forte natae rei ita erat, ut vocandus esset in ius quaestor. (13.13.1–2)

> When I emerged from the nooks and crannies of books and teachers into the midst of men and into the light of the forum, I recall it being asked in the workplaces at Rome of those who publicly teach and give *responsa* about the law whether a

---

[40] The theoretical aspects of *consilium* and *responsa* as an intellectual process are more suppressed in the *Noctes* than there is room here to explore, but the text's general question-and-answer structure (see Pr. 25 and the phraseology of the *capita rerum*, on which Riggsby (2007)) is suggestive in this light. On 14.2, see Holford-Strevens (2003), pp. 294–5.

[41] Gunderson (2009), pp. 68–70.

[42] Cf. Gunderson (2009), p. 72.

quaestor of the Roman people could summon a praetor into court. This was not being discussed as a leisurely academic inquiry, but it happened to be actually relevant to a case that had arisen, as a quaestor was to be summoned into court.

The power of magistrates to summon one another was also at stake in Labeo's refusal at 13.12. Gellius tells us that the emergent consensus of the jurists in 13.13 is that the *maiestas* of the quaestor's office protects him from a summons.

> sed ego, qui tum adsiduus in libris M. Varronis fui, cum hoc quaeri dubitarique animadvertissem, protuli unum et vicesimum rerum humanarum in quo ita scriptum fuit: [. . .] (13.13.4)

> But since I was at that time always reading the books of Marcus Varro, when I noticed that this thing was being investigated and in doubt, I brought out volume 21 of his *Human Antiquities* in which this is written: [. . .]

Varo's declaration about which magistrates may be summoned, in combination with another passage of the same work (13.13.5), makes it clear that the quaestor may be summoned after all, and Gellius settles the debate by having the relevant passages read out of his Varro (13.13.6: *utraque igitur libri parte recitata, in Varronis omnes sententiam concesserunt*).[43] An antiquarian has come to the rescue, and contemporary juristic discourse is set straight by a proper respect for and interest in the historical status of institutions and offices; in short, Gellius here enacts the same value which has made the juristic authors he reads such an effective source of antiquarian knowledge. So although the youthful Gellius, new to his judicial duties, sometimes strays across disciplinary boundaries, he brings back uniquely valuable knowledge with the kind of interdisciplinary reading we see here – wide and synthetic in both jurisprudence *and* antiquarianism and grammar.

On the one other occasion at which current legal questions are recalled, jurists are nowhere to be seen. *Noctes* 3.16 considers the possible variations in the term of pregnancy in a set of interlocking interpretive frameworks: archaic literature as cultural evidence, traditions of linguistic interpretation, and the interpretation of archaic medical literature (Hippocrates). The legal implications of this question are various, with the upper limit touching on *postumi* as well as *infamia* for a wife who does not respect the mourning period and the lower limit – specifically, the vexed question of eight-month pregnancy – having bearing on the *ius trium liberorum*.[44] Gellius's discussion here is lengthy, involved and assertive: he hunts down in Varro an Aristotelian explanation for the differing accounts in poetry (3.16.5– 6, 3.16.13), goes toe-to-toe with known grammatical offender Caesellius

---

[43] Gunderson (2009), pp. 177–8.
[44] For various ramifications, see Hanson (1997), p. 589; Treggiari (1991), p. 29; Gardner (1986), p. 51; Milnor (2005), p. 153.

Vindex for misinterpreting Livius Andronicus (3.16.11), integrates his own recent literary reading (3.16.13), pits laughable *grammatici* against the Latinising Favorinus to apply Homeric evidence (3.16.15–19), and, having learned from the commentary of Sabinus about the interpretation of Hippocratic aphorism (3.16.7–8) offers his own exegesis of that vitally but vaguely authoritative author (3.16.20).

Gellius indicates both the specific legal ramifications of this otherwise somewhat aimless discussion and the authority for the approach he takes to it with personal recollections. Besides book learning, he recalls learning about an actual case at Rome (3.16.12); Gellius emphasises his autopsy of Hadrian's rescript and the claim the emperor makes there to having consulted the opinions of philosophers and doctors (as advertised by Gellius in his heading for the piece, *cap.* 3.16).[45] The approach is hardly unique; the *Digest* preserves a ruling of Antoninus Pius and an opinion of Paul that both attest to the currency of the problem and the consultation of Hippocratean evidence.[46] Gellius recalls another legal investigation, too, the ultimate judgment in which he omits (3.16.21) as a test to the reader (who has just read Gellius's pronouncement of an authoritative principle that should account for all permutations of the question, at 3.16.20).[47] He then closes with a story from Masurius Sabinus by way of Pliny the Elder about a praetor who ruled with obvious ignorance of all this material (3.16.23); for Pliny, the length of pregnancy was wondrous, but Gellius finds wonder in the absurdity of the praetor's assertion that the law has fixed no limit on pregnancy. There are some questions, Gellius shows, that have no need of juristic opinion, and every need of wide, careful reading of all kinds of literature.

5. GELLIUS MEETS THE JURISTS

Thus far I have omitted those rare occasions on which Gellius depicts himself meeting a living jurist. He seems to lack juristic teachers, but is not blind to the presence of jurists in contemporary Rome (although Apollinaris's reference to jurists *quos adhibere in consilium iudicaturi soletis* at 12.13.2 is suggestive – there *were* jurists in his judicial *consilium*, but they do *not* appear in the *Noctes*). The two main encounters with jurists – 16.10 with an anonymous *iuris peritus* and 20.10 with Sextus Caecilius – are much commented upon and peripheral to my discussion here, but a brief discussion will shed some light on the themes that have emerged from Gellius's treatment of juristic reading. Just as Gellius's encounters with flesh-and-blood *grammatici* teach him the scepticism he brings to the grammatical writings

---

[45] On Hadrian and ruling on wills, see Honoré (1994), pp. 13–18.

[46] D.38.16.12 (Pompon. 30 Quint. Muc.) and 1.5.12 (Paul. 19 Resp.), respectively.

[47] 3.16.20: . . . *quod aliquando ocius fieret, non multo tamen fieri ocius, neque quod serius, multo serius.*

of Verrius Flaccus and Caesellius Vindex, his run-ins with jurists resonate closely with his handling of juristic literature, and encapsulate perfectly his values for that reading.

Perhaps the best illustration of the Gellian Favorinus's role as cipher/ *provocateur* for Gellius is *Noctes* 20.1, in which he openly claims (20.1.9) the sceptic's right to play at ignorance in order to elicit a learned disquisition. His criticisms of the obscure cruelty of the Twelve Tables compel the famously learned (20.1.1) Sextus Caecilius to defend their continued relevance; obscurity, Caecilius points out, is created at the point of reception (20.1.5–6), and the cruelty is ameliorated when we consider the nature of linguistic and customary change throughout history, and indeed the intervening legal history which has reconciled the spirit and letter of the Tables to contemporary values. Favorinus boasts of his reading of the Tables (20.2.4) as well as juristic commentary on them (20.2.13), and his learning earns him an embrace.[48] Caecilius's speech wins the approval of all (20.1.55), an unusually explicit endorsement for the *Noctes*.[49] Caecilius is not an intimate of the author's, but his excellence has a clear rationale: the kind of jurist who pays attention to the Twelve Tables (and whatever other ancient law and jurisprudence goes with it) will necessarily know much about the history of Roman customs and practice.[50]

The other jurist at 16.10 proves a corollary.[51] When a word in Ennius, read in public, requires elucidation, Gellius makes the turn toward authority that often presages disappointment as he asks a friend of his *ius civile callens* to explain it. A pun on the man's juristic authority accompanies his refusal (16.10.4: *. . . cum illic se iuris, non rei grammaticae peritum esse respondisset . . .*) as he pleads disciplinary boundaries, and Gellius must remind him that the word appears also in the Twelve Tables – that, in fact, Ennius has taken it from that source (16.10.5).[52] The man sneers at the archaism: 'I would have to explain and interpret this if I had studied the law of the Fauns and Aborigines', he says (16.10.7), arguing that he is only responsible for the laws that are currently binding (16.10.8).[53] When a passing poet is able to easily explain the word, the lesson becomes clear: Latin is the purview of any Roman intellectual, a jurist who disdains the Twelve Tables (and, we may infer, its accompanying tradition of interpretation and scholarship) will be ignorant of the language that is a common cultural property.

Between 20.1, the virtuoso performance of the rare excellent jurist, and 20.2, the grammatical assistance offered by a juristic book with which we

---

[48] 20.1.20, for which compare his response to Fronto at 2.26.20.
[49] On 20.10, see Holford-Strevens (2003), pp. 127–9 and Keulen (2009), pp. 170–4.
[50] Gunderson (2009), pp. 79–84.
[51] On 16.10, see most fully Nörr (1976). See also Gunderson (2009), pp. 157–8.
[52] For the plea that a word is outside one's purview, cf. the *grammaticus* of 19.10.
[53] The allusion to mythic history is familiar from *N.A.* 1.10 as shorthand for risible obscurity.

began, we have a complete illustration of Gellius's relationship with juristic knowledge. But if we are in search of an 'origin story' for this relationship, the necessary coda is 20.10, in which a young Gellius takes a question about a legal phrase to a *grammaticus*. The exchange inverts 16.10: the *grammaticus* claims only to interpret literature, Gellius responds that the phrase appears in Ennius, and the *grammaticus* begs off again:

> cum hos ego versus Ennianos dixissem, 'credo' inquit grammaticus 'iam tibi. sed tu velim credas mihi Quintum Ennium didicisse hoc non ex poeticae litteris, set ex iuris aliquo perito. eas igitur tu quoque' inquit 'et discas, unde Ennius didicit.' usus consilio sum magistri [. . .] (20.10.5–6)

> When I had quoted these lines of Ennius, the grammarian said, 'I believe you now. But you believe me when I tell you Quintus Ennius learned this phrase not from reading poetry, but from some jurist. Therefore you should go and learn from the same source as Ennius'. So I took the teacher's advice [. . .]

Gellius's description of the defeated authority as nonetheless a *magister* reminds his reader there is still a lesson to be learned here. And Gellius learns it, resolving to append to his discussion 'what I have learned from jurists and their writings' on the grounds that it is unseemly (*non oportet*) to be ignorant of the meaning of the legal phrases one encounters in everyday business (20.10.6). This enquiry too leads us to the Twelve Tables (20.10.8). That ancient code, then, and all the study, interpretation and legislation that follows with it – collectively, the study of jurisprudence as Gellius believes it is best done – bestows a kind of learning that offers not only access to common cultural property but also the language and formulae that surround one in everyday life, just as Crassus said. This fact is learned first-hand in an experience as formative as his first encounter with an unreliable *grammaticus* (6.17).

6. CONCLUSIONS

No small part of the *Noctes*'s enduring charm for modern readers is accounted for by the deft way Gellius builds, cumulatively, his recalled and current authorial personae. Piece by piece, we are given glimpses of someone with a vague biography but distinct interests, from whom performances of and opportunities for learning prompt increasingly recognisable responses. And so it is that we know what is going on when we read the following:

> edicta veterum praetorum sedentibus forte nobis in bibliotheca templi Traiani et aliud quid requirentibus cum in manus incidissent, legere atque cognoscere libitum est. (11.17.1)

> The edicts of the ancient praetors just happened to fall into my hands one day when I was sitting in the library of Trajan's temple, looking for something else entirely, and it pleased me to read and get to grips with them.

This is the very *mira quaedam in cognoscendo suavitas et delectatio* that Cicero's Crassus assured his audience accompanies legal study (*De Oratore* 1.193). It is not part of the training of an orator; it is, instead, the turn toward authority, the pursuit of 'immense portraits of antiquity', that ensures for a man of learning, responsibility and legal *negotium* an awareness of Roman custom, values and language throughout history. And it is, in Crassus's terms, a direct encounter with the Roman cultural heritage that has made them the rulers of the world.

Why read jurists in the *Noctes*? It is very rarely to help answer a legal question – those may well have other answers. The question is instead, why *not* read jurists? Why deprive oneself of the impressive antiquarian and linguistic learning, the unique insight into values and institutions, and the surprising and interesting material that lurks in the pages of Labeo, Capito, Sabinus and others? Juristic literature is, in the classic formulation of advertisements for breakfast cereals in the United States, *part of this complete diet* – a distinct and irreplaceable element of a larger intellectual lifestyle for the learned gentleman of Antonine Rome. Gellius shows us a library lifestyle in which the jurists' books are available to the curious reader, and indicates how they contain the answers to questions as well as the kind of material and knowledge with which one can set oneself apart from the herd.

The jurists understand ancient speech and *mos maiorum* because these are essential to the interpretation of law. Gellius fixates on this antiquarian quality in jurisprudence and expands it – in spite of the rising tide of intellectual professionals, most notably *grammatici*, who seem to haunt him with their restrictive self-definition, he knows the disciplines never had true boundaries.[54] He identifies a distinction among contemporary jurists between those who still regard the Twelve Tables (and accompanying traditions) as relevant, and those who use the *lex Aebutia* (16.10.8) as an excuse to ignore them; and into that distinction, which might seem like one of intra-disciplinary concerns, inserts a provocative and assertive claim to key cultural values.[55] The right sort of jurists, for various reasons, are those who take advantage of the deep and authoritative claim to antiquarian enquiry that characterises their profession.

The elite intellectual gentleman has studied certain disciplines in his education, and in his social life has the optional acquaintance of experts in both these and others. This generates a wide array of questions with an equally wide array of stakes. Gellius is interested to short-circuit certain assumptions about which disciplines can answer which questions, and thus the law teaches non-legal knowledge as much as non-legal knowledge helps with the practice of law. Gellius is perhaps concerned with no moment in one's intellectual lifestyle more than when a question has arisen and the student's hand

---

[54] Harries (2006), p. 180.
[55] For the Twelve Tables did not belong to the jurists alone: Harries (2006), p. 172.

hovers uncertainly in front of the bookshelf. The professional title of the author is as poor a guide as the title of the book: a Roman curious about his customs or language would do well to reach for a book on law.

BIBLIOGRAPHY

Frier, B. W., *The Rise of the Roman Jurists: Studies in the Pro Caecina* (1985).

Gunderson, E., *Nox Philologiae: Aulus Gellius and the Fantasy of the Roman Library* (2009).

Harries, J., *Cicero and the Jurists: From Citizens' Law to the Lawful State* (2006).

Hanson, A. E., 'The eight months' child and the etiquette of birth: *obsit omen!*', *Bulletin of the History of Medicine*, 61.4 (1987), p. 589.

Holford-Strevens, L., *Aulus Gellius: An Antonine Scholar and his Achievement*, rev. edn (2003).

Gardner, J. F., *Women in Roman Law and Society* (1986).

Honoré, T., *Emperors and Lawyers*, 2nd edn (1994).

Keulen, W., *Gellius the Satirist* (2009).

Lao, E., 'Luxury and the creation of a good consumer', in R. K. Gibson and R. Morello (eds), *Pliny the Elder: Themes and Contexts* (2011), p. 35.

Leeman, A. D. and Pinkster, H., *De oratore Libri III / M. Tullius Cicero. Band II* (1981).

Marache, R., *La Critique Littéraire de Langue Latine et le Développement du Gout Archaïsant au IIe Siècle de Notre Ère* (1952).

Milnor, K., *Gender, Domesticity, and the Age of Augustus* (2005).

Murphy, T., 'Pliny's *Naturalis historia*: the prodigal text', in A. J. Boyle and W. J. Dominik (eds), *Flavian Rome: Culture, Image, Text* (2003), p. 301.

Nörr, D., 'Der Jurist im Kreis der Intellektuellen: Mitspieler oder Aussenseiter? (Gellius, *Noctes Atticae* 16.10)', in D. Medicus and H. H. Seiler (eds), *Festschrift für Max Kaser zum 70. Geburtstag* (1976), p. 57.

Stevenson, A. J., 'Gellius and the Roman antiquarian tradition', in L. Holford-Strevens and A. Vardi, *The Worlds of Aulus Gellius* (2004), p. 118.

Swain, S., 'Bilingualism and biculturalism in Antonine Rome', in L. Holford-Strevens and A. Vardi, *The Worlds of Aulus Gellius* (2004), p. 3.

Treggiari, S., *Roman Marriage: Iusti Coniuges from the Time of Cicero to the Time of Ulpian* (1991).

Vardi, A., 'Gellius against the professors', *ZPE*, 137 (2001), p. 41.

Vessey, D. W. T., 'Aulus Gellius and the cult of the past', *ANRW*, II.34.2 (1994), p. 1863.

Chapter 3

Artes Urbanae: *Roman Law and Rhetoric*

Olga Tellegen-Couperus and Jan Willem Tellegen

1. INTRODUCTION

Modern Romanists generally assume that Roman law was completely separate from rhetoric. Whereas Roman law was a science, rhetoric was not. Rhetoric was a skill developed by the Greeks that was used by advocates to pervert the truth. The Roman jurists did not need rhetorical arguments to support their case: *stat pro ratione auctoritas*. They never wanted to have anything to do with rhetoric.[1]

In the twentieth century, this view has been challenged several times. First Johannes Stroux and later Theodor Viehweg argued – be it in different ways – that Roman law was closely connected to rhetoric.[2] Their ideas triggered much discussion, but failed to convince the majority of Roman law scholars. Over the past ten years or so, we have also tried to demonstrate that Roman law and rhetoric were closely connected, but so far, our work has not changed the commonly held view either.[3] The reason may be that we have not yet addressed the basic assumption that Roman law was a science and rhetoric was not. We will do so now.

The assumption that Roman law was a science is based on another supposition: that the concept of science, including legal science, already existed in classical Antiquity. However, it was only in the sixteenth century that legal science as we know it now came into being.[4] It originated in the minds of the French legal humanists, for example Donellus. In the words of Peter Stein, 'he assumed that Justinian's law must be logical even though it did not appear to be so, and applied himself to identifying what he conceived

---

[1] Cf. Schulz (1946), p. 54. A more differentiated approach is in Crook (1995), pp. 40–1.

[2] Johannes Stroux, 'Summum ius summa iniuria, Ein Kapittel aus der Geschichte der interpretatio iuris' intended for the *Festschrift P. Speiser-Sarasin*, Leipzig 1926, which never appeared in its entirety. The work was reprinted in *Römische Rechtswissenschaft und Rhetorik* (1949), pp. 9–66. Viehweg (1974).

[3] For instance, in Tellegen-Couperus and Tellegen (2000), pp. 171–202; Tellegen-Couperus and Tellegen (2006), pp. 381–408; Tellegen-Couperus and Tellegen (2007), pp. 231–54. It all began with Tellegen (1982).

[4] Cf. Feldman (2009), pp. 109–20; remarkably, she does not refer to Roman law or rhetoric at all.

to be its underlying rational structure'.[5] In the seventeenth and eighteenth centuries, various orderings of the civil law were made, showing the influences of natural law and the Enlightenment. In some countries, for example Austria and France, they resulted in codifications. The last step was made by the founder of the German Historical School, Friedrich Carl von Savigny. Focusing on the works of the second-century classical jurists, he tried to ascertain the central principles of Roman law and created the new scientific system of present-day Roman law.[6]

When the codifications of the nineteenth and twentieth centuries turned Roman law into a historical phenomenon, scholars – now called Romanists – began to apply this legal system to Roman law as well. Because classical Roman law was regarded as the basis of modern private law, it was supposed to share the same rules and principles. However, some of these rules and principles did not belong to classical Roman law. At the same time, Roman legal practice was familiar with rhetoric, but rhetoric was excluded by modern legal science. Consequently, problems arose when legal sources like Gaius' Institutes and Justinian's Digest were studied. These problems were sometimes 'solved' by adapting the text to the theory, for instance, by declaring words or sentences in the Digest to be sixth-century interpolations.[7] Sometimes, however, they were not solved at all because the rhetorical aspects of, for instance, the controversies in the Institutes of Gaius were ignored. Problems also arose when so-called rhetorical sources like the pleas of Cicero were studied. These problems were solved by regarding the references to legal practice as biased and therefore as unreliable. As a result, a Roman law was (re)constructed that was not always in accordance with the sources.

In this chapter, we will first discuss the theories put forward by Stroux and Viehweg, adding our comment. Then we will deal with the role of rhetoric in Gaius' Institutes and in Justinian's Digest. We hope to make it clear that Roman law was not a science in the modern sense and that law and rhetoric belonged together as two sides of the same coin: legal practice.

2. THE THEORIES OF STROUX AND VIEHWEG

Johannes Stroux (1886–1954) was a German classicist and historian. In 1926, he published a paper entitled '*Summum ius summa iniuria*, ein Kapitel aus der Geschichte der *interpretatio iuris*'. In the introduction to the paper, Stroux described the various stages of legal development in Greek and Roman society.[8] Originally, there was only the oral tradition of law. In both cultures,

---

[5] Stein (1999), p. 80.
[6] Stein (1999), pp. 104–27.
[7] Stein (1999), pp. 128–9.
[8] Stroux (1949), pp. 9–12.

this stage was followed by that of recording law in order to protect it against arbitrariness and distortion, as well as against time. Its being unchangeable seemed to guarantee the essence of the law, and the interpretation of the law necessarily had to serve that purpose. Over time, however, the words of the law hardened whereas life went on and society changed. Neither the inter-pretation of the law by judges nor its application by others could provide the much needed innovation. Then, next to the law came equity. In Rome, the praetorian edict became the instrument to make *aequitas* a fundamen-tal legal principle. According to Stroux, the aphorism *summum ius summa iniuria*, 'the greatest right is the greatest wrong', is like a war cry indicating that positive law without equity is no law. As such, it was first formulated by Cicero, but the idea originated in Greek culture. One could even say that it belongs to all times and all places.

Stroux suggested that it was through Hellenistic philosophies and rheto-ric that Rome was influenced by the idea behind the aphorism *summum ius summa iniuria*. Here, however, the contrast between strict law and equity was incorporated into legal practice and, in that way, had stimulated legal devel-opment.[9] Rhetoric provided the means for implementation, particularly the so-called *status* doctrine.

We know the *status* doctrine because it is described by Cicero in his *De inventione* but it may have been developed in the second century BCE by the Greek rhetorician Hermagoras.[10] It basically deals with the question of how to defend oneself against an accusation: by focusing on the facts or on the law. The latter category is particularly interesting when the words of the law are not clear and have to be interpreted. This can happen if the words are ambiguous, if the words of the law do not seem to reflect the intention of the lawgiver, if there are two applicable laws that contradict each other, or if the words of a law do not refer to a particular case but can be interpreted by analogy so that they do. According to Stroux, this system did not only apply to the interpretation of laws, but also to wills, stipulations, and other 'formal gefasste rechtsgeschäftliche Willensäusserungen'.[11] Stroux presented two examples to illustrate how the aphorism *summum ius summa iniuria* worked in legal practice: the famous *causa Curiana* and Cicero's speech *pro Caecina*.[12] In both cases, the *status* of *verba – voluntas* was applied. In both cases, the jurists argued for an interpretation according to the *verba*, the orators for the *voluntas*. In both cases, equity won.

Stroux noticed that Roman jurisprudence then also changed into a legal science, and he wondered whether this happened under the influence of rhet-oric as well. In his time, it was generally assumed that the scientific approach

[9]　Stroux (1949), p. 20.
[10]　Stroux (1949), pp. 23–40.
[11]　Stroux (1949), p. 33.
[12]　Stroux (1949), pp. 42–8.

to law was provided by Hellenistic philosophy, and particularly by the Stoa. Stroux admitted that Stoic philosophy was very influential in Rome, but not its dialectic. He assumed that rather the New Academy and the Peripatetic School supported the development of Roman legal science. Again, rhetoric provided the means, as is shown by the methodological work called *Topica* which Cicero wrote for his friend, the jurist Trebatius. By drawing up an abstract *Topica* – that is, a scientific theory of argumentation – the orators offered the jurists a means to systematise their casuistic opinions.[13] Stroux concluded that the fact that Justinian's *Corpus Iuris* does not contain a comprehensive theory of *interpretatio iuris* does not prove that such a theory did not exist in classical Roman law, but that Justinian, in his new codification, wanted to exclude all signs of interpretation: he even wanted to make interpretation superfluous.[14]

There are two comments we would like to make on Stroux's theory. First, we think that Stroux made an important contribution to the rediscovery of classical Roman law by connecting rhetoric to law, but we are surprised to notice that he still regarded the jurists and the orators as thinking in completely different ways: the jurists focused on form and the orators focused on justice. Second, Stroux was right in assessing that Cicero's *Topica* is a methodical work that could be helpful to jurists, but he still adhered to the idea that the jurists of the late Republic developed a legal science, a '*Methodenlehre*'. It was Viehweg who, several decades later, questioned exactly this point, whether law could really be organised as a systematic science.

Theodor Viehweg (1907–88) was Professor of Philosophy and Sociology of Law at the Johannes Gutenberg University at Mainz, Germany. His approach to the relationship between law and rhetoric was very different from that of Stroux. In his book *Topik und Jurisprudenz*, Viehweg 'contrasted the deductive systematic intellectuality that has been influential since Descartes and the more contextual problem oriented style inherited from classical rhetoric'.[15] On the basis of examples drawn from two millennia of legal history, he concluded that the rhetorical or topical approach is more suitable for law. In the context of this chapter, we will focus on the first part of his book, where Viehweg dealt with Greek and Roman Antiquity.

Because the concept of *topica* was practically unknown in his time, Viehweg first wanted to discover its meaning and therefore turned to the works of Aristotle and Cicero on this subject (§2). He noticed that Aristotle did not present his *Topica* as part of logic but as belonging to dialectics. In this work, Aristotle offered a catalogue of ways of reasoning that could help in a discussion of any problem whatsoever to draw conclusions from sentences that were probably true. Cicero, in his *Topica*, did not add this

[13] Stroux (1949), pp. 51–2.
[14] Stroux (1949), pp. 65–6.
[15] Cf. the blurb of the English translation of Viehweg (1993).

philosophical context but only created a catalogue of arguments that were based on probability and that could be used in daily life. Viehweg concluded that *topica* can be described as a *techne* of problem-oriented thinking that had been developed by rhetoric.

Next, Viehweg analysed the concept of *topica* (§3). He assumed that a problem is any question that seems to allow more than one answer, and that only relevant questions need to be answered. The problem is brought into the context of a more or less explicit and extensive deduction from which the answer is inferred. This context can be called a system. In short, solving a problem involves classing it into a system. If an attempt is made to solve a problem by focusing on system A, then only some problems can be solved, the others cannot: they will no longer be regarded as real problems. If, on the other hand, an attempt is made to solve a problem by focusing on the problem, systems A, B, C and so on may be taken into consideration. *Topoi* are points of view that can help when choosing a particular system or way of reasoning. Some *topoi* can be used to solve all sorts of problems; others are particularly suited to solving legal problems.

Viehweg then turned to the Roman *ius civile*. 'It is well known', he wrote, 'that *ius civile* [Roman law] is rather disappointing to deductive systematiz-ers' (§4). The texts in the Digest, for instance, belong to contexts that are problem-oriented rather than system-based. Consequently, the concepts and rules developed by the *ius civile* cannot be readily systematised; they must be understood to form part of topical thinking. *Topica* tends to collect points of view and summarise them in catalogues. *Ius civile* did the same, for law. The jurists proceeded to formulate propositions that could be used as *topoi*. According to Viehweg, the so-called *regulae* provide a good example of such propositions. At times, they were collected and summarised. Viehweg thought that the last section of the Digest, book D.50.17, constituted such a catalogue.

Can Roman law be problem-oriented and still be qualified as a science? Viehweg used the Aristotelian distinction between *techne* (art) and *episteme* (science) to answer this question; he concluded that the Roman jurists themselves regarded *ius* as an art. In his view, jurists and orators applied the same method of working which derived from Aristotle's dialectics. Viehweg stressed that the latter had nothing to do with Stoic dialectics which were closely connected to the mathematic intellectuality of Antiquity: in the structure of the *ius civile*, no trace of the Stoic Chrysippus can be found.[16]

Viehweg went several steps further than Stroux in connecting law and rhetoric. In our view, he demonstrated convincingly that Roman law was characterised by a problem-oriented way of working, and that the jurists and the orators applied the same topical approach. However, we have two

---

[16] Viehweg may not have noticed that Cicero, in *Topica* 54, refers to the Stoic dialectics; see the comment by H. M. Hubbell in his translation of Cicero's *Topica* (1976), p. 422.

points of criticism; both regard his connecting *topica* and Roman law. First, Viehweg did not see that Cicero's *Topica* cannot really be compared to that of Aristotle, let alone be qualified as inferior. As Robert Gaines has demonstrated, it contains various ways of finding arguments ordered in a systematic way meant for legal practice.[17] Secondly, Viehweg was wrong in qualifying the *regulae* as *topoi* of Roman law. They are concrete precedents rather than abstract ways of reasoning.[18] In our view, it is certainly possible to find *topoi* in legal sources like Gaius' Institutes and Justinian's Digest. In the following two sections, we will apply Viehweg's theory to these sources.

3. LEGAL SCIENCE AND RHETORIC IN GAIUS' INSTITUTES

If the Roman jurists had created a legal science that was independent from rhetoric, it must be possible to find traces of a scientific system in the legal literature of the classical period. However, this is not so simple. Our main source of information for classical Roman law is Justinian's Digest, but the framework of that source does not really correspond to what in modern times is regarded as a system. We will return to the Digest in the next section. There is, however, another source that did seem to reflect the system of Roman law and to exclude rhetoric: the Institutes of Gaius.

Gaius' Institutes, an elementary textbook of Roman law, was written in the second century.[19] It was structured in a simple way, dividing the law into 'persons', 'things' and 'actions'. About the author, Gaius, we know next to nothing. The textbook must have been popular because various later editions have been published and because sections have been quoted in the *florilegia* of the fourth and fifth centuries and in Justinian's Digest of the sixth century. It was even used as a model by the Byzantine law professors when Justinian ordered them to compose a new textbook, the (Justinianic) Institutes. However, for many centuries after the fall of the Roman Empire, the work itself was not available.

The first complete manuscript of Gaius' Institutes was discovered in Verona in 1816, by B. G. Niebuhr. Before that time, Roman law had been studied for more than six centuries on the basis of Justinian's Digest, Codex, and Institutes.[20] As was pointed out in the introduction to this chapter, the sixteenth century had witnessed the rise of legal science based on the *Corpus Iuris Civilis*. The rediscovery of Gaius' Institutes, therefore, took place

---

[17] Gaines (2002), pp. 445–80, particularly pp. 469–76.

[18] For instance, the *regula* about expenses and assets of something (D.50.17.10) (Paul. 3 ad Sab.): *Secundum naturam est, commoda cuiusque rei eum sequi, quem sequentur incommoda*) may form a proposition in a specific form of reasoning, whereas *topoi* as presented by Cicero contain general points of view like the argument of time, cause and effect, authority, and so on.

[19] See Gordon and Robinson (1988), pp. 7–13.

[20] As of the fifteenth century, these books came to be called *Corpus Iuris Civilis*, as opposed to the *Corpus Iuris Canonici*.

after, in countries like France and Austria, the new codifications had been introduced and, in the German *Länder*, Savigny had just begun to create '*das heutige römische Recht*'. It will be clear that the rediscovery of Gaius' Institutes caused a shock among the Romanists. The text was partly familiar to them through the Institutes of Justinian. However, it was also partly new because it referred to legal concepts and procedures that no longer existed in the sixth century and that had been left out of Justinian's Institutes. Therefore, Gaius' Institutes provided a lot of new information on Roman law and its history.

There were two major issues in Gaius' Institutes that puzzled the Romanists. First, the system of Roman law that had been developed over the centuries and that was based on the division of rights *in rem* (*dominium* and *iura in re aliena*) and rights *in personam* (obligations) could not really be recognised in the work of Gaius. And yet, it should be there. Secondly, throughout his textbook, Gaius mentioned approximately twenty controversies between leading Roman jurists which referred to as many unsolved legal problems. If the Roman jurists had created a system that could provide the one correct solution for every legal problem, there could not have been controversies, let alone in a law textbook. In the following, we will first analyse how the Romanists have tried to solve the system-related problem and give our comment. Then we will discuss the problem of the controversies and show that it can be solved by connecting it to rhetoric.

The system of Roman law in Gaius' Institutes

In his *Römische Rechtsgeschichte*, Max Kaser, one of the leading Romanists of the twentieth century, described the essence of legal science. In his view, it was the development of legal concepts that are well determined as to content and clearly separated from each other, and that are ordered and linked together in a logical system.[21] Under the influence of the Greek dialectical method, the Roman jurists had developed such concepts and such a system, but their way of working had remained casuistic. The one exception to this rule was Gaius. In his Institutes, he divided the subject matter into *personae* and *res*, that is, into legal subjects and legal objects, or, into the law of persons (including family law) and the law of property (*Vermögensrecht*). The subdivision of things into *res corporales* and *res incorporales* gave the first impulse to dividing the law of property into things, inheritance and obligations. This first step towards a system can still be traced in the codifications of our day, according to Kaser.

It is clear that the essential element for Gaius' Institutes is the subdivision of things into *res corporales* and *res incorporales*. In 2.13, Gaius describes

---

[21] Kaser (1967), p. 164: 'Zum Wesen einer solchen gehört die Entwicklung inhaltlich genau bestimmter und von einander abgegrenzter juristischer Begriffe und ihre Ordnung und Abstimmung aufeinander in einem von der Sachlogik bestimmten System'.

corporeal things as tangible things, such as land, a slave, a garment, gold, silver, and so on. In the next section, Gaius describes the incorporeal things:[22]

> Incorporeal are things that are intangible, such as exist merely in court, for example an inheritance, a usufruct, obligations however contracted. It does not matter that corporeal things are comprised in an inheritance, or that the fruits gathered from land (subject to a usufruct) are corporeal, or that what is due under an obligation is commonly corporeal, for instance land, a slave, money; for the rights of inheritance, usufruct, and obligation themselves are incorporeal [. . .]

In modern Romanist literature, it is assumed that the word *res* and therefore also the distinction between *res corporales* and *res incorporales* refers to legal objects. However, this distinction is commonly regarded as illogical. The *res corporales* would be legal objects, that is, objects of ownership. However, ownership is a right. Therefore, the right must be identified with the object, and ownership must be regarded as a *res corporalis*. The *res incorporales* should be legal objects, too, but then it would be unclear what the objects were. This problem was solved by regarding the *res incorporales* as (subjective) rights.[23] Consequently, the phrase 'quae in iure consistunt' in the first line of Inst. 2.14, is translated by most scholars as 'that exist in a right'.[24] With the distinction between *res corporales* and *res incorporales*, Gaius was supposed to have referred to the distinction between *dominium* and *iura in re aliena*. In other words, he had done a bad job.

In our view, this interpretation is rather far-fetched.[25] It goes wrong at the

---

[22] Inst.Gai. 2.14: Incorporales sunt, quae tangi non possunt, qualia sunt ea, quae [in] iure consistunt, sicut hereditas ususfructus obligationes quoquo modo contractae. Nec ad rem per[tinet quod in hereditate res corporales con]tinentur, et fructus, qui ex fundo percipiuntur, corporales sunt, et quod ex aliqua obligatione nobis debetur, id plerumque corporale est veluti fundus homo pecunia: nam ipsum ius successionis et ipsum ius utendi fruendi et ipsum ius obligationis incorporale est: text edition by David (1964), p. 36. Our translation is based on that by de Zulueta (1946), p. 69. The main difference is the translation of *in iure* in the first line as 'in court'. In the following, we will explain why we prefer this translation.

[23] It is interesting to see how, in the past 100 years, this distinction has been dealt with in textbooks of Roman law. They all interpret *res incorporales* as (subjective) rights, but all have problems explaining the distinction. See, for instance, Salkowski (1898), p. 204; van Oven (1948), p. 138; Arangio Ruiz (1960, repr. 1978), pp. 162–3; Jolowicz and Nicholas (1972), p. 412; Villers (1977), p. 253; Kaser (1989), p. 90; Borkowski and du Plessis (2005), pp. 153–4, (2010, 4th edn), pp. 151–2). Some think it originated in Greek grammar and/or philosophy. Two do not mention the distinction at all, namely Schulz (1951) and de Francisci (1968).

[24] Some scholars translate it as 'that exist in law'. This phrase caused a lot of discussion, particularly because it is not quite certain that the phrase contained the preposition 'in'. According to David and Nelson (1954–68), p. 240, it did. For an overview and renewed discussion, see Nicosia (2009), pp. 821–35.

[25] In this vein, see Tellegen (1994), pp. 35–55. According to Bretone (1999), p. 284, this interpretation is *'fantasiosa'*. For us, however, it would be fanciful to explain that *res* means something other than 'things', let alone that Gaius would use it to refer to 'legal objects' as well as 'subjective rights'.

very beginning, with the assumption that the concepts *personae* and *res* are to be interpreted as referring to legal subjects and legal objects, respectively. We think they do not. In the first book of his Institutes, Gaius describes the three categories of *status* that refer to persons (freedom, citizenship and family) and how a person's *status* can change. He does not describe the capacity of a person to perform a legally valid act or to have property. Consequently, the word *personae* cannot mean 'legal subjects' but only 'persons'.

In the second and third books, Gaius deals with the *res*. At the beginning of book II, he mentions a number of distinctions of things, all the time explaining why a particular distinction is relevant. He does not describe what qualifies as a legal object. Gaius defines the *res corporales* as things that can be touched, and the *res incorporales* as things that cannot be touched but that exist *in iure*. The relevance of this distinction is explained in Inst 2.28: incorporeal things cannot be transferred by tradition, the informal way of transferring property, but only by means of *in iure cessio*. This legal concept, however, originated in the law of procedure. For a proper understanding of the distinction between *res corporales* and *res incorporales*, it must be borne in mind that, in his Institutes, Gaius did not only deal with *personae* and *res*, but also with *actiones*. In our view, this distinction can only be explained in its context, that is, in connection with the *in iure cessio* as part of the Roman law of procedure.

The *in iure cessio* begins like a normal procedure *per formulas* before the praetor, when the plaintiff claims the usufruct (or another *res incorporalis*) from the defendant. This phase of the procedure is called '*in iure*'. The praetor asks the defendant whether he also claims the usufruct. The defendant may keep silent or indicate that he does not do so. Then the praetor will assign the usufruct to the plaintiff and a transfer of the usufruct will have taken place. The defendant can also indicate that he does want to claim the usufruct; then the praetor may grant a *formula*, and a regular trial (*apud iudicem*) may follow. In short, *res incorporales* can be the object of a transfer and of a procedure.

The procedure to claim the usufruct makes it clear that, in this connection, the word *res* cannot be taken to mean 'rights'. The *formula* of a *vindicatio ususfructus* was based on that of the *reivindicatio* (to claim *dominium*, property) but it was slightly adapted. Let us compare both *formulae*. According to the reconstruction of Lenel, the *formula* of the *reivindicatio* ran as follows:[26]

> X must be judge. If it appears that the thing at stake belongs to Aulus Agerius according to the *ius Quiritium*, and if this thing has not been restituted by the order

---

[26] Lenel (1927), pp. 185–6. 'Iudex esto. Si paret rem qua de agitur ex iure Quiritium Auli Agerii esse neque ea res arbitrio iudicis Aulo Agerio restituetur, quanti ea res erit, tantam pecuniam iudex Numerium Negidium Aulo Agerio condemnato, si non paret absolvito'. In the pattern *formula*, the name of the plaintiff is always given as Aulus Agerius, and that of the defendant as Numerius Negidius. The translation of this *formula* is our own.

of the judge to Aulus Agerius, then the judge must condemn Numerius Negidius to pay so much money to Aulus Agerius as this thing is worth. If it does not appear, then he must absolve him.

The formula of the *vindicatio ususfructus* is:[27]

X must be judge. If it appears that Aulus Agerius has the right of usufruct on that land that is at stake and if this thing has not been restituted to Aulus Agerius, then the judge must condemn Numerius Negidius to pay so much money to Aulus Agerius as this thing is worth, if it does not appear then he must absolve him.

In the first part of the *reivindicatio*, the thing that is claimed is referred to as *res*, a *res corporalis*. In the *vindicatio ususfructus*, however, the thing that is claimed is referred to as *ius*, that is, the right of usufruct that rests on someone else's land. In the latter part of the *formula*, the word *res* is used, but then it indicates the thing at stake, the *res incorporalis*. Apparently, the words *ius* and *res* are used as synonyms. By adapting the *formula*, it became possible to claim a usufruct in court. Consequently, the word *res* in Gaius Inst. 2.12–14 cannot be taken to mean 'rights'.

Now the meaning of the phrase '*quae in iure consistunt*' becomes clear: it refers to the first part of the formulary procedure, before the praetor, which is called *in iure*. The *res incorporales* only exist *in iure*, 'in court'. Gaius did a good job when he added this explanation: it helped to clarify a simple distinction which he made for his elementary textbook.

The fundamental mistake made by modern Romanists is their assumption that Gaius is dealing with subjective rights. This concept was unknown to Gaius; it originated only between the fourteenth and sixteenth centuries.[28] Gaius, and the other Roman jurists for that matter, had a completely different way of thinking than present-day civil-law jurists. It must be concluded that Gaius' Institutes did not reflect the system of subjective rights of modern civil law and that the system that was used does not qualify as legal science in the modern sense.

The controversies in Gaius' Institutes

The second issue that puzzled the Romanists was the twenty or so controversies mentioned in Gaius' Institutes. These controversies existed between the two law schools that had emerged in Rome in the early Principate, the

[27] Lenel (1927), p. 190: 'Iudex esto. Si paret Aulo Agerio ius esse eo fundo qua de agitur uti frui neque ea res arbitrio iudicis Aulo Agerio restituetur, quanti ea res erit, tantam pecuniam iudex Numerium Negidium Aulo Agerio condemnato, si non paret absolvito'.
[28] Villey (1946–7), pp. 201–27. According to the same author, it was William of Ockham who first introduced the concept of subjective right. Feenstra (1989), pp. 111–22 suggests it was Donellus.

Sabinian or Cassian school and the Proculian school.[29] The leaders of these schools defended opposite positions over several points of private law. How could they do so, if there was only one correct solution to a legal problem? Moreover, the jurists in question gave arguments to support their opinions. Why would they do so if they normally did not because, according to Schulz, *stat pro ratione auctoritas?* The leaders of the schools may have had the *ius respondendi ex auctoritate principis* and will have had a lot of authority. Finally, some of these controversies were solved by a compromise, a *media sententia*. How could such a solution be fitted into a system that allowed only one correct solution?

Ever since the discovery of the manuscript of the Institutes, dozens of scholars have tried to solve the problem of the controversies. Most of them did so from a dogmatic perspective on Roman law, trying to find one overall interpretation that could bring the controversies within the system of Roman law. However, they did not succeed in finding one interpretation that could explain all the controversies. They have not adapted their way of working until recently.

A few years ago, Tessa Leesen wrote a monograph about the controversies in Roman law.[30] She suggested that they could be explained by connecting them to rhetoric. Her main thesis was that jurists, like orators and lawyers, made use of the art of rhetoric, and of its argumentative theory, the *topica* as developed by Cicero and Quintilian, to make their opinions persuasive. By analysing the twenty-one controversies in Gaius' Institutes, she was able to demonstrate how, in these cases, the jurists used topical arguments to support their view. There was not one correct solution, but the opinions of both jurists could be defended without one of them losing his integrity. We will give one example that is discussed by Leesen, namely, that of the controversy on *specificatio* mentioned in Gaius, Inst. 2.79:[31]

> On a change of *species* also, we have recourse to *naturalis ratio*. If, therefore, you have made wine, or oil, or grain from my grapes, olives, or ears of corn, the question is asked whether this wine, oil, or grain is mine or yours. In like manner, if you have made some vase of my gold or silver or if you have constructed a boat, or a cupboard, or a bench from my planks. In like manner, if you have made a garment from my wool or if you have made mead from my wine and honey or if you have a plaster or an ointment from my drugs, the question is asked whether what you have thus made from my material is yours or is mine. Some think that the material and the substance have to be taken into consideration, that is, the manufactured article is considered to belong to the owner of the material. And

---

[29] In modern literature, the very *raison d'être* of the law schools is also controversial, cf. Stein (1999), p. 17, but see also Tellegen-Couperus (1990), pp. 95–7.

[30] Leesen (2010).

[31] Leesen (2010), pp. 70–90. For the Latin text here and in the following, see http://www. TheLatinLibrary.com (accessed 13 February 2012) under *Ius Romanum*.

this opinion is above all preferred by Sabinus and Cassius. Others, however, think that the object belongs to him who created it; this is the view held above all by the authorities of the other school. However, they also think that he who owned the material and the substance has the *actio furti* against him who stole it and also a *condictio* against the same person because, although it is no longer possible to bring a *vindicatio* when things have perished, they may be the object of a *condictio* against thieves and certain other possessors.

The text forms part of a discussion on the different means of acquisition of ownership based on *naturalis ratio*. The first example has become classic: When somebody (A) makes wine by processing the grapes of somebody else (B) without mutual agreement, a problem of ownership arises: does the owner of the grapes (B) or the maker of the wine (A) become owner of the wine? The owner of the grapes will claim ownership of the wine from the maker who is in possession, and he will do so by means of a *reivindicatio*. The Sabinians supported B's claim, the Proculians defended the view that A had become the owner.

Gaius does not explicitly mention the arguments used by the Sabinians and the Proculians, but they have come down to us via the Digest in the second book of the so-called *Res Cottidiana sive aurea*, a fourth-century version of Gaius' Institutes. The relevant text, D.41.1.7.7, runs as follows:

> When someone has made for himself something from another's material, Nerva and Proculus think that the maker owns that thing, because what has been made previously belonged to no one. Sabinus and Cassius rather think that the *naturalis ratio* requires that the person who has been the owner of the material also becomes the owner of what is made from his material, since nothing can be made without the material: if, for example, I make some vase from gold, silver or bronze, or a garment from your wool, or mead from your wine and honey, or a plaster or an ointment from your drugs or wine, oil or grain from your grapes, olives or ears of corn. Nevertheless, there is also a *media sententia* of those who correctly think that, if the thing can be returned to its material, the better view is that propounded by Cassius and Sabinus. If it cannot be returned, Nerva and Proculus are sounder. Thus, for example, a finished vase can be returned to its raw mass of gold or silver or bronze. It is not possible, however, to return wine, oil or grain to grapes and olives and ears of corn. Neither can mead be returned to honey and wine or plasters or ointment to drugs. It seems to me, however, that some have said correctly that there should be no doubt that the grain, shaken from someone's ears of corn, belongs to him whom the ears of corn have come from. For since the grain, that is contained in the ears of corn, has its own perfect form, the one who has shaken out the ears of corn does not make a new form. But he uncovers what already exists.

This text shows that both schools base their claim on the *naturalis ratio*, so there is no fundamental difference.

In the course of time, various explanations of this controversy have been offered. The most typical one is that based on philosophy: it has been argued that the Sabinians were influenced by the Stoa and the Proculians by Aristotle and the Peripatos. Other scholars explained it by the conservative-progressive antithesis, some stating that the Sabinians were conservative and the Proculians progressive, others that it was the other way around.

According to Leesen, both the Proculians and the Sabinians used topical arguments. Cicero's *Topica* and particularly Quintilian's *Institutio oratoria* helped her find the relevant *topoi* or, in Latin, *loci*. She reconstructed the reasoning of the Proculians with the *locus ab adiunctis*:

- What has been made did previously not belong to anyone.
- Therefore what someone never had, he has not lost.
- B is the owner of the material, i.e. the grapes.
- Therefore, B cannot vindicate the *nova species*, i.e., the wine.

The Sabinians used the *locus ex causis* to support their argument:

- Since nothing can be made without the material,
- the ownership of a *nova species* (e.g. wine, oil, or grain) must be granted to the owner of the *materia* (i.e. to the owner of the grapes, olives, or ears of corn).
- B is the owner of the material.
- Therefore, B is the owner of the *nova species*.

In D.41.1.7.7, the *media sententia* is mentioned that was supposed to be a compromise between the two positions. If a thing has been made from some material but cannot be reduced to its material, then the opinion of the Proculians must be followed and the thing be regarded as belonging to the maker. However, this compromise is not very convincing because it is equally reasonable to state that the material is still present in the *nova species* and that therefore the wine belongs to the owner of the material. Yet it was this *media sententia* that was approved by Justinian and was included in his Institutes (Inst 2.1.25).

In this and other controversies, the leaders of the Sabinian and the Proculian schools defended two opposite positions on a legal problem with arguments offered by rhetoric, that is, with topical arguments. Both positions were reasonable. The controversies were included by Gaius in his elementary textbook on Roman law. For him, and for his students, the relationship between Roman law and rhetoric was a matter of course.

4. LEGAL SCIENCE AND RHETORIC IN JUSTINIAN'S DIGEST

Justinian's Digest is generally regarded as reflecting the culmination of Roman legal thought. It contains fifty books divided into titles. Each title consists of texts taken from the work of one or more jurists who lived in a period ranging from about 100 BCE to 250 CE. In these texts, the jurists

summarise legal problems and indicate how they should be solved, sometimes also referring to other jurists who do or do not hold the same opinion.
The works of the classical jurists have not been preserved; we know them
because they were included in collections made between the fourth and sixth
centuries, the most important one being the Digest.

On 15 December 530, Emperor Justinian I ordered his Minister of Justice,
Tribonian, to make a compilation of classical Roman law.[32] In the Byzantine
Empire, the writings of the classical jurists were still used to support or
deny legal claims but the content and authenticity of the texts were often
dubious. The new collection, the Digest, was intended to solve that problem.
Tribonian and a dozen experts were given wide powers: they were allowed
to select texts that were suitable for inclusion, to delete superfluous and outdated elements, and to solve contradictions. To structure the collection, they
used the same order that had been used by the classical jurists themselves,
that of the praetorian edict.

Since the second century BCE, when the new praetor *urbanus* started his
year of office, he published an edict in which he announced for what types
of claims he would allow a procedure, and how such claims and possible
defences could be worded in a *formula*.[33] In the course of time, the edicts
had grown into a body of law that was ordered more or less according to the
formulary procedure. No edict has come down to us, but from the time of
S. Sulpicius Rufus, a prominent jurist of the late Republic, the jurists used
the edict as a frame of reference to order their opinions. They published
their collections under the title *Digesta*, *Responsa*, *Quaestiones*, and the like.[34]
In the third century, the formulary procedure was replaced by imperial
jurisdiction, but the substantive law remained applicable. Therefore, it made
sense for Tribonian and his compilers to use the structure of the edict for
ordering the opinions of the classical jurists.

As we described in the previous section, the jurists of modern times preferred the structure of Gaius' Institutes to create a new system of Roman
law. However, Roman law as described in Justinian's Digest was regarded
as the high point of Roman legal science. The question then arose how it
could be established that Roman law was a science. This is the subject of the
famous monograph by Franz Horak, *Rationes decidendi*, published in 1969.[35]
In this book, Horak discusses some 300 texts in order to ascertain whether
Roman law was a science. Horak adheres to the commonly held view that
rhetoric is irrelevant in this context.

In the following, we will first summarise Horak's view, adding our

---

[32] See Tellegen-Couperus (1990), pp. 141–4.
[33] On the formulary procedure and the activities of the jurists, see Tellegen-Couperus (1990),
     pp. 53–62.
[34] On the basis of these works, Lenel (1927) has been able to reconstruct the praetorian edict.
[35] Horak (1969). The second part has never been published.

comments. Then we will discuss a Digest text that, in his view, 'proves' the scientific character of Roman law. We will demonstrate that it does not do so and that it can only be properly explained by connecting it to rhetoric.

Legal science in Justinian's Digest

Whereas Kaser in his definition of legal science only mentioned the existence of a dogmatic system, Horak also required a context of justification (*Begründungszusammenhang*). He described justification as a combination of sentences that are connected in such a way that one is considered explicitly as a logical consequence of the other. This connection may exist because a conclusion is drawn from a premise, or because one sentence is connected with another, argumentative one. Horak took into account only those motivations that were explicitly qualified as such. In his view, there is a constant interaction between the system and the justification.

According to Horak, it was essential to distinguish the context of justification from the context of discovery. The latter concept serves to find an argument, and particularly requires intuition. The former serves to prove a logical reasoning to be correct. For legal science, only the context of justification is relevant. Nowadays, however, there is a tendency to involve facts and values in legal reasoning, for instance by using analogy, so that law can only partially be regarded as a science. In this connection, Horak discussed Viehweg's book.

There are various reasons why Horak disagreed with Viehweg. One of them is that Viehweg does not distinguish between the context of justification and the context of discovery. As a result, he applies *topica* to an indiscriminate range of cases and veils the contrast between legal understanding and normative legal policy. According to Horak, Aristotle's *Topica* and its historical derivations hardly contribute to scientific understanding as a method to find an argument, and do not do so at all as a method to prove a logical argument to be correct or not.

The main part of Horak's book consists of the analysis of about 300 texts dating from the late Republic that contain some form of argumentation. They are divided into two groups. In the first group, the argumentation consists of deduction from a certain premise, for instance the application of a general or individual legal norm, the conclusion from a legal rule, or deduction from a certain legal concept. In the second group, the argumentation is not so clear. Here, for instance, the premise is uncertain or the deduction is not compelling like arguing from analogy. Only for the first category can the *rationes decidendi* be qualified as scientific. Therefore, Roman law can only partially be regarded as a science. Although Horak does not want to draw a general conclusion from texts that only belong to the late Republic, he suggests that the Roman jurists reached the same scientific level as jurists of our day.

We would like to make a few comments on Horak's monograph. First, Horak regarded two elements as essential requirements for establishing the existence of a legal science: a kind of system and a context of justification; he analyses the texts as to the context of justification, but he does not specify the system of Roman law. Second, we doubt whether it really makes sense to distinguish between the context of justification and the context of discovery in connection with *topoi*; the *topos* is relevant not only to law-finding but also to justify a decision, a rule or a subsumption.[36] Third, just like Viehweg, Horak dramatically underestimated Cicero's *Topica*. In the previous section, we demonstrated that the controversies described in Gaius' Institutes could only be explained by connecting them to topical argumentation.

In the following, we will try to assess whether Horak's conclusion about the scientific character of Roman law is correct. Horak dealt with the 300 or so texts in an order beginning with the one that provides the best evidence of the scientific character of Roman law, and ending with the one that is least fit to do so. In the context of this chapter, we want to discuss one of his texts. It seems to make sense to focus on the very first one.

Legal reasoning in D.43.19.3pr

The first category of texts discussed by Horak consists of those that include justifications by applying a legal norm. Horak qualified this category as the most obvious way of justification for the modern lawyer, since it is a simple subsumption under a general or individual norm. In the late Republic, there were not as many laws as there are today, so the Roman jurists did not have much to do in the way of justification by simple subsumption. Consequently, this first category includes but a few texts and has hardly anything attractive to offer as to law.

For the first category, justifications by applying a general norm, Horak admits that it has been difficult to find suitable texts. Indeed, there is only one that qualifies: D.43.19.3pr:[37]

> Ulpian in book 70 Edict. Hence, also Labeo writes as follows: If you have right-fully been having the use of a road from me, and I sell the farm through which the road you used went, and then the buyer prohibits you, then even if you are held to have used it by stealth from him (for whoever uses a road when prohibited, uses it by stealth), the interdict is still available to you within a year, because in this year you will have used it not by force or stealth or *precarium*.

Digest title D.43.19 deals with the edictal clause about the private right of way in person and with cattle. It consists mainly of texts taken from the 70th book of Ulpian's commentary on the praetorian edict. In this text, Ulpian

---

[36] In the same vein, Wieacker (1970), pp. 339–55, particularly p. 352; Honoré (1973), p. 59.

[37] Translation from Watson (1985).

quotes Labeo, a jurist who lived at the time of Emperor Augustus. The facts are relatively simple. Plaintiff A claims to have a right of way through his neighbour's land. The previous neighbour has sold the land to B, probably without telling him about the servitude. When B sees A walking on his land, he forbids him to do so. A turns to the praetor and asks him to grant the interdict *De itinere actuque privato*. It is granted, but the new neighbour does not comply, and a trial follows.

The *interdictum De itinere actuque privato* was a praetorian remedy prohibiting interference with rights of way. It protected anyone who, in the year before the interdict was issued, had used the way not by force or stealth or *precario*.[38] In the opening text of title D.43.19, it is formulated as follows:[39]

> The Praetor says: I forbid the use of force to prevent you from using the private right of way in person or with cattle that is in question, which you have used this year not by force or stealth or *precario* from him.

According to Horak, the interdict posed a general norm and the only thing the jurist Labeo had to do was subsume the facts under this norm. The only condition for applying the interdict would be that the plaintiff had used the right without force, stealth or *precario* during the previous year, even if he had done so only during a short time. Later wrongful use did not exclude the interdict. This is Horak's interpretation of the case.

In our view, this is not simply a case of subsumption. If so, it would not have been necessary to interpret the wording of the interdict. However, the wording is not clear. When is someone acting *clam*, with stealth? How is the time limit of one year to be understood? Labeo admits that someone who is using the servitude after the owner has prohibited him from doing so is acting *clam*. Still, he argues that the interdict should protect that person. The time limit of one year is vague but Labeo does not specify whether even a short time within that year is sufficient. Here, Horak refers to Ulpian who, in another text, argued that even a short time like thirty days would be sufficient. Apparently, the words 'with stealth' and 'in this year' were subject to discussion.

In the procedure, both parties would have presented arguments to support their views. A claimed that B should stop hindering him from using the right of way because, in the past year, he had used it *nec vi nec clam nec precario*. B could put forward two arguments. First, he could deny that the interdict was applicable because, after he had forbidden A to use the road

---

[38] *Precarium* was a contract consisting of the gratuitous grant of the enjoyment of land or movables, the grantor being able to terminate the arrangement at any time. Cf. Borkowski and du Plessis (2005), p. 309, (2010, 4th edn), p. 308.

[39] D.43.19.1pr: 'Praetor ait: Quo itinere actuque [privato], quo de agitur, [vel via] hoc anno nec vi nec clam nec precario ab illo usus es, quo minus ita utaris, vim fieri veto'. Translation based on Watson (1985).

through his farm, A had still done so and therefore had acted with stealth. Second, he could state that the interdict should not be taken literally. During the previous year, A had hardly used the road or not at all and it would be unreasonable to let him be protected by the interdict. The purpose of the interdict was to protect the use of a servitude on a regular basis.

A could reply to the second argument that the interdict does not specify a minimum time limit for using the interdict, and that it therefore should be applied in his case. Moreover, what is 'a minimum'? A could refer to the paradox of the *sorites* introduced by the Greek philosopher Eubulides;[40] it was not until 200 years later that Ulpian fixed it at thirty days. It was more difficult for A to refute B's first argument; even Labeo himself had to admit that. However, Labeo succeeded to convince the judge that the words of the interdict allowed it to be granted to A.

From the above, it is clear that the interdict in question does not provide a certain premise and that Labeo's text does not present a case of subsumption. The interdict was interpreted by one party according to the letter, by the other party according to the intention. In terms of the status theory of rhetoric, the status *scriptum – sententia* was used. The text therefore does not present a case of legal science.

5. CONCLUSION

If we are right to suppose that Roman law was not a science in the modern sense and that it was closely connected to rhetoric, then new fields of research open up. The accepted method of researching Roman law will change. It is no longer necessary to (re)construct the system of Roman law as has been done over the past five centuries or to try to accommodate opinions of jurists that seem to deviate from the regular pattern. It is no longer necessary to try to explain why the same jurist had a different opinion in another, similar case. It is no longer necessary to keep Cicero out of the way.

What remains is the notion that the Roman jurists reached a remarkably high level of sophistication in creating law. However, it will now be interesting to discover how they argued legal problems from both sides; in the Digest, there are a number of texts showing such discussions. It will be interesting to see whether so-called rhetorical sources can contribute to understanding the development of Roman law. Unfortunately, it will hardly be possible to assess whether the actual presentation of a point of view in a trial influenced the outcome: a bad *actio* could completely undermine a good legal argument, and vice versa.

It will be necessary to acquire some knowledge about the various rhetorical systems that were taught to young Romans belonging to the upper class,

[40] Döring (1998), p. 211. The *sorites* paradox is mentioned by Cic. *Acad.* 2.49: '[B]y adding a single grain at a time they make a heap'.

some of whom we now know as jurists. Here is a problem, for there is not much literature on classical rhetoric, particularly not on rhetoric in a legal context.[41] But a problem can be regarded as a challenge, and we hope this chapter may inspire scholars to take it up and study Roman law from a legal and rhetorical perspective.

BIBLIOGRAPHY

Arangio Ruiz, V., *Istituzioni di diritto romano*, 14th edn (1960, repr. 1978).

Borkowski A., and du Plessis, P., *Textbook on Roman Law*, 3rd edn (2005).

Bretone, M., *I fundamenti del diritto romano. Le cose e la natura* (1999).

Crook, J. A., *Legal Advocacy in the Roman World* (1995).

David, M., *Gaius Institutiones*, 2nd edn (1964).

David, M., and Nelson, H. L. W., *Gaius Institutionum Commentarii IV, Kommentar, 2. Lieferung* (1954–68).

de Francisci, P., *Sintesi storica del diritto romano*, 4th edn (1968).

de Zulueta, F., *The Institutes of Gaius* (1946).

Döring, K., 'Eubulides aus Milete', in *Der neue Pauly. Altertum*, 4 (1998), p. 211.

Feenstra, R., '*Dominium* and *ius in re aliena*: The origins of a civil law distinction', in P. B. H. Birks (ed.), *New Perspectives on the Roman Law of Property. Essays in honour of Barry Nicholas* (1989), p. 111.

Feldman, R., *The Role of Science in Law* (2009).

Frost, M. H., *Introduction to Classical Legal Rhetoric* (2005).

Gaines, R. N., 'Cicero's *Partitiones Oratoriae* and *Topica*: Rhetorical Philosophy and Philosophical Rhetoric', in J. M. May (ed.), *Brill's Companion to Cicero. Oratory and Rhetoric* (2002), p. 445.

Gordon, W. M. and Robinson, O. F., *The Institutes of Gaius* (1988).

Honoré, A. M., 'Legal reasoning in Rome and today', *Cambrian LR*, 4 (1973), p. 59.

Horak, F., *Rationes decidendi. Entscheidungsbegründungen bei den älteren römischen Juristen bis Labeo*, vol. I (1969).

Jolowicz, H. F., and Nicholas, B., *Historical Introduction to the Study of Roman Law*, 3rd edn (1972).

Kaser, M., *Römische Rechtsgeschichte* (1967).

Kaser, M., *Römisches Privatrecht*, 15th edn (1989).

Leesen, T. G., *Gaius meets Cicero. Law and Rhetoric in the School Controversies* (2010).

Lenel, O., *Das edictum perpetuum*, 3rd edn (1927).

Nicosia, G., '*Ea quae iure consistunt*', in A. Palma (ed.), *Scritti in onore di Generoso Melillo*, vol. II (2009), p. 821.

Salkowski, C., *Institutionen. Grundzüge des Systems und der Geschichte des römischen Privatrechts*, 7th rev. edn (1898).

---

[41] Frost (2005) has some interesting chapters on the history of rhetoric, but does not make any reference to Roman law at all. Tellegen-Couperus (2003) contains some twenty-five papers dealing with the twelve books of Quintilian's *Institutio Oratoria* from a legal and a rhetorical point of view.

Schulz, F., *History of Roman Legal Science* (1946).

Schulz, F., *Classical Roman Law* (1951).

Stein, P., *Roman Law in European History* (1999),

Stroux, J., *Summum ius summa iniuria, Ein Kapittel aus der Geschichte der interpretatio iuris*, in: *Römische Rechtswissenschaft und Rhetorik* (1949), p. 9.

Tellegen-Couperus, O., and Tellegen, J. W., 'Law and rhetoric in the *Causa Curiana*', *Orbis Iuris Romani*, 6 (2000), p. 171.

Tellegen-Couperus, O., and Tellegen, J. W., '*Nihil hoc ad ius, ad Ciceronem*', RIDA, 53 (2006), p. 381.

Tellegen-Couperus, O., and Tellegen, J. W., 'Achieving justice by twisting the truth', in A. Corbino (ed.), *Studi per Giovanni Nicosia*, vol. 8 (2007), p. 231.

Tellegen-Couperus, O., *A Short History of Roman Law* (1990).

Tellegen-Couperus, O. (ed.), *Quintilian and the Law* (2003).

Tellegen, J. W., *The Roman Law of Succession in the Letters of Pliny the Younger* (1982).

Tellegen, J. W., '*Res incorporales* et les codifications modernes du droit civil', *Labeo* 40 (1994), p. 35.

van Oven, J. C., *Leerboek van Romeinsch privaatrecht* (1948).

Viehweg, T., *Topik und Jurisprudenz. Ein Beitrag zur rechtswissenschaftlichen Grundlagenforschung*, 5th rev. edn (1974).

Viehweg, T., *Topics and Law. A Contribution to Basic Research in Law* (1993).

Villers, R., *Rome et le droit privé* (1977).

Villey, M., 'L'idée du droit subjectif et les systèmes juridiques romains', RHD, 24–5 (1946–7), p. 201.

Watson, A. (ed.), *The Digest of Justinian*, 4 vols (1985).

Wieacker, F., 'Review of Horak, *Rationes Decidendi*', in ZSS (rom. Abt.), 90 (1970), p. 339.

Chapter 4

The Senatus Consultum Silanianum: Court Decisions and Judicial Severity in the Early Roman Empire

Jill Harries

1. INTRODUCTION

In status-conscious ancient Rome, while legal discourse aspired to fairness (*aequitas*),[1] the poor were more cruelly punished, when convicted of criminal conduct, than the rich,[2] and the slave's legal protection was almost non-existent compared with that of the free man or woman.[3] In some respects, Roman attitudes to slavery were benign: good slaves could be freed by will or in the master's lifetime; freedmen were often close confidants of their masters, as Tiro was of Cicero; and the manumitted slave might live to see his descendants prosper as full Roman citizens. But master-slave relationships were not always so harmonious: a slave-owning society could never be entirely at ease with itself. A specific source of concern was that, in wealthy households, the master and his family would be heavily outnumbered by his slaves. And disaffected slaves, it was feared, might either kill the master themselves or connive at his killing by others.

A policy of deterrence was the answer. One element in this was the Senatus Consultum (SC) Silanianum, which was passed in 10 CE, and modified over time by a series of court decisions, supplemented by juristic interpretations. The Roman Senate had, through its resolutions (*senatus consulta*), a role as a legislator, which became more significant after the popular assemblies ceased to function late in the reign of Augustus (30 BCE to 14 CE).[4] But where its own interests were at stake, the Roman Senate made its decisions not on the basis of the kind of dispassionate legal thinking we might associate with Roman law as a discipline, but in line with its own emotions, social attitudes and prejudices. Whatever their personal relationships with their slave establishment, senators were terrified of 'Slaves' in the abstract. The reaction of the Younger Pliny, early in the second century

---

[1] Cf. Ulpian at D.1.1.1.1 (Ulpian. 1 Inst.) that law is the 'art of the good and the fair' (*ars boni et aequi*).
[2] See Garnsey (1970).
[3] For the convention that slaves should not be treated with excessive harshness, see Inst.Gai. 1.53; Garnsey (1996), pp. 90–3. On slaves' right of asylum, see Garnsey (1996), pp. 95–6.
[4] See Talbert (1984), pp. 431–59.

CE, to the brutal murder by his slaves of an admittedly cruel master, was representative of this attitude:[5] even kind and considerate masters were in danger, he wrote, because slaves were not reasoning beings but followed their instincts, like animals.

The evolution of the SC Silanianum therefore provides a useful case study of the impact of elite self-interest on the development of law. But it should be emphasised that, in some respects, the elite behaviours revealed in their reactions to master-murder are extreme. Other voices were more understanding, notably those of philosophers like Seneca,[6] who emphasised the shared humanity of master and slave, although none challenged the institution of slavery as such. Legal discourse acknowledged the 'quality' of slaves as people, although sometimes only because this affected their value as property: the damages, for example, that could be sued for because of an injury to a slave would be assessed in terms of his *qualitas*, as honest and entrusted with important responsibilities or, alternatively, as a notorious convict.[7] Under the Early Empire, the killing of slaves by masters could qualify as homicide[8] and, in the second century, cases of maltreatment of slaves by their masters could reach the attention of provincial governors, even of emperors. In 152 CE Antoninus Pius listed a series of cases of abuse, which had come to the attention of the governor of Baetica in southern Spain; in all three cases, the complaints of the slaves were taken seriously – in part because disaffected slaves were less valuable – and their abusive masters (or mistresses) cautioned or punished.[9]

The SC Silanianum is peculiarly harsh, designed to address exceptional situations, in which slaves had (apparently) got out of control. Perhaps because it was they who were most threatened, senators were the most active in the extension of the application of the SC, through senatus consulta and decisions reached by them acting as a court. Through these and the occasional verdict issued by provincial governors, who in the first and second centuries CE were also senators, the elite as a collective, rather than the jurists, controlled its implementation, and their fears, as we shall see, created new and, in general, harsher precedents. The history of the SC Silanianum, therefore, does not only document the effect of senatorial self-interest on a specific aspect of slave law, that of master-murder; it also provides an illustration of the importance of court-made law for legal evolution. The spectacle is not an edifying one. Little heed seems to have been paid to legal precision or to such residual human rights as slaves might still claim. Separate issues became

[5] Plin. *Ep.* 3.14.
[6] Sen. *Ep.* 47 and *Ben.* 3.18 and 20; Garnsey (1996), pp. 67–9.
[7] D.47.10.15.44 (Ulpian. 77 ad Ed.).
[8] Suet. *Claud.* 25.2; D.40.8.2 (Modestin. 6 Reg.)
[9] D.1.6.2 (Ulpian. 8 de Off. Procos.); *Coll.*3.3.1–6 (Ulpian. 8 de Off. Procos.); Inst 1.8.1. For an argument that legal policy towards slaves was consistently harsh (i.e. more in line with the attitudes that drove the SC Silanianum), see Watson (1983), pp. 53–65.

confused and, on at least one occasion, procedures designed to ensure that the processes of investigation, interrogation and conviction were carried out in the right order, and punishment inflicted on the right people, seem to have been casually disregarded.

The SC Silanianum was also of interest to jurists although, as we shall see, it was categorised in a characteristically technical and specialist way, as a civil law matter. But for the attitudes that drove its evolution, we must rely on Roman senatorial writers, especially the *Annales* of the advocate and historian Tacitus, and the *Letters* of his contemporary the Younger Pliny. Both flourished under the Flavians (r. 69–96) and Trajan (r. 98–117). Pliny died in around 112 CE and Tacitus' *Annales* are the product of the end of Trajan's reign and the early years of Hadrian (from 117). As senators and prominent orators, they observed the reactions of their colleagues to events; Pliny in particular also shows their social assumptions at work by voicing them as his own. But, although both Tacitus and Pliny knew some law, they did not write as legal specialists. Theirs, therefore, is the perspective on law of the intelligent layman, who appreciated from their own experience that law was not the preserve only of lawyers, and that the Senate had considerable discretion to act in matters concerning itself, as it saw fit. It was also the perspective of literary craftsmen, masters of allusion, who reshaped the raw material of law and history as commentary on their times.

Although not the main decision-makers, the jurists, especially Ulpian, have an important role as a supplement and a corrective to a record dominated by senatorial decisions. It is they, rather than Pliny or Tacitus, who reveal that part of the difficulty with interpreting the SC was that the meanings of key terms, which could affect the scope and severity of its implementation, were disputed. Ulpian's analysis – which is contained in his commentary on the praetorian edict, as codified in c 130 CE – was the last significant stage in the development of law based on the SC Silanianum, although later texts provide extra information on how some questions, still live in Ulpian's time, were resolved.[10] Jurists, with the significant exception of C. Cassius Longinus (suffect consul in 30 CE), were not directly involved in the main stages in the evolution of the law on master-murder after 10 CE, which were the SC Claudianum or Neronianum in 57 CE; the controversial execution of the slave *familia* of the murdered Pedanius Secundus in 61 CE; a debate recorded in a letter of the Younger Pliny concerning the fate of the *familia* of a dead senator, the cause of whose death was disputed, in 105 CE; and a court decision made by the *legatus*, Trebius Geminus, which was validated by its incorporation into juristic commentary.

---

[10] Later modifications and explanations are contained in Paul. *Sent.* 3.5 and C.6.35.

2. 'VETUS MOS': CUSTOMARY LAW BEFORE THE SC SILANIANUM

In his account of the execution of the slaves of the murdered Pedanius Secundus, Tacitus did not ascribe their deaths to the provisions of the SC Silanianum but to 'ancient custom' (*vetus mos*).[11] As an advocate, Tacitus knew his law. He knew also the difference between unwritten customary law and statute – and that the relationship between the two was far from straightforward and required frequent clarification. Adultery was a good example: adulterous wives had 'customarily' been punished by their families, but Augustus had, in 18 BCE, introduced a criminal court to try alleged offenders, and probably stipulated the penalty of confiscation of property and exile on separate islands.[12] Despite this, custom persisted. For example, when recording the sentence passed in 17 CE at the suggestion of Tiberius on Appuleia Varilia by her family for adultery, Tacitus refers to the ancestral customary practice of exile beyond the 200th milestone from Rome.[13] Tacitus' treatment of the episode makes a clear distinction between the statute on the one hand and the procedures and penalties established by the customary law, that preceded it and still (thanks to Tiberius) ran in parallel with the Augustan reform.

As Tacitus was fully capable of drawing the line between customary legal practice and formal legal enactment, we would expect similar care from him in his treatment of the Pedanius Secundus episode; 'vetus mos' was not to be identified with the SC Silanianum, because it was something different. This does not establish beyond doubt that the SC made no mention of the penalties that awaited slaves, under customary law, for failure to protect. The point is that it was not responsible for their introduction and that they were incidental to its main purpose, which, as we shall see, was to instruct the praetor, or investigating magistrate, on the rules governing conduct of the *quaestio*, the investigation into the causes of the master's death and who (if anyone) was responsible.

Little is known of legal practice in cases of master-murder under the Republic, but two incidents are indicative. One was the reaction of the slaves and freedmen of Marcus Marcellus, the ex-consul, to the murder of their master by a known individual with a grievance in Athens in 45 BCE.[14]

---

[11] Tac. *Ann.* 14.42.

[12] Paul. *Sent.* 2.26.14. On the Augustan adultery law, see Treggiari (1991), pp. 277–90.

[13] Tac. *Ann.* 2.50.4: 'ut exemplo maiorum propinquis suis ultra ducentesimum lapidem removerentur suasit'. Cf. Suet. *Tib.* 35, allowing jurisdiction 'in line with ancestral custom' (*more maiorum*) by the family council in cases of adultery where no public prosecution was forthcoming; and Tac. *Ann.* 13.32.3 on the trial in 57 CE of Pomponia Graeca by her husband and family council for adultery 'in line with ancient established practice' (*prisco instituto*).

[14] Cic. *Fam.* 4.12.3.

They ran away, and 'very few' were left, when the body was discovered. We do not know specifically what consequences were anticipated by Marcellus' *familia*; clearly, even though the murderer was not a member of the *familia*, they were terrifying enough for the slaves and freedmen to prefer the risks of running away to those of staying put.

The second, from a later source and therefore possibly anachronistic, is of more interest, as it shows a Republican jurist's awareness of what the consequences to a slave might be of a master taking his own life. After the defeat of Brutus and Cassius at Philippi in 42 BCE, Pacuvius Labeo, father of the more famous jurist Antistius Labeo, committed suicide with the assistance of a slave. However, he manumitted the slave first, so that the slave could not be entrapped by the customary sanction that he should be punished, as a slave, for failing to, in effect, protect the master from himself.[15] It is possible that Appian, writing long after the passing of the SC Silanianum, has allowed his account to be influenced by later developments. However, the likeliest original source for the anecdote, if not an invention, would be a reliable one, Pacuvius' son, Antistius Labeo, who would follow his father in keeping a sturdily 'Republican' distance from the new Augustan order.[16]

3. THE SC SILANIANUM, 10 CE

The sponsor of the Senatus consultum Silanianum was the consul of 10 CE, one C. Junius Silanus, a member of a distinguished senatorial family.[17] His cousin, Marcus, would also be consul nine years later and Marcus' daughter, Junia Lepida, would marry the distinguished jurist and suffect consul of 30 CE, C. Cassius Longinus, who, in 61 CE, would play a prominent and controversial role in the further evolution of the application of the SC Silanianum. Perhaps he may even have felt some sense that his family 'owned' the resolution or should, at the very least, have some privileged say in its interpretation.[18]

Despite the seriousness of master-murder, and the setting-up under the SC of a *publica quaestio*, which would be conducted under the conventions governing criminal offences, the framework within which juristic discussion of the SC would be conducted was that of private or civil law. As part of its regulation of the *quaestio* process, the SC contained provisions, to

---

[15] Appian. *H.R.* 4.135; D.29.5.1.22 (Ulpian. 50 ad Ed.) states that the SC Silanianum does not apply in cases of suicide except if done in the presence of a slave who could have intervened but failed to do so. See also Paul. *Sent.* 3.5.4.

[16] Tac. *Ann.* 3.70 and 75 (his freedom of speech contrasted with the servility of Ateius Capito); Aulus Gellius, *N.A.* 13.12.1 (traditionalism of Labeo as a lawyer); Dio, *H.R.* 54.15.7–8 (distance from Augustus).

[17] Syme (1986), 'The Junii Silani', pp. 188–99 and Tables XII and XIII.

[18] This may also be the reason for Pliny's addressing of his letter on his own difficulties with the SC to Cassius' pupil, Titius Aristo (*Ep.* 8.14, discussed below).

be enforced by the praetor, which prevented the opening of the will of the deceased. These were incorporated at some point into the praetorian edict and were commented on by Ulpian and others in the context of the Edict, not of the law on homicide. Later sources, such as Paulus' *Sententiae* (3.5) and Justinian's Digest (29.5), followed his lead and incorporated interpretation of the SC Silanianum into discussion of how wills should be administered and under what conditions they should not be opened.

The instruction of the SC to the praetor declared that, where a master had been killed by open violence, the will of the deceased should not be opened, until an investigation (*quaestio*) into the death had been completed.[19] The purpose of this was to prevent any possible murderer hoping to benefit from the will from profiting from its provisions, if they were implemented prior to investigation, trial and conviction. This was especially relevant to slaves manumitted in the will. As the will would not be opened prior to the *quaestio*, the slaves who hoped for freedom would remain slaves, and thus subject to the other provisions of the SC, until the truth was known.

There was clearly, therefore, an obligation on the heirs not to open the will and confiscation of property would follow if the heirs were shown to have failed in their duty.[20] That obligation could, however, be breached, owing to ignorance, which was excusable.[21] The failure had implications; implementation of legacies or manumissions in the will could benefit a murderer or his associates and was a failure of duty, in that the heir denied himself the power to 'avenge' the death of the testator. The integrity of the will was not, therefore, a technical matter; it also reflected the social requirement on a dutiful heir to exact justice and punish the guilty.[22] Still, an heir could not be held liable forever and, in 11 CE, a rider to the SC imposed a time limit of five years on the lodging of a complaint against him.[23] Nor, as Severus Alexander ruled in 232, could an heir be held liable if the killers could not be traced.[24]

What were the circumstances in which the SC Silanianum would apply? Ulpian's commentary shows that four terms (at least) in the (now lost) text required elucidation. *Dominus*, he wrote, referred to the man who had full ownership (*proprietas*), not the usufruct, and the protection of the law should be extended to the *filii familias*, the sons of the household, and the

---

[19] D.29.5.3.18 (Ulpian. 50 ad Ed.) (the opening of a will of a man said to be *occisus*): 'edicto cavetur, priusquam de ea familia quaestio ex senatus consulto habita suppliciumque de noxiis sumptum fuerit'.

[20] D.29.5.3.5 (Ulpian. 50 ad Ed.); 29.5.8 (Paul. 46 ad Ed.); 29.5.9 (Gaius 17 ad Ed. Prov.); 29.5.15 (Marcian. 1 Delat.); 49.14.14 (Gaius 11 ad Leg. Iul. Pap.).

[21] D.29.5.3.22 (Ulpian. 50 ad Ed.).

[22] Cf. Paul. *Sent.* 3.5.2: it befits the honour of the heir that he does not allow the death of the testator, by whatever means, to pass unavenged ('honestati enim heredis convenit qualemcumque mortem testatoris inultam non praetermittere').

[23] D.29.5.13 (Venul. Saturn. 2 de Pub. Iud.).

[24] C.6.35.7 (a. 232).

other children in power (*in potestate*) – as well as, perhaps, those who were not.[25] *Servi*, slaves, liable for interrogation, included also slaves who might achieve their freedom under arrangements already made, and slaves of a son, even when part of the son's independently owned property as a soldier (*peculium castrense*).[26] There were also debates about the liability of the slaves of spouses (who were liable) and of fathers-in-law, who were not, although Ulpian and others disagreed.[27]

Moreover, masters could die without being killed (*occisus*). Antistius Labeo, who could have been present at the debate, when the SC was agreed, stated that there had to be visible evidence that force had been used.[28] Poison, therefore, by definition a secret crime, did not, initially, activate the SC, unless there was evidence that it had been forcibly administered. This exemption, however, had been overturned by the end of the third century.[29] Nor, in Ulpian's view, was it applicable if a master committed suicide in private, although the slaves were expected to intervene, if they knew about it. And, finally, there was the question of where the slaves were. Those liable were described as 'under the same roof' (*sub eodem tecto*), which evoked further discussion about how far away a slave could be, and still be liable. The 'roof' became a mobile concept; slaves in attendance (and therefore not under a roof) were liable if their master was killed on a journey away from home.[30] Here judges' law through court decisions made an unwelcome intervention. According to another jurist, cited by Ulpian, 'it had often been adjudged' (*sic esse saepe iudicatum*) that being under the same roof could apply to anyone close enough to hear a cry for help. Ulpian did not agree: the strength of voices, he said, varies.[31] The last word on this lay with Justinian who, in 532 CE, ruled that, as the ancients had failed to provide an adequate definition of 'sub eodem tecto', henceforward all slaves who were within shouting distance of the master, wherever he and they were, would be liable, be that 'in the house, on the road or in the countryside'.[32]

---

[25] D.29.5.1.1; 6; 8 (Ulpian. 50 ad Ed.).

[26] D.25.5.1.4–5; 14 (Ulpian. 50 ad Ed.).

[27] D.29.5.1.15–16 (Ulpian. 50 ad Ed.).

[28] D.29.5.1.17 (Ulpian. 50 ad Ed.).

[29] D.29.5.1.18 (Ulpian. 50 ad Ed.) (poison); D.29.5.1.19 (forcible administration of poison); Paul. *Sent.* 3.5.2; not only were men deemed to be killed (*occisus*) when lethal force applied 'per vim aut per caedem' but also when a man is killed by poison ('sed et is qui veneno necatus dicitur').

[30] D.29.5.1.31 (Ulpian. 50 ad Ed.); Paul. *Sent.* 3.5.6: 'Sed et hi torquentur, qui cum occiso in itinere fuerunt'.

[31] D.29.5.1.27 (Ulpian. 50 ad Ed). However, the hard line taken by Ulpian's anonymous judges was endorsed by Paul. *Sent.* 3.5.7: Slaves from close by, if they failed to bring help to the master on hearing his cries for help, when they could have done, are punished ('Servi de proximo si, cum possent ferre, auditis clamoribus auxilium domino non tulerunt, puniuntur').

[32] C.6.35.12 (a. 532): 'ex quocumque loco sive in domo sive in via sive in agro possent clamorem audire vel insidias sentire et non auxilium tulerint'.

4. THE POWER OF FEAR

The primary purpose of the SC Silanianum was deterrence. Early in the
third century, Ulpian, who was not a senator, set the passing of the SC
Silanianum and its successor resolutions firmly in the context of masters'
fears for their own safety:

> cum aliter nulla domus tuta esse possit, nisi periculo capitis sui custodiam dominis
> tam ab domesticis quam ab extraneis praestare servi cogantur, ideo senatus con-
> sulta introducta sunt de publica quaestione a familia necatorum habenda.[33]

> As no household could be secure in any way other than that the slaves should be
> compelled under pain of capital punishment to offer protection to their masters
> from dangers both from those within the house and from outsiders, for this
> reason, senatorial resolutions were passed concerning the public investigation
> (*quaestio*) to be conducted taking evidence from the *familia* of the persons killed.

The subject of the SC, then, was the procedures governing the running of the
quaestio. However, embedded in the tradition, as it had evolved by Ulpian's
time, was a fundamental confusion, between the investigative process (*quaestio*), established by the SC, and the infliction of punishment on the guilty.
How, in such a context, was guilt to be defined? The opening part refers to
the punishment, which, under Tacitus' 'ancient custom', awaited slaves who
failed to protect their masters from danger, when they could have done; they
were compelled to protect him 'periculo capitis sui'. But the second part
refers specifically to the court of investigation, *quaestio*, established by the SC
Silanianum and its successors. As part of this process, slaves resident 'under
the same roof' (*sub eodem tecto*) would become liable to judicial interrogation,
which, for slaves, entailed the automatic use of torture,[34] a rule which had
the incidental effect of violating the principle established by Augustus and
his successors that torture should not be used as a first resort.[35] The primary
purpose of the *quaestio* process was not to punish the slaves for failing to
protect their masters but to find out what they knew about the murderer
and his accomplices.[36] Eligibility for judicial torture should not have meant,

---

[33] D.29.5.1pr (Ulpian. 50 ad Ed.).
[34] D.48.18 on *quaestio* (interrogation) procedure contains extensive regulations on which
slaves were liable for interrogation/torture; voluntary confessions of slaves implicating their
masters were invalid (D.48.18.18.5 (Paul. 5 *Sent.*)).
[35] D.48.18.1pr and 1 (Ulpian. 1 de Off. Procos.), from Ulpian, *On the Duties of the Proconsul*,
which goes on to list slaves liable, or not, in other criminal judicial contexts.
[36] Cf. Buckland (1908), p. 96, who confuses the investigative roles of the *quaestio* with the (punishment for) the failure to protect, but does observe the distinction between judicial torture
and punishment: 'the basis of the liability to torture was that they did not render help. The
torture was not punishment; it was a preliminary to the *supplicium* that awaited the guilty
person. Not doing his best to save the *dominus* justified torture; more than that would of
course be needed for the conviction of the murderer'.

in itself, that the interrogated were automatically liable for punishment for failure to prevent the death.

One source for the confusion was that the two categories of slave, those who were liable for the *quaestio* and those who should face punishment for failure to protect, were virtually co-extensive. The slaves 'under the same roof' who might know about the murder were the same unfortunate individuals who should have protected him. Slaves resident not 'under the same roof' could not have intervened and, in general, were not likely to know anything useful either. Nor should the fate of the murderer him/herself be ignored. The failure to protect was a different order of wrongdoing from being directly or even indirectly involved in the killing itself – yet the slaves who did nothing and the murderer faced the same penalty. These three elements, then – the eligibility for interrogation, the liability for punishment for failure to protect, and liability for the death – became, from 10 CE, inextricably linked, owing to confusion in the Senate and the courts and, behind it all, elite masters' fear of their own slaves. By the time of Ulpian, the all-important distinction between *quaestio* and *supplicium* had disappeared and regulations on punishment were also now ascribed, perhaps erroneously, to the original text of the SC:

> Hoc autem senatus consultum eos quidem, qui sub eodem tecto fuerunt **omnimodo punit**, eos vero, qui non sub eodem tecto, sed in eadem regione non aliter nisi conscii fuissent.[37]

> This senatus consultum inflicts punishment (*omnimodo punit*) on those who were under the same roof but those who were not under the same roof but merely in the same region, it does not (punish), unless they were complicit in the deed.

There were also wider social assumptions at work. Punishments inflicted on the lower orders, slave and free, were designed to cause pain, to degrade and humiliate.[38] The idea of torture as punishment was therefore already present in the Roman penal system and would find further expression, for example in the tortures of Christian martyrs who were 'punished' by torture in the context of the *quaestio*, as well as in the arena, for failing to recant. But, as we have seen, there were other aspects of the SC Silanianum too, notably lack of clarity on the definitions of words and phrases, which were reinterpreted by successive legislative decision-makers, expanding its application in the general direction of increased severity. Students of law in Late Antiquity and the era of Justinian's *Corpus Iuris Civilis* (compiled 529–34 CE) are familiar with the apparent excesses of the late Roman judge, as evidenced in the infliction of extreme penalties on criminals, and the extension of the use of

---

[37] D.29.5.1.26 (Ulpian. 50 ad Ed.). The conventions of juristic shorthand would allow for the subsuming of the punitive aspect into the application of the SC, even if it were not covered in the original text.

[38] Millar (1984), pp. 124–47; Millar (2002), pp. 120–50.

judicial torture up the social scale[39] But Roman justice was always harsh; the expanded implementation of the SC Silanianum over the first century CE both foreshadows and helps to explain the judicial severity of the later centuries of the Roman Empire.

The SC Silanianum, like many Senatus consulta of the first century CE, was primarily concerned with providing instructions to the magistrate about a process. Its main focus, therefore, was on the *quaestio*, by which the violent death of a *dominus* would be investigated and the killer(s) punished. The 'liability' of slaves under the SC's provisions on the *quaestio* was to be interrogated under torture to find out what they knew. Coexisting with the resolution, however, was a separate convention, enshrined in older customary law, that slaves who failed to protect their masters, were liable for punishment. While it is possible that this was also acknowledged in the SC, it was not germane to its primary purpose. However, given the overlap of the categories of slave liable for judicial torture and those liable, under *vetus mos*, for execution, it was not likely that they would remain distinct for long.

5. THE MURDER OF PEDANIUS SECUNDUS, 61 CE

In 61 CE, the application of the SC and the customary law, which preceded it, was tested in a *cause célèbre*. Four hundred slaves from the *familia* (household establishment) of the murdered city prefect of Rome, Pedanius Secundus, were condemned to execution for failing to protect him, in line with 'ancient custom'. The killer, one of the slaves, was known and his motive, while disputed, was agreed to be a private grudge. While a large crowd assembled outside to demonstrate their disapproval at the apparent inhumanity of the sentence, within the Senate, the now aged C. Cassius Longinus, jurist and former suffect consul (in 30 CE), rose to defend the decision. The historian Tacitus, who would have had access to the original text in the *Acta Senatus*, the proceedings of the senate, reworked the speech to draw attention to the wider implications of the incident.[40] Cassius, as characterised in the speech, is Tacitus' most vivid representation of the senator as jurist, whose austere reputation acts to legitimise the raw emotion, which his argument in effect condoned. The speech thus exemplifies (some) Roman views on masters and slaves, the function of punishment, and the humanity, or lack of it, of *princeps*, senate and people.

In Tacitus' version of Cassius' speech, a socio-legal justification for *severitas* is combined with the self-portrait of a speaker who glories in being out of line with contemporary *mores*, despising modernity and intervening only when the need was greatest. However, it should also be recognised that Tacitus' Cassius is a literary creation. Like other jurists who delved into

---

[39] MacMullen (1986), pp. 147–66.
[40] Tac. *Ann.* 14.43–44. See Nörr (1983), pp. 187–222; Wolf (1988).

the meaning of obscure words in the Twelve Tables and the darker recesses of Roman antiquarian lore,[41] Cassius is represented as a stereotypical conservative. He was also a relic of the Roman Republic in another sense. The namesake of, and in some sense related to, C. Cassius Longinus, the assassin of Caesar, Tacitus' Cassius is the self-proclaimed embodiment of ancient Republican virtue. His high standards had already been evidenced in his strict governance of the army in Syria,[42] and he would later be implicated in a plot by his nephew by marriage, L. Silanus, against Nero and exiled;[43] one count against him was that he had images of the assassin Cassius in his house, an indication that he aspired to follow his example.[44] Yet the decisions of Cassius the jurist which survive suggest that he had a strong sense of fairness and could take the more lenient option: the status of athletes, for example, was safeguarded by his ruling that they competed for glory (*virtus*) not money; and no one, he said, should be compelled to undertake a curatorship of an estate against his will (although some thought otherwise).[45]

Cassius' speech, in Tacitus' representation, is therefore an assertion of ancient Republican integrity, against the debasement of public discourse by mistaken modern values. He is a throwback, but empowered by the fact that what he seeks to advocate and protect is 'ancient custom'. Behind this is a more sinister reality. Cassius' advocacy is not of 'ancient custom' but, as so often with Roman advocates, his reading of it. His justification for the execution – or judicial murder – of the 400 was based, not on a jurist's scrupulous reading of text, but simply on fear. Masters were afraid of their slaves, he said, and always had been, although the risks were greater now, because slaves were now drawn from many lands and cultures. According to the speaker, the slave *familia* had also demonstrably failed to protect their master: surely, Cassius argued, the murderer must have let slip some words, or someone should have noticed that he had acquired a weapon, or seen him making his way through the house with his light. In short, the other slaves had a duty to disclose what they knew, and must be controlled through fear of the consequences to them of failure. While Cassius conceded that the

---

[41] See, in brief, Harries (2006), pp. 85–90.

[42] Tac. *Ann.* 12.12.1.

[43] Tac. *Ann.* 16.7–9.

[44] O'Gorman (2000), pp. 59–60: '(Family *imagines*) . . . represent both the glorious past and the possibility of its repetition in the future . . . The images of Cassius do not stand for a dead past but one which is dangerously contiguous with the present'.

[45] D.3.2.4pr (Ulpian. 6 ad Ed.): 'Athletas autem Sabinus et Cassius responderunt omnino artem ludicram non facere; virtutis enim gratia hoc facere'; D.42.7.2.3 (Ulpian. 65 ad Ed.): 'Quaeritur, an invitus curator fieri potest: et Cassius scribit neminem invitum cogendum fieri bonorum curatorem; quod verius est'. He did, however, take a hard line on interpretation of the *Lex Julia* on *res repetundae* (restitution of the proceeds of extortion), arguing that a senator convicted under the law could not act as a witness (D.1.9.2 (Marcell. 3 Dig.): 'Cassius Longinus non putat ei permittendum qui propter turpitudinem senatu motus nec restitutus est, iudicare vel testimonium dicere, quia lex Iulia repetundarum hoc fieri vetat').

execution of innocent people was unjust, the fate of a few individuals was justified as contributing to the public good (*utilitas publica*) as a whole.

Cassius' authority, as both lawyer and ex-consul, and his advocacy of punishment as a means of deterrence carried the day. 'No one individual dared', wrote Tacitus, to contradict him, but pleas were nonetheless forth-coming from anonymous protesters among the crowd on the grounds of the numbers, age and sex of the victims.[46] Humanity and severity were in direct conflict. Cassius' arguments based on fear anticipate the formulation by Ulpian, as do his comments on the liability of slaves to execution on the grounds that they should have known or noticed something and therefore disclosed what they knew in time to prevent the murder. They had failed, in other words, in their duty to protect, as originally enshrined in customary law.

This, it may be suggested, was the point at which the procedural provi-sions of the SC Silanianum converged fully with customary law on the pun-ishment of slaves for failure to protect. For Tacitus combines reference to 'ancient custom' with the phraseology of the SC: it was the *familia* 'under the same roof,' which, under *vetus mos*, was liable to punishment.[47] But neither Tacitus, nor his Cassius, cited specific clauses in the SC to validate Cassius' argument. And Tacitus could have done; he knew of the SC, as he records a clarification introduced by, probably, the SC Neronianum or Claudianum in 57 CE, that when a master was killed, even slaves manumitted by will could be subject to the *quaestio* and punished (although it is not clear than one inevitably followed from the other).[48]

The SC Neronianum and the aftermath of Pedanius' murder are mile-stones along a road leading towards increased judicial severity. The SC of 57 expanded the scope of the SC Silanianum by making slaves manumitted by will liable to the *quaestio*; and the precedents created by the executions in 61 were still more serious in their implications. One was that the slaves were executed even though the identity of the murderer was known. Secondly, children, it seems, were not spared; later interpretations, if not the SC itself, exempted children 'under age' from liability to the *quaestio* or punishment, although they could be frightened into telling what they knew.[49] And thirdly, perhaps most significantly for the future, a new debate was opened up on the definition of *familia*. For one over-zealous senator, Cingonius Varro, proposed that the freedmen 'under the same roof' should also be banished from Italy. This was firmly vetoed by Nero; compassion might not have altered 'ancient custom' (*antiquus mos*) but harsh innovations, he said, had

---

[46] Tac. *Ann.* 14.45.1: 'ut nemo unus contra ire ausus est'.

[47] Tac. *Ann.* 14.42.2: 'quae sub eodem tecto mansitaverat'.

[48] Tac. *Ann.* 13.32. See also Paul. *Sent.* 3.5.6, which, as was standard by his day, conflates judicial torture and punishment.

[49] D.29.5.1.32–33 (Ulpian. 50 ad Ed.).

no place.[50] Though the threat to freedmen, whom all would have agreed were part of the *familia*, was, for the time being, averted, it would return.

6. PLINY THE YOUNGER IN THE SENATE, 105 CE

In 105, an unassertive jurist, Titius Aristo, who had been an auditor of the great Cassius and a commentator on his work, was the recipient of Pliny's thoughts, conveyed at some length, on the writer's conduct of a senatorial vote.[51] The matter at issue was the decision taken on the fate of the freed-men of a dead senator, the consul Afranius Dexter. Written after the event, the letter presented Aristo with a *fait accompli*. He could agree with Pliny, whose line of conduct in relation to the vote is justified in a series of agi-tated rhetorical questions, object, or abstain from comment: his reaction is not on record. A large part of the letter is also taken up with an explana-tion as to why the question needed to be asked in the first place; thanks to Domitian, the Senate had become poorly educated and unable to understand how to take decisions properly. This problem, as we shall see, was more fundamental than Pliny acknowledged.

Placed in the centre of book 8, the letter is pivotal and designed, not merely as a technical query, but as a literary exercise.[52] As Whitton argues, the opening profession of ignorance is designed to dazzle, the 'digression' on the 'enslavement' of the Senate to Domitian and its consequent ignorance of its own procedure is a commentary on the body of the letter, the unfettered judgment of a free Senate, no longer 'exiled', exercised over real slaves. But this was how Pliny hopes that his contemporary readership will react. To them, his rescuing of the freedmen from the worst penalty, death, in favour of exile, would read like mercy. But, as will be argued below, Pliny's conduct, and that of the Senate, falls short in a number of key respects. The observa-tion that the Senate had lost the ability to make sensible judgments about voting could be extended to its failure to appreciate why legal procedures should be conducted in the right order and that, in particular, a verdict of guilt or innocence should be formally reached and recorded before sentence is pronounced. Perhaps this was even part of Pliny's intention; the Senate's ignorance, the result of past tyranny, was even more all-encompassing than the author could openly admit.

Pliny's account dodges a number of relevant questions. First, had it been

---

[50] Tac. *Ann.* 14.45.2: 'censuerat Cingonius Varro ut liberti quoque, qui sub eodem tecto fuis-sent, Italia deportarentur. Id a principe prohibitum est, ne mos antiquus, quem misericordia non minuerat per saevitiam intenderetur'.

[51] Plin. *Ep.* 8.14. For Aristo as Cassius' *auditor*, see D.4.8.40 (Pompon. 11 ex Var. Lect.) and for his *notae* on Cassius' works, D.7.1.7.3 (Ulpian. 17 ad Sab.); 7.1.17.1 (Ulpian. 18 ad Sab.); for his unobtrusive demeanour and wide-ranging culture, see Plin *Ep.* 1.22.

[52] For its wider literary and cultural significance and relation to Tacitus, see Whitton (2010), pp. 118–39.

proved, at the time of the vote, that a crime had been committed? The cause of Dexter's death, which was agreed to be unnatural, was uncertain and Pliny cites three possibilities: suicide by his own hand; murder at the hands of his household; and suicide, but by their agency in obedience to his orders.[53] According to Pliny, at the time that the Senate chose to debate the matter, responsibility for the death was still unknown. Was the death suicide? Were the slaves in a position to prevent it? Where the slaves were at the time is not stated; a more considerate suicide, if such he was, might have ensured that the slaves and freedmen were out of the house at the time (and therefore unable to supply assistance or prevent him). Pliny does not know, but he should have done. Answers to those questions were directly relevant to the fate of the slaves, as well as the freedmen; all might be liable to judicial torture but it was still, in theory, possible for them or others to prove that they were unable to intervene.

Secondly, and assuming that a crime had been committed, were the freedmen liable on grounds of failure to protect? As we have seen, 'customarily' members of the *familia* of masters who were killed, and who took no action to protect them, even against themselves in cases of suicide, were liable to be executed. Before 61, the question of the liability of freedmen, as members of the *familia*, for interrogation and punishment had not, apparently, been raised. Nero's decision in 61 had held the line that slaves were liable to punishment but freedmen were not. Forty years later, however, the question was still a live one and the Senate were invited, again, to adjudicate on whether the freedmen of a man, who had died violently, should suffer as a consequence of his death.

Thirdly, had the *quaestio*, to be conducted by the praetor or some other magistrate, already taken place? Or was it, or a further stage of it, to take place in the future? Pliny makes no reference to a preliminary investigation, yet the narrowness of the question under debate, the fate of the freedmen, suggests that there had been an enquiry of some kind, which had been inconclusive. On the other hand, the decisions reached by the Senate as to liability of both slaves and freedmen to the *quaestio* suggest that some part of the investigation, if not the main part, was still to come. Regardless of the outcome, the Senate, would proceed on the basis of unproven assumptions to pass judgment as to the guilt or innocence, not only of the freedmen but of the slaves as well, without waiting for the *quaestio* to run its course. With the verdicts still unresolved, it was not surprising that the senators themselves were far from unanimous as to the guilt or innocence of the freedmen, whose fate they were to decide.

Why was the outcome of the *quaestio* anticipated? The senate seem to have proceeded on the basis of an understanding that, as Dexter had been 'killed',

---

[53] Plin. *Ep.* 8.14.12: referebatur de libertis Afrani Dextri consulis, incertum sua an suorum manu, scelere an obsequio perempti.

his *familia* were liable to punishment for their failure to protect, regardless of the circumstances of his death, which were still unknown. In terms of the mention in the SC of the *familia* of the *occisus*, the man killed, the hardliners were technically correct. Freedmen were also members of the *familia*. Whether inclusion of the freedmen in the *quaestio* (or as liable automatically to punishment for failure to protect) was the intention of the original drafters of the SC is another matter; had they been liable, Pacuvius Labeo's freeing of his slave to save him from answering for his master's suicide would have had no beneficial effect.

Sitting as a court, the Senate, including Pliny, whose humanity did not extend to the slave element in the *familia*, disposed of the slaves without controversy. They were liable to torture in the *quaestio* and would then be executed, not for the crime (which had yet to be proved) but, presumably, for failing to keep the master alive. While this may reflect practice at the time, it was out of line with juristic opinion later; suicide, as we have seen, did not make the *familia* automatically liable for torture or for punishment, unless they were in a position to intervene. But worse was to come. All agreed also that the freedmen were also liable to interrogation; this may have generated the Trajanic decision recorded by the jurists, that those freed in the master's lifetime were liable to the *quaestio*.[54] This did not automatically entail torture: Ulpian later stated that the term *quaestio* referred to the whole interrogation process, not solely to *tormenta*.[55] But the potential extension of judicial torture up the social scale in the context of master-murder, without apparently much reflection or, on this occasion at least, any debate, was characteristic of the court decisions that would further this process and erode the immunities even of the elite from judicial torture in Late Antiquity.

When the time to vote on the fate of the freedmen arrived, Pliny faced two problems. One, which he did not admit, was that the Senate had pre-empted the conclusions of the *quaestio* as to guilt or innocence. Secondly, a majority of the Senate favoured punishment of some kind, either the death penalty or exile (*relegatio*), and assumed the guilt of the freedmen, but a substantial minority, Pliny included, favoured acquittal, believing them innocent, or at least not liable for failure to protect. His disagreement with the other two groups was fundamental: the divergence concerned not the punishment but the verdict. The supporters of the death penalty and banishment then threatened to make common cause, and use tactical voting to remove the option of acquittal first. Pliny, despite constant interruptions, insisted that the three proposals be taken separately, the main proponent of the death penalty then

[54] Cf. D.29.5.10.1 (Paul. 1 ad SC Silan.): it was resolved under the deified Trajan that those freedmen whom the deceased had freed during his lifetime should also be subject to the *quaestio* ('sub divo Traiano constitutum est de his libertis quos vivus manumiserat quaestionem haberi').

[55] D.29.5.1.25 (Ulpian. 50 ad Ed.).

abandoned his proposal and compromised on exile because he was afraid that acquittal would have a plurality if the three were taken separately. Despite some doubts expressed by scholars in recent decades, it is clear that the result was the compromise: exile or relegation.[56]

A rapid reading of Pliny's letter leaves the impression of a writer eager to celebrate his own moderation. The reality, from a modern standpoint, is less appealing. Pliny made no attempt to protect the slaves, unlike the demonstrators against the executions in 61; he condoned the use of the *quaestio* for the freedmen as well as the slaves; and he failed to admit the possibility that Dexter's death was a suicide that could not have been prevented, a question that could perhaps have been clarified if the *quaestio* process had first run its course. Instead, the Senate had rushed to judgment, pre-empting the verdict of the *quaestio* both on the cause of death and the liability, if any, of the *familia*. On the issue of principle concerning the freedmen, Pliny also failed. Although he believed the freedmen innocent, he was forced to acquiesce in their punishment. Thus not only was Cassius' legacy of *severitas* with regard to the fate of the slaves left intact, but the Neronian precedent of clemency towards the freedmen was also, arbitrarily, reversed.

7. THE SC SILANIANUM IN THE SECOND CENTURY CE

The muttered protests of the crowd, who objected to the execution of the slaves of Pedanius in 61, is evidence that the increasing severity in the implementation of the SC Silanianum did not go unchallenged. But they would not be the dominant voices in the debate. Such evidence as survives for its evolution in the second century suggests that the issue of liability was still a live one and that (some) judges continued the expansion of its operation, while at least one emperor, Marcus Aurelius, sought to reverse the trend.

Judicial decisions by provincial governors and their reasoning are seldom cited by name and that of the *legatus* Trebius Geminus on the meaning of a key phrase in the SC is an exception.[57] In a treatise on the public or criminal courts – a reminder that the SC bears on public as well as civil or private law – the jurist Maecianus described the reasoning behind Geminus' decision to execute a slave boy who was under-age (*impubis*), despite the convention that children were not liable under the SC Silanianum. Geminus' justification was based on the circumstances of the murder, and on an original reading of the SC's phrase 'under the same roof'. The under-age slave had slept in his murdered master's room, at his very feet, and yet had not raised the alarm or even informed on the murder afterwards. In Geminus' view, this undermined the usual immunity of the *impubis*; the boy, who admittedly was too young to assist, was nearly an adult and was old enough to understand what

---

[56]   Whitton (2010), pp. 118–19.
[57]   D.29.5.14 (Maecian. 11 de Pub. Iud.).

was going on. He should therefore have taken action to call for help and not have preserved his silence afterwards. Secondly, 'he believed' that the SC protected those *impuberes* who were merely under the same roof – not those who were in close attendance on the master, and who therefore were in a position to act. Such under-age children, provided they understood what was happening, were not, he argued, exempt from punishment under the law.

Geminus' decision, and the reasons for it, moved the reading of the SC further in the direction of judicial severity, expanding its scope and undermining a traditional exemption from both torture and punishment. The definition of being 'too young', he argued, no longer depended on the physical condition of being *impubis* but on a new, more subjective test, the expected level of understanding. Moreover, the shelter afforded by the roof had, again, shifted. All those not 'under the same roof' were, of course, already exempt from the *quaestio*, unless shown to be complicit. Within the group under the same roof, who were in general liable, an exemption hitherto had been granted to *impuberes*. But this *impubis* had not simply been under the same roof, he had been in the same room (and therefore able to assist by calling for help, which he did not). At a stroke, some parts of a household sheltered by the same roof had become more endangered than others.

All the documented decisions and debates of the Roman Senate, acting as a court, and of other judges, such as Geminus, tend in one direction: an expansion of those categories of socially inferior people liable for judicial torture and punishment under new readings of the SC and a general willingness to implement the decree in its harshest form, rather than opt for a more merciful approach. By contrast, as we have seen, the emperor Nero (or his legal advisers) had refused to bow to pressure to expand the application of the SC to freedmen, although the benefits of his decision were largely eroded in the decades that followed. It was therefore perhaps not a coincidence that the Roman Senate, which had been collectively responsible for the increased harshness of the SC over the years, was the recipient of an *oratio*, or legal speech, which went against that trend.

Marcus Aurelius (r. 161–80), unlike, say, Pliny and his Senate, is perhaps the only later legislator to show awareness of the all-important distinction between the investigation process under the *quaestio* and the infliction of punishment. Marcus' Stoic philosophy provided a distinctive perspective; regardless of status, only the wise man could be truly free.[58] Perhaps this motivated his insistence on the rights of innocent slaves as set out in an *oratio* (formal address on legal matters) to the Roman Senate. The speech addressed a situation in which, we may assume, the *quaestio* had taken place and slaves found innocent by the process were left in a position to benefit

---

[58] Garnsey (1996), pp. 134–8, arguing that Stoics did not (by implication) believe in 'natural slavery'.

from the master's will; not all, therefore, were expected to be put to death just because they were part of the *familia*.[59] If they were shown later to have been freed and to have benefited from the dead master's will, the will's provisions for them and their children should be honoured. Marcus' views were still current in the early sixth century and were revisited, endorsed and tidied up on a matter of detail in a constitution of the emperor Justinian, issued in 531.[60]

8. CONCLUSION

The subject of the SC Silanianum was an emotive one for the Roman elite; its subject was the process that would ensure their safety (it was hoped) when alive and, at worst, avenge them when violently dead. While under the Republic, the *familia* of a murdered man could expect judicial interrogation and perhaps punishment for their failure to protect, the SC Silanianum regulated the procedure of the *quaestio*, which would establish the truth and punish the guilty. While its clauses may have referred in passing to the liability of the *familia* for failure to protect, rather than for the murder itself, this was not its main purpose. Its stipulation that the heirs should not open the will prior to the *quaestio*, on pain of confiscation of the property by the fiscus, provoked extensive juristic commentary and established the place of the SC Silanianum in juristic interpretation of civil and praetorian law on wills and their administration. That the lawyers privileged the question of the will over that of the lives of the *familia* says much about (some) Roman juristic priorities.

As time passed, different elements in the investigative and punitive process became confused. Slaves were liable to judicial torture, because slave evidence in criminal cases was always taken under torture; in addition, under 'ancient custom', they were liable to punishment, for failure to protect. It followed that the *familia* of a murdered man, resident under the same roof, or close enough, in some sense, to intervene, and who failed to help, would suffer the death penalty, whatever the degree of individual guilt, and regardless of whether the identity of the murderer had been discovered. The result was the infamous execution in 61 of Pedanius' *familia* of 400 slaves, including, it appears, women and children, the last a direct violation of rules on the liability of minors.[61]

In a parallel development, the application of the *quaestio* was extended to

---

[59] This could of course refer to the slaves not '*sub eodem tecto*', who were not in a position to have provided assistance.

[60] C.6.35.11 (a. 531). Another constitution in the same section revisits the definition of '*sub eodem tecto*', complaining about the failure of the ancients to provide clear guidance as to its meaning.

[61] D.29.5.1.32 (Ulpian. 50 ad Ed.).

other elements in the *familia*, including freedmen. By Pliny's time, freedmen also fell foul of the general confusion of liability for the *quaestio* with liability for punishment; the freedmen of Dexter, against whom nothing had been proved, were duly, if controversially, exiled. And the slaves hauled before Geminus' court found that the under-age exemption from execution no longer applied, if the child happened to be in the wrong place at the wrong time.

It would be going too far to assume, on the basis of two examples, Nero and Marcus Aurelius, that emperors were less inclined to judicial severity than the Roman Senate of the early empire or the courts. Hadrian, indeed, provides one counter-example, ruling that slaves capable of assisting their masters should do so, even at their own risk, as slaves must learn not to prefer their own safety to that of the master; a slave girl may not be physically capable of taking on a murderer, but she can cry out for help.[62] But emperors were not driven, as senators were, by waves of collective emotion, or even panic and, while senators had friends, like Titius Aristo, who knew the law, emperors could employ the best lawyers available on their advisory councils, to give them learned, but also dispassionate, guidance.

By contrast, the behaviour of the Senate and of such judges as we know of is consistent in its resolve to maximise the scope of the SC Silanianum and its efficacy as a deterrent. Pliny's colleagues, scared as they doubtless were already by the death of Dexter, would also have recalled the murder of Larius Macedo, battered to death by his slaves in the bath-house, the occasion, noted above, of Pliny's comment that even kind masters were not safe from their brutish slaves.[63] The Senate's contribution to court-made law was the product of emotion, even panic; the effects were profound and not always salutary. Yet, rational or not, they contributed by their decisions to the evolution of court-made law, one element that would contribute over time to the increased judicial severity evidenced in Late Antiquity.

Finally, the story of the SC suggests questions of how we should read law in literature. Students of Classics are familiar with the techniques of literary allusion. Perhaps we should look harder at legal allusions as well, the web of connections silently woven by and within the consciousness of the Roman reader. Allusion can play strange tricks with chronology. Tacitus' *Annales* were aimed at a readership alive in the second decade of the second century and aware of recent controversies on the SC; readers in c 120 of his account of 61 (and Nero's exemption of the freedmen) would have been conditioned by their recollections of the Dexter case in 105. And one jurist, more than any other, was associated with how the SC Silanianum was read and implemented. When Tacitus gave Cassius' speech pride of place in his account of the executions in 61, the message was that he, like Cassius (and,

[62] D.29.5.1.28 (Ulpian. 50 ad Ed.).
[63] Plin. *Ep.* 3.14.

later, Ulpian), saw masters' fears of their slaves as the prime motive for the implementation of the law as deterrent. And it was surely no coincidence that Titius Aristo, Pliny's addressee in 105, was Cassius' pupil. Decades after his death (c 70 CE), the austere ghost of a man, who embodied the stern values of a lost Republic, was, for both Pliny and Tacitus, still a force to be reckoned with.

BIBLIOGRAPHY

Buckland, W. W., *The Roman Law of Slavery* (1908).

Garnsey, P., *Social Status and Legal Privilege in the Roman Empire* (1970).

Garnsey, P., *Ideas of Slavery from Aristotle to Augustine* (1996).

Harries, J., *Cicero and the Jurists. From Citizens' Law to the Lawful State* (2006).

MacMullen, R., 'Judicial savagery in the Roman Empire', *Chiron*, 19 (1986), p. 147.

Millar, F., 'Condemnation to hard labour in the Roman Empire from the Julio-Claudians to Constantine', *Papers of the British School at Rome* 52 (1984), p. 124; and F. Millar, *Government, Society and Culture in the Roman Empire* (2002).

Nörr, D., 'C. Cassius Longinus, der Jurist als Rhetor (Bermerkungen zu Tacitus, Ann. 14.42–45)', *Historia Einzelschriften* 40 (1983), p. 187.

O'Gorman, E., *Irony and Misreading in the Annals of Tacitus* (2000).

Syme, R., *The Augustan Aristocracy* (1986).

Talbert, R. J. A., *The Senate of Imperial Rome* (1984).

Treggiari, S., *Roman Marriage. Iusti Coniuges from the Time of Cicero to the Time of Ulpian* (1991).

Watson, A., 'Roman slave law and Romanist ideology', *Phoenix*, 37 (1983), p. 53.

Whitton, C. L., 'Pliny, Epistles 8,14: Senate, slavery and the *Agricola*', JRS, 100 (2010), p. 118.

Wolf, J. G., *Das senatus consultum Silanianum und die Senatsrede des C. Cassius Longinus aus dem Jahre 61 n. Chr.* (1988).

Part II

Interactions between Legal Theory and Legal Practice

Chapter 5

Laws' Empire: Roman Universalism and Legal Practice

Caroline Humfress

1. INTRODUCTION: CITIES AND EMPIRE

Sometime in the late third or possibly early fourth century, a rhetorician, writing in Greek, probably in the Roman provinces of the East, composed a treatise on epideictic rhetoric (the rhetoric of praise and blame). Transmitted under the name of Menander of Laodicea (a city in south-west Asia Minor), the treatise advises orators on how to praise gods, peoples and cities according to a long and technical tradition of encomiastic speech. There are explicit references to Isocrates' *Panathenaicus*, various works by Plato, the 'encomium on Sicily' in Cicero, and orations by Aelius Aristides on both Rome and Athens. Amongst other subjects, we find specific advice on how an orator should assess the actions of a city, according to the four classical philosophical virtues: courage, justice, temperance (*sophrosune*) and practical wisdom (*phronesis*).[1] After a lengthy discussion concerning how a city's actions should be praised according to the virtue of justice, and some brief pointers concerning praise for temperance 'in public life' and then in relation to the household, the discussion turns to the virtue of practical wisdom:

> In the public sphere, we consider whether the city accurately lays down legal conventions and the subject matter of the laws – such as inheritances by heirs and other topics covered by the laws. (This aspect, however, is now redundant, because we use the universal laws of the Romans.) Within the private sphere, the issue is whether there are many famous rhetors, sophists, geometricians, and representatives of other sciences that depend on practical wisdom.[2]

According to the author of this late Graeco-Roman treatise, praising cities for the display of practical wisdom in the legal sphere was an outdated activity. Public officials in the cities of the East no longer exercised their

---

[1] (Ps-)Menander, *Treatise* I.III.361–5; Russell and Wilson (1981), pp. 60–70. Heath (2004), pp. 127–31 argues that *Treatise* I should not be attributed to Menander of Laodicea.

[2] (Ps-)Menander, *Treatise* I.III.364, lines 10–16; Russell and Wilson (1981), p. 68. For discussion of this passage, see Nutton (1978), pp. 214–15; Carrié (2005), p. 274; Mélèze Modrzejewski (1982), p. 350; and Garnsey (2004), pp. 148–9.

practical wisdom in framing their own laws and legal procedures, because the inhabitants of their cities used 'the universal laws of the Romans'. Thus whereas Isocrates (fourth century BCE) and Aristides (mid second-century CE) could both use 'the topic of laws' to amplify their praise of a city, rhetoricians working under the later Roman empire apparently did not need to bother. The orator could now only praise a city for its *ēthē* (customs).[3] The implication is that by the late third century CE, the Graeco-Roman cities in the East had lost whatever autonomy they had previously possessed as lawgivers.

The question of to whom these Graeco-Roman cities had lost their law-making powers seems to find an answer in a second late Roman rhetorical treatise, also transmitted under the name of Menander of Laodicea and copied with the first treatise in the manuscripts.[4] This second treatise addresses the orator directly as 'the voice of the city', and includes a section on how to construct a formal speech of praise for an emperor (*basilikos logos*). As in an encomium for a city, praise for the actions of an emperor should be set out according to the four virtues.[5] Under 'justice', the orator should praise an emperor's 'mildness towards subjects, humanity towards petitioners, and accessibility', as well as commending him for sending 'governors around the nations, peoples, and cities, [who are] guardians of the laws and worthy of the emperor's justice, not gatherers of wealth'.[6] With regard to the emperor's practical wisdom (*phronesis*), the orator should say that it surpasses that of all other men on earth, hence:

> Of his legislative activity, you should say that his laws are just, and that he strikes out unjust laws and himself promulgates just ones. 'Therefore, laws are more lawful, contracts between men are more just'.[7]

---

[3] (Ps-)Menander, *Treatise* I.III.363, lines 7–14; Russell and Wilson (1981), p. 67. The context is how to praise a city with respect to the topic of 'fair dealing towards men', one of three subdivisions within the virtue of justice (the other two subdivisions are piety towards the gods and reverence towards the dead): 'If the citizens neither wrong foreigners nor do harm to one another and have customs that are equal and fair and laws that are just, they will manage their city with the highest degree of excellence and justice. Nowadays, however, the topic of laws is of no use, since we conduct public affairs by the universal laws of the Romans. Customs (*ēthē*), however, vary from city to city, and form an appropriate basis for an encomium'.

[4] This second treatise survives in the manuscript tradition alongside (Ps-)Menander, *Treatise* I but they do not seem to have been written by the same individual; see Heath (2004), pp. 128–9.

[5] (Ps-)Menander, *Treatise* II.373, lines 5–8; Russell and Wilson (1981), p. 84.

[6] (Ps-)Menander, *Treatise* II.375, lines 8–10 and lines 18–21; Russell and Wilson (1981), pp. 88–90.

[7] (Ps-)Menander, *Treatise* II.375, lines 24–8; Russell and Wilson (1981), p. 90. Compare Themist. *Orat.* 1.15b, *Orat.* 5.64b and *Orat.* 15.187a. Early Christian writers also make various uses of this (Hellenistic kingship) ideology; for discussion, see Nasrallah (2010), pp. 119–63; Buell (2002); and Chadwick (1993).

The 'topic of laws' was thus seen to have excellent potential in terms of amplifying praise for a Late Roman Emperor's actions, in stark contrast to praise for a city, where, as we have seen, it counted as a futile exercise.[8] As far as our late Graeco-Roman orator was concerned, emperors, not cities, made laws.

Book I of Gaius' Institutes, an elementary legal textbook composed in the mid-second century CE, lists a number of sources for Roman law, past and present: 'laws' of the Roman people *(leges)*; enactments of the plebeians *(plebiscita)*; resolutions of the senate; constitutions of the emperors; 'the edicts of those who have the right to issue edicts' (which would include consuls, praetors, aediles and governors of provinces); and the responses of jurisprudents.[9] Each of the sources named by Gaius remained relevant to learning Roman law and doing Roman law – in different ways and to differing extents – throughout the later Empire. For good reasons, however, modern Roman historians – like late Roman orators – tend to focus upon the emperors themselves:

> L'empereur a le quasi monopole du droit. La loi au troisième siècle, ce sont les décisions impériales qui, à l'époque postclassique, seront qualifiées par le terme de lex qui désigne la source principale et presque exclusive du droit.[10]

Moreover, the juristic sources give the impression that imperial decisions could be interpreted as having a universality that other sources of law lacked. For example, in book 25 of his commentary on the praetor's edict, the Severan jurist and imperial bureaucrat Ulpian refers to an imperial rescript, issued by Hadrian, which laid down monetary penalties against anyone who buried a body in a city, as well as any magistrate who allowed the practice, but, Ulpian continues:

> What if the municipal law allows burial in the city? We must consider whether, in the light of Imperial rescripts, this provision has to be departed from; for the rescripts are of general scope and Imperial legislation has its own force and should apply everywhere.[11]

From at least the late second century CE Roman jurists had begun to copy imperial rescripts together systematically, an activity that was continued in the *codices* of the late third-century legal experts (and probably imperial

---

[8] A point made again in (Ps-)Menander, *Treatise* II in the section on 'The speech of arrival' for an imperial governor at 386, lines 1–4; Russell and Wilson (1981), pp. 108–10: 'If there had still been a need for lawgiving, it [namely, the city which the governor is entering] would have legislated for mankind universally, as Sparta and Athens did once for the Greeks'. See also Slootjes (2006), p. 112.

[9] Inst.Gai.1.1.2; compare D.1.2.2, 12 (Pompon. 1 Enchirid.).

[10] Coriat (1997), p. 70.

[11] D.47.12.3.5 (Ulpian. 25 ad Ed.).

officials) Gregorius or Gregorianus and Hermogenianus, both cited as models for the later fifth-century imperial Codex Theodosianus.[12]

Before the promulgation of Justinian's 'Corpus Iuris Civilis', however, jurists did not approach imperial constitutions as exclusive sources of Roman law. In fact, before the Justinianic reforms to the legal curriculum, students at law schools (such as those at Beirut, Rome and Constantinople) had apparently 'barely begun to read Imperial pronouncements after four years of study [. . .]'.[13] Nonetheless, late Roman legal experts – whether giving *responsa* to private individuals or employed as various types of officials within the imperial bureaucracy – certainly worked within a legal and administrative system that functioned with the emperor at its apex.[14] What Hopkins terms 'the symbolic unity of the Roman emperor' is thus as important to our understanding of Roman law under the empire, as it is to our understanding of politics, administration and religion.[15]

There can be no doubt that in the course of the first three centuries of the empire, Roman law had expanded from the city of Rome and Italy into the provinces. Processes associated with 'municipalisation' and 'provincialisation' led to rapid developments in (what we now term) administrative and fiscal law under the early Empire, as well as contributing to a marked expansion in the scope of the imperial bureaucracy. One estimate for the numbers of imperial officials operating between c 250 and 400 CE gives a rise 'from about 250 overall to at least 3,000 per generation in each half of the Empire, a twenty-fold increase'.[16] In particular, emperors and their officials had an empire-wide concern for the maintenance of law and order and for the efficient extraction of tax revenue and other fiscal burdens. Moreover, as Brélaz argues: 'Law and order are, together with taxation, the main attributes of sovereignty and the most visible demonstrations of the power of an authority'.[17] Hence, in terms of an ideology of Empire-building, taxation and a concern for the maintenance of public law and order should be understood as unifying and 'universalising' forces.[18]

---

[12] On the late second-century collection of Papirius Iustus, see Franciosi (1972). On the later third-century *codices*, see Sperandio (2005); Cenderelli (1965); and CTh.1.1.5pr with Scherillo (1934). See also Honoré (1994), and more generally on the 'idea' of an exclusively 'imperial' law, Riccobono (1949).

[13] Justinian, *Institutes* pr: 'Until now even the best students have barely begun to read imperial pronouncements after four years of study; but you have been found worthy of the great honour and good fortune of doing so from the beginning and of following a course of legal education which from start to finish proceeds from the emperor's lips'. See also Digest, *Const. Omnem*, 1.

[14] Liebs (1987); Liebs (1989); and Liebs (2002) discuss jurists in the Western provinces. Honoré (1998) and Honoré (2004) argue for a special relationship between legal expertise and government in the East.

[15] Hopkins (1978).

[16] Heather and Moncur (2001), p. 31.

[17] Brélaz (2008), p. 45.

[18] On the army, see Galsterer (1986), p. 26; Demougeot (1981); and Palmer (2007). On taxation, see Hobson (1993), p. 197; Eck (2000), p. 282; and Carrié (2005), pp. 275–6.

In practice, imperial officials tended to work through, or alongside, local elites. *Civic* elites, where they existed, were particularly important: 'From the administrative point of view the Roman world empire was a union of urban communities; the city was the foundation on which imperial administration rested'.[19] Whilst different models of imperial and local civic interaction developed in distinct geographical regions of the early empire, all Roman cities had some administrative responsibilities in terms of executing orders and judgments from imperial officials. Epigraphic evidence from the Eastern empire, however, suggests a marked shift in relations between cities and central government dating from the mid-third century CE, when inscriptions honouring imperial governors begin to outweigh those dedicated to local officials.[20] Carrié is right to reject the idea of a 'pre-conceived political programme of authoritarian centralization' under the Severi; we should likewise be wary of attributing an 'out-and-out bureaucratization of the administration' to the age of Diocletian and Constantine.[21] Nonetheless, it is noteworthy that when local governments performed legal administrative functions in the later third and early fourth centuries, they did so increasingly under the supervision of or in tandem with imperial officials. For example, the text of the *Pauli sententiae* which circulated in various copies and editions in the late Roman West, states that municipal magistrates can arrest fugitive slaves and 'transfer them to the office of the governor or the province or proconsul' (1.6a.4); that municipal magistrates, 'if they have the legal power', can emancipate and manumit slaves (2.25.4); and that an heir can be compelled by a municipal magistrate to enter upon and transfer an estate, on request of the beneficiary of a *fideicommissum*, 'on the authority of the governor' (5.5a.1). Late Roman imperial constitutions also refer to the duties of municipal magistrates with regard to the administration of testamentary bequests and the performance of manumissions and guardianships, as do a number of fourth- and fifth-century papyri from Egypt. Municipal magistrates were involved, along with imperial officials, in prosecutions against Christians in the early fourth century, as well as later prosecutions against Christian schismatics and heretics.[22] There is also some evidence for city councils and municipal magistrates judging legal cases on their own authority, although the main subject of petitions to *boulai* (city councils) in third and fourth-century Egypt concerned municipal liturgies, in particular

---

[19] Wolf (2006), p. 443. See, in general, Nörr (1969); Gascou (1999); Eich (2005); and Camodeca (2006).

[20] Robert (1948), discussed by Nutton (1978), pp. 219–20; Saller (1982), p. 168 and Rouché (1998).

[21] Carrié (2005), pp. 275–6 and 282.

[22] For the evidence on municipal magistrates being involved in the persecution of Christians, see Carrié (2005), p. 289 with n. 85. On the prosecution of schismatics and heretics, see Humfress (2007), pp. 243–68.

attempts to avoid nominations and burdens.[23] The fact that an imperial constitution, issued in 412 and addressed to the Proconsul of Africa, forbids duumvirs from extending 'the power of their fasces' (i.e., their jurisdictional authority) outside the limits of their own municipalities, implies that municipal magistrates still had jurisdictional powers to abuse.[24] Nonetheless, as Denis Feissel has demonstrated, between 324 and 610 CE a mere handful of inscriptions survive which record legal acts undertaken at either a municipal or provincial level (i.e., at provincial assemblies).[25] In the later Roman legal epigraphy, then, the focus is almost exclusively on what Feissel terms 'les actes de l'État imperial'.

Given the emphasis on imperial law and state jurisdiction within late Roman epigraphy, in addition to the promulgation of centralised imperial law codes – coupled with fourth-century developments establishing 'new' imperial legal officials within the localities, such as the *defensor civitatis* and 'new' central 'Palatine' legal offices, such as the imperial *Quaestor* – it begins to seem absurd *not* to assume that all law and legal practice in the later Roman empire was subject to the universal control of the emperors and their bureaucrats.[26]

2. CONTEXTUALISING 'THE UNIVERSAL LAWS OF THE ROMANS': THE EARLY EMPIRE

> Our problem is then: was Rome at all interested in producing a single juridical framework for the whole Empire, or at least for all Roman citizens living in any part of the Empire? Did they want Superinius Aquila of Cologne and Aurelius Bonosus of Carthage to live under the same system of laws?[27]

Galsterer's problem, as outlined in the quotation above, is central to the question of legal universalism under the early Empire: did 'Rome' seek to impose a uniform application of Roman law in the provinces?[28] Supposing for the moment that our Graeco-Roman rhetorician, Ps-Menander, was right to imply that local law had been displaced by Roman law by the late third/early-fourth centuries, does it necessarily follow that this was a consequence of imposition from above? In terms of private law ('inheritances by heirs and other topics'), Ps-Menander's *Treatise* I states only that the inhabitants of the

---

[23] Bowman (1971), p. 113. P.Oxy LIV 3758 records a case heard before the *logistes* in 325; Liban. *Orat.* 11.139 refers to the *boule* of Antioch judging a legal case. See also the epigraphical sources listed by Feissel (2009), pp. 99–102.

[24] CTh.12.1.174 = C.10.32.53 (412 CE); cf. D.50.1.26 (Paul. 1 ad Ed.).

[25] Feissel (2009).

[26] On *defensor civitatis*, see Frakes (2001); on imperial *Quaestor*, see Harries (1988); and Faro (1984). See in general Meyer (2004), pp. 217, 252, 296. On 'imperial law', see Vessey (2003); a review article of Honoré (1998); Harries (1999); and Matthews (2000).

[27] Galsterer (1986), p. 23; see also Galsterer (1999).

[28] Stolte (2001), p. 169 discussing Galsterer.

Eastern cities made use of the 'universal laws of the Romans'; it does not tell us that Roman private law was forced upon them by imperial officials, or indeed by any other kind of official.

Ps-Menander's treatise, however, was composed after 212 CE and the promulgation of Caracalla's Constitutio Antoniniana (an imperial edict granting Roman citizenship to almost all free inhabitants of the Roman empire).[29] As such, the brief comments that Ps-Menander makes on the 'universal laws of the Romans' have been cited as evidence for the fact that Roman law *was* imposed on the vast majority of the free inhabitants of the empire, as a result of Caracalla granting them Roman citizenship.[30] Roman historians and legal scholars from Mitteis onwards have suggested, to widely varying effects, that Caracalla's Constitutio Antoniniana required large numbers of provincials to order their private relations with each other according to Roman law.[31] Thus Ando, for example, states that: 'Caracalla's grant of citizenship to all freeborn residents of the empire in 212 CE will have dramatically altered the legal landscape: any and all earlier provincial edicts will have had to be entirely rewritten'.[32] Having accepted some kind of necessary link between the extension of Roman citizenship and the 'state' imposition of Roman law, other scholars place Caracalla's edict at the apex of historical processes that reach back into the Roman Republic. Bispham, for example, links the Constitutio Antoniniana to the provisions of late Republican and early imperial municipal charters and relates both in turn to the extension of Roman law and citizenship to Italy and the provinces:

> How far, and how quickly, the new *municipia* picked up the *ius ciuile* is, then, an important question, and one which recurs again and again as Roman citizen-ship spreads across the Empire, right up to the aftermath of the Constitutio Antoniniana. One would like to know, in particular, whether Rome was proac-tive and *dirigiste*, enforcing the adoption of the *ius ciuile* and other provisions of universal application in the new *municipia*, or whether it was left up to the communities themselves to mug up on it as best they could.[33]

---

[29] See Sasse (1958); and Wolff (1976).

[30] Talamanca (1971).

[31] Mitteis (1891), esp. pp. 160–6, arguing that the Constitutio Antoniniana was part of a pro-grammatic attempt to replace existing local laws (*Volksrecht*) with Roman law (*Reichsrecht*).

[32] Ando (2006), p.178. Compare Lintott (1993), p. 154: 'Only after Caracalla gave Roman citizenship to almost all the free population of the empire (in AD 212 on the usual view), can Roman law be said to have been, at least in theory, the law of the empire', and Honoré (2004), p. 113: 'With the constitutio Antoniniana Roman law had became a universal law'. Rowlandson and Takahashi (2009), p. 117, state that sibling marriage in Egypt ended abruptly when the Constitutio Antoniniana made it 'illegal' (i.e., it was not permitted by Roman law and virtually all were now Roman citizens).

[33] Bispham (2007), pp. 205–6. Compare Gardner (2001). On the 'Roman private law' clauses within the Flavian municipal charters, see Gonzaleź (1986), in particular *lex Irnitana* chapters 93, 10B 52–102C and 85; Johnston (1987); Rodger (1990); Lamberti (1993); Tomlin (2002); Wolf (2006); and Nörr (2007).

Looking forward from the Constitutio Antoniniana, most scholars express doubts as to the success of Caracalla's (supposed) attempt at legal universalism. As Yiftach-Firanko questions with respect to law in Graeco-Roman Egypt:

> In 212 the Antonine Constitution turned the provincial population into Roman citizens. Formally, it subjected all its inhabitants to the precepts of Roman law. Yet did this change in status also mean a profound change in the legal practices in Egypt?[34]

Virtually none of the vast secondary literature questions the premise that once an individual or community had been granted Roman citizenship, they were henceforth required to use Roman law to govern their private relations.[35]

To assume that the Roman authorities aimed at the unification of law through the extension of citizenship is, in fact, one aspect of what Galsterer has rightly identified as 'a tendency among the legal historians of the unification school [namely, Mitteis, Arangio-Ruiz, Wolff, and so on] to assign motives to the Roman state which are taken unselfconsciously from the modern national state as it developed in the nineteenth and twentieth centuries'.[36] In reality, no state act obliged Roman citizens to use Roman private law.[37] Citizenship should be understood rather 'as an enabling mechanism, offering access to the judicial procedures and remedies of the society at different levels'.[38] The papyrological record, alongside other sources, certainly provides a wealth of evidence for individuals and communities engaging in numerous different ways with Roman private law, both before and after 212 CE; but the reasons why they did so need to be sought from below.[39] Those who had more at stake than others in terms of land-owning and 'elite' sociopolitical status may have been more likely to seek out the remedies and

---

[34] Yiftach-Firanko (2009), p. 543; see also Yiftach-Firanko (2009), p. 554 on the use and adaptation of the *stipulatio* clause in Egypt after 212 CE.

[35] Exceptions are Schönbauer (1931) and Schönbauer (1937), both contra Mitteis. See also Seidl (1973); Galsterer (1986); Cotton (1993); Meyer (2004), p. 183; Garnsey (2004), pp. 146–7; and Carrié (2005), pp. 274–5.

[36] Galsterer (1986), p. 24.

[37] Mélèze Modrzejewski (1993), p. 998.

[38] Garnsey (2004), p. 155. For a broader contextualised reading of Roman citizenship, see Dench (2005), pp. 93–151.

[39] For 'new' papyri from the Roman Near East (provinces of Syria; Mesopotamia; Arabia; Judaea/Syria Palaestina), see Cotton, Cockle, and Millar (1995), including relevant texts from P. *Euphr*: see Cotton, Cockle and Millar, nos 24–9; P. *Dura*: see Cotton, Cockle and Millar, nos 44 and 45; P. *Bostra*: see Cotton, Cockle and Millar, no. 171; and *Pap. Colon.*; see Cotton, Cockle and Millar, no. 173. See also Cotton and Yardeni (1997); Cotton (2006); Kraemer (1958) = P. *Nessana* III; Arjava, Buchholz, and Gagos (2007) = P. *Petra*. For Egypt, see also now Richter (2008). For the later West, see Tjäder (1955); Wessel (2003); and Velázquez Soriano (2000), esp. document nos 8, 39, 40A and 40B.

protections of Roman law, or to be enmeshed in them already. The establishment of economic rights and entitlements to property; the agreement and
regulation of contracts; and the negotiation of a host of other material interests might demand the use of specifically Roman legal instruments within
any particular context. Moreover, as John Crook notes, the *de controversiis
agrorum*, one of 'the least-discussed' of the handbooks of Frontinus (first
century CE), 'shows what a lot of litigation was generated by land, with its
questions of ownership, boundaries and taxation'.[40] This activity, however,
still does not amount to the emperor or Roman 'state' officials *requiring*
individuals to use Roman law because they were Roman citizens.

   Caracalla's grant of citizenship to virtually all free inhabitants of the
empire would have certainly increased the number of individuals who
had the right (*ius*) to make use of Roman law, *qua* citizens. Prior to 212 CE,
however, there were also various types of legal mechanisms that gave 'non-
citizens' the ability to make use of some Roman legal concepts and practices.
According to Gaius' *Institutes*, every individual was either slave or free:
some were free by birth (*ingenui*) and some were made free through a grant
of freedom (*libertini* or *liberti*, 'freedmen'). A free man or woman was either
a Roman citizen; or a 'Latin' (i.e., holding the *ius Latii*); or a peregrine, a
foreigner or 'alien', who might in turn be a citizen of some other specific peregrine community.[41] As a class, Latins had some of the juridical *iura* (rights)
of full citizenship: in particular the right to make a contract with a Roman
which would then be enforceable according to Roman law (*ius commercii*).
As Woolf states: 'In this, and in other respects, Latins had access to Roman
law, even if Roman law was in practice probably interpreted in the light of
local traditions'.[42] Nor were foreigners (*peregrini*) entirely outside the Roman
legal system. *Ius gentium* ('law of the peoples') referred to 'those legal habits
which were accepted by the Roman law as applying to, and being used by,
all the people they met, whether Roman citizens or not'.[43] The elaboration
of this concept enabled jurists to define certain interactions between peregrines, Latins and citizens as being under Roman jurisdiction: for example,
peregrines could acquire ownership through 'natural' modes of acquisition
(*traditio, occupatio, accessio*); slavery was also *iure gentium*, all peoples had it
– although there were aspects of the (Roman) law of slavery which were peculiar to the Roman *ius civile* alone. Moreover, according to Gaius' Institutes
4.37, a legal fiction enabled foreigners to either sue or be sued 'as if' they were

---

[40] Crook (1995), p. 53. See now Campbell (2000) and Cuomo (2007), pp. 103–30 discussing the
      expertise of land surveyors vis à vis legal experts (including jurists) in resolving boundary
      disputes.
[41] On the Roman law of status, see Crook (1967), pp. 36–67 including a lucid discussion of the
      relative status of 'Coloniary Latins' and 'Junian Latins'. On the *ius latinum*, see also Kremer
      (2006).
[42] Woolf (1998), p. 67.
[43] Crook (1967), p. 29.

Roman citizens, in certain actions. At Rome, the *praetor peregrinus* handled litigation between foreigners and citizens and probably also cases where foreigners were the only parties – such cases were judged according to, what the jurists termed, 'honesty and fairness' (in the *iudicia bonae fidei*).[44] Within the city of Rome and across the Empire, contact with foreigners and 'aliens' was unavoidable, especially in terms of commerce, business dealings, and so on. The Roman senate, the jurists, the emperors and their officials were well aware of a world of private legal transactions involving 'non-citizens', and recognised the need to regulate those transactions from within the Roman legal system itself. From the perspective of the *peregrinus*, on the other hand, a grant of Roman citizenship would have by no means necessarily implied a first contact with Roman law.

Certain historical developments within Roman law and legal practice were peculiar to the city of Rome; one such fundamental development was the *ius honorarium*, a branch of law developed by the urban praetor (and other magistrates at Rome) in order to 'support, supplement and correct the civil law'.[45] In theory, the edictal remedies developed under the authority of the urban praetors were only valid for Rome and its environs, because this was the limit of the urban praetors' own jurisdiction. It thus became necessary to develop mechanisms through which Roman citizens throughout Italy and the provinces could access important praetorian innovations, as and when they were developed (for example, the praetorian remedy *bonorum possessio*, 'possession of goods').[46] This was partly achieved through imperial constitutions, juristic commentary and *responsa*, and partly through the actions of imperial officials within the provinces. This is a much contested topic, but provincial governors – or magistrates of at least praetorian standing – were apparently responsible for promulgating provincial edicts, primarily for the benefit of Roman citizens within their own jurisdiction. The contents of the 'provincial edicts' seem to have essentially mirrored those of the urban praetors at Rome, with some variation. The stabilising of the urban praetorian edict around 125 CE (the *edictum perpetuum*) prompted the writing of relatively large-scale edictal commentaries, such as that by Ulpian under the Severans.[47] The fact that Gaius wrote a commentary on 'the provincial edict' may imply a similar type of juristic development. Imperial constitutions and governors' edicts could also contain legal and administrative measures directed to a single province, or part of a province – what was technically termed *Provinzialrecht* ('provincial law') in nineteenth-century Romanist

---

[44] For discussion, see Turpin (1965).
[45] D.1.1.7.1 (Papinian. 2 Def.).
[46] See Watson (1971) and for the later Empire, Pulitanò (1999).
[47] Ulpian's ad edictum apparently had a wide circulation under the later Empire, with numerous fragments found in papyri; in addition, the *Fragmenta Berolinensia* possibly indicates a postclassical edition; for further discussion, see Purpura (1995).

scholarship.[48] Again this 'provincial law' – as far as it goes – was elaborated piecemeal and in response to specific situations. In sum, as even this brief sketch highlights, we cannot think in terms of a 'ready-made' Roman law being exported *en bloc* from Rome to the provinces, either before or after 212 CE. As recent studies and critiques of the concept of 'Romanisation' have demonstrated, particularly with respect to religion, urbanism and cultural identity: 'imperialism was a dialectic in which both sides played a part'.[49] The same insight can be developed with respect to 'Roman' law and legal practice.

According to the beneficial ideology – which advertised power relations of mutual benefit to both ruler and ruled – emperors were the ultimate bestowers of gifts and largesse, as well as dispensers of justice.[50] They regularly granted general acts of amnesty in criminal matters (*indulgentia*) as well as dispensing special legal privileges and exemptions to individual petitioners on a daily basis. In terms of private law (inheritance, family, property, contracts, commerce, and so on), petitioners throughout the Roman provinces also looked to the emperors and imperial officials for decisions on individual situations and case specific responses.[51] They thus contributed to, in the words of Fergus Millar, 'the formation of a body of rules which were in principle valid throughout the Empire'.[52] As Millar also stresses, however, 'the body of rules thus created was not so much enforced by any apparatus of government as available for use by interested parties making claims or bringing suits, and then by officials, or Emperors, giving rulings in response'.[53] The question for us, then, is not so much whether 'Superinius Aquila of Cologne' and 'Aurelius Bonosus of Carthage' had the same system of laws enforced upon them by Rome; but rather why 'Superinius Aquila of Cologne' or 'Aurelius Bonosus of Carthage' used Roman law, as and when they did, in any specific context or situation. Re-framing Galsterer's problem in this way demands asking much broader questions concerning Roman private law and its 'reception' in the provinces under the early Empire. It also necessitates exploring what other alternatives – and limitations – existed on the ground, in specific localities, in terms of maintaining socio-legal order and handling conflict.

How and to what extent any given individual, before or after 212 CE, either could make use of, or would want to make use of, Roman private

---

[48] See Amelotti (1999).

[49] Revell (2009), p. 191; also Mattingly (2002).

[50] Nutton (1978); also Stolte (2002).

[51] See Hauken (1998); Connolly (2010), pp. 137–58; and Gascou (2004). For the later Empire, see Fournet and Gascou (2004); and Fournet (2004). Petitioners also variously looked to Roman military officials, as discussed by Peachin (2007).

[52] Millar (1983), p. 78.

[53] Millar (1983), p. 78. See also Carrié (2005), pp. 273–6 and Arjava (1999) on the 'penetration' of Roman family law into Egypt.

law would have depended on a combination of various economic, political, cultural and socio-legal factors. What kinds of access any specific individual, group or community had to (Roman) legal advice, to notaries and/or to Roman legal officials needs to be considered.[54] Juridical capacity, gender, and socio-economic status are also relatively obvious determinants (although how they functioned in practice under both the early and later empires is often less than clear).[55] Neither juridical capacity nor socio-economic status should be thought of as static phenomena within an individual's lifespan: slaves could become freedmen; a *filius familias* could become *sui iuris*; *honestiores* and *potentiores* could suffer a loss of status, and so on. Patronage was fundamental, alongside the expectation that elite social status would be given its proper due within Roman legal processes.[56] Individuals, and groups, would also have weighed the costs and benefits – in terms of time, money and social status – of using Roman private law, relative to any specific situation.[57] Lodging a formal case before a Roman official was a particularly costly option: alongside the payment of necessary tips and fees to various officials, petitioners had to reckon with the possibility of a lengthy wait for justice – P. Euphrates 1 (246 CE) registers a complaint from the villagers of Beth Phouraia (Syria Coele) that they had waited for over eight months in Antioch for a decision from the governor.[58] An appeal to an imperial official, or a general reference to 'the law of the emperors' in a petition, however, could function as a marker of elite status and/or as a deliberate advertisement of loyalty to imperial authority. To use an example from the later Roman period, Joelle Beaucamp has demonstrated from papyrological evidence that the elite in Justinianic Egypt were more likely than those lower down the social strata to invoke substantive Roman law principles and imperial constitutions, throughout their legal dealings. She concludes that: 'closeness to Imperial law was therefore connected to social conditions'.[59] The Byzantine Egyptian elite may have had better access to imperial law, in the sense of better access to legal expertise, but they also had sociological reasons for aligning themselves with texts of law promulgated by the emperors.

Existing social structures and traditional local practices would also have influenced the way in which individuals engaged – or not – with Roman law principles and/or practices. For example, justice could be sought from the god(s), via a local temple, priest or holy man or through 'self-help' activities

---

[54] For the early Empire, see Kantor (2009).

[55] On gender, see Grubbs (2002) and Bannon (2001); on socio-economic status, see Garnsey (1970) and Humfress (2006).

[56] On patronage, see now Garnsey (2010).

[57] On the time and expense associated with Roman litigation in particular, see Kelly (2006), pp. 138–85.

[58] Cotton and Eck (2005), p. 41.

[59] Beaucamp (2007), p. 286.

such as cursing.[60] More generally, within any given community, disagreements may usually have been heard before a local 'big man', for example a senatorial landowner, a tribal chief, or community elder(s). Depending on the context or situation, local 'big men' might have intervened in disagreements and disputes with some awareness of Roman legal principles and practices (such as, for example, formal arbitration). It is just as likely, on the other hand, that a local big man would seek to resolve a dispute using local knowledge alone and employing general socio-cultural norms – thus providing a type of 'justice' in which the parties to the dispute were more likely to acquiesce.[61] The social density of any given community – in a city, village, rural area, 'great estate', and so on – could also determine whether any use was made of Roman legal procedures or institutional structures.[62] As numerous modern studies in social anthropology, micro-economic theory and law have shown, socio-legal order can be maintained in a 'tight-knit' community or group with little or no recourse to formal law. In a 1991 monograph, for example, Ellickson showed how contemporary boundary and cattle trespass disputes in Shasta County, California were settled in the context of long-established and continuing social relationships and groupings, highlighting the role of 'strategic' gossip, the threat of violence and the appeal to 'community elders'.[63] This perspective also provides a crucial context for the development of the Christian '*episcopalis audientia*', the 'bishop's hearing'.[64] Finally, violent self-help should not necessarily be thought of as simply an alternative to Roman law and state-sanctioned coercion. Imperial officials took breaches in public law and order very seriously, if and when they came to their attention; 'private' violence, however, could also work in conjunction with Roman law. For example, an individual might attempt to enforce a property claim by violently seizing possession as a prelude to lodging a court case for rightful ownership; or seek out a Roman legal remedy for possession, and then use private violence to enforce it. All of the various factors discussed so far could change over time, as well as differ from one locality to the next – and each, of course, needs to be understood as operating in relation to the others, in any given context.

When we do find individuals using Roman law – whether in Rome or the provinces – that engagement could take place on a number of different levels, each implying various types of legal knowledge. First, in the broadest sense, Roman concepts of property, contract, trust, inheritance and so on were not just 'legal' concepts, they were also part of a broader socio-cultural

---

[60] Chaniotis (2009). See also Tomlin (1998) and Versnel (2010).

[61] For discussion of potentially relevant 'Roman' socio-cultural norms, particularly in the context of elite behaviour, see Barton (2001).

[62] Shaw (2000), p. 373 notes the 'vast tracts of cityless lands that had to be controlled through the agency of local landowners and their domains'.

[63] Ellickson (1991). See also Galanter (1981), pp. 17–25.

[64] This argument is explored in Humfress (2011).

repertoire.[65] Hence, for example, we find the technical Latin phrase *sine dolo malo* translated into Greek and inscribed on 'confession inscriptions' in Lydia and Phrygia (first to third centuries CE).[66] Or we find early Christian authors, such as Tertullian and Cyprian in North Africa, developing theological ideas by working through Roman legal metaphors.[67] Second, on a more specific level: 'Law may be used as a cookbook from which we learn how to bring about desired results – disposing of property, forming a partnership, securing a subsidy'.[68] Until at least the Age of Justinian, there was no clear set of authoritative Roman legal 'cookbooks' to work from: hence the 'recipe' being followed would have differed according to access to legal advice, local practices, specific situations, and so on. Moreover, as the legal anthropologists Franz and Keebet von Benda-Beckmann explain, with reference to modern ethnographic studies:

> In each arena actors make more or less constrained choices. They may avoid any use of law, opting for non-legal means. They may opt for one law and exclude others; they may also use more than one law. They may sharply distinguish legal systems, or efface their boundaries, or develop hybrid forms. Most of the time, people just go along in their daily routines without reflecting on [the] law that has shaped these routines, their social relationships and attitude [. . .][69]

Seen from the perspective of the individual actor, then, specific Roman legal forms could be used to transform an everyday occurrence – the making of a promise, the offering of a loan, a gift of property – into something that could then be viewed (plausibly) as a Roman 'legal' act, whether by other parties to the transaction, or by an imperial official, or in a Roman court, and so on. This is perhaps the situation that we find in the first-century BCE *Tabula Contrebiensis*, in which a judgment is preceded by two technical Roman *formulae*, despite the fact that the 'underlying dispute did not rely on Roman law';[70] or, similarly, with the evidence for third-century CE Egyptians inserting Roman *stipulatio* clauses into their 'Greek' contract documents.[71] Individuals might also make use of Roman institutionalised practices by having a contract drawn up according to a specific Roman structure, maybe employing specialist notaries or copyists where available, whilst expressing the contents of that document in non-technical Latin, or Greek, or Aramaic, or Hebrew, and so on.[72] Imperial constitutions and juristic writings had to develop

---

[65] Fögen (2002).
[66] Chaniotis (1997), pp. 382–4.
[67] Humfress (2007), pp. 174–5.
[68] Galanter (1981), p. 12.
[69] Benda-Beckmann and Benda-Beckmann (2006), p. 24.
[70] Birks, Rodger, and Richardson (1984).
[71] See Yiftach-Firanko (2009), p. 554.
[72] For Roman documentary forms, see Ciulei (1983); Cotton (2003); Meyer (2004), pp. 170 and 180–2; and Meyer (2007).

various principles to decide upon the 'legality' of such agreements, if and when they were tested in the Roman courts. Individuals might equally opt for a 'Roman' procedure, such as appointing an arbitrator *ex compromisso* (by formal agreement), at the same time as deciding the dispute itself according to 'local' norms.[73] In all these examples, the focus is on what any given actor's particular use and/or adaptation can tell us about how Roman law functioned within a specific 'local' framework, or even just with respect to a single case.

Those who went to the trouble and expense of litigating a dispute through a Roman court (or courts), or petitioning a Roman official or emperor, would be judged, in general, according to Roman legal principles. Emperors, jurists and Roman officials under the Early Empire did take some established customs, 'ancient practices' and even 'peregrine laws' into account. For example, an imperial rescript promulgated on 26/27 March, 224 CE informs a certain Aper, a veteran, that whether the ruins of a house could be legally turned into a garden or not (thus changing the original land use) would be decided by the provincial governor on the basis of 'what has usually been done in the town in similar cases'.[74] Determining certain long-established local practices might also be essential to deciding cases according to Roman legal principles; for example, as in C.3.34.7 (286 CE), which refers to respecting 'ancient practices' and 'established customs' in determining the right (servitude) to take water. In fact, according to Ulpian's commentary on the praetorian edict, taking the customary practices of an urban neighbourhood into account could be an essential part of *aequitas* (equity).[75] Certain practices, however, could be judged by the emperors and their officials to be 'non-Roman' – as and when they came to their attention.[76] There is also (limited) evidence for some petitioners addressing questions to the emperors with 'Greek' legal principles in mind. Other petitioners had done their Roman law homework, or else had found someone else to do it for them: a 294 CE rescript, addressed to a certain Fronto, instructs him to 'cite the response of the jurist Papinian and the opinion of others whom you [sc. Fronto] have mentioned' and to set up the defence of fraud (C.5.71.14). A certain Mucianus had likewise apparently copied an opinion of Papinian

---

[73] On arbitration *ex compromiso*, see Roebuck and De Loynes de Fumichon (2004), pp. 174–85.
[74] C.8.10.3; see also C.8.52.1 which probably relates to the same case. Compare D.1.3.32 (Iulian. 84 Dig.) and D.1.3.33 (Ulpian. 4 de Off. Procos.).
[75] D.25.4.1,15 (Ulpian. 24 ad Ed.) with specific reference to determining the paternity of a newborn child, according to a list of praetorian formalities.
[76] C.5.5.2 (285 CE, to Sebastina): the praetor's edict brands a man who has two wives with infamy, thus having two wives should be punished; C.8.46.6 (288 CE, to Hermagenes): a Greek custom of publicly disowning children is 'not approved by Roman laws'. For the restriction of Jewish marriage under the Late Empire, see C.1.9.7 (393 CE to Infantius, Count of the Orient) and more generally C.5.5.4 (to Andromachus, Count of the Private Estate). Millar (2008), p. 126 discusses a Jewish marriage contract (*ketubah*), dated 417 CE and written in Aramaic, from Antinoopolis, Egypt.

into his petition to the emperors (C.6.37.12, 240 CE). In general, classical jurists – addressing themselves perhaps to a particular 'elite' top section of society – agreed that those who made use of Roman law could not then plead ignorance of Roman law as a defence. Ulpian, again commenting on the praetorian edict, specifically on time limits for claiming praetorian possession of an estate, goes further:

> Pomponius says that the knowledge which is necessary is not such as is exacted from persons learned in the law, but is what anyone can acquire, either by himself or through others; that is to say, by taking the advice of persons learned in the law, as the diligent head of the household should do.[77]

In sum, a culture of 'professional' Roman law was by no means irrelevant to legal practice within the provinces of the empire, but it was not determinant of it either. Even if we were to suppose that individuals had unlimited access to relevant jurisprudential texts and legal expertise (in some cases, a big 'if'), we still need to acknowledge what Wickham terms 'a constant dialectic between local practices and organized legal knowledge'.[78]

Since at least Mitteis and Schönbauer, Roman historians have in fact acknowledged the existence of other types of 'organized legal knowledge' existing alongside Roman law in certain provinces of the early Empire: 'Greek law', 'Egyptian law', 'Jewish law', 'Nabatean law', what Mélèze Modrzejewski terms 'Hellenistic law', and so on.[79] Much of this scholarship, however, tends to be based upon what Lauren Benton (in a different context) describes as a 'stacked legal systems or spheres' model: a model that imagines a number of 'ordered, nested legal spheres or systems', with state law, in our case to be understood as Roman law, 'capping the plural legal order' through its ability to establish a monopoly on violence.[80] Benton argues that this 'stacked' model is fundamentally flawed because individuals on the ground engage in 'rampant boundary crossing' across legal systems or spheres:

> Legal ideas and practices, legal protections of material interests, and the roles of legal personnel (specialized or not) fail to obey the lines separating one legal system or sphere from another. Legal actors, too, appeal regularly to multiple legal authorities and perceive themselves as members of more than one legal community. The image of ordered, nested legal systems clashes with wide-ranging legal practices and perceptions.[81]

---

[77] D.38.15.2.5 (Ulpian. 49 ad Ed.); compare D.37.1.10 (Paul. 2 ad Sab.).
[78] Wickham (2003), p. 4.
[79] See, in general, Tuori (2007). On 'Nabatean law', see Cotton (2009); on 'Coptic law' as a misleading concept, see Papaconstantinou (2009), p. 450 with fn. 16.
[80] Benton (2002), p. 8. See also Benton (2007).
[81] Benton (2002), p. 8.

This argument can be developed with respect to the first-century 'Babatha archive', a collection of papyri, found in the Nahal Hever cave in the Judaean desert, consisting primarily of legal family documents including contracts of loan, marriage contracts and deeds of sale and gift – variously written in Jewish, Greek, Aramaic and Nabatean Aramaic languages. Babatha's archive (and the accompanying archive of Salome Komaise) has generated a great deal of scholarly discussion concerning what type of law might have governed the legal situations envisioned in these papyri: whether it was Jewish, Rabbinic, Hellenistic, or Roman.[82] The question of the 'legal identity' of the Babatha archive has also been linked to questions concerning the 'identity' of Babatha herself: was she more Jewish, Hellenistic or Roman? Comparatively little work, however, has been done on how Babatha might have attempted to strategically range across different types of law and legal institutions in order to achieve an outcome favourable to her interests. A 2005 essay by Satlow, focusing on marriage payments and succession strategies in the Judaean desert documents, begins to explore this alternative perspective:

> I have tried to avoid explaining the papyri in the light of Rabbinic or 'Hellenistic' law or practice. I have done this not because I believe, a priori, that such comparisons are methodologically unsound; indeed in this particular case the rabbinic material nicely illustrates and confirms some of the suggestions offered here. Rather, my goal has not been to see how 'Jewish' or 'Hellenistic' Babatha and her friends were, but to try to understand a family at work, negotiating the mundane and treacherous terrain of money and familial relationships.[83]

Likewise, Elizabeth Meyer and Hannah Cotton have both drawn attention to the fact that:

> Babatha was a woman who fled to the Nahal Hever cave with no fewer than three Greek translations of the Roman formula of the *actio tutelae* in her leather pouch, so it is easy to believe that she was investigating the legal possibilities of the Roman legal system in Arabia for the likes of herself, and trying to exploit the opportunities it offered to the best of her abilities.[84]

Babatha's use of both Rabbinic and Roman law thus becomes evidence for (her access to) a kind of 'multi-legal' knowledge or at least a 'multi-legal' awareness – through which she attempted to achieve certain specific goals.[85] Franz von Benda-Beckmann has developed a similar argument on the basis

---

[82] See, for example, Cotton (2002); Cotton and Eck (2005); and Mélèze Modrzejewski (2005).

[83] Satlow (2005), p. 65.

[84] Meyer (2007), pp. 62–3; also Cotton (2002), p. 18: 'Rome's subjects could and would seek Roman justice whenever they believed that it would be more effective, more advantageous, and more just than the local one'.

[85] On 'multi-legal' awareness, compare, for example, Pirie (2006) on Tibetan Pastoralists.

of ethnographical fieldwork in contemporary Western Sumatra; working in the field, legal anthropologists were:

> forced to contextualize, [to] see how different categories of actors were influenced by, and made use of, different legal bodies in different contexts of interaction. In order to do this systematically, they had to dissociate categories of actors from the categories of law to which the actors 'belonged' by normative construction, that is, the farmer from his/her customary law; the bureaucrat from his state law; the religious functionary from his religious law. Only then could they see that farmers used, or were influenced by, state law; bureaucrats by traditional law etc. Empirical research further showed that the relations between the elements in a plural legal whole could be different; people could distinguish legal subsystems and choose between them, or accumulate them, or create new combined legal forms and institutions, while other actors, in other contexts, would act differently.[86]

There seems to be real potential for developing this kind of legal anthropological methodology further with respect to the much broader vista of legal practice revealed to us by papyrological evidence, epigraphical data and other first to third-century sources (including 'Patristic' texts). This approach leads us firmly away from the idea of an empire-wide imposition of Roman law potentially or actually governing the legal behaviour of Rome's subjects; rather, it will reveal them, as groups or individuals, negotiating the structures of Roman law and choosing – in so far as they were able – to engage with them, or not.

3. ROMAN LAW AND THE LATER EMPIRE: DEVELOPING A LEGAL ANTHROPOLOGICAL APPROACH

> I ask of your illustrious knowledge, whether there is one law for advocates and another for retired advocates, one equity for Rome and another for Matar?[87]

These questions, written in an early fifth-century letter addressed to a practising advocate by a retired advocate (*ex togato*), were intended to be understood rhetorically: according to the questioner at least, when two such learned individuals had a dispute with each other, their sense of equity, of 'fairness' and right dealing, should be the same whether the conflict unfolded at Rome or in the environs of their home town of Matar in Africa Proconsularis. Whilst some important modern scholarship has explored the kind of out-of-court negotiations and 'extra-legal' strategies that our two elite fifth-century North Africans were engaged in here, law in the Later Roman Empire is more usually associated with the unified legal system of the Emperor and

---

[86] Benda-Beckmann (2009), p. 32.
[87] *Ep. ad salvium PL* 20.243C-D. For discussion of this letter and its background, see Lepelley (1989), pp. 240–51; and Sirks (1999).

their imperial magistrates (as well as other legal officials operating from within the imperial bureaucracy).[88]

What is most visible in the late Roman legal evidence is, naturally, the product of the 'central' imperial government (imperial constitutions and law codes), and the imperially-sponsored institutional Christian church (especially with respect to the development of a specific *ius ecclesiasticum* and the early beginnings of a 'canon law').[89] Moving from the principate to the dominate, we seem to shift from a legal world of 'citizens' to one of 'citizens and subjects': 'As the Roman Empire expanded, the state became ever more intrusive in seeking to resolve the disputes of its citizens . . . The judge under the Empire in the provinces was an extension of state power and a symptom of the expanded role of the state in the lives of its citizens and subjects'.[90] This is a trend that appears to culminate in the sixth-century emperor Justinian's insistence that he alone is the sole interpreter of the law and the source of both Roman and ecclesiastical jurisprudence, alongside his confirmation of the canons of the Christian church themselves as civil laws.[91] However, even if, for the sake of the argument, we were to equate *all* late Roman law with imperial law, a 'legal anthropological' perspective is still essential to understanding how that law functioned in practice. As Chris Wickham has argued with reference to courts and conflict in medieval Tuscany:

> Even if we restricted our interest to the impact of Roman law, we would have to recognize that its nature and extent depended on the choices of the members of different local communities (whether litigants, lawyers or judges) as to how to approach law, and what law (if any) to use [. . .] These were cultural choices, whether conscious or unconscious, made inside locally specific realities; the social processes that generated them must be studied before anything else. There was everywhere, furthermore, a constant dialectic between local practices and organized legal knowledge: each affected the other. What we need to study in order to understand this dialectic is how people approached courts and arbitrations, with what expectations, and which strategies they used to get their way.[92]

---

[88] On late Roman out-of-court negotiation and formal arbitration, see Gagos and Van Minnen (1995); Harries (2003); and Harries (2007), pp. 28–42. Studies for the post-Roman West are, of course, more numerous, for example: Davies and Fouracre (1986); Wormald (1998); Rosenwein (1999); Brown (2001); Brown and Gorecki (2004); Karras, Kaye, and Matter (2008); and Rio (2009).

[89] See Gaudemet (1985); Gaudemet (1983); Gaudemet (1979); Crogiez-Pétrequin, Jaillette and Huck (2009); and Aubert and Blanchard (2009).

[90] Harries (2003), p. 71. Garnsey (2004), pp. 140–50 rightly stresses that citizenship and its various gradations still functioned as important legal mechanisms in the later Roman empire.

[91] C.1.14.12, Justinian to Demosthenes PP (529 CE); Digest, *Const. Deo Auctore*, 6; Justinian, Institutes pr.; Justinian, Novel 9pr (535 CE) and Justinian, Nov.131.1 (545 CE). Compare C.1.14.11 (474 CE). On Roman and Canon law in the age of Justinian, see the introductory chapter to Van der Wal and Stolte (1994).

[92] Wickham (2003), p. 4.

This kind of legal anthropological approach foregrounds individual parties, their perceptions of action and the choices that they make within any given socio-cultural situation, whilst still taking account of law codes, 'state' institutions and legal officials where relevant. It thus contrasts with what the legal sociologist Marc Galanter characterised as a legal-centralist perspective: 'The view that the justice to which we seek access is a product that is produced – or at least distributed – exclusively by the state [. . .]'.[93] If we set to one side a (nineteenth- and early twentieth-century) state-based theory of law that puts official law codes, formal legal institutions and the state *at the core* of all social order, then the idea of legal universalism under the Later Empire has the potential to look quite different.

What is at stake in developing a legal anthropological approach, rather than adopting a legal-centralist perspective, can be demonstrated via a brief analysis of the concept of 'legal practice' itself. If we adopt a legal-centralist starting point, then exploring legal practice inevitably involves some kind of questioning as to how far the 'law-in-the-books', or indeed unwritten customary law, relates to the law-in-action.[94] Exploring legal practice thus becomes an exercise in 'gap analysis': does the law on the ground match the official law as promulgated, or at least as transmitted, in the books? If not, how big are the gaps and why might they exist?[95] Late Roman historians, for example, tend to ask to what extent late Roman imperial constitutions – or even the canons of church councils – were applied in practice, and whether they were used correctly or not; in other words, we go to the 'legal' texts, then we look at law in practice, we inevitably find gaps, and try to account for them.[96] A 'legal anthropological' approach, on the other hand – where we try to understand legal processes as socio-cultural processes – does not neglect the 'law-in-the-books' (whether imperial codes, juristic writings), but seeks rather to contextualise that 'state' law in terms of a much broader understanding of legal practice. From a legal anthropological perspective, for example: 'The principal contribution of courts to dispute resolution is providing a background of norms and procedures against which negotiations and regulation in both private and governmental settings take place'.[97] Individuals bargain and strategise 'in the shadow of the law', hence, in the words of Galanter: 'The courts (and the law they apply) may thus be said to confer on the parties what Mnookin and Kornhauser call a "bargaining endowment," i.e., a set of "counters" to be used in bargaining between disputants.'[98] All of this activity, moreover, takes place in the context of

[93] Galanter (1981), p. 1.

[94] On the concept of 'customary law' as 'unwritten law', see Schulze (1992), pp. 13–14.

[95] On 'gap analysis', see Hartog (1985), p. 925 with fn.94 and Galanter (1981), p. 5.

[96] This was the methodology that I (unconsciously) followed in Humfress (2005) and Humfress (2006b). Compare Arjava (2003–4) and Stolte (2009).

[97] Galanter (1981), p. 6.

[98] Galanter (1981), p. 6. The reference is to Mnookin and Kornhauser (1979).

what Galanter terms 'indigenous ordering' or 'indigenous law', a 'social ordering that is indigenous – i.e., familiar to and applied by the participants in the everyday activity that is being regulated'.[99] For the later Roman Empire we might think of a particular Christian community within the city of Constantinople, or a specific trade association at Carthage, and so on. In order to explore 'law in practice', we first have to take account of who is using the formal/official law, in the context of what 'indigenous order' or 'indigenous law' and to what ends. As Galanter concludes:

> I am not trying to turn legal centralism upside down and place indigenous law in the position of primacy. Instead I suggest that the relation of official and indigenous law is variable and problematic. Nor do I mean to idealize indigenous law as either more virtuous or more efficient than official law. Although by definition indigenous law may have the virtues of being familiar, understandable, and independent of professionals, it is not always the expression of harmonious egalitarianism. It often reflects narrow and parochial concerns; it is often based on relations of domination; its coerciveness may be harsh and indiscriminate; protections that are available in public forums may be absent.[100]

A legal anthropological approach, then, acknowledges that rule-systems and their measures of enforcement were effectively spread throughout Late Roman society. Its starting point would be an attempt to reconstruct the field of late Roman legal practice from the perspective of individual actors, groups or communities, given their respective 'horizons of the possible': who they were, where they were and what kinds of indigenous ordering structured their lives – *as well as* their access to different types of formal legal 'knowledge' and imperial institutional structures.

4. CONCLUSION

Official Roman (or Graeco-Roman) sources envisage a world ruled by the universal law of Rome and its emperors. However, the central government of Rome, whether in the early or the late empire, before or after the edict of Caracalla, did not control the lives of all its subjects in the sphere of law, and did not attempt to do so. It is more profitable to look at the issue of law and legal practice from the bottom up, and to ask *whether*, how and why Rome's subjects, as individuals or as groups, availed themselves of the Roman legal system – given that from the third century CE, the sphere of Roman law had expanded, and that the bulk of the inhabitants of the empire (most of those who were free) had rights, as Roman citizens, to access it. Such an enquiry takes us well beyond the imperial law codes into papyri, inscriptions and diverse literary texts (including the works of the

---

[99] Galanter (1981), p. 17.
[100] Galanter (1981), p. 25.

Church Fathers, a rich source of evidence for legal or extra-legal behaviour at the local level); and it leads us to explore the ways in which Roman law and legal knowledge were used and adapted to local conditions and needs, or simply bypassed, as diverse other strategies were employed for settling disputes and securing order. A legal anthropological approach is an essential complement to and corrective of the legal-centralist perspective that is dominant in late Roman legal studies. 'The main point may be, that law never was one and that, however sublime justice may be, law is a complex of systems of social control among other complexes of systems of social control'.[101]

BIBLIOGRAPHY

Amelotti, M., 'Reichsrecht, Volksrecht, Provinzialrecht. Vecchi problemi e nuovi documenti' *SDHI*, 65 (1995), p. 211.

Ando, C., 'The administration of the Provinces', in D. S. Potter (ed.), *A Companion to the Roman Empire* (2006), p. 177.

Arjava, A., 'Die römische Vormundschaft und das Volljährigkeitsalter in Ägypten', *ZPE*, 126 (1999), p. 202.

Arjava, A., 'Law and life in the sixth-century Near East', *Acta Byzantina Fennica*, 2 (2003–4), p. 7.

Arjava, A., Buchholz, M. and Gagos, T. (eds), *The Petra Papyri*, vol. III (2007).

Aubert, J.-J., and Blanchard, P. (eds), *Droit, religion et société dans le Code Théodosien* (2009).

Bannon, C., *The Brothers of Romulus: Fraternal Pietas in Roman Law, Literature and Society* (2001).

Barton, C. A., *Roman Honor: The Fire in the Bones* (2001).

Beaucamp, J., 'Byzantine Egypt and imperial law', in R. S. Bagnall (ed.), *Egypt in the Byzantine World 300–700* (2007), p. 271.

Benton, L., *Law and Colonial Cultures: Legal Regimes in World History 1400–1900* (2002).

Benton, L., 'Empires of exception: history, law, and the problem of imperial sovereignty', *Quaderni di Relazioni Internazionali*, 8 (2007), p. 54.

Birks, P., Rodger, A., and Richardson, J. S., 'Further aspects of the *Tabula Contrebiensis*', *JRS*, 74 (1984), p. 45.

Bispham, E., *From Asculum to Actium* (2007).

Bowman, A. K., *The Town Councils of Roman Egypt* (1971).

Brélaz, C., 'Maintaining order and exercising justice in the Roman provinces of Asia Minor', in B. Forsén and G. Salmeri (eds), *The Province Strikes Back: Imperial Dynamics in the Eastern Mediterranean* (2008), p. 45.

Brown, W., *Unjust Seizure: Conflict and Authority in an Early Medieval Society* (2001).

Brown, W. and Gorecki, P. (eds), *Conflict in Medieval Europe: Changing Perspectives on Culture and Society* (2004).

---

[101] Van den Bergh (1969), p. 350.

Buell, D. K., 'Race and universalism in early Christianity', *Journal of Early Christian Studies*, 10.4 (2002), p. 429.

Camodeca, G., 'La prassi giuridica municipale. Il problema dell'effettività del diritto romano', in *Gli Statuti Municipali* (2006), p. 515.

Campbell, J. B., *The Writings of the Roman Land Surveyors* (2000).

Carrié, J.-M., 'Developments in provincial and local administration', in A. K. Bowman, P. Garnsey and A. Cameron (eds), *The Cambridge Ancient History*, 2nd edn, vol. XII, *The Crisis of Empire* A.D. 193–337 (2005), p. 269.

Cenderelli, A., *Ricerche sul 'Codex Hermogenianus'* (1965).

Chadwick, H., 'Christian and Roman universalism in the fourth century', in L. R. Wickham and C. D. Bammel (eds) *Christian Faith and Greek Philosophy in Late Antiquity. Essays in Tribute to George Christopher Stead* (1993), p. 26.

Chaniotis, A., 'Ritual performances of divine justice: the epigraphy of confession, atonement and exaltation in Roman Asia Minor', in H. M Cotton, R. G. Hoyland, J. J. Price and D. J. Wasserstein (eds), *From Hellenism to Islam. Cultural and Linguistic Change in the Roman Near East* (2009), p. 115.

Ciulei, G., *Les triptyques de Transylvanie: études juridiques* (1983).

Connolly, S., *Lives Behind the Laws: the World of the Codex Hermogenianus* (2010).

Coriat, J.-P., *Le Prince Législateur* (1997).

Cotton, H. M., 'Jewish jurisdiction under Roman rule: Prolegomena', in M. Labahn and J. Zangenberg (eds), *Zwischen den Reichen: Neues Testament und Römische Herrschaft* (2002), p. 5.

Cotton, H. M., '"Diplomatics" or external aspects of the legal documents from the Judaean desert', in C. Hezser (ed.), *Rabbinic Law in its Roman and Near Eastern Context* (2003), p. 49.

Cotton, H. M., 'The Yadin Papyri (P. Yadin) 1961–2004', in The Hebrew University of Jerusalem (ed.), *In Memory of Yigael Yadin 1917–1984 Lectures Presented at the Symposium on the Twentieth Anniversary of his Death* (2006), p. 31.

Cotton, H. M., 'Continuity of Nabatean law in the Petra papyri: a methodological exercise', in H. M Cotton, R. G. Hoyland, J. J. Price and D. J. Wasserstein (eds), *From Hellenism to Islam. Cultural and Linguistic Change in the Roman Near East* (2009), p. 154.

Cotton, H. M., and Eck, W., 'Roman officials in Judaea and Arabia and civil jurisdiction', in R. Katzoff and D. M. Schaps (eds), *Law in the Documents of the Judaean Desert* (2005), p. 23.

Cotton, H. M. and Yardeni, A. (eds), *Aramaic, Hebrew and Greek Documentary Texts from Nahal Hever and Other Sites, with an Appendix Containing Alleged Qumran Texts (The Seiyâl Collection II) Discoveries in the Judaean Desert*, vol. 27 (1997).

Cotton, H. M., Cockle, W. E. H., and Millar, R., 'The papyrology of the Roman Near East: a survey', *JRS*, 85 (1995), p. 214.

Crook, J., *Law and Life of Rome: 90 B.C. – A.D. 212* (1967).

Crook, J., *Legal Advocacy in the Roman World* (1995).

Crogiez-Pétrequin, S., Jaillette, P., and Huck, O. (eds), *Le Code Théodosien: diversité des approches et nouvelles perspectives* (2009).

Cuomo, S., *Technology and Culture in Greek and Roman Antiquity* (2007).

Davies, W. and Fouracre, P., *The Settlement of Disputes in Early Medieval Europe* (1986).

Demougeot, E., 'Restrictions à l'expansion du droit de cité dans la seconde moitié du ive siècle', *Ktema*, 6 (1981), p. 381.

Dench, E., *Romulus' Asylum: Roman Identities from the Age of Alexander to the Age of Hadrian* (2005).

Eck, W., 'Provincial administration and finance', in A. K. Bowman, P. D. A. Garnsey and D. Rathbone (eds), *The Cambridge Ancient History*, 2nd edn, vol. XI, *The High Empire A.D. 70–192* (2000), p. 266.

Eich, P., *Zur Metamorphose des politischen Systems in der römischen Kaiserzeit. Die Entstehung einer 'personalen Bürokratie' im langen dritten Jahrhundert* (2005).

Ellickson, R. C., *Order Without Law. How Neighbours Settle their Disputes* (1991).

Faro, S., 'Il questore imperiale', *Koinonia*, 8 (1984), p. 133.

Feissel, D., 'Les actes de l'État imperial dans l'épigraphie tardive (324–610): prolégomènes à un inventaire', in R. Haensch (ed.), *Selbstdarstellung und Kommunikation: Die Veröffentlichung staatlicher Urkunden auf Stein und Bronze in der römischen Welt* (2009), p. 97.

Fournet, J.-L., 'Entre document et littérature: la pétition dans l'antiquité tardive', in D. Feissel and J. Gascou (eds), *La pétition à Byzance. Centre de Recherche d'Histoire et Civilisation de Byzance*, Monographies 14 (2004), p. 61.

Fournet, J.-L., and Gascou, J., 'Liste des pétitions sur papyrus des Ve–VIIe siècles', in D. Feissel and J. Gascou (eds), *La pétition à Byzance. Centre de Recherche d'Histoire et Civilisation de Byzance*, Monographies 14 (2004), p. 93.

Frakes, R. M., *Contra potentium iniurias: the defensor civitatis and Late Roman Justice* (2001).

Franciosi, G., 'I 'libri viginti constitutionum' di Papirio Giusto', in *Studi in Onore di G. Grosso*, vol. 5 (1972), p. 149.

Fögen, M. T., *Römische Rechtsgeschichten. Über Ursprung und Evolution eines sozialen Systems* (2002).

Gagos, T. and van Minnen, P., *Settling a Dispute. Towards a Legal Anthropology of Late Antique Egypt* (1995).

Galanter, M., 'Justice in many rooms: courts, private ordering, and indigenous law', *Journal of Legal Pluralism and Unofficial law*, 19 (1981), p. 1.

Galsterer, H., 'Roman law in the provinces', in M. H. Crawford (ed.), *L'impero romano e le strutture economiche e sociali delle province* (1986), p. 13.

Galsterer H., 'Statthalter und Stadt im Gerichtswesen der westlichen Provinzen', in W. Eck (ed.), *Lokale Autonomie und römische Ordnungsmacht in den kaiserzeitlichen Provinzen vom 1. bis 3. Jahrhundert* (1999), p. 243.

Gardner, J. F., 'Making citizens: the operation of the *Lex Irnitana*', in L. de Blois (ed.), *Administration, Prosopography and Appointment Policies in the Roman Empire* (2001), p. 215.

Garnsey, P. D. A., 'Roman citizenship and Roman law in the Late Empire', in S. Swain and M. Edwards (eds), *Approaching Late Antiquity, The Transformation from Early to Late Empire* (2004), p. 133.

Garnsey, P. D. A., 'Roman patronage', in S. McGill, C. Sogno and E. Watts (eds),

From the Tetrarchs to the Theodosians. Later Roman History and Culture 284–450 CE (2010), p. 33.

Garnsey, P. D. A., *Social Status and Legal Privilege in the Roman Empire* (1970).

Gascou, J., 'Unités administratives locales et fonctionnaires romains. Les données des nouveaux papyrus du Moyen Euphrate et d'Arabie', in W. Eck (ed.), *Lokale Autonomie und römische Ordnungsmacht in den kaiserzeitlichen Provinzen vom 1. bis 3. Jahrhundert* (1999), p. 61.

Gascou, J., 'Les pétitions privées', in D. Feissel and J. Gascou (eds), *La pétition à Byzance. Centre de Recherche d'Histoire et Civilisation de Byzance*, Monographies 14 (2004), p. 141.

Gaudemet, J., *La formation du droit séculier et du droit de l'église aux iv et v siècles*, 2nd edn (1979).

Gaudemet, J., 'Collections canoniques et codifications', *Revue de Droit Canonique*, 33 (1983), p. 81.

Gaudemet, J., *Les sources du droit de l'église en occident du iie au viie siècle* (1985).

Gonzaleź J., 'The *Lex Irnitana*. A new copy of the Flavian municipal law', *JRS*, 76 (1986), p. 147.

Grubbs, J. E., *Women and the Law in the Roman Empire. A Sourcebook on Marriage, Divorce and Widowhood* (2002).

Harries, J., 'The Roman Imperial Quaestor from Constantine to Theodosius II', *JRS*, 78 (1988), p. 148.

Harries, J., *Law and Empire in Late Antiquity* (1999).

Harries, J., 'Creating legal space: settling disputes in the Roman Empire', in *Rabbinic Law in its Roman and Near Eastern Context* (2003), p. 63.

Harries, J., *Law and Crime in the Roman World* (2007).

Hartog, H., 'Pigs and positivism', *Wisconsin Law Review*, 4 (1985), p. 899.

Hauken, T., *Petition and Response: An Epigraphic Study of Petitions to Roman Emperors, 181–249* (1998).

Heath, M., *Menander. A Rhetor in Context* (2004).

Heather, P., and Moncur, D., *Politics, Empire and Philosophy in the Fourth Century. Select Orations of Themistius* (2001).

Hobson, D. W., 'The impact of law on village life in Roman Egypt', in B. Halpern and D.W. Hobson (eds), *Law, Politics and Society in the Ancient Mediterranean World* (1993), p. 193.

Hopkins, K., 'Divine emperors or the symbolic unity of the Roman emperor', in K. Hopkins (ed.), *Conquerors and Slaves: Sociological Studies in Roman History*, vol. 1 (1978), p. 197.

Honoré, T., *Emperors and Lawyers, Second edition, with a Palingenesia of Third-Century Imperial Rescripts 193–305* AD (1994).

Honoré, T., *Law in the Crisis of Empire 379–455* AD: *The Theodosian Empire and its Quaestors* (1998).

Honoré, T., 'Roman law 200–400 AD: from cosmopolis to Rechtstaat?', in S. Swain and M. Edwards (eds), *Approaching Late Antiquity. The Transformation from Early to Late Empire* (2004), p. 109.

Humfress, C., 'Law and legal practice', in M. Maas (ed.), *The Cambridge Companion to the Age of Justinian* (2005), p. 161.

Humfress, C. (2006a), 'Poverty and Roman law', in R. Osborne and M. Atkins (eds), *Poverty in the Roman World* (2006), p. 183.

Humfress, C. (2006b), 'Civil law and social life', in N. Lenski (ed.), *The Cambridge Companion to the Age of Constantine* (2006), p. 205.

Humfress, C., *Orthodoxy and the Courts* (2007).

Humfress, C., 'Bishops and lawcourts in Late Antiquity: how (not) to make sense of the legal evidence', *Journal of Early Christian Studies*, 19.3 (2011), p. 375.

Johnston D., 'Three thoughts on Roman private law and the *lex Irnitana*', *JRS*, 77 (1987), p. 62.

Kantor, G., 'Knowledge of law in Roman Asia Minor', in R. Haensch (ed.), *Selbstdarstellung und Kommunikation: Die Veröffentlichung staatlicher Urkunden auf Stein und Bronze in der römischen Welt* (1999), p. 249.

Karras, R. M., Kaye, J., and Matter, E. A. (eds), *Law and the Illicit in Medieval Europe* (2008).

Kelly, C., *Ruling the Roman Empire* (2006).

Kraemer, C. J., *Excavations at Nessana III. The Non-Literary Papyri* (1958).

Kremer, D., *Ius Latinum. Le concept de droit latin sous la république et l'empire* (2006).

Lamberti, F., *Tabulae Irnitanae : municipalità e ius Romanorum* (1993).

Lepelley, C., 'Trois documents méconnus sur l'histoire sociale et religieuse de l'Afrique romaine tardive, retrouvés parmi les spuria de Sulpice Sévère', *Antiquités Africaines*, 25 (1989), p. 235.

Liebs, D., 'Römische Jurisprudenz in Africa im 4. Jh. n. Chr.', ZSS (rom. Abt.), 106 (1989), p. 201.

Liebs, D., *Römische Jurisprudenz in Gallien (2 bis 8 Jahrhundert)* (2002).

Liebs, D., *Die Jurisprudenz im spätantiken Italien (260–640 n.Chr.)* (1987).

Lintott, A. W., *Imperium Romanum: Politics and Administration* (1993).

Matthews, J. F., *Laying Down the Law: A Study of the Theodosian Code* (2000).

Mattingly, D. J., 'Vulgar or weak "Romanization", or time for a paradigm shift?', *JRA*, 15 (2002), p. 536.

Mélèze Modrzejewski, J., 'Ménandre de Laodicée et l'Edit de Caracalla', in J. Mélèze Modrzejewski and D. Liebs (eds), *Symposium 1977. Vorträge zur griechischen und hellenistichen Rechtsgeschichte* (1982), p. 335. [Reprinted with original pagination in Mélèze Modrzejewski, J., *Droit imperial et traditions locales dans l'Egypte romaine* (1990)].

Mélèze Modrzejewski, J., 'Diritto romano e diritti locali', in A. Schiavone (ed.), *Storia di Roma* III/2 (1993), p. 985.

Mélèze Modrzejewski, J., 'What is Hellenistic law? The documents of the Judaean desert in the light of the papyri from Egypt', in R. Katzoff and D. M. Schaps (eds), *Law in the Documents of the Judaean Desert* (2005), p. 7.

Meyer, E. A., *Legitimacy and Law in the Roman World* (2004).

Meyer, E. A., 'Diplomatics, law and Romanisation in the documents from the Judaean desert', in J. W. Cairns and P. J. du Plessis (eds), *Beyond Dogmatics. Law and Society in the Roman World* (2007), p. 39.

Millar, F., 'Empire and city, Augustus to Julian: obligations, excuses and status', *JRS* 73 (1983), p. 76.

Millar, F., 'The many worlds of the late Antique Diaspora: supplements to the Cambridge History of Judaism vol. IV', *Journal of Jewish Studies*, 59.1 (2008), p. 120.

Mitteis, L., *Reichsrecht und Volksrecht in den östlichen Provinzen des römischen Kaiserreichs, mit Beiträgen zur Kenntniss des griechischen Rechts und der spätrömischen Rechtsentwicklung* (1891).

Mnookin, R. H., and Kornhauser, L., 'Bargaining in the shadow of the law: the case of divorce', *The Yale Law Journal*, 88 (1979), p. 950.

Nasrallah, L. S., *Christian Responses to Roman Art and Architecture* (2010).

Nörr, D., *Imperium und Polis in der Hohen Prinzipatzeit*, 2nd edn (1969).

Nörr, D., '*Lex Irnitana C. 84 IXB 9–10: neque pro socio aut fiduciae aut mandati quod dolo malo factum esse dicatur*', ZSS (rom. Abt.), 124 (2007), p. 1.

Nutton, V., 'The beneficial ideology', in P. D. A. Garnsey and C. R. Whittaker (eds), *Imperialism in the Ancient World* (1978), p. 209.

Palmer, B., 'The Imperial presence: government and army', in R. S. Bagnall (ed.), *Egypt in the Byzantine World 300–700* (2007), p. 244.

Papaconstantinou, A., '"What remains behind": Hellenism and Romanitas in Christian Egypt after the Arab conquest', in H. M. Cotton, R. G. Hoyland, J. J. Price and D. J. Wasserstein (eds), *From Hellenism to Islam. Cultural and Linguistic Change in the Roman Near East* (2009), p. 447.

Peachin, M., 'Petition to a centurion from the NYU Papyrus Collection and the question of informal adjudication performed by soldiers', in A. J. B. Sirks and K. A. Worp (eds), *Papyri in Memory of P. J. Sijpesteijn* (2007), p. 79.

Pirie, F., 'Legal complexity on the Tibetan Plateau', *Journal of Legal Pluralism and Unofficial Law*, 53/54 (2006), p. 77.

Pulitanò, F., *Ricerche sulla 'bonorum possessio ab intestato' nell'età tardo-romana* (1999).

Purpura, G., *Diritto, Papiri e Scrittura* (1995).

Revell, L., *Roman Imperialism and Local Identities* (2009).

Riccobono, S., 'Il problema del ius novum (extraordinarium) nella dottrina romanistica del secolo XIX e XX', *Circolo Giuridico*, N.S. 20 (1949), p. 162.

Richter, T. S., *Rechtssemantik und forensische Rhetorik*, 2nd edn (2008).

Rio, A., *Legal Practice and the Written Word* (2009).

Robert, L., 'Epigrammes relatives à des gouverneurs', *Hellenica*, 4 (1948), p. 35.

Rodger A., 'The jurisdiction of local magistrates: chapter 84 of the Lex Irnitana', *ZPE*, 84 (1993), p. 147.

Roebuck, D., and de Loynes de Fumichon, B., *Roman Arbitration* (2004).

Rosenwein, B., *Negotiating Space. Power, Restraint and Privileges of Immunity in Early Medieval Europe* (1999).

Rouché, C., 'The functions of the governor in Late Antiquity: some observations', *Antiquité Tardive*, 6 (1998), p. 31.

Rowlandson, J., and Takahashi, R., 'Brother-sister marriage and inheritance strategies in Greco-Roman Egypt', *JRS*, 99 (2009), p. 104.

Russell, D. A., and Wilson, N. G., *Menander Rhetor. A Commentary* (1981).

Saller, R., *Personal Patronage under the Early Empire* (1982).

Sasse, C., *Die Constitutio Antoniniana: eine Untersuchung über den Umfang der Bürgerrechtsverleihung auf Grund des Papyrus Giss. 40.1.* (1958).

Satlow, M. L., 'Marriage payments and succession strategies in the documents from the Judaean desert', in R. Katzoff and D. M. Schaps (eds), *Law in the Documents of the Judaean desert* (2005), p. 51.

Scherillo, G., 'Teodosiano, Gregoriano, Ermogeniano', in E. Albertario (ed.), *Studi in Memoria di Umberto Ratti* (1934), p. 247.

Schönbauer, E., 'Reichsrecht gegen Volksrecht? Studien über die Bedeutung der Constitutio Antoniniana für die römische Rechtsentwicklung', ZSS (rom. Abt.), 51 (1931), p. 277.

Schönbauer, E., 'Reichsrecht, Volksrecht und Provinzialrecht', ZSS (rom. Abt.), 57 (1937), p. 309.

Schulze, R., '"Gewohnheitsrecht" und "Rechtsgewohnheiten" im Mittelalter – Einführung', in G. Dilcher and R. Schulze, *Gewohnheitsrecht und Rechtsgewohnheiten im Mittelalter* (1992), p. 9.

Seidl, E., *Rechtsgeschichte Ägyptens als römischer Provinz* (1973).

Shaw, B., 'Rebels and outsiders', in A. K. Bowman, P. D. A. Garnsey and D. Rathbone (eds), *The Cambridge Ancient History*, 2nd edn, vol. XI, *The High Empire A.D. 70–192* (2000), p. 361.

Sirks, A. J. B., 'The Epistula ad Salvium, appended to a letter of Sulpicius Severus to Paulinus: observations on a recent analysis by C. Lepelley', *Subseciva Groningana* 6 (1999), p. 75.

Slootjes, D., *The Governor and his Subjects in the Later Roman Empire* (2006).

Sperandio, M. U., *Codex Gregorianus: origini e vicende* (2005).

Stolte, B., 'The impact of Roman law in Egypt and the Near East in the third century AD: The documentary papyri. Some considerations in the margin of the Euphrates papyri (P.Euphr.)', in L. de Blois (ed.), *Administration, Prosopography and Appointment Policies in the Roman Empire* (2001), p. 167.

Stolte, B., 'Jurisdiction and the representation of power, or the emperor on circuit', in L. de Blois et al. (eds), *The Representation and Perception of Roman Imperial Power. Proceedings of the Third Workshop of the International Network Impact of Empire (Roman Empire, c. 200 B.C. – A.D. 476)* (2002), p. 261.

Stolte, B., 'The social function of law', in J. Haldon (ed.), *A Social History of Byzantium* (2009), p. 76.

Talamanca M., 'Su alcuni passi di Menandro di Laodicea relativi agli effetti della "constitutio Antoniniana"', in *Studi in Onore di Edoardo Volterra*, vol. 5 (1971), p. 433.

Tjäder, J.-O., *Die nichtliterarischen lateinischen Papyri Italien aus der Zeit 445–700* (1955).

Tomlin, R. S. O., 'The Curse Tablets', in B. Cunliffe (ed.), *The Temple of Sulis Minerva at Bath, volume 2: The Finds from the Sacred Spring* (1998), p. 59.

Tomlin, R. S. O., 'The Flavian municipal law', ZPE, 141 (2002), p. 281.

Tuori, K., 'Legal pluralism and the Roman empires', in J. W. Cairns and P. J. du Plessis (eds), *Beyond Dogmatics. Law and Society in the Roman World* (2007), p. 39.

Turpin, C. C., 'Bonae fidei iudicia', *Cambridge LJ*, 23 (1965), p. 260.

van den Bergh, J., 'Legal pluralism and Roman law', *The Irish Jurist*, 4 (1969), p. 338.

van der Wal, N., and Stolte, B., *Collectio Tripartita: Justinian on Religious and Ecclesiastical Affairs* (1994).

Velázquez Soriano, I., *Documentos de época visigoda escritos en pizarra (sigl. vi–viii) 2 volumes. Monumenta Palaeographica Medii Aevi: Series Hispanica* (2000).

Versnel, H. S., 'Prayers for justice in East and West: recent finds and publications', in R. L. Gordon and F. M. Simón (eds), *Magical Practice in the Latin West* (2010), p. 275.

Vessey, M., 'Sacred letters of the law: the emperor's hand in Late Roman (literary) history', *Antiquité Tardive*, 11 (2003), p. 345.

von Benda-Beckmann, F., and von Benda-Beckmann, K., 'The dynamics of change and continuity in plural legal orders', *Journal of Legal Pluralism and Unofficial Law*, 53–4 (2006), p. 1.

von Benda-Beckmann, F., 'Riding the centaur? Reflections on the identities of legal anthropology', in M. Freeman and D. Napier (eds), *Law and Anthropology. Current Legal Issues vol. 12* (2009), p. 13.

Watson, A., *The Law of Succession in the Later Roman Republic* (1971).

Wessel, H., *Das Recht der Tablettes Albertini* (2003).

Wickham, C., *Courts and Conflict in Twelfth-Century Tuscany* (2003).

Wolf, J. G., 'The Romanization of Spain: the contribution of city laws in the light of the *Lex Irnitana*', in A. Burrows and A. Rodger (eds), *Mapping the Law. Essays in Memory of Peter Birks* (2006), p. 439.

Wolff, H., *Die Constitutio Antoniniana und Papyrus Gissensis 40.1* (1976).

Woolf, G., *Becoming Roman: the Origins of Provincial Civilization in Gaul* (1998).

Wormald, P., *Legal Culture in the Early Medieval West* (1998).

Yiftach-Firanko, U., 'Law in Graeco-Roman Egypt; Hellenization, fusion, Romanization', in R. Bagnall (ed.), *The Oxford Handbook of Papyrology* (2009), p. 541.

Chapter 6

The Concept of Conubium *in the Roman Republic*

Saskia T. Roselaar

1. INTRODUCTION

During their conquest of Italy, the Romans devised various legal instruments to regulate their relations with people who did not possess Roman citizenship. One of the issues that needed regulation was marriage: laws had to be formulated to enable marriage between people from different political entities, and to lay down rules for the regulation of inheritance in such unions.

It is often assumed that the main instrument devised by the Romans to regulate marriage with *peregrini* – a term which included Latin and Italian allies, as well as other non-citizens – was *conubium* or *ius conubii*, which might be translated as a 'right to marry each other'. It is usually assumed that *conubium* was a right that could be granted by Rome to non-citizens, and permitted them the use of certain legal instruments related to marriage, which were otherwise only available to citizens. The presence of *conubium* was especially important because of its implications for inheritance law. If a marriage was not concluded legally, any children would not be recognised and therefore would not be the automatic heirs of the parents. This meant that the legality of marriage remained important throughout Roman history. Unfortunately, our sources for *conubium* in the Republic are extremely scanty; for the Empire there is much more information available, but we cannot assume that *conubium* in this period followed the same rules as before. Nevertheless, some sources exist that claim to be describing very early Roman history, although their reliability is questionable.

Here I will review the legal possibilities for marriage between Romans and non-citizens in the Republic, especially the idea that *conubium* with Roman citizens was a privilege granted to people with Latin status. Thus, the relations between the legal framework and the practical side of marriage will become clear. I will argue that many long-standing assumptions about marriage between Romans and aliens in the Republic cannot hold; in particular, the idea that Latins enjoyed widespread *conubium* with Romans seems to me very unlikely. This has important implications for our ideas concerning social relations between Romans and their allies in Italy.

2. *CONUBIUM* UNDER THE EMPIRE

First of all we must investigate the basic meaning of the term *conubium*, which was derived from *con* + *nubere* ('marry + to/with'). The usage of *conubium* as a shorthand for 'marriage' occurs occasionally from the late Republic onwards, for example in Livy's description of the war between Romans and Sabines. The Sabine women tell their fathers: 'If you are weary of these ties of kindred, these marriage-bonds (*si conubii piget*), then turn your anger upon us; it is we who are the cause of the war, it is we who have wounded and slain our husbands and fathers'.[1] Cicero describes the development of ties between people, leading to the growth of states: 'Then follow in turn marriages (*conubia*) and connections by marriage, and from these again a new stock of relations, and from this propagation and growth states have their beginnings'.[2] This meaning becomes much more common in the later Empire, for example in Augustine: 'It is perhaps not absurd to call it "marriage" (*conubium*), if (the union) has been agreeable to them up to the death of one of them'.[3] It was also used in this way in official texts: 'It seems unworthy for men who do not possess any rank to descend to sordid *conubia* with slave women'.[4] However, for the Republican period and the early and middle Empire, *conubium* usually denotes a legal right or privilege to conclude marriage.

Conubium as a legal right is widely discussed in imperial sources; however, it should be kept in mind that we cannot assume that the same rules applied during the Republic. A starting point is the Rules of Ulpian, written down in the third century CE. Ulpian states:

> A rightful marriage exists, when between those who contract a marriage there is *conubium* [. . .] *Conubium* is the ability to take a wife. Roman citizens have *conubium* with Roman citizens, but with Latins and *peregrini* only if this has been granted. With slaves there is no *conubium*.[5] Between parents and offspring to a certain grade *conubium* never exists[6] [. . .] If *conubium* applies, the children always follow the (status of) the father; if *conubium* does not apply, they pertain to the condition of the mother, except that from a *peregrinus* and a Roman citizen woman a *peregrinus* is born, because the *Lex Minicia* ordered that one born from a *peregrinus* on one

---

[1] Liv. *Hist.* 1.13. Tacitus uses it thus in *Hist.* 3.34: Cremona, through 'the many connections and intermarriages formed with neighbouring nations (*adnexu conubiisque gentium*), grew and flourished'. See *Hist.* 4.65: 'Those who in former days settled here and have been united to us by marriage' (*nobiscum per conubium sociatis*). Similar meanings in Verg. *Aen.* 3.136, 4.168, 7.96, 7.333, 12.821; *Cul.* 299; Stat. *Theb.* 7.300; *Silv.* 1.2.195.

[2] Cic. *Off.* 1.54.

[3] Augustin. *Bon. Con.* 5.

[4] CTh.12.1.6 (318 CE); Prudent. *c. Symm.* 2.617. See Volterra (1950), pp. 368–9.

[5] Treggiari (1991), p. 44 thinks marriage between free and freed was not forbidden in the Republic.

[6] See Corbett (1930), pp. 47–51.

side should follow the condition of the inferior parent. From a Roman citizen and a Latin woman a Latin is born, and from a free man and a slave woman a slave, because in these cases there is no *conubium*, and they therefore follow the status of the mother.[7]

Gaius in the second century gives much the same regulations:

Roman citizens are understood to have contracted legal marriage and to have children born from it in their power, if they have married Roman citizen women or Latin or peregrine women with whom they have the right of marriage. For it happens that, because the right of marriage results in children following their father's status, not only do they become Roman citizens, but they are also in their father's power.[8]

Therefore, the rule was that '*conubium* always means that he who is born follows the condition of the father'.[9]

Therefore, someone enjoying *conubium* would be able to contract a *iustum matrimonium* according to the rights of Roman citizens. Thus, *conubium* was 'the right to contract a marriage with a foreigner which will be upheld in a Roman court of law, with full validity of testamentary power and paternity rights'.[10] Roman citizens could always marry each other, unless there was a legal impediment.[11] However, being a Roman citizen did not automatically carry *conubium* with everyone else; it was a condition that had to exist between both people.[12] Marriage with a Latin or peregrine was only possible

[7] Ulpian. *Reg.* 5.2: 'Iustum matrimonium est, si inter eos, qui nuptias contrahunt, conubium sit [. . .] 3. Conubium est uxoris ducendae facultas. 4. Conubium habent cives Romani cum civibus Romanis; cum Latinis autem et peregrinis ita: si concessum sit. 5. Cum servis nullum est conubium. 6. Inter parentes et liberos infinite cuiuscumque gradus conubium non est [. . .] 8. Conubio interveniente liberi semper patrem sequuntur, non interveniente conubio matris conditioni accedunt, excepto eo, quod ex peregrino et cive Romana peregrinus nascitur, quoniam lex Minicia ex alterutro peregrino natum deterioris parentis condicionem sequi iubet. 9. Ex cive Romano et Latina Latinus nascitur, et ex libero et ancilla servus, quoniam, cum his casibus conubia non sint, partus sequitur matrem'. For marriage between freedmen and their patrons, see D.24.2.11pr-2; 23.2.45.4–6; 25.7.1pr (all Ulpian. 3 ad Leg. Iul. et Pap.); C.5.5.1; for pupils, see C.5.6.1. See Serv. *Aen.* 1.73: *Conubium est ius legitimi matrimonii.* See Gardner (1986), pp. 32–6; Treggiari (1991), pp. 37–43; Evans-Grubbs (2002), pp. 154–5.

[8] Inst.Gai.1.56–7: 'Iustas autem nuptias contraxisse liberosque iis procreatos in potestate habere cives Romani ita intelleguntur, si cives romanas uxores duxerint vel etiam Latinas peregrinasve cum quibus conubium habeant, cum enim conubium id efficiat ut liberi patris condicionem sequantur, evenit ut non solum cives Romani fiant sed et in potestate patris sint'. See 1.76–80; C.5.27.11pr.

[9] Inst.Gai.1.81: 'Semper conubium efficit ut qui nascitur patris condicioni accedat'.

[10] Sherwin-White (1973), pp. 33–4. See Corbett (1930), p. 24: '*Conubium* is said to exist between a man and a woman when they are capable of legal intermarriage'.

[11] De Visscher (1952), p. 405. For *conubium* as a right awarded to discharged soldiers, see Inst. Gai. 1.57 with Corbett (1930), pp. 39–42; Sherwin-White (1973), p. 268; Mirkovic (1986); Treggiari (1991), p. 44.

[12] De la Chevalerie (1954), pp. 272–3.

if *conubium* had been granted to them, individually or to a whole people or city, by the Roman state.[13]

Children from such a marriage followed the citizenship status of the highest-ranked partner, at least after the *Lex Minicia* was introduced (see below). Children from a *iustum matrimonium* were in *patria potestas*; without lawful marriage, they were fatherless and *sui iuris*.[14] This had important consequences for inheritance rights: in case of intestate death, the first heirs were the *sui heredes*, that is those who were *in potestate* (legitimate children who had not been emancipated) or *manus* (wives married *in manus*, see below);[15] they now became *sui iuris*. Illegitimate children were not in *patria potestas* and therefore were not *sui heredes*. If there were no *sui heredes*, the intestate heirs would be, first, the *agnati proximi* (male relatives on the father's side), then the *gentiles*.[16] All *sui*, male or female, took equal shares. A woman could not have *sui heredes*, since she did not have *patria potestas*.[17] Therefore, in a marriage without *conubium*, there was no automatic succession between parents and children on intestacy in Roman law.[18] Furthermore, after the death of one partner, the remaining partner could only claim the estate if the marriage was valid, and only if there were no *heredes* or *agnates*.[19] Wives married *sine manu* and who were *sui iuris* could be appointed heirs, but only by a will; they were not intestate heirs.[20] Furthermore, if someone was not a Roman citizen *sui iuris*, he could not make a will. Making a will was an act of the *ius civile*, and therefore *peregrini* could not make one, nor inherit from a Roman by law.[21]

In practice, it was difficult to check whether *conubium* existed between two intended partners; at the census a man had to declare that he had a wife 'to his best knowledge' (*ex sententia*);[22] since, if he were married without *conubium*, he would not have a legal wife, the question likely intended to ask whether he was legally married. However, the censors could not easily check the truthfulness of the answer; if the husband and/or wife were Roman citizens, it would have been possible to check previous census lists to see if they had been registered before as such. For a Latin or *peregrinus*, the only

---

[13] Volterra (1950), pp. 357–8; Crook (1967), p. 40; Gardner (1986), pp. 142–4; Evans-Grubbs (2002), pp. 18–21; Frier and McGinn (2004), p. 32.

[14] Inst.Gai.1.87.

[15] Fayer (2005), pp. 197–222 points out that marriage and *conventio in manus* were not necessarily part of the same process nor occurred at the same time.

[16] Treggiari (1991), pp. 28–9; Saller (1994), p. 163; Gardner (1998), pp. 15–16; Frier and McGinn (2004), pp. 322–4.

[17] Inst.Gai.3.1–8. See Watson (1971), p. 175; Gardner (1986), pp. 190–4; Evans-Grubbs (2002), p. 219; Frier and McGinn (2004), pp. 339–40.

[18] Treggiari (1991), pp. 49–50.

[19] D.38.11.1pr (Ulpian. 47 ad Ed.). See Cic. *Top.* 4.20.

[20] Treggiari (1991), p. 383.

[21] Watson (1971), pp. 22, 26, 33; see in general Kaser (1960), pp. 695–7.

[22] Sulp. *ap.* Gell., N.A. 4.3.2; Gell. N.A. 4.20.3; Dion. Hal. 2.25.7; Cic. *De Or.* 2.260. See Treggiari (1991) p. 58.

option was to check local census records, but this would have been cumbersome or impossible. Therefore, it may regularly have occurred that a couple discovered they were not legally married, even if they thought they were. The discovery that no *conubium* existed with a betrothed was a valid reason to end the engagement.[23] Under the Empire there were regulations about marriage in error, since this may have occurred frequently:

> If a Roman citizen man has married a Latin or peregrine wife through ignorance, because he believed that she was a Roman citizen, and has begotten a son, the child is not in his power, because he is not even a Roman citizen, but either a Latin or peregrine [. . .] By a decree of the Senate it is permitted to prove a case of error, and so the wife also and the son arrive at Roman citizenship, and from that time the son begins to be in his father's power [. . .] Likewise, if a Roman citizen woman has married a peregrine man through error, as if he were a Roman citizen, it is permitted to her to prove a case of error, and so also her son and her husband arrive at Roman citizenship, and equally the son begins to be in his father's power.[24]

The most important aim was to ensure that children were legitimate, because having legitimate children, and therefore making sure they were legal intestate heirs, was the most important goal of marriage.

3. CONUBIUM AMONG CITIZENS IN THE EARLY REPUBLIC

The sources suggest that a concept of *conubium* already existed in the early Republic, and that some of its elements were similar to those we encounter in later sources.

In 445 BCE debate erupted about intermarriage between patricians and plebeians: 'C. Canuleius, a tribune of the plebs, introduced a law with regard to the intermarriage of patricians and plebeians. The patricians considered that their blood would be contaminated by it and the special rights of the houses thrown into confusion'.[25] Canuleius then held a speech in which he argued:

> In one of these laws we demand the right of intermarriage, a right usually granted to neighbours and foreigners – indeed we have granted citizenship, which is more than intermarriage, even to a conquered enemy [. . .] Was not this very prohibition of intermarriage between patricians and plebeians, which inflicts such serious injury on the commonwealth and such a gross injustice on the plebs, made by the decemvirs within these last few years? [. . .] They are guarding against our becoming connected with them by affinity or relationship, against our blood being allied with theirs [. . .] If your nobility is tainted by union with us, could you not have kept it pure by private regulations, by not seeking brides from the plebs, and not

[23] Sen. *Ben.* 4.27.5. See Treggiari (1991), p. 158.
[24] Inst.Gai.1.67.
[25] Liv. *Hist.* 4.1.2.

suffering your sisters or daughters to marry outside your order? [. . .] That this should be prohibited by law and the intermarriage of patricians and plebeians made impossible is indeed insulting to the plebs [. . .] For, as a matter of fact, what difference is there, if a patrician marries a plebeian woman or a plebeian marries a patrician? [. . .] Of course, the children follow the father.[26]

Dionysius states that the *decemviri* in the Twelve Tables of 451–50 BCE forbade marriage (*epigamia*) between patricians and plebeians; *epigamia* may be a translation of *conubium*, or at least of the concept as it existed in Dionysius's own time.[27] It is likely that patricians and plebeians in earlier periods did in fact marry each other, and that the ban on doing so was only a result of an increasing movement by the patricians to separate themselves from the plebeians.[28] Already for the very start of Roman history, Livy describes *conubium* as a legal concept that could be shared by different peoples:

Rome had now become so strong that it was a match for any of its neighbours in war, but its greatness threatened to last for only one generation, since through the absence of women there was no hope of offspring, and *there was no right of intermarriage with their neighbours* [. . .] Romulus sent envoys amongst the surrounding nations to ask for alliance and the right of intermarriage on behalf of his new community.[29]

Of course most of these stories are legendary, so they do not offer real evidence for a legal concept of *conubium* in this early period.[30]

It is likely that this episode was constructed later as an element of the 'Struggle of the Orders' between patricians and plebeians, possibly on the basis of misunderstood evidence. Forsythe, for example, argues that the idea of a marriage ban between the classes was based on a later obligation for priests to marry by the rite of *confarreatio*, which Livy might have understood as being the result of an earlier limitation on marriage between patricians and plebeians.[31] The class struggle was not limited to Rome, but was considered by later authors to be an element of society in Latium in general. Livy relates that in 443 BCE a conflict erupted in Ardea, because

---

[26] Liv. *Hist.* 4.3.4–4.11.

[27] Dion. Hal. 10.60. See Twelve Tables 11.1; Dion. Hal. 11.2.2; Cic. *Rep.* 2.63. See Volterra (1950), p. 373; Catalano (1965), p. 99.

[28] Corbett (1930), p. 30, however, states that intermarriage occurred from 445 BCE onwards apparently misunderstanding Livy.

[29] Liv. *Hist.* 1.9.1–2: '... nec cum finitimis conubia essent. Tum ex consilio patrum Romulus legatos circa vicinas gentes misit qui societatem conubiumque novo populo peterent'. Ov. *Fast.* 3.195–200 also says that 'rights of intermarriage' were granted to foreigners: 'Rights of intermarriage are granted to distant peoples, / yet none wished to marry a Roman' ('extremis dantur conubia gentibus, at quae Romano vellet nubere, nulla fuit').

[30] Cornell (2005).

[31] Forsythe (2005), p. 229.

two young men were courting a girl of plebeian descent celebrated for her beauty. One of them, the girl's equal in point of birth, was encouraged by her guardians, who belonged to the same class; the other, a young noble captivated solely by her beauty, was supported by the sympathy and good-will of the nobility.[32]

If we assume that Romans and Latins at this time shared *conubium* (see below), then it appears that *conubium* would have been especially important for the nobility as a mechanism by which they created alliances throughout Latium, while not permitting the members of their class to reduce its power by marrying plebeians.[33] In any case, it is likely that the ban on marriage between patricians and plebeians was lifted shortly after 445 BCE, since there is much evidence for marriage between the two groups in the later Republic.[34]

4. CONUBIUM BETWEEN ROMANS AND LATINS BEFORE 338 BCE

A commonly held belief among modern scholars is that *conubium* was essential for a legal marriage between Romans and *peregrini*. A special group of *peregrini* were the Latins, and it is usually assumed that *conubium* existed between them and the Romans before and after the Latin War of 341–38 BCE.

Our earliest evidence for *conubium* in a non-legendary context appears in Livy's description of the settlement of Latium by the Romans in 338:

> Lanuvium received the full citizenship [. . .] Aricium, Nomentum, and Pedum obtained the same political rights as Lanuvium. Tusculum retained the citizenship which it had had before. [. . .] Antium [. . .] [was] admitted to citizenship. [. . .] The rest of the Latin cities were deprived of the rights of intermarriage, free trade, and common councils with each other ('ceteris Latinis populis conubia commerciaque et concilia inter se ademerunt'). Capua [. . .] was given *civitas sine suffragio*, as were also Fundi and Formiae.[35]

This passage is crucial in our study of *conubium*, although we should keep in mind that it was written 300 years after the events it describes. Nevertheless, Livy's detailed enumeration of Latin towns and their varying treatments suggest that he had reliable details available regarding the privileges and punishments they received. The phrasing suggests that most of the Latins (apart from those retaining their privileges) were deprived of *conubia* and *commercia*

---

[32] Liv. *Hist.* 4.9.
[33] De Visscher (1952); see De la Chevalerie (1954), p. 280.
[34] Gardner (1986), p. 32.
[35] Liv. *Hist.* 8.14: 'Lanuvinis civitas data sacraque sua reddita [. . .] Aricini Nomentanique et Pedani eodem iure quo Lanuvini in ciuitatem accepti [. . .] Et Antium [. . .] civitas data. [. . .] Ceteris Latinis populis conubia commerciaque et concilia inter se ademerunt. Campanis [. . .] Fundanisque et Formianis [. . .] civitas sine suffragio data'.

generally, both those with Rome and with each other, whereas the *concilia* were *inter se*, that is between the Latin towns.[36]

Dionysius mentions that *isopoliteia* existed between Romans and Latins in the period before 338 BCE, and that they had received this through the *Foedus Cassianum* of 493 BCE: 'All the Latins, to whom we lately granted equal rights of citizenship, will be on our side, fighting for this commonwealth as for a country now their fatherland'.[37] In combination with Livy's passage for 338 BCE, this leads to the assumption that before 338 *conubium* was a reciprocal right, which not only granted a Latin the right to marry a Roman, but also a Roman to marry a Latin, and for Latins between themselves to marry each other. This would be in keeping with the principle of *isopoliteia* as claimed by Dionysius. Some assume that this was the result of individual treaties between Rome and the Latin cities, or of a grant by Rome;[38] however, in the early Republican period, there is no reason to assume that Rome was very much stronger than the other Latin towns, and that therefore this grant was a hegemonic permission emanating from Rome, as it would later become. In any case, it is likely that marriage between Romans and Latins already existed very early in the Republic.[39]

The Latin War of 341–38 BCE marked a fundamental change in the relationship between Rome and the Latins. Before this war, Rome had not been powerful enough to impose its will on other states – at least in theory; we can see growing interference by Rome and resulting dissatisfaction among the allies from the early fourth century. Now, however, Rome was the most important power in central Italy, and could take one-sided, hegemonic decisions about the rights of its allies (or rather subjects), as is clear from Livy's description of Rome's decisions in 338 BCE.

In 306 BCE, according to Livy,

---

[36] Sautel (1952), pp. 38–9 assumes that all these rights were valid between the Latin towns, not with Rome. De Visscher (1952), p. 417 suggests that Latins were still allowed to marry into Roman families, but not amongst each other; this would have strengthened Rome's control over the Latins. However, the text suggests that they were deprived of *conubium* generally, including with Rome.

[37] Dion. Hal. 7.53.5. This speech was held during the trial of Coriolanus in the early fifth century. Similarly, in 8.35.2 Coriolanus demands that 'the Romans will . . . give [the Volsci] equal rights of citizenship: as they have done in the case of the Latins'. In 6.63.4, citing a speech held by Brutus before the *Foedus*, Dionysius suggests that the Latins did not yet have equal rights: 'I say nothing of the thirty cities of the Latin nation, which would be only too glad to fight our battles by reason of their kinship, if you would but grant them equal rights of citizenship, which they have constantly sought'. See also 8.70.2, 8.72.5, 8.74.2, 8.75.2, 8.76.2; see 4.58.3 for *isopoliteia* between Romans and Gabii. For the *Foedus* itself, see Dion. Hal. 6.95.2, where, however, he does not mention marriage rights.

[38] Mommsen, cited in De Visscher (1952), p. 405.

[39] De Visscher (1952), pp. 406–7; Dixon (1992), p. 79; Forsythe (2005), pp. 184. Humbert (1978), p. 97 thinks that *isopoliteia* was the same as Roman citizenship, but it is not clear why Latins would have desired Roman citizenship.

three of the Hernican communities – Aletrium, Verulae, and Ferentinum – had their municipal independence restored to them as they preferred that to the Roman franchise, and the right of intermarriage with each other was granted them (*suae leges redditae conubiumque inter ipsos*), a privilege which for a considerable period they were the only communities amongst the Hernicans to enjoy. The Anagnians and the others who had taken up arms against Rome were admitted to the *civitas sine suffragio*, were deprived of their municipal self-government and the right of intermarriage (*concilia conubiaque adempta*).[40]

Sherwin-White argued that 'if *civitas sine suffragio* implied the equation of its holder to a *civis Romanus* in all but political rights, then the Anagnini would automatically have shared in the *conubium* with the other Hernici which all *cives Romani* enjoyed'.[41] However, this is not what Livy says: he states that Anagnia was deprived of *conubia* and *concilia*. It is likely that the *concilia* were again *inter se*, as in 338 BCE; for the *conubia* we do not have evidence, but since the Hernici had been admitted to the *Foedus Cassianum* on equal terms with the Latins, we can assume they had enjoyed the same rights, namely *commercium* and *conubium*, with Rome. This they would now have lost.[42] The other towns received *conubium* with each other (*inter ipsos*), not with Rome, so we cannot conclude that all Hernici were now allowed to marry Romans. We see here again a clear indication of Rome's growing power, which allowed her to make unilateral decisions about which legal rights were granted to her allies; any rights should therefore be seen as privileges granted by Rome, which could be taken away at any point. This development became even more pronounced in the later Republic.

5. CONUBIUM IN THE LATER REPUBLIC

A persistent assumption for the later Republic is that Latins enjoyed many privileges in their relations with Rome; these are usually cited as *conubium*, *commercium*, and the *ius migrationis*. *Conubium* would have constituted a privilege that could be granted to Latins (and *peregrini*), which would have allowed them to contract valid marriages with Romans. This would mean that a Roman could marry those Latins and *peregrini* who either individually or as a group had received *conubium* with Rome. It is almost universally believed that the Latins as a collective had been granted *conubium* by the *Foedus Cassianum* and that they retained this after 338.[43] Sherwin-White,

---

[40] Liv. *Hist.* 9.43.23.
[41] Sherwin-White (1973), p. 49.
[42] De Visscher (1952), p. 417 believes they only lost the right of intermarriage with each other.
[43] Crook (1967), p. 44; Sherwin-White (1973), pp. 32–7; pp. 109–16; Humbert (1978), pp. 98–108; Treggiari (1991), pp. 44–5; Crawford (1992), p. 36 who assumes that this remained unchanged since the *Foedus Cassianum*; Capogrossi Colognesi (1994), pp. 16–23;

for example, thinks that *Latinitas* became 'the path to Roman citizenship, and almost a secondary form of the *civitas* itself'.[44] He argues that 'for the Republican period before the Social War there can be no doubt. The statement in Livy [...] implies that these rights persisted between Latin and Roman'. However, I have argued above that the *commercia* and *conubia* that the Latins lost referred to all rights, both between Romans and Latins and between Latins themselves, while the *concilia* that were taken away were common councils between Latins only.[45] Livy clearly states that the Latins were now deprived from *commercia* and *conubia* with Rome, and it is nowhere indicated that they regained these rights later.

Therefore, there is in fact no reason to assume that the Latins were privileged over other allies in their contacts with Rome after this year. The evidence in fact suggests that Latins were placed on the same footing as all other *peregrini*. Livy states that in 169 BCE 'there were two portents which were not taken into consideration, one because it occurred on private, the other on foreign soil' (*in agro peregrino*).[46] The 'foreign soil' in question was the Latin colony of Fregellae. Furthermore, Gaius states: 'The *Lex Minicia* classes as *peregrini* not only foreign races and peoples but also those called Latins; it also applied to the other Latins, who had their own communities and cities and were in the category of *peregrini*'.[47] There has been some debate over the date of the law, but it is likely that it should be dated to shortly before 90 BCE,[48] showing that in the late Republic Latins were considered *peregrini*.

The privilege of *conubium* between inhabitants of different Latin towns is another debated issue; Livy suggests that the Latins were deprived of this right in 338 BCE. However, Servius Sulpicius refers to a particular betrothal procedure among Latins: 'The man who was to take the woman

---

Cornell (1995), pp. 295–7; Forsythe (2005), p. 290. Coşkun (2009), pp. 35–6, n. 70 argues that the ban on marriage between Latins issued in 338 BCE did not last long, although there is no evidence that it was lifted. Watson (1971), p. 27 argues that Latins could receive inheritances from Romans, but it is not clear why this should be the case.

[44] Sherwin-White (1973), p. 98.

[45] This is not considered by Sherwin-White, who actually omits the word *concilia* from his quote: Sherwin-White (1973), pp. 109–10.

[46] Liv. *Hist.* 43.13.6.

[47] Inst.Gai.1.79. The passage may be interpreted in two ways: either the Latins were always classed as *peregrini* or they were only interpreted as such in this law. However, it is more likely that the definition was not created only for the *Lex Minicia*, but was valid in other cases as well; see Catalano (1965), pp. 278–87.

[48] Cherry (1990), pp. 248–50; Treggiari (1991), p. 45; Dixon (1992), p. 124. Coşkun (2009), p. 38, fn. 80 argues it should be dated after 90 BCE or even in the imperial period, but gives no arguments. A date shortly before 90 BCE fits well with other laws passed at the same time, which all aimed to restrict the rights of Italian allies. This may reflect a desperate attempt by the Roman state to maintain a barrier between it and other Italians, who increasingly demanded more rights. The *Lex Licinia Mucia* of 95 BCE, which expelled *peregrini* from the Roman census lists, is another example of such a law.

to wife made a formal promise'. If the marriage was cancelled, 'he who had asked for her hand, or he who promised her, brought suit on the ground of breach of contract', and a fine was payable. Sulpicius adds that 'this law of betrothal was observed up to the time when citizenship was given to all Latium by the *Lex Iulia*' (i.e., 90 BCE).[49] It may be that this was a custom of the *prisci Latini* and had earlier been shared by Romans; the Latin colonies seem not to have been involved.[50] This passage is sometimes used to argue that all Latins possessed *conubium* with each other, although Sulpicius does not say that marriage occurred between *different* Latin peoples; the partners could very well have been of the same Latin group. There is therefore no positive evidence that Latins were allowed to marry each other after 338.

The problem of the possession of *conubium* by Latins should be connected to that regarding the other two privileges they are commonly assumed to have had: *commercium* and the *ius migrationis*. However, the possession of both these privileges by the Latins has recently been questioned. Regarding the *ius migrationis*, in two well-known episodes from 187 BCE and 177 BCE the Romans were asked by some Latin towns to return to them people who had moved to Rome; Rome then ordered the Latins to return home.[51] However, if the Latins had possessed *ius migrationis*, these expulsions make no sense. If Latins had the right to migrate to Rome, then the Roman state could not expel them.[52]

I have argued elsewhere that it is also unlikely that the Latins, as a rule, held *commercium*,[53] apart from those who were settled in colonies of Latin status. It is likely that a similar arrangement pertained to *conubium* as well. A passage dating to 177 BCE has been interpreted as showing evidence for the widespread existence of *commercium* among the Latins:

> The law entitled the Latin allies to become Roman citizens as long as they left a son of their own at home [. . .] To avoid the necessity of leaving a son at home, men would hand their sons over as slaves (*mancipio dabant*) to anyone with Roman citizenship, on the condition that the sons would be manumitted; as freedmen they would become citizens. Men with no offspring to leave behind adopted sons to become Roman citizens.[54]

---

[49] Sulp. *ap.* Gell. *N.A.* 4.4. See Corbett (1930), pp. 9–15.

[50] Coşkun (2009), p. 37 fn. 76.

[51] Liv. *Hist.* 39.3.4–5; 41.8.6–12; 41.9.9–12; 42.10.3; Cic. *Sest.* 13.30.

[52] Broadhead (2001) in more detail; Coşkun (2009), pp. 107–10. Laffi (1995), p. 51 thinks that *ius migrationis* was a privilege granted to all Latins at the time of the *Foedus Cassianum*, but in that case it would have been abolished in 338; furthermore, there is no reason why the Romans would care about the population levels of Latin towns other than colonies, since they were not of strategic importance.

[53] Roselaar (forthcoming).

[54] Liv. *Hist.* 41.8.8–10. See Laffi (1995) for a detailed discussion of this passage.

The expression *mancipio dabant* seems to suggest that *peregrini* (in this case, Latins) who sold their sons as slaves – which were *res mancipi* – to Roman citizens were admitted to *mancipatio*, and therefore that they held *commercium*.[55]

However, the passage should be considered in the light of the *ius migrationis*. It is thought that Latins were allowed to migrate to Rome and thereby take up Roman citizenship. However, from Livy's passage, it is clear that this was not as simple as is often thought: if Latins had been allowed to migrate to Rome, they would not have needed to resort to such ingenious methods of gaining citizenship for their sons. It is more likely that we should identify a specially privileged group within the Latins, namely the inhabitants of the Latin colonies. Since many Latin colonists were originally from Rome,[56] it would make sense that they were allowed to return to Rome if they left a son behind in their colony. This would make it more attractive for Romans to join a colony, because they would have an opportunity to return; for the state this assured that the colonies, which were strategically important for the Romans, remained up to strength.[57] Those of Latin origin who joined a colony may have been granted the same right, to encourage them to join and as a reward for services to the Roman state.[58]

I suggest that the Latin colonists may have been granted the right to use *mancipatio* as a special privilege, like the right to migrate if they left a son in the colony. It is possible that they were also granted *commercium*. This would have been necessary especially for reasons of inheritance: if many settlers were of Roman origin, then it was to be expected that they would receive inheritances from or want to bequeath them to family members who had remained Roman citizens. *Commercium* was needed to receive inheritances, since inheritances might include *res mancipi*.[59] However, *commercium* was not sufficient to arrange inheritances with their Roman relatives: *conubium* would be necessary as well.

That indeed some Latin colonies enjoyed special inheritance privileges is clear from a passage in Cicero:

> Sulla himself passed a law respecting the rights of citizenship, avoiding any taking away of the legal obligations and rights of inheritance of these men. For he orders the people of Ariminum to be under the same law that they have been. Who does

---

[55] Galsterer (1976), p. 103; Sherwin-White (1973), p. 109.

[56] Sherwin-White (1973), p. 27; Luraschi (1979), pp. 261–2, 272–81; Cornell (1995), pp. 367–8.

[57] The Romans were adamant about the need to keep up the strength of the colonies; in the case of Roman citizens' colonies, intricate regulations existed to keep the colonist contingent up to strength; see Roselaar 2009.

[58] Broadhead (2001).

[59] Inst.Gai.2.210 indeed states that *peregrini* could not inherit, but see Mayer-Maly (2003), p. 6.

not know that they were one of the twelve colonies and that they were able to receive inheritances from Roman citizens?[60]

It appears that twelve colonies had the right to inherit from Romans, including Ariminum, and that the rest did not. Such inheritances could not have been possible without *conubium*, so this passage suggests that there were, at least in Cicero's time, twelve colonies with *conubium*. A commonly held theory is that they were the last twelve Latin colonies, founded from 268 BCE onwards; the first of these was Ariminum.[61]

However, there are problems with this interpretation. Firstly, Cicero's words *eodem iure esse, quo fuerint Ariminenses* do not sound as if the Ariminenses had a clearly defined set of rights; it sounds more like an ad-hoc measure, possibly a Sullan innovation applying only to Ariminum. Furthermore, it is strange that the last twelve colonies, which were furthest away from Rome, received more rights than others closer to Rome. Their rights would not have been very useful, because they would not interact with Romans so much. Since there is no indication anywhere in the sources before Cicero that there was a difference in status between Latin colonies, I am inclined to believe that Cicero is referring to an innovation by Sulla which affected twelve colonies.[62]

---

[60] Cic. *Caec.* 102: 'Deinde quod Sulla ipse ita tulit de civitate ut non sustulerit horum nexa atque hereditates. Iubet enim eodem iure esse quo fuerint Ariminenses; quos quis ignorat duodecim coloniarum fuisse et a ciuibus Romanis hereditates capere potuisse?' See Catalano (1965), p. 109; Luraschi (1979), pp. 281–99.

[61] Bernardi (1973), pp. 76–88. The others would be Beneventum, Firmum Picenum, Aesernia, Brundisium, Spoletium, Placentia, Cremona, Thurii Copia, Vibo Valentia, Bononia and Aquileia. However, there is debate about the status of some other towns, especially Luna and Luca; if either of them was a Latin colony, as is assumed by some (see Roselaar (2010), p. 325), then the total of twelve would not add up. Watson (1971), p. 27 argues that it was only by Sulla that the rights of Ariminum were extended to other cities, but Cicero does not say this. Corbett (1930), pp. 24–6 argues that Ariminum and eleven other colonies had an inferior status, rather than more rights. However, if anything, they would have had more rights than other colonies, since they could inherit and others could not. Sherwin-White (1973), pp. 102–4 is indecisive, but does not believe that the twelve towns enjoyed other rights than the rest of the Latin colonies. Coşkun (2009), pp. 34–9 with fn. 70, 80; 64–70 with fn. 192; 119; 146–7; 169 fn. 522 argues that the *ius XII coloniarum* included *commercium*, *conubium*, *nexum*, *enktesis*, the *ius testamenti factio*, and *ius hereditatis captio*, and was created in the 120s BCE. Because the *ius civitatis adispiscendae per magistratum*, which Coşkun assumes to have been created in this period, made many local elites citizens, Latins in the same colonies would have had problems in dealing with their own townsmen, so the *ius XII coloniarum* was created to deal with this problem. It is unclear, however, why only twelve colonies were granted this; Coşkun suggests it may have been granted individually to each colony at their request. The *ius civitatis adispiscendae per magistratum* is another thorny problem; Sherwin-White (1973), p. 112, argues that it was created in the early first century. I am inclined to agree with Bradeen (1959) that citizenship *per magistratum* was not automatically granted to Latins at all during the Republic.

[62] Antonelli (2006) argues that they were the twelve towns in which Sulla had founded colonies; however, we do not know how many colonies Sulla established.

There would, in that case, be no evidence for the possession of *conubium* by any colony before Sulla, but the idea that the Latin colonies received this right, together with *commercium* and the *ius migrationis*, is in my view attractive. I suggest that Latin colonists were the only group in possession of these three rights, which would on the one hand make sure that the manpower of the colonies remained up to strength, and at the same time make joining a colony more attractive because existing family ties were not sundered by the change of status from Roman to Latin.[63]

A second problematic group were the *cives sine suffragio*. Since they were *cives*, they would fall under the Roman *ius civile* and therefore have *conubium* with Romans.[64] In the case of Anagnia in 308 BCE, the grant of this right was clearly intended as a punishment, which makes it unlikely that they were given the privilege to marry Romans. However, the Capuans, who had received it as a reward in 338 BCE, clearly did marry Romans. They joined Hannibal in the Second Punic War, but before they decided to defect,

> the only circumstances which prevented them from immediately revolting were the old established right of intermarriage (*conubium vetustum*) which had led to many of their illustrious and powerful families becoming connected with Rome and the fact that several citizens were serving with the Romans.[65]

After Rome recaptured Capua in 211 BCE, its leaders were punished with the loss of their *civitas*. They appealed to the Romans, stating that 'they were for the most part Roman citizens, connected with Roman families by intermarriage (*conubio vetusto*)'.[66] There is indeed some evidence for marriage between Romans and Campanians: Pacuvius Calavius, the leader of Capua in the Second Punic War, had married a daughter of Appius Claudius, and Calavius' daughter had married one of the Livii.[67] The daughter of Fabius Maximus Rullianus married Atilius Calatinus, another Campanian noble.[68]

The situation of the Campanians had not yet been resolved in 188 BCE. As Livy states,

> the censors had obliged the Campanians to register for the census at Rome, since it had not been clear earlier where they should register. The Campanians now requested that they might be allowed to take wives who were Roman citizens and

---

[63] Bernardi (1973), p. 68 argues that there was no *conubium* between the colonists of different colonies, but this is unlikely, since members of the same family might go to different colonies.

[64] Sherwin-White (1973), p. 46.

[65] Liv. *Hist.* 23.4.7.

[66] Liv. *Hist.* 26.33.3. A Roman ambassador in 200 BCE, according to Liv. *Hist.* 31.31.11, pointed out to the Macedonians that 'we had forged links with [the Campanians] first by a treaty, subsequently by marriage and family ties (*deinde conubio atque cognationibus*), and finally by granting them citizenship'.

[67] Liv. *Hist.* 23.2.6.

[68] Val. Max. *Mem.* 8.1.9.

that any who had taken them be permitted to keep them; and they also asked that any children born to them before that date be considered as legitimate and able to inherit. Both requests were granted.[69]

This shows clearly that the Campanians, who at this time held the status of *peregrini*, did not have *conubium* before they made this request, for in that case they would not have had to ask for recognition of their marriages.[70]

It is clear from this passage that a grant of *conubium* was a unilateral decision made by the Roman state: it could grant this privilege to an individual or group at its own discretion. As in the case of Capua, the Senate could also take away the privilege whenever it wanted, especially as a punishment to disloyal allies. In this way grants of *conubium* – like grants of other privileges, like *commercium*[71] – functioned as a tool to maintain Rome's hegemony over its allies. This is itself makes it very unlikely that all allies, or even all Latins, possessed this right;[72] if that were the case, Rome would have found it more difficult to use *conubium* as a tool of government. All attestations in fact refer to individual cases. The use of *conubium* and related privileges was, I suggest, first and foremost a hegemonic tool, and not an element of 'Romanisation'; it simply privileged some people over others in their relations with Rome, but did not always make them any more 'Roman' in their cultural outlook – Latin colonists of Roman descent would have a 'Roman' mindset already; other Latin colonists, however, may have been proud of their new privileged status, and thus grants of legal privileges may have engendered a new feeling of *Romanitas* among certain groups in Italy. It is clear that *conubium* was a closely guarded privilege, as was Roman citizenship itself.

For example, a grant of *conubium* to a specific group was made in 171 BCE:

> A deputation from Spain arrived, who represented a new race of men. They declared themselves to be sprung from Roman soldiers and Spanish women who were not legally married (*cum quibus conubium non esset*) [. . .] The senate decreed that they should send in their own names and the names of any whom they had manumitted to L. Canuleius, and they should be settled on the ocean shore at

---

[69] Liv. *Hist.* 38.36: 'Campani . . . petierunt, ut sibi cives Romanas ducere uxores licere, et, si qui prius duxissent, ut habere eas, et nati ante eam diem uti iusti sibi liberi heredesque essent'.

[70] De la Chevalerie (1954), p. 277. Volterra (1950), p. 367 fn. 57 argues that being counted in Rome meant that they gained citizenship, but this is not necessarily the case. It only means that they were registered in a separate group by the censors at Rome, since there was no Capuan administration that could have done the job.

[71] Roselaar (forthcoming).

[72] Corbett (1930), pp. 26–8 and Volterra (1950), p. 380 argue that Rome had to grant *conubium* to every treaty partner separately; however, they still assume that eventually all allies received it. In fact, if only a few allies held *conubium*, there would be no reason why it should be part of the treaties with allies; on the other hand, it was possibly a standard item in charters of Latin colonies.

Carteia, and any of the Carteians who wished to remain there should be allowed to join the colonists and receive an allotment of land. This place became a Latin colony and was called the 'Colony of the Libertini'.[73]

What we see here is a kind of retrospective grant of *conubium*: the marriages were recognised in a sense, since the sons were considered legally born; however, they did not receive Roman citizenship, as their fathers had held, but only Latin status. If their parents had received full 'retrospective' *conubium*, the men should have been made *peregrini*, since children of a Roman man and a peregrine woman with *conubium* followed the mother's status and so were *peregrini* (see below). Apparently this was felt to be inappropriate for the situation, and indeed the *lex Minicia* shortly afterwards changed this law. We see again that the Roman state could unilaterally make whatever grants it wished from its hegemonic position.

In 186 BCE the Senate decided that the freedwoman prostitute Hispala Faecenia, who had assisted Romans in the Bacchanalian affair, 'be permitted to marry a free-born man, and that whosoever married her suffer thereby no prejudice or loss of status'.[74] The absence of *conubium* in her case was due to her freed status rather than the fact that she was not a citizen; nevertheless, the Senate could, again, simply decide that such objections were taken away. Citizenship and *conubium* could also be granted separately: in 89 BCE some Spanish cavalry were granted Roman citizenship, but not *conubium*; this would mean that they could not marry Roman women.[75] Thus, it is clear that the Roman state could decide whatever it wished in regard to its civic rights: it could grant all rights separately, to specific peoples, groups, or individuals.

As for the Italian *socii*, there is no indication that they as a group possessed *conubium*, as is sometimes assumed for *commercium*. Diodorus suggests that some Italian *socii* also enjoyed *conubium*: in a battle during the Social War, soldiers from both parties recognised each other as 'men whom the law governing intermarriage had united in this kind of friendly tie'.[76] Some scholars argue that all *socii* already possessed *conubium*,[77] but this is very unlikely; some of the Italian rebels may have been Latins or *cives sine suffragio*.

An important change in marriage rights was introduced by the *Lex Minicia*, possibly dated to before 90 BCE (see above). Before this law, if there was no *conubium* between two people, they were not legally married, and the child took its mother's status. If there was *conubium*, it took the father's status. Therefore, children of a Roman mother and non-Roman father without *conubium* had been Roman citizens, since according to the

---

[73] Liv. *Hist.* 43.3.1–4.

[74] Liv. *Hist.* 39.19.5. See Humbert (1987). Volterra (1950), p. 358 and De Visscher (1952), p. 403 are therefore wrong that *conubium* was not an individual right, but only that of a group.

[75] ILS 8888. See Mirkovic (1986), p. 171.

[76] Diod. 37.15.2. See Sherwin-White (1973), p. 125.

[77] Galsterer (1976), p. 103; contra Bernardi (1973), p. 83; Coşkun (2009), p. 38 fn. 78.

ius gentium, illegitimate children followed the mother. In the case of a valid marriage, children took the status of the father.[78] Therefore, children of a Roman woman and a peregrine man with *conubium* had been *peregrini*, since *conubium* meant that children followed the father. This was seen as somewhat of a paradox; therefore, the *lex Minicia* enacted that when there was no *conubium*, the child followed the parent with the lowest status. Nothing changed for cases in which the father was a citizen: a Roman father and a peregrine mother without *conubium* had a peregrine child, while a peregrine father with *conubium* and a Roman mother had a Roman child, as had been the case earlier.[79]

Another legal development related to marriage and inheritance rights was the growing prevalence of marriages *sine manu*, which gradually replaced those with *manus*; by the mid-first century BCE, if not earlier, *sine manu* was the most common form of marriage.[80] With *manus*, a woman who married passed from the *potestas* of her father to that of her husband; the husband would then have complete control over her possessions, and upon her death these would be inherited by his family. If a woman was married *in manu*, her father could only give her a dowry, and she would have no right to an inheritance on her father's death; when married *sine manu*, she could inherit from him. *Sine manu*, a woman remained in her father's *potestas*, to which she returned in the case of her husband's death; her possessions would be inherited by her family on her father's side.[81]

The earliest reference to *sine manu* marriage dates to 204 BCE, when the *Lex Cincia* limited gifts between husband and wife.[82] It is also referred to by Ennius[83] and in Cato's comments on the *Lex Voconia* of 169, which allowed women to have their own property.[84] An increase in *sine manu* marriages occurred possibly after the divorce of Carvilius Ruga around 230 BCE, who was, apparently, the first to divorce his wife for reasons other than those laid down in the Twelve Tables.[85] Because no laws existed for this situation, the wife and her father did not have a legal action to claim the return of her

[78] Corbett (1930), p. 97; Sherwin-White (1973), ch. 15; Coşkun (2009), p. 34.
[79] Inst.Gai.1.76–8. Ulpian and Gaius also say that if either parent was peregrine, the child was peregrine, but this refers to parents without *conubium*. See Gardner (1986), p. 31; Treggiari (1991), pp. 45–7; Frier and McGinn (2004), p. 32.
[80] Kaser (1960), p. 324; Dixon (1992), p. 40; Evans-Grubbs (2002), p. 21.
[81] Dixon (1992) pp. 40, 74.
[82] FV 302. However, the Twelve Tables 6.5 (cited in Inst.Gai.1.111) already refer to the avoidance of *manus*: if a woman did not sleep in the marital bed for three nights per year (the so-called *ius trinoctium*) she would avoid entering into *manus* and stay instead in her father's control. See Gardner (1986), pp. 12–13; Lewis and Crawford (1996), pp. 661–2.
[83] *Her.* 2.24.38: a father is given authority to end his daughter's marriage.
[84] Gell. *N.A.* 17.6.1.
[85] Dion. Hal. 2.25.7; Plu. *Quaest. Rom.* 14; *Romulus* 35.3–4; *Numa* 25.12–13; Val. Max. 2.1.4; Gell. *N.A.* 4.3.1–2, 17.21.44.

dowry. When divorce became more common, the *cautiones rei uxoriae* and *actio rei uxoriae* were created.[86] A marriage *sine manu* had other advantages for a *paterfamilias*, who would in most cases make the decisions about his daughter's marriages.[87] If his daughter was widowed young, he would be able to arrange her next marriage to his advantage, since she was still under his *potestas*. The fact that she was still entitled to a share in her father's inheritance would enable the father to make decisions about his fortune up to the moment of his death. The development of *sine manu* marriages would therefore be in keeping with the availability of larger fortunes towards the end of the third century, over which a *paterfamilia*s would wish to retain control.[88]

It is possible that the *Lex Minicia* was passed for the same reasons that caused the increase in *sine manu* marriages, namely a growing preoccupation with regulations regarding inheritances. This indicates a growing desire to make sure that the increasingly large fortunes accumulated in this period remained in the hands of the same family; on the part of the Roman state, it suggests a desire to ensure that wealth remained in the hands of Roman citizens. *Conubium* would be a part of this development, because it would ensure that *peregrini* would not have access to Roman wealth: children of a marriage in which one of the partners was a non-Roman would, as *peregrini*, not be able to inherit from a Roman citizen. In this sense, *conubium* and other privileges worked as an important element of separation between Romans and others, rather than as a mechanism of integration. This fits in with the very restricted admittance of *peregrini* to Roman citizenship in general, as we have seen.

6. CONCLUSION

I have reviewed some common ideas about *conubium* in the Roman Republic. *Conubium* as a legal concept originated quite early in the history of the Republic, since by 338 it was an established privilege that could be granted to others. *Conubium* underwent some important innovations in the Republican period, for example the *Lex Minicia*. Gradually it developed from a loosely defined custom, as it was before the Latin War, to a strictly

---

[86] Kaser (1960), pp. 337–8; Gardner (1986), pp. 48–9; Dixon (1992), p. 45.

[87] Gardner (1986), pp. 45–6.

[88] Looper-Friedman (1984), pp. 293–5; Gardner (1998), pp. 40–1; Jacobs (2009), pp. 109–10. Some have seen this development as a liberation of women from male control (see discussion in Dixon (1992), pp. 20, 30–1). However, when this development took place, women were still expected to be under the *tutela* of a man, and the erosion of *tutela* as a practical limitation on women's powers had not yet begun; see Crook (1986); Dixon (1986); (2002), pp. 77–88; Gardner (1986), pp. 16–22; Dodds (1991–2). The 'liberation of women' cannot therefore have been the aim of those who, in the third and second centuries, chose marriages *sine manu* instead of with *manus*.

delineated instrument of Roman hegemony, used to keep a close watch on allies and subjects.

The Roman state was completely hegemonic in its decisions; it could grant *conubium* in combination with citizenship or separately, to groups, individuals, or peoples. There is no evidence for a widespread grant of *conubium* to Latin and/or Italian allies; however, I argue that the inhabitants of Latin colonies did enjoy this right, because it was important to maintain the strategic function of these colonies. The *cives sine suffragio* also shared in this right because they participated in the Roman *ius civile*.

We may conclude that the absence of *conubium* was an important mechanism of separation between Romans and colonial Latins and, on the other hand, the other Latins and allies. It is likely that the limited possibilities for access to Roman wealth, and the wish to be able to inherit from Roman citizens, formed an important drive in the desire for Roman citizenship that *peregrini* felt in the late Republic. This may have been one of the reasons that drove the Italian allies to revolt in the Social War; I hope to explore this issue further in future work.[89]

BIBLIOGRAPHY

Antonelli, L., 'Silla, Ariminum e lo ius duodecim coloniarum', in L. Braccesi (ed.), *Ariminum. Storia e archeologia* (2006), p. 241.

Bernardi, A., *Nomen Latinum* (1973).

Bradeen, D. W., 'Roman citizenship *per magistratum*', CJ, 54 (1959), p. 221.

Broadhead, W., 'Rome's migration policy and the so-called *ius migrandi*', CCG, 12 (2001), p. 69.

Capogrossi Colognesi, L., '*Ius commercii, conubium, civitas sine suffragio*. Le origini del diritto internazionale privato e la romanizzazione delle comunità latino-campane', in A. Corbino (ed.), *Le strade del potere* (1994), p. 3.

Catalano, P., *Linee del sistema sovrannazionale romano* (1965).

Cherry, D., 'The Minician law: marriage and the Roman citizenship', *Phoenix*, 44 (1990), p. 244.

Corbett, P. E., *The Roman Law of Marriage* (1930).

Cornell, T. J., *The Beginnings of Rome. Italy and Rome from the Bronze Age to the Punic Wars (c. 1000–264 BC)* (1995).

Cornell, T. J., 'The value of the literary tradition concerning archaic Rome', in K. A. Raaflaub (ed.), *Social Struggles in Archaic Rome: New Perspectives on the Conflict of the Orders* (2005), p. 47.

Coşkun, A., *Bürgerrechtsentzug oder Fremdenausweisung? Studien zu den Rechten von Latinern und weiteren Fremden sowie zum Bürgerrechtswechsel in der Römischen Republik (5. bis frühes 1. Jh. v. Chr.)* (2009).

Crawford, M. H., *The Roman Republic* (1992).

[89] I would like to thank Luuk de Ligt, Egbert Koops and Boudewijn Sirks for discussions about the issue of *conubium*.

Crook, J. A., *Law and Life of Rome: 90 B.C.–A.D. 212* (1967).

Crook, J. A., 'Women in Roman succession', in B. Rawson (ed.), *The Family in Ancient Rome: New Perspectives* (1986), p. 58.

De la Chevalerie, A., 'Observations sur la nature du "conubium" et la situation juridique des Campaniens avant et après les guerres d'Annibal', *RIDA*, 3.1 (1954), p. 271.

Dixon, S., 'Family finances: Terentia and Tullia', in B. Rawson (ed.), *The Family in Ancient Rome: New Perspectives* (1986), p. 93.

Dixon, S., *The Roman Family* (1992).

Dixon, S., *Reading Roman Women. Sources, Genres and Real Life* (2001).

Dodds, J., 'The impact of the Roman law of succession and marriage on women's property and independence', *Melbourne University Law Review*, 18 (1991–2), p. 899.

Evans-Grubbs, J., *Women and the Law in the Roman Empire. A Sourcebook on Marriage, Divorce and Widowhood* (2002).

Fayer, C., *La familia romana: aspetti giuridici ed antiquari. Parte 2: Sponsalia, matrimonio, dote* (2005).

Forsythe, G., *A Critical History of Early Rome: from Prehistory to the First Punic War* (2005).

Frier, B. W., and McGinn, T. A. J., *A Casebook on Roman Family Law* (2004).

Galsterer, H., *Herrschaft und Verwaltung im republikanischen Italien. Die Beziehungen Roms zu den italischen Gemeinden vom Latinerfreuden 338 v. Chr. bis zum Bundesgenossenkrieg 91 v. Chr.* (1976).

Gardner, J. F., *Women in Roman Law and Society* (1986).

Gardner, J. F., *Family and familia in Roman Law and Life* (1998).

Humbert, M., *Municipium et civitas sine suffragio. L'organisation de la conquête jusqu'à la Guerre Sociale* (1978).

Humbert, M., 'Hispala Fecenia et l'endogamie des affranchis sous la République', *Index*, 15 (1987), p. 131.

Jacobs, A., 'Carvilius Ruga v uxor: a famous Roman divorce,' *Fundamina*, 15:2 (2009), p. 92.

Kaser, M., *Das römische Privatrecht I: das altrömische, das vorklassische und klassische Recht* (1960).

Laffi, U., 'Sull'esegesi di alcuni passi di Livio relativi ai rapporti tra Roma e gli alleati Latini e Italici nel primo quarto del II sec. a.C.', in A. Calbi and G. Susini (eds), *Pro poplo arimenese* (1995), p. 43.

Lewis, A. D. E., and Crawford, M. H., 'Twelve Tables', in M. H. Crawford (ed.), *Roman Statutes* II (1996), p. 555.

Looper-Friedman, S. E., 'The decline of *manus*-marriage in Rome', *TvR*, 44 (1984), p. 281.

Luraschi, G., Foedus, ius Latii, civitas: *aspetti costituzionali della Romanizzazione in Transpadana* (1979).

Mayer-Maly, T., 'Commercium', *TvR*, 71 (2003), p. 1.

Mirkovic, M., 'Die Entwicklung und Bedeutung der Verleihung des Conubium', in W. Eck and H. Wolff (eds), *Heer und Integrationspolitik. Die römische Militärdiplome als historische Quelle* (1986), p. 167.

Mousourakis, G., *The Historical and Institutional Context of Roman Law* (2003).

Roselaar, S. T., *Assidui or proletarii? Property in Roman Citizen Colonies and the Vacatio Militiae*, Mnemosyne 62 (2009), p. 609.

Roselaar, S. T., *Public Land in the Roman Republic: a Social and Economic History of* ager publicus *in Italy, 396–89* BC (2010).

Roselaar, S. T., 'The concept of *commercium* in the Roman Republic', *Phoenix*, (forthcoming).

Saller, R. P., *Patriarchy, Property, and Death in the Roman Family* (1994).

Sautel, G., 'Essai sur la notion romaine de 'commercium' à l'époque ancienne', in G. Sautel, Y. Bongert and B. Perrin (eds), *Varia. Études de droit romain* (1952), p. 1.

Sherwin-White, A. N., *The Roman Citizenship* (1973).

Treggiari, S., *Roman Marriage. Iusti coniuges from the Time of Cicero to the Time of Ulpian* (1991).

Volterra, E., 'La nozione giuridica del *conubium*', in *Studi in memoria di Emilio Albertario*, vol. 1 (1950), p. 347.

de Visscher, F., '"Conubium" et "civitas"', *RIDA*, 1 (1952), p. 401.

Watson, A., *The Law of Succession in the Later Roman Republic* (1971).

Chapter 7

Financial Transactions by Women in Puteoli

Éva Jakab

1. CHANGING TIMES AND METHODOLOGIES

Sed fugit interea, fugit irreparabile tempus[1] – in formulating these famous lines, the focus of Virgil's contemplation was human feelings and their change-able nature, but his wise observation can equally be applied to history: time marches on and new historical periods replace the old ones. Each period has its own typical social values which include ideas about legal policy or the proper view of certain legal institutions. Historians and lawyers are necessarily children of their own age – their reasoning is in various ways influenced by their social, cultural and economic environment. It is very likely that topics such as 'women and society' or 'women and law' have always been highly sensitive to (and often deeply manipulated by) the ideological and cultural background in which they are treated.

The present chapter focuses on some of the ways in which women participated in business in ancient Rome. It is obvious that the topic is intimately connected with the issue of the role of women in Roman life and Roman law – their advantages and disadvantages. As is commonly known, modern teaching of and research into Roman law remains to a large extent dominated by the fascinating private law theory of the nineteenth century known as 'Pandectism'. The extent to which our ideas about the social role and economic activities or possibilities of Roman females are still shaped by bourgeois morals of the nineteenth century and by the principles of Roman law manuals written by (mostly conservative) men is an interesting question. In order to gain some insight into this, a brief survey of work on this period is required. Let us look at the works of some of the most famous authors. Rudolph von Jhering, for example, seems to have delighted in sketching a highly honourable picture of Roman ladies (*matronae*). He described them with much respect, but at the same time banished them to the stage of almost idealised creatures:

> Kein Volk der alten Welt, die Griechen nicht ausgenommen, hat dem weiblichen Geschlecht einen so würdigen Platz in der Gesellschaft angewiesen als die Römer

---

[1] Verg. *Geor.* 3,284.

[. . .] Das weibliche Geschlecht war nach Ansicht der Römer dem männlichen nicht bloß völlig ebenbürtig und daher in sozialer Beziehung um nichts zurückgesetzt, [. . .] sondern es war ein Gegenstand höherer Achtung, es stand eine Stufe über dem männlichen.[2]

In discussing matters such as *patria potestas* and *manus*, it is worth noting that Jhering only surveyed sources concerning a few aristocratic and heroic Roman ladies. An entirely different picture of the social status of Roman women emerges in the popular textbook by Dernburg, written towards the end of the nineteenth century:

Der Mensch ist männlichen oder weiblichen Geschlechts [. . .] Der Mann gehört dem öffentlichen Leben an, der Beruf der Frau weist sie auf das Haus. Zehlreiche öffentliche Rechte und Pflichten, die dem Manne zukommen, hat daher die Frau nicht [. . .] Selbst die Verbote, wonach Frauen nicht intercedieren dürfen, insbesondere das S. C. Velleianum, werden von den Römern darauf zurückgeführt, dass Frauen dem öffentlichen Leben fern stehen, denn die Intercessionen, – d. h. der Eintritt in die Schulden Dritter, um diesen Kredit zu verschaffen, – galten in Rom als bedingt durch die politische Stellung des Mannes und durch die Beziehungen, welche diese veranlasste.[3]

This passage is a very clear statement of what women were expected to be – the last few sentences of the short chapter from which the quotation was taken also give a hint of the law in force during the time of Dernburg (which might have been present in the subconscious mind of the author when formulating his opinion): 'Dies wurde gemeines Recht. Für Handelsfrauen gelten aber die Intercessionsbeschränkungen nicht; sie wurden neuerdings in den bei weitem meisten Landen Deutschlands gesetzlich für alle Frauen aufgehoben'.[4] For all the respect that gentlemen felt for their honourable ladies at the *fin de siècle*, it is clear that they rather wished to avoid confronting them in everyday business life. Most of the famous lawyers could not help looking at the ancient sources with a certain prejudice, originating in the morals of their own age.

Modern textbooks of Roman law even now emphasise the subordinate status of women in ancient Rome, although the whole treatment has become much more sophisticated: 'bleibt die allgemeine Regel [. . .] dass Frauen zeitlebens unter Gewalt stehen [. . .] Die rechtliche Stellung der Frau, auch der unverheirateten, wird mehr und mehr verselbständigt [. . .]'.[5] Textbooks in the English tradition were always less concerned about highly systematised theory and kept closer to the sources: 'The general principles of the perpetual *tutela* of women were the same as those of *tutela impuberum* [. . .] this institution is an uncompromising expression of *tutela* as in the interest

---

[2] Jhering (1880), pp. 203–4.
[3] Dernburg (1896), pp. 128–9.
[4] Dernburg (1896), p. 129.
[5] Kaser (1971), pp. 268–9.

of the tutors, lifelong, because the interest in the inheritance is lifelong, since a woman can have no *sui heredes* [. . .]'.[6]

Looking at the sources, there is undoubtedly a strong tendency towards restrictive measures against women in Roman law, such as *patria potestas* (the power or control of the father, which included the power over death and life), *manus* (control of the husband over the wife in marriage), perpetual *tutela mulieris* (guardianship of women) which existed from the time of the Twelve Tables if a woman was *sui iuris*, as well as measures introduced later such as the above-mentioned *Senatus Consultum Velleianum* which forbade women from acting as personal surety for anyone.[7] Nevertheless, an emerging tendency to grant liberties in private law for women, especially from the beginning of the Principate, can also be detected in the sources, as in the laws of Augustus with the *ius liberorum*, the sceptical view of Gaius relating the sense of guardianship over women or his description of how easy it was for women to change their tutors if they were dissatisfied with the current one (to all these rules we will return below).

In the history of law, new legislation usually follows an earlier development in legal life: the legislator satisfies a certain demand created by social and economic changes. If Augustus felt obliged to grant some liberties in relation to legislative acts for women, it can be considered as a strong argument that a similar or equivalent practice must have already existed in everyday legal life. At the end of the Republic, there may have been legal customs that acted 'against the law' – and they may have been tacitly and commonly tolerated.

Without going into detail, it is sufficient to mention the tension between the 'law in books' or 'law in codex' and the 'law in action' – this is well known in modern comparative law but it was less considered until now in legal history.[8] Legal life consists not only of written laws (or theoretical, highly sophisticated decisions of jurists); the individual who forms part of a certain society also lives in a legal environment or legal culture.[9] Friedman explained this distinction through his famous comparison between law and language (both being socially bounded phenomena):

> A dictionary is full of obsolete, archaic words, alternative forms, unused and common words, all jumbled together. Only the person who actually speaks the language is a sage guide to usage [. . .] The dictionary gives some hints, but not enough [. . .] Similarly, for legal systems: they are very different in real life, from the way they appear in formal texts. Study of legal culture must begin with the living law.[10]

---

[6] See Buckland (1939), p. 101.
[7] See on this aspect Gardner (1995), pp. 234–5.
[8] See, for example, Zweigert-Kötz (1996), p. 10 *passim*.
[9] Legrand (2001), p. 396 *passim*.
[10] Friedman (1990), p. 53.

In this chapter I will attempt to sketch a new picture about women and their financial transactions, focusing on the sources from 'real life'. Apart from written law and highly developed jurisprudence, legal documents offer a fascinating vista of 'living law', reports of useful tricks and legally dubious methods – phenomena of a legal culture 2,000 years ago.

2. THE BEGINNINGS

The story of the special group of sources I will deal with began with a dramatic event. In August in 79 CE, the ancient volcano Vesuvius, which dominated the bay of Naples, unexpectedly erupted. The lovely Campanian landscape with its flourishing small towns, profitable agricultural units (*villae rusticae*) and fashionable country houses was taken by surprise by the extraordinary power and destruction of the eruption. Streaming lava, raining ash and a disastrous conflagration destroyed all life in a few hours. Pliny the Younger reports the earthquake and eruption in impressive language (6,16):

> The buildings around us were shaking [. . .] and we were very scared that they would collapse [. . .] Also we saw the sea dragged back into itself and then apparently driven back by the shaking of the earth [. . .] Indeed, the shoreline had retreated, and many sea creatures were stranded on the dry sand. In the other direction a terrible black cloud, split by jagged and quivering bursts of fiery air, gaped open to reveal tall columns of flame [. . .][11]

This vivid description comes from an eye-witness: at the time of the eruption the author was staying with his uncle, Pliny the Elder,[12] very close to the event. The older Pliny served as the commander of the Roman fleet, stationed at Misenum; his close relatives visited him for a pleasant stay at the seaside.

Pliny the Elder, a keen researcher of nature, acted seemingly without fear. The scientist in him was curious, and the commander felt it his duty to rescue human life – and sacrifice his own (6,16):

> My uncle, a man of great intellectual curiosity, decided that this was a phenomenon of great importance, which had to be investigated at closer quarters [. . .] He took some warships out to sea, taking his place on board to help [. . .] Soon ash was falling on the ships, hotter and thicker as they drew nearer [. . .] Meanwhile fires erupted from different points all over Mount Vesuvius, and the towering flames gave off a light whose brightness and clarity contrasted with the shadows of the night [. . .] For the buildings were being shaken by frequent and strong tremors, and they seemed to move to and fro as if they had been shifted from their foundations [. . .] Then the flames and the smells of sulphur that preceded them

---

[11] Translation by Berry (2007), p. 24.
[12] Pliny the Elder published a huge encyclopaedia c. 77–9 CE, the *Naturalis historia*.

made the others decide to flee and woke up my uncle. Leaning on two slaves, he got up, and straight away he collapsed [. . .][13]

There was no help for the terrified population: an elementary *vis maior* ('accident of nature or human violence'),[14] the natural disaster wiped out all life in a zone of 10 to 20 km. However, the impact of these forces of nature was to prove lucky for later generations, especially for archaeologists, historians and legal historians. Although Pompeii and Herculaneum, the most important among the surrounding settlements, were lost to the Romans, they survived well preserved for posterity. Some archaeologists call them 'frozen in time' – the valuable evidence of ancient culture remained mostly untouched, covered with a thick coating of petrified volcanic lava and ash.[15] The modern archaeological sites and museums offer a fascinating mosaic of living, working or contracting in first-century Italy. The topic of the current study will comprise but one segment from this mosaic: the monetary transactions of women in everyday legal life.

3. *TABULAE* – AN ANCIENT WRITING MATERIAL

The Romans usually set up their legal documents on wooden tablets (*tabulae*). This is a special Roman type of preserving evidence which might have had some sacral roots.[16] What did *tabulae* look like? Generally, one side of a thin, small wooden tablet (their usual size was approximately 10×15 cm) was slightly indented and covered with a wax (or shellac) coating set into the rectangular indentation.[17] The scribe wrote with a metallic pen (called a *stylus*) on the waxed surface. It is obvious that this technology was imperfect, and could not be trusted to offer infallible proof before a court: the wax might have been warmed up and the letters could easily have been erased or 'corrected' by someone who did not flinch at forgery.

Meanwhile, notary practice developed two types of *tabulae* to avoid such tricks: the *diptychon* and *triptychon*. A *diptychon* consists of two tablets, a *triptychon* of three. In each type, the legally relevant text was written on the two interior wax faces, then closed by a string and sealed by witnesses. The seals must not be broken or cut unless before court.

It is astonishing that such simple wooden tablets survived a powerful volcanic eruption and can be read today. Admittedly, the originals are mostly very damaged, full of holes and cracks. In spite of this, they deliver highly valuable sources about our topic.

There are three significant finds of writing tablets excavated in the

---

[13] Translation by Berry (2007), p. 22.
[14] Crook (1967), p. 114.
[15] Berry (2007), p. 26.
[16] See Meyer (2004), pp. 44–63.
[17] Wolf (2010), pp. 19–20; Wolf and Crook (1989), pp. 10–14.

environs of Mount Vesuvius.[18] The first finds (counting c 153 pieces) consisted of tablets that belonged to a banker, well known in his day: Lucius Caecilius Iucundus. They were discovered in 1875 in a Pompeian house. Most of them are receipts drawn up at auctions conducted by his banking house. Two further tablets were found in 1887 – these present the documents of a certain Poppaea Note, a freed woman of Priscus.[19] Among them are some extremely interesting pieces of evidence for a legal historian: for example, a *mancipatio fiduciae causa* (pledge with transfer of ownership) of two slave boys and an acknowledgement of a debt (published already in *FIRA* III as no. 91, 91b). The second, bigger discovery produced several groups of tablets from Herculaneum (published long ago by G. Pugliese-Carratelli and V. Arangio-Ruiz).[20]

The third significant find of tablets (in some ways the most important of them) was discovered in 1959, during the construction of a highway between Naples and Salerno, in a remote building close to Pompeii.[21] The original stage and function of the house remains uncertain. The archaeologists found part of a peristyle and a number of rooms alongside it, with adjoining *triclinia* (dining rooms). It is very likely that the location was severely damaged in the earthquake of 62 CE. A number of objects found in the rooms show that in 79 CE, it was still under repair.[22] In one of the *triclinia* lay the remains of a boat, an iron anchor, and some oars, as well as a wicker basket containing writing tablets.[23] It is likely that these items had been stored there provisionally during the construction work.

It is significant that all the tablets relate to business conducted in Puteoli, not in Pompeii. They were first known as the tablets of Murécine (the name of the spot where they were found), but later became known as the Sulpicii Archive. The name relates to the family (*familia*) of the Sulpicii, businessmen from Puteoli who are preserved as protagonists or intermediaries in most of the documents.

This chapter deals only with the above-mentioned third group of sources, the famous Archive of the Sulpicii. The story of the conservation and publication is a complicated one. The archaeological report originally mentioned almost 300 tablets, but there are only 137 items listed in the inventory of the Museum in Pompeii. The first partial readings of the tablets was made known to the world in a speedy publication by Carlo Giordano and Francesco Sbordone, though regrettably of rather poor quality.[24] It was Giuseppe Camodeca who advanced new methods and made the greatest progress in

---

[18] See Gröschler (1997), pp. 22–32; Meyer (2004), pp. 126–7.
[19] For her whole story, see Metzger (2000) with further evidence.
[20] See Camodeca (1999), p. 15 *passim*.
[21] Camodeca (1999), pp. 11–14; Andreau (1999), p. 71 *passim*.
[22] Gröschler (1997), p. 31.
[23] Meyer (2004), p. 126 *passim*.
[24] See Camodeca (1999), p. 15.

reading and re-editing the tablets. He undertook a systematic reading of all the tablets, both those that had already been published, and the rest. Then, in 1999, he produced an excellent revisited publication of the whole archive. Furthermore, the research of Lucio Bove,[25] Joseph Georg Wolf[26] and John A. Crook[27] merits a mention. There are also several valuable new studies by historians and legal historians, some of which I will mention in passing in the following short analysis.

Let us turn to the sources. The new volume of Camodeca contains 127 tablets. Of these, ninety-five are well preserved and the rest (thirty-two tablets) are rather heavily damaged. The documents cover a period of thirty-two years: the oldest is dated 29 (or possibly 26) CE and the latest 61 CE. Although they were found in a building located close to the river port of Pompeii, they do not concern business conducted in that city. Most of them describe business transactions in the small town of Puteoli, a busy port in the bay of Naples (located 12 km from Naples and 6 km from Baiae). In the first century, Puteoli was the most important and most heavily frequented port for Rome and the whole of Italy. Ships bringing grain from Egypt mostly docked here.[28] There is no explanation as to how and why these documents were brought into the above-mentioned villa, close to Pompeii.

We are well informed about the protagonists in these tablets. The tablets belonged, as I mentioned above, to the family of the Sulpicii: Caius Sulpicius Faustus, Cinnamus, Eutychus and Onirus. It is well known from the documents that they were freedmen or the freedmen of freedmen or – possibly – the sons of freedmen.[29] Without doubt, all of them were deeply involved in some kind of banking – the documents report several types of commercial transactions. The phenomenon of freedmen heavily involved in industrial and commercial activities was not unusual in Rome.[30] Some of them became very wealthy and several were moderately wealthy. Freedmen were commonly employed also as intermediaries, as business agents.[31] On the other hand, among the clients of the Sulpicii we find tradesmen, shippers, freedmen, slaves and peregrines, and we are especially interested in the female ones. Whether the Sulpicii were *argentarii* (bankers with extended operations in every kind of financial transactions)[32] or simply *faeneratores* (moneylenders) remains disputed (a question to which we shall return).[33]

Camodeca re-edited 127 tablets in his volume. Summarising their contents,

[25] See Bove (1984) with a detailed analysis.
[26] See Wolf (2010), pp. 15–16, with a good survey of earlier publications.
[27] See especially Crook (1978), p. 229 *passim*.
[28] See Jakab (2000), pp. 245–6.
[29] See Andreau (1999), p. 73; for the social background, see also Camodeca (1993), pp. 342–5.
[30] See Garnsey (1981), pp. 362–6, with trifling evidence.
[31] See especially Garnsey (1981), p. 364.
[32] See, for example, Camodeca (1999), p. 22 *passim*.
[33] For the discussion, see Andreau (1999), p. 75 *passim*.

thirty-nine *tabulae* (41%) deal with legal procedure or arbitration, and fifty-six (59%) with legal transactions (loans, receipts, pledges, rents, money transfers). I have selected ninety-seven tablets (75%) for a larger project in progress, restricted to documents with texts complete enough to obtain a good account of the legal perspective.

4. WOMEN IN BUSINESS?

In the rich material from the Archive of the Sulpicii, twenty-three tablets (24%) record legal transactions performed by women. This simple statistic already hints at the importance of women in the business life of Puteoli. Women as contracting parties are involved in twenty-one tablets; in two further tablets they are indirectly involved.

Serva, liberta, domina: our protagonists come from very different segments of the population. Some of them are slaves and objects of contracts, like Fortunata in TPSulp. 90–3: Marcia Aucta, her owner, pledged her for a debt and the creditor put her up for auction after the debt fell due. We are well informed about this auction, for the announcement of it is recorded in several tablets. There are also several freedwomen contracting their own business with the Sulpicii. A good example is Patulcia Erotis, a *liberta* acting as *domina auctionis* (owner of the merchandise sold by the auctioneer).[34] In the preserved document, Patulcia confirms that she has received 19,500 sestertii, the auction price for an unknown article owned by her (unfortunately the text is incomplete). This was a significant amount at that time: it could have been the price of 40 tons of grain or ten to forty slaves on the market (depending on their quality).[35] A further example of a freedwoman in business is a certain Marcia Fausta taking a loan of 2,000 sestertii from the Sulpicii.[36]

A freeborn lady, Caesia Priscilla (in TPSulp. 58 and 71), seems to have belonged to the upper-middle class of Puteoli. Her credit with the bank was remarkable too: her financial transactions (loans, remittances, deposits) amounted to 24,000 sestertii.

Finally, there were also distinguished ladies of high birth involved in Puteoli business life: Domitia Lepida and Lollia Saturnina, representatives of the Roman senatorial aristocracy, seem to be the most prominent of them. Domitia was the daughter of L. Domitius Ahenobarbus[37] and the sister of Cn. Domitius Ahenobarbus;[38] their grandmother was Octavia. As we see,

[34] TPSulp. 82.
[35] Duncan-Jones (1982), p. 346.
[36] TPSulp. 99.
[37] C. D. Ahenobarbus, the son of Cn. D. Ahenobarbus, was married to Antonia; he was *consul* in 16 BCE, *proconsul Africae* in 12 BCE; see Cancik and Schneider (1996).
[38] He was married to Agrippina in 28 CE – and their son was Nero. Cn. Domitius Ahenobarbus became consul in 32 CE; Cancik and Schneider (1996), vol. 3, p. 755.

they were already closely connected by birth with the family of the Emperor; Domitia also became the aunt of the later Emperor Nero.[39] Domitia Lepida was first married to Valerius Messalla Barbatus, later to Faustus Cornelius Sulla and finally to Caius Appius Iunius Silanus. The daughter of Domitia Lepida was the famous Valeria Messalina who wed the Emperor Claudius. Ancient authors characterised her as rich, scheming and unscrupulous.[40]

Domitia was the owner of admired estates, among them a famous villa at Baiae and Ravenna with fishponds, and probably the *horti Domitiae* across the Tiber in Rome. She also owned some *praedia* (plots of land) in Puteoli, on which were built grain storehouses financed by private investors. TPSulp. 46 records the rent of a stall in this very storehouse (*locatio conductio*). Another tablet, TPSulp. 79, preserves a pledge of grain in a storehouse with Domitia's name mentioned again as the owner of the location.

The wording of the documents makes it clear that the aristocratic Domitia Lepida was only the owner of the plots. It is very likely that an investor (who is of no consequence in this context) built storehouses on the grounds to let to tradesmen. The plot belonged further to Domitia Lepida who might have had a share in the profit.[41] Nevertheless, neither Domitia herself nor one of her dependants took part in the business drawn up in the documents cited above. Her name (as owner of the plot) served merely for the correct identification of the location.

The other lady of high birth mentioned in the sources was Lollia Saturnina, the sister of the more famous Lollia Paulina, who was the wife of the Emperor Gaius (Caligula).[42] Lollia Saturnina was married to D. Valerius Asiaticus, who also owned a pretty villa at Baiae. Her husband reached the honour of being a *consul suffectus* in 35 CE and *consul* in 46 CE. One of her freedmen, a certain Marcus Lollius Philippus, is mentioned in two Puteoli tablets (TPSulp. 54 and 73). TPSulp. 54 is a *chirographum* of Marcus Lollius Philippus about a loan: he received 2,000 sestertii and promised to return it. It is very likely that the freedman acted here for himself; the small amount is a strong argument in support of such an interpretation. In the other tablet, Gnostus, a slave of Lollia Saturnina, paid to Caius Sulpicius Cinnamus a certain amount (the text is damaged in this part).[43] Remarkably, the payment was carried out for the account of Marcus Lollius Philippus. Jane Gardner supposed financial difficulties on the part of the freedmen in the background:

> Has Lollius perhaps been conducting some business on behalf of Lollia, acting as her agent, *procurator*? It is possible; then, for some reason, he was unable to carry

[39] See also Gardner (1999), pp. 12–13.
[40] Cancik and Schneider (1996), vol. 3, p. 743.
[41] Buckland (1939), p. 167 speaks of a 'building lease'.
[42] See Camodeca (1999), p. 172; also Gardner (1999), p. 14.
[43] TPSulp. 54 and 73.

through some necessary payment (for a debt which he incurred in his own name, but could recover from her later), so Lollia is having to intervene and pay directly, since, if Lollius was her mandatary, she was ultimately liable to provide the money to carry out the deal. However, given the evidence for Lollius' previous business difficulties and shaky credit rating, it is perhaps more likely that as his patroness she is helping out a needy client.[44]

I do not agree with this reading of this short legal document. Gardner's interpretation seems rather hypothetical and does not convince. It seems more likely that the freedman Marcus Lollius Philippus maintained good connections with the household and staff of his former owner. The business connections might have remained despite the change of legal status. It is very likely that M. Lollius Philippus and Gnostus (who was a slave of Lollia Saturnina) were involved in some type of common business (Gnostus probably using his *peculium*). The document delivers a good example of mixed activities between freedmen and their former 'families'. Gnostus might have paid back a debt of M. Lollius Philippus to the bank of the Sulpicii – such money transactions were not rare and were done to avoid the disadvantages of cash payments. Lollia Saturnina, the high-born lady, might have had nothing to do with the whole affair – I do not see any evidence for a necessary personal involvement on her side.

As we see, the tablets of Puteoli indicate that members of the emperors' families and of the household of senators were investing money through the Sulpicii.[45] It can be supposed that the slaves and freedmen acted as intermediaries in these financial transactions. The loans agreed in this way were – as Andreau assumed – simply money investments, because the aristocracy was interested first of all in interest-bearing investments.[46]

5. WOMEN IN CLASSICAL ROMAN LAW

Our examination will focus on the legal content of Puteoli business transactions carried out by women. What type of contracts did women conclude with the Sulpicii? What is the typical legal position of women in these contracts? Which are the most convenient legal constructions chosen by women taking part in everyday business?

It is commonly known – and recorded in every manual of Roman law – that women had to have a guardian (*tutor*) and needed authorisation from their guardian throughout their lives if they were *sui iuris* (not under *potestas*). J. A. Crook summed up the main features of this *tutela mulierum* (guardianship over women) as follows:

---

[44] Gardner (1999), p. 14.
[45] Andreau (1999), p. 26.
[46] Andreau (1999), p. 90 *passim*.

Males were released from guardianship when they reached puberty, since they were then capable of having children of their own who would legitimately exclude the agnates [. . .] Women were never released (for even if married – except with *manus* – they were *sui iuris*, and their husband was not their guardian). Astonishment at this fact would be misplaced; subjection of women's legal acts to some male authority was virtually universal in antiquity. What does need comment is that this lifelong guardianship was whittled away by legal devices, though as a formality it hung grimly on.[47]

Legal acts requiring authorisation from a guardian were, for example, the alienation of *res mancipi*,[48] making a valid will and any contract that placed the woman under an obligation (for example, taking of credit, granting personal security).[49] Gaius pointed out the main rules of this guardianship as follows (Inst.Gai.1.144):

> Parents are permitted to appoint testamentary guardians for their children who are subject to their authority, who are under the age of puberty, and of the male sex; and for those of the female sex, no matter what their age may be, and even if they are married; for the ancients required women, even if they were of full age, to remain under guardianship on account of the levity of their disposition.[50]

As we see, ancient lawyers usually reasoned for the necessary guardianship over women based on the argument of *levitas animi* or *inbecillitas sexus*. The (from a modern perspective) degrading statement was not a particularly reasonable argument; it looks more like a popular *topos*. The very idea of 'female weakness' already existed in the works of the great philosophers of classical Athens.[51] At Rome, a similar idea existed as may be seen in the description of Cicero's well-known and resolute wife, Terentia, who fearlessly managed her fortune 'like a man'.[52] Be that as it may, by the mid-second century CE, Gaius seems rather sceptical of the continued necessity of *tutela mulierum* (Inst.Gai.1.190):

> There does not seem to be any good reason, however, why women of full age should be under guardianship, for the common opinion that because of their levity of disposition they are easily deceived, and it is only just that they should be subject to the authority of guardians, seems to be rather apparent than real; for

---

[47] Crook (1967), p. 114.

[48] To the ancient group of *res mancipi* belonged real estates, slaves, easements (*servitutes*) and draught animals (*iumenta*). But also the old, traditional way of recording wills was an act of *mancipatio*; see Kaser-Knütel (2005), pp. 327–8.

[49] Generally Crook (1967), p. 115; for personal security in the *tabulae Pompeianae*, see Andreau (1994), p. 48.

[50] The translations of all texts quoted from Gaius follow F. de Zulueta, *Gaius Institutions with an English Translation and Commentary* (1946).

[51] Arist. *Polit.* 1260a; see also Kaser-Knütel (2005), p. 314.

[52] Cic. *Fam.* 14,8,2.

women of full age transact their own affairs, but in certain cases, as a mere form, the guardian interposes his authority, and he is often compelled to give it by the *praetor*, though he may be unwilling to do so.

During the Roman Empire some constitutions (especially the legislation of Augustus) had freed mothers with three or four children from the obligation of having a guardian.[53] The weakened practice of women's guardianship is well demonstrated in a short document, which records the granting of a guardian by the prefect of Egypt:[54]

> Q. Aenulius Saturninus, prefect of Egypt, at the request of C. Terentius Sarapammon, granted a guardian to Maevia Dionysarion in accordance with the lex Iulia et Titia and the *senatusconsultum*, to wit M. Iulius Alexander – this grant not being to the prejudice of any legitimate guardian '. . .' I, Maevia Dionysarion, have requested the above-named guardian, Iulius Alexander, as stated. I, Gaius Iulius Heracla, have written this on her behalf, she being illiterate.[55]

The small piece of papyrus deals with an unusual situation: obviously the woman involved, a certain Maevia Dionysarion, had no guardian for a current business. Therefore the magistrate, the local authority, the prefect of Egypt appointed one, a certain Iulius Alexander, for the purpose. It is remarkable that Maevia formally requested it. The wording which at first sight seems complicated ('this grant not being to the prejudice of any legitimate guardian . . .') refers to the general rule of legal hierarchy in guardianship.[56]

As we have seen above, modern textbooks of Roman law promote a systematic view of legal institutions utilising strict definitions. By contrast, the ancient sources offer a rather more sophisticated treatment of the same subject. I would raise the question if the first or the second issue – or probably a third one – can be confirmed through the documents of everyday legal life (through the so-called 'law in action'). I wonder whether the strongly systematic approach of the course books is in fact confirmed by business practice. The traditional view gives the impression that women were almost totally excluded from business; that they could not act at all without the authorisation of a guardian. Did they really act in every legal (or money) transaction with a guardian as is commonly supposed? Were women in business disadvantaged at all?

As a working hypothesis, let us assume that there might have been some,

[53] Inst.Gai.1.194: 'Moreover, a freeborn woman is released from guardianship if she is the mother of three children, and a freedwoman if she is the mother of four, and is under the legal guardianship of her patron. Those who have other kinds of guardians, as, for instance, Atilian or fiduciary, are released from guardianship by having three children'.
[54] *FIRA* III no. 25.
[55] Translation from Crook (1967), pp. 114–15.
[56] See Inst.Gai.1.173 and 1.186–7.

probably widely established, artful ways of contracting in practice, which could eliminate the strongly discriminating rules of positive law.

6. WOMEN IN LEGAL LIFE

I have selected five tablets from the rich material of the Archive of the Sulpicii, comparing them with a few fragments from the works of Roman jurists as legal background. It is widely accepted that the Sulpicii should be considered predominantly *faeneratores*.[57] Let us start with a fragmentary document in which the banker acts – without any doubt – as moneylender (TPSulp. 58):

> prae[t]er HS vigintì millia | nummum in rationem | Priscil[l]ae d[o]minae meae; | eaque HS quatuor millia, | (5) quae su[p]ra s[cr]ipta [s]unt, | proba recte darì fide rogavit | C(aius) Sulpicius F[a]ustus fide promisi | Pyramus Caesiae Priscillae ser(vus)
>
> . . . except the 20,000 sestertii for the account of my *domina* Priscilla; that the 4,000 sestertii, written above, be given properly and in good coin, asked for faith by Caius Sulpicius Faustus, promised for faith by Pyramus, the slave of Caesia Priscilla.

The document was part of a *triptychon* (a document which consisted originally of three waxed tablets), but only one tablet is preserved with a piece of the interior side. It shows the ending of a contract (the beginning of the text is lost) with the impression of seals of witnesses on the verso. The deed was drawn up in Puteoli (as confirmed in line 9). It is a *stipulatio* concluded between Caius Sulpicius Faustus and Pyramus, one of the slaves of a certain Caesia Priscilla (line 8). The *stipulatio* counts as one of the oldest and most useful Roman contracts: it was an oral request and promise. Gaius called it an obligation *verbis* – a contract concluded simply by words (Inst.Gai.3.92): 'An obligation is verbally contracted by question and answer, as for instance: "Do you solemnly agree to give it to me?" "I do solemnly agree." "Will you give it?" "I will give it." "Do you promise?" "I do promise" . . .' The mutual conversation (question and response) becomes the very contract; writing or witnesses were in no way necessary, though a written record might be the best way of keeping evidence of it.[58]

Obviously the banker, Faustus paid out 4,000 sestertii in cash to Pyramus, and called for a stipulation of its repayment.[59] It seems very likely that the agreement was a loan, a *mutuum*. However, the deed drawn up for the

---

[57] Andreau (1999), p. 76: 'The third hypothesis, which is my preference, is that they were moneylenders (*faeneratores*), but not traders (either never traders, or traders no longer, having decided to devote themselves solely to moneylending)'.

[58] For the legal background see Finkenauer (2010), pp. 28–30.

[59] For the legal background of the combination, see Gröschler (2006), p. 286.

creditor puts only the fact of the payment (*numeratio*) in writing, without recording the type of the contract concluded between the parties.

A *mutuum* was called in ancient Rome a 'real contract': the handing over of money for the return of its equivalent. Theoretically, one could not charge for the loan. If somebody wanted to contract for interest, it had to be done by a separate stipulation. This explains why the two formulas are usually mixed in the Archive of the Sulpicii.

Unfortunately, almost the whole text is lacking in TPSulp. 58; nonetheless, the tablet remains important for us, being a transaction involving a woman. Therefore we need a similar record for reconstructing its main legal terms. TPSulp. 50 seems to be suited to our purposes. (TPSulp. 50, 9 November 35 CE):

> M(arcus) An[tonius M(arci) f(ilii)] M[a]ximus [scripsi] me accce=|pi[sse et deber] e C(aio) Sul[pi]cio Fau[sto HS] ∞ ∞ n(ummum), | (5) [quae ab eo mutua] et n[umerata a]cc[epi] [e]aq[ue HS ∞ ∞] nummu[m, q(uae) s(upra) s(cripta) s(unt), p(roba) r(ecte) | d(ari)stip[ulat]us est C(aius) Su[lpicius Faustus spopo]ndì | eg[o] M(arcus) Anton[ius Maximus ---]

> . . . I, Marcus Antonius, son of Marcus Maximus have written that I have received and owe to Caius Sulpicius Faustus 2,000 sestertii, that I have received from him in cash as a loan; and that 2,000 sestertii, written above, be repaid properly and in good coin, questioned for faith by Caius Sulpicius Faustus and promised for faith by Marcus Antonius Maximus.

It is a mixed formula again combining the typical features of two different types of documents: *chirographum* and *testatio*. Gaius notes that in the Greek-speaking world (which had long been used to treating a contract as a writing) 'deeds of hand', acknowledging debt and promising payment, were accepted as contractually in force (Inst.Gai.3.134):

> Praeterea litterarum obligatio fieri videtur chirographis et syngraphis, id est, si quis debere se aut daturum se scribat, ita scilicet, ut, si eo nomine stipulatio non fiat. Quod genus obligationis proprium peregrinorum est.

> Furthermore, literal obligation appears to be created by *chirographa* and *syngrapha*, that is to say documents acknowledging a debt or promising a payment, of course on the assumption that a stipulation is not made in the matter. This form of obligation is special to peregrines.

A *chirographum* (*cheirographon*) was a very common type of document, written in the first person singular (it means subjectively styled), and mostly by the debtor's own hand, without witnesses.[60] The debtor acknowledged owing somebody something (for example, a certain amount of money). On the contrary, a *testatio* was drawn up always in the third person (objectively styled), mostly by a scribe, and was consequently sealed by witnesses.

---

[60] For exceptions, see Jakab (2011), p. 287.

The first part of our text records a receipt of Marcus Antonius, written in his own hand. It was an acknowledgment of handing over 2,000 sestertii from Cinnamus as a loan (cash payment, from hand to hand, through a *numeratio*). It was followed – as usual – by a stipulation (*testatio* with witnesses). It is remarkable that the stipulation also was formulated in the first person singular in our tablet.

It is commonly considered as a threefold document producing two legal actions: receipt, acknowledgement of a debt and stipulation of repayment. In my opinion, in accordance with Gaius (3.134), there might be three different *causae obligationis*: the cash payment among the parties concluded a loan (*mutuum*), the mutual conversation of repayment of an obligation *verbis* (*stipulatio*) and the *chirographum*, this special type of constitutive legal document according to Hellenistic legal practice an *obligatio litteris* (a contract by writing) with an additional third possibility of claim before court.[61]

Let us summarise in brief. TPSulp. 50 presents a well preserved deed recording a loan contract carried out by one of the Sulpicii. The banker paid out hard currency at the cash desk of his bank house and insisted upon a legal document (business as usual). Most deeds about loans were drawn up following the same formula. Furthermore, it can be assumed that a scribe or an employee of the Sulpicii usually prepared the exterior side of the *tabulae* (as mentioned above, this side was only a summary of the agreement without procedural relevance). The debtor took it as a model and drew up the interior side mostly in his own hand.[62] This partly automatic way of drafting legal documents is a strong argument that the loan of Caesia Priscilla might have followed a similar structure.

Armed with this knowledge, we can return to the first document (TPSulp. 58). It can be assumed that this deed also contained all three legal foundations (*causae obligationis*) observed above – with three different possible actions for the creditor to choose from. Of course, the burden of proof is different in each action (as the fact of cash payment, the written acknowledgement or the oral question and promise).

As we have noticed, in our first document (TPSulp. 58), a slave called Pyramus concluded the loan contract with Caius Sulpicius Faustus, although he mentioned the name of his owner, Caesia Priscilla. It was a useful feature of Roman law that slaves could act without any difficulties as contracting parties. However, the possibilities of a lawsuit were slightly different in business involving slaves.

It is worth looking briefly at a further document showing how it worked (TPSulp. 56, 7 March 52 CE):

---

[61] See Jakab (2011), pp. 286–9; the mixed type of the document was overlooked by Gardner (1999), p. 15.

[62] See Jakab (2011), p. 289 with further evidence.

Niceros colonorum coloniae | Puteolanae servus arcarius | scripsi me accep[i]
sse mutu«os» et | debere C(aio) Sulpicio [Ci]nnamo HS [∞]| nummos eosque HS
mille nummos, qui s(upra) s(cripti) s(unt), p(robos) r(ecte) d(ari) k(alendis) Ìulis
| primis {p(robos) r(ecte d(ari)} fide rogavit C(aius) | Sulpicius Cinnamus, fide
promisi | Niceros col(onorum) col(oniae) servus arcarius.

> . . . I, Niceros, *servus arcarius* of the *colonia* Puteoli, have written that I have
> received as a loan and owe to Caius Sulpicius Cinnamus 1,000 sestertii. And that
> those 1,000 sestertii, written above, shall be repaid properly and in good coin on
> 1 July, and be repaid properly and in good coin has been asked by Caius Sulpicius
> Cinnamus and duly promised for faith by me, Niceros, *servus arcarius* of the
> *colonia* Puteoli [. . .]

This deed reports a loan contract between the banker Cinnamus and
Niceros, a slave, owned by the municipality of Puteoli.[63] Niceros specified
his profession in the deed; this was a common identification method in the
ancient world. Niceros was a *servus arcarius*, a minor clerk administering
matters involving public money in Puteoli. It is unclear whether he might
have used the 1,000 sestertii, borrowed in this document, privately. In all
likelihood he contracted on behalf of his *peculium* (a kind of personal property granted to a slave from his master), but he might have contracted also
for his owner or employer.[64]

This tablet was again drawn up with a mixed formula – similar to those
observed above (a combination of a *chirographum* and a *testatio*). There are
also three different *causae obligationis* (*numeratio*, *chirographum*, *stipulatio*)
in the detailed wording of the contract. However, everything acquired by a
slave belonged automatically to his master (*dominus* or *domina*) according to
Roman law. In our case, if Niceros was owned by the *colonia* of Puteoli, the
municipality became the owner of every piece of coin acquired by him as a
loan. Going by this, a claim for repayment must have been brought against
the owner of the slave-debtor, in this case the *colonia* of Puteoli.[65]

Having finished this short excursion, we are now equipped to return to
the legal transaction of Priscilla in our first text (TPSulp. 58). The extremely
fragmentary document can be reasonably explained in light of the structure
of TPSulp. 50 and 56, just analysed. It can be assumed that the *tabulae* about
the loan raised by Pyramus also contained a *chirographum* (*scripsi me accepisse
et debere*) followed by the promise of repayment (stipulation).

However, the number of persons involved in the legal transaction is

---

[63] For a detailed analysis, see Gröschler (2006), pp. 261–2.
[64] For typical types of agency, see Aubert (1994), p. 30 *passim*.
[65] In line 11, the promise of Niceros is formulated as a *fidepromissio* which agrees with the rules
      of classical Roman law. The solemn ancient form of stipulation using the word *spondeo* was
      confined to Roman citizens. However, non-citizens were allowed very early to replace it with
      fide promittere or *fide iubere*.

unusual – not two, but three participants: Faustus, Pyramus and Caesia Priscilla. It is not clear whether Pyramus borrowed the money for himself (on behalf of his *peculium*) or vicariously for his *domina* (owner). And which action(s) could be raised from this contract or from the very document?

We have seen above in our third loan on *tabulae* (TPSulp. 56) that a slave need not necessarily represent his owner. On the contrary, the slave was able to act also on his own (in fact, within the financial limits of his *peculium*). Slaves in business were commonly accepted everywhere in the Roman Empire. Also Pyramus the slave might have raised 4,000 sestertii without any trouble from the bank of the Sulpicii for himself. In this case Pyramus might have had the same legal situation as Niceros above (see TPSulp. 56). Indeed, Camodeca argued precisely for this explanation: he assumed that the phrase *in rationem* needs to be related to the 20,000 sestertii already due from Priscilla and has nothing to do with the case at issue.[66]

However, there are some arguments against this solution: especially the pre-existing debt of 20,000 sestertii in line 1 and the phrase next to it: *in rationem Priscillae dominae meae* (lines 2–3). Obviously it refers rather to the new debt of 4,000 recorded in the present document. This seems to me more reasonable, considering the usual meaning of *rationes*.

Rationes were account books widely used by Romans in first-century Italy. All transactions, especially financial ones, were carefully recorded on wooden tablets or papyrus and kept by every economic unit: a household, *villa rustica* or bank.[67] Ulpian, the leading jurist of the third century, specifies its meaning as follows: 'a *ratio* is a transaction involving two aspects, giving and receiving, credit and debit, incurring and discharging an obligation on one's own account . . .'[68] In the case at issue, it must have been the bank account of Priscilla regarding her credit and debit with the Sulpicii. In my opinion, the phrase ascertains that the 4,000 sestertii (as the former 20,000) were charged to her account. Taking this into account, the obligation (loan contract) needs to be considered as concluded between Faustus and Priscilla – and not Pyramus, who acted merely as the receiver of the money.[69]

At this point it is necessary to risk some remarks on the social background. Although we do not know anything about the social status of Caesia Priscilla, the large sum of money suggests that she might have been rather wealthy. However, the *domina* involved in the business seems to have been careful to avoid any public appearance at a bank to withdraw money. Instead, she sent her slave to pick up the cash credited for her. Her reserved manner is typical of female behaviour in ancient society, where ladies of a

---

[66] Camodeca (1999), p. 149.
[67] See Jakab (2009), pp. 39–46.
[68] D.2.13.6.3 (Ulpian. 4 ad Ed.).
[69] Unclear is the opinion of Gardner (1999), p. 15 – was it a business with a *peculium* or on behalf of Caesia Priscilla?

certain standing and property were not accustomed or expected to act almost publicly.[70]

However, the banker must have insisted upon drawing up the loan contract properly, according to usual business practice. It meant – as we have seen above – always a stipulation of repayment by the debtor, too. Because a stipulation (a mutual, oral question and promise) was impossible in her absence, the only remaining choice was that Pyramus, the slave of Priscilla, had to conclude it. Indeed, this fact slightly altered the proper way of instituting an action in a future lawsuit.[71]

In the tablets we have examined thus far, the Sulpicii acted as moneylenders. However, there are several *tabulae* that record money transactions without mentioning the name of a Sulpicius. It can be supposed that the bank took part in these transactions as well. Before continuing our panorama of businesswomen, let us survey briefly the usual operations of bankers in ancient Rome. A short survey can be useful for a better understanding of the legal and economical context.

Ulpian, one of the best known classical Roman lawyers, summed up the main operations of small bankers dealing with problems of insolvency – related of course to a concrete trial (D.16.3.7.2):

> Quotiens foro cedunt nummularii, solet primo loco ratio haberi depositariorum, hoc est eorum qui depositas pecunias habuerunt, non quas faenere apud nummularios vel cum nummulariis vel per ipsos exercebant.

> Whenever moneylenders become insolvent, it is customary for account of the depositors to be taken first, that is, of those who had money on deposit, not money at interest with the moneylenders, or invested in conjunction with the moneylenders, or left with them to make use of it.[72]

The case deals with *nummularii* – these were small-style bankers occupied mostly with money exchange, although they also sometimes engaged in interest-bearing investment. During their usual business transactions, they repeatedly accepted deposits from their clients. Ulpian found it important to distinguish between two main types of agreements: the banker might have paid interest on the capital or he might not have.[73] In the latter case, the customer was interested first of all in safe custody (safekeeping), and in the former case, in profit (interest-bearing).

According to the regular rules of deposit in Roman law, the depositary was not entitled to use the object deposited, and to do so was a breach of

---

[70] Gardner (1995), p. 257 *passim*.

[71] Instead of a direct action against the *promissor* from the stipulation (*actio ex stipulatu*), it could be brought in rather as an *actio quod iussu* against his owner Priscilla – however, with the same result.

[72] The English translations from the Digest follow Watson (1985).

[73] For banking, see Andreau (1999), p. 90 *passim*.

contract.[74] In general, however, bankers wished to make use of the money. In this case, the depositary was not obliged to return the identical coins left in his custody but the equivalent value (*eiusdem generis*).[75] With some hesitation, Papinian confirmed that agreements of such type were widely used and, without any doubt, in force, according to the opinion of a vast majority (D.16.3.24): 'for if it was agreed that the equivalent sum be repaid, then the matter exceeds the very well-known limits of a deposit'. In this special type of deposit, the depositary was able to use the coins kept by him, and in this case he came under an obligation to pay interest.

Nevertheless, Ulpian analysed not only two, but three types of possible agreements among bankers and their clients. The legally relevant differences among these three types emerged most clearly if the bank failed. Those whose money had not been touched and who could identify it as theirs could simply claim their property back. Those whose money had been used but who had not received any interest had a preferential claim in case of insolvency. Those receiving interest ranked together with the usually long line of ordinary creditors of the banker. Ulpian's decision seems to suggest that there was really a range of possibilities open to a Roman who had cash to spare, and which option he chose would have depended on the risk he was prepared to accept.

However, this is not the place for a long discussion about banking in ancient Rome. For our sources, the wooden tablets from the Archive of the Sulpicii, it is only relevant that a regular client might have invested money 'at' the banker, 'with' the banker or 'through' the banker. In the first case, the bank acted as paying agent, while in the second the bank, so to speak, borrowed the money from the client against interest (and all risk remained with the bank). In the third case, the customer transferred the money to a bank and authorised the banker to invest it at a good rate of interest (here the bank acted as an agent and the risk remained with the customer).

Let us scrutinise in the next *tabulae*, concerning transactions by women, if Ulpian's model of banking meets the transactions of the Sulpicii. There is, for example TPSulp. 71 (26 March 46 CE), again a fragmentary preserved financial transaction with Caesia Priscilla, the lady already presented above:

> C(aius) Iulius Amarantus scripsi | [me] accepisse ab Py[ramo] | [Caesiae] Priscillae servo s[e]stertia tria millia | nummum ex epistula

> . . . I, Caius Iulius Amarantus have written that I have received from Pyramus, the slave of Caesia Priscilla, 3,000 sestertii in accordance with the *epistula*.

As we see, almost all the protagonists count as old acquaintances: Pyramus was also introduced above, in our first *tabula*. In the waxed tablet at hand,

---

[74] Kaser-Knütel (2005), pp. 196–8.
[75] Crook (1967), p. 209.

he might have revisited the bank on the order of his female proprietor, Caesia Priscilla. It is very likely that he acted here vicariously for his wealthy *domina*. The document contains a *chirographum* of a certain Caius Iulius Amarantus about a cash payment, hand to hand. The last line gives a hint of the existence of a certain *epistula*, a private or business letter. It seems likely that this very letter laid down the *causa* of the payment, the detailed agreement between the parties.

Lucio Bove argued that the legal content must have been a loan contract (*mutuum*): Priscilla could have played the role of the creditor and Amarantus the role of the debtor.[76] Camodeca refused this interpretation and noticed that there was neither a stipulation nor any other promise of repayment, therefore the parties must have changed their roles in the business: Priscilla might have been the debtor and Amarantus the creditor receiving the repayment from her.[77]

As the fragmentary text is short, it could provide some further possible interpretations – relying on the role of an *epistula* in legal transactions. Reading the decisions of the Roman jurists, it seems very likely that *epistulae* were special types of documents, and not mere synonyms of *chirographum* (as considered earlier, for example, by Leopold Wenger).[78] An *epistula* could have been especially useful in credit transactions between more than two parties who contracted merely on confidential terms. There is plenty of evidence for this special function of *epistula*; and it leads also in the above quoted tablet of Caesia Priscilla to a possible new concept of the facts. It seems to me that the following aspects should be especially considered: the *tabula* was preserved in the archive of a bank; the *epistula* mentioned at the end must have been of legal relevance; legal transactions were usually recorded in more than a single document; furthermore it was not rare that more than two parties were involved in money transactions.

In summary, I see two further possibilities for reconstructing the legal relations among the parties. In the first case, Priscilla might have deposited a larger amount of money with the Sulpicii. Pyramus, her slave, could raise and pay out the 3,000 sestertii, recorded here, in cash directly at the cash desk of the bank, from the account of Priscilla, to Amarantus. We can better understand the legal structure supposed above if we use the next text as a possible model for it (D.16.3.28):

> Caecilius Candidus Paccio Rogatiano suo salutem. viginti quinque nummorum quos apud me esse voluisti, notum tibi ista hac epistula facio ad ratiunculam meam ea pervenisse: quibus ut primum prospiciam, ne vacua tibi sint: id est ut usuras eorum accipias, curae habebo.

---

[76] Bove (1984), p. 162.
[77] Camodeca (1999), p. 170.
[78] Wenger (1953), p. 736.

> Caecilius Candidus to Paccius Rogatianus, greetings. As to the 25 sestertii, which you wished to be lodged with me, I inform you by this letter that they have been entered on my account. I shall attend to this sum as soon as possible, to see that you do not have it lying idle [producing no return]. That is, I shall take care of it that you get interest on it.

A certain Caecilius Candidus (probably a banker) wrote a short memorandum (a surprisingly informal business letter) to his client. He assured him that a certain amount of money arrived on his account and that he would do his best to invest it with good profit. Assuming the same model, it can be supposed that Amarantus wrote the *epistula* mentioned and he might have received the cash payment. However, he also issued a *chirographum* (preserved in TPSulp. 71) as a receipt. But can it be reasonably supposed that two different records were made about the same payment? In my opinion, it does not need to be a contradiction. It was very common in everyday legal life to issue separate documents about each stage of a transaction. The present *chirographum* (TPSulp. 71) recorded the act of carrying out the cash payment between Pyramus and Amarantus (the slave paid out the money entrusted to him). Independent of that, Amarantus could have issued another document (called an *epistula*) summing up the terms of the agreement and acknowledging the receipt of the money for Priscilla (who was his real contracting party in this case). Nevertheless, it is not clear what type of contract was concluded between the parties; it was probably a loan or a deposit. In a future lawsuit, the *chirographum* would have entitled Priscilla to sue for repayment only of the equivalent of the sum paid out (this denotes exactly 3,000 sestertii without any interest). The aforementioned *epistula*, with the exact terms of their contractual relations, might have contained a different type of contractual obligation with better terms for Priscilla: for example, a money deposit which would have entitled her to also sue for interests and remedy. Accepting this hypothesis, we would have new evidence for the occupation of the Sulpicii as paying agents, and probably Amarantus as a private agent for money investments.

However, there is also another possible solution for TPSulp. 71. The *epistula* (mentioned in line 7) might have been written by Priscilla, as well. Here we can use a different legal structure depicted by Marcellus, deciding a rather complicated case (D.46.1.24):

> Lucius Titius cum pro Seio fratre suo apud Septicium intervenire vellet, epistulam ita emisit: Si petierit a te frater meus, peto des ei nummos fide et periculo meo.

> When Lucius Titius wished to stand surety for his brother, Seius to Septicius, he sent a letter in these terms: 'If my brother seeks an advance from you, I ask you to give him the money, relying on my honour and at my risk'.

There is a business letter again: the short note of a certain Lucius Titius (a typical name in a blank form) showing how informally and effectively *epistulae* might have been used in complicated legal structures. According to this model, the facts behind the fragmentary receipt of Amarantus might have been as follows: Priscilla would have asked and authorised her slave, Pyramus, to give Amarantus a helping hand (paying out 3,000 sestertii to him), from his (Pyramus') *peculium* but at her (Priscilla's) risk. She may have wanted to avoid acting openly as a creditor, being a lady of distinguished birth or delicate social status. Possibly Amarantus belonged to a lower social class, and she was reluctant to publicly cast herself as being involved in business with him. The Sulpicii would have acted here again as paying agents and discrete intermediaries at the same time. The legal relation, produced by an agreement and a mandatory payment, is close to a personal surety (Priscilla would be a guarantor for Amarantus at Pyramus). However, there can be no valid legal obligations between a *domina* and her slave.

Let us move forward, leaving Caesia Priscilla for the present to examine some further money transactions of female 'managers' in ancient Puteoli. There was a certain Gaia Primigenia who obviously also preferred discreet business through bankers (TPSulp. 105, 9 March 56 CE):

> si[· ·]++++[---]+um | [· ·]S++[· ·]+++stipula[tus]s [e]s[t] | C(aius) Sulpicius Cinn[amu]s, quì se | procuratorem G[· · ·]ae Primìgeni=|ae esse [di]cebat, spopondit | C(aius) Ìulius Atimetus.

> . . . [promise has been called] by Caius Sulpicius Cinnamus, who declared that he is the procurator of Gaia Primigenia, promised by Caius Iulius Atimetus.

In this tablet, the bank of the Sulpicii acted finally as a contracting party. Cinnamus (one of the members of the younger generation of the Sulpicii) concluded a *stipulatio* with a certain Caius Iulius Atimetus. The document is heavily damaged. Camodeca set it under the title *Negotia incerta et fragmenta*, among texts of no consequence. Despite its condition, it can yet deliver some useful information. It is evident from line 4 that a certain Gaia Primigenia was the contracting party (*liberta* or *domina*, it is not clear). Cinnamus acted here simply as her *procurator* (private agent) as mentioned explicitly in line 4. Gaia Primigenia might have deposited a certain amount of money with the Sulpicii and authorised Cinnamus to invest it on short-term interest-bearing terms. It seems very likely that Cinnamus (and not Gaia Primigenia) concluded the present loan contract with Atimetus – and it could have fitted as a very reasonable solution for a lady in ancient Puteoli. However, the banker might have charged the interest (paid by Atimetus as debtor) immediately to the account (*ratio*) of Gaia Primigenia.

Let us take another look at Ulpian's sophisticated model of usual banking activities in ancient Rome. Of all the possible models, Gaia Primigenia's business (TPSulp. 105) seems to adhere to this structure: Cinnamus, the banker might have acted as a careful agent, investing money for his client (money deposited with him) for a good profit. The usual risk (which is the possible insolvency of the debtor) remained in this case always with the client, thus in our case with Gaia Primigenia.

There is a further tablet (TPSulp. 99, 28 February 44 CE) with a rather fragmentary textual record of the financial transactions of a certain Marcia. Camodeca suggested completing her name for Marcia Fausta; she might have been a *liberta*, a freedwoman. The text is heavily damaged, yet Camodeca reconstructed it ingeniously using similar formulas. It looks very likely that Marcia was the debtor in a loan contract, concluded with M. Octavius Fortunatus. The bank of the Sulpicii might have been involved in the business again as a simple paying agency. It is remarkable that Marcia acted with her guardian (*tutor*), a certain Epichares (line 10).

It will have come to our attention that all our businesswomen have acted without a guardian. Thinking in terms of modern Roman law textbooks, there must have been guardians also in TPSulp. 58, 71 and 105. We shall return to this problem later in the summary, where I will try to offer a reasonable explanation for the missing guardians.

Returning to Marcia, we see that she received here a relatively small sum of 2,000 sestertii. She was obliged to repay it in three instalments: the first one between 15 March and 5 April, the second one on an unknown date, and the third one on 1 May. The document was drawn up on 28 February 44 CE. The legal transaction between the parties can be reconstructed as follows: M. Octavius Fortunatus (probably a freedman) might have deposited a certain amount of money with the bank of the Sulpicii (as a kind of current account). Later, he concluded a loan contract with Marcia, crediting her 2,000 sestertii for a short term of two months with repayment in three instalments. The money was withdrawn by Marcia (and her guardian) at the bank of the Sulpicii. The Sulpicii were involved in the business again as a simple paying agency.

Finally, we must look at some money transactions between ladies of interest in Puteoli: a certain Titinia Antracis and Euplia. The wooden tablet was titled by the scribe as *Tabellae Titiniae A[ntracidis]*:[79]

Exp(ensos)| Eupliae Theodori f(iliae) [HS ∞ DC] | Meiliacae tutore aucto[re] | Epichare Aphrodisi f(ilio) Athe[niensi]; | petiit et numeratos acce[pit] | domo ex r[i]sco | Acceptos | Risco (vac.) [HS ∞ DC]; | Eos HS ∞ DC nu[mmos, qui s(upra) s(cripti) s(unt)], | interrogant[e Titinia Antracide], | fide sua esse ius[sit Epichares Aphrodisi] | f(ilius) Athenensis p[ro Euplia Theodori f(ilia)] | Meliacae Ti[tiniae Antracidi] | Act[um Puteolis . . .

The Tablets of Titinia Antracis | paid out | to Euplia, daughter of Theodorus, 1,600 sestertii | from Melos, with authorization of her guardian | Epichares, son of Aphrodisius, from Athens, | she asked and received in cash | from home, out of the cash desk. | Received | to the cash desk, 1,600 sestertii | and those 1.600

---

sestertii written above | questioned by Titinia Antracis | for his faith promised Epichares Aphrodisius' | son from Athens for Euplia the daughter of Theodorus | from Melos to Titinia Antracis | acted in Puteoli.

The present *triptychon* is well preserved, but difficult to explain. It is of some interest that there are two further texts concerning loans of Euplia in the Archive.[80] The remarkable title 'Tabellae of Titinia Antracis' and further typical phrases in accounting (such as *exceptos, acceptos*) give some hints as to its explanation. It looks rather like an unusual, almost unknown type of evidence, an extract from an account book (*rationes*). There were three persons involved in the money transaction: Titinia, Euplia and Epichares. The ladies formed the parties concluding a contract while the only man, Epichares, acted as the guardian and guarantor for Euplia. Euplia was very likely a woman of Hellenistic-Greek origin; her guardian might have been her husband but could also be a third person.[81]

Modern scholars have argued for the interpretation of the legal content being a simple loan between the ladies: Titinia was the creditor and Euplia the debtor.[82] However, this interpretation offers no possible solution for the role played by the Sulpicii in the matter. It is also very strange that the parties chose this unusual formula instead of a regular loan (as cited above, for example, with Caesia Priscilla). For a more satisfactory explanation, Peter Gröschler suggested that it must have been a transaction not between two, but rather three parties.[83] The payment might have been carried out at the cash desk of a bank. In this case, the first lines would record simply a payment with the usual terminology of accounting. Euplia, a freeborn peregrine woman from Asia Minor (Melos), might have acted as the receiver of the cash money and the debtor named for its repayment. She acted properly with her guardian, Epichares – who is also of Greek nationality (and probably her husband as already mentioned above).[84] Jane Gardner supposed that the document appears 'to be written by a man, also a Greek, Epichares of Athens'. This seems too speculative – I do not see any evidence in the text for Epichares' writing the deed. Accepting the thesis that the document is an extract from the account book of the bank, it might have been written rather by a scribe of the very bank.

Epichares acted also as guarantor (personal surety) for Euplia. Gardner assumed that 'the addition of a guarantor usually indicates either that the creditor is not satisfied that the borrower's credit is good, or that the debt is otherwise unsecured'.[85] For a similar situation, she quoted TPSulp. 64 and

---

[80] TPSulp. 61 and 62.
[81] See Gardner (1995), p. 16.
[82] See Bove (1984), p. 150 *passim*; Wolf (2010), p. 85.
[83] Gröschler (1997), pp. 67–96; his thesis is accepted also in Rowe (2001), p. 230.
[84] Gardner (1999), p. 17.
[85] Gardner (1999), p. 18 *passim*.

argued that N. Castricius Agathopus should have been Faecia's tutor. For a better understanding, I should print here the heavily damaged text: '. . . sunt, interrogante [T]itinia | Basilide, fide sua esse iussit | N(umerius) Castricius Agathopus pro Fa[e]cia . . .' As we see, the short fragment preserved does not give any hint of the legal or personal connections between the parties. As for the gender-specific importance of guarantors for loans received by women, Gardner combined here guardianship and guarantee in a confusing manner: 'Moreover, for women with tutors, there is at least a presumption of good credit, since . . . a woman could not take on obligations without the consent of her tutor . . .'[86] From the legal point of view, both personal and real surety seems to have been equally used and broadly accepted in the Roman world. However, personal surety was rather typical for Roman deals while Greeks preferred pledges. Considering this, I do not see any gender-specific or socially shaped phenomenon in the fact that Epichares acted as guarantor for Euplia in TPSulp. 60.

Furthermore, there is a financial transaction involving a woman drawn up following the same formula – without mentioning any *tutor*. In TPSulp. 63 (also a *nomen arcarium*), a certain Magia Pulchra borrowed the remarkably large sum of 30,000 sestertii from Caius Sulpicius Cinnamus. Camodeca suggested that Magia might have earlier given birth to at least three children, therefore she enjoyed the Augustan *ius liberorum*.[87] Unfortunately, the text is seriously damaged from line 14; the letters preserved seem to introduce the usual stipulation of a guarantor: *Idem spo[pondit]* . . . We do not know anything about the life and pains of Magia Pulchra. However, the mere evidence of acting here without tutor seems to me not conclusive for the assumption that she must have been the mother of at least three children.

But let us return to Titinia Antracis, Euplia and Epichares in TPSulp. 60. The two entries (*exp.* – *acp.*) cannot stand for the same money transaction, in my opinion. Neither legally nor economically would it have made good sense. On the contrary, I argue that the relatively small sum of 1,600 sestertii was paid out in cash from the cash desk of the bank – and immediately taken in to the same cash desk.[88]

All *tabellae* documents show a formula that is rare in ancient Italy. However, there are some Greek papyri from Roman Egypt with a similar structure. Double entries in the account books of banks were usual, if the party was an old client of the same bank, carrying out the whole transaction. It might have worked well in everyday life, assuming that the debtor immediately deposited the money, just received on his account, with the same bank.

---

[86] Gardner (1999), p. 21.
[87] Camodeca (1999), p. 158.
[88] Gardner (1999), p. 17 assumed here a failure of the scribe and interpreted the entries *exp.* and *acp.* as synonym phrases.

There is a fitting example of this structure in a papyrus document, an extract from an account book of a bank:[89]

> To Apollonios, son of Hestiodoros, which to Ariston,
> son of Antipatros (paid out) 700 from Ariston, son of Antipatros (received) 700.

It is remarkable that there are five further documents of the same type, as the text just explained (TPSulp. 60) in the Archive of the Sulpicii and two further deeds in waxed tablets from Herculaneum.[90] Six of these eight documents record money transactions by women. Until now, nobody has taken notice of this surprising fact. The phenomena can be reasonably explained by the desire of women for discretion, as pointed out already above. Female participants in business tried to avoid personal appearances at public places. Acting through a bank could offer a discreet and useful alternative to this problem.

To summarise: as mentioned in the introduction above, in ancient Rome women had to have guardians for the entire duration of their lives (*tutores*). The acts needing a guardian's authorisation were alienation of *res mancipi* (mainly land and slaves); making a will; and any contract that put the woman under an obligation. This was the law as taught and learned in several textbooks.

However, we have just surveyed several *tabulae* from Puteoli containing contracts, receipts and other financial transactions by women from different segments of population – and only a few of them include the authorisation of a guardian. How was this possible?

It is well known that Augustus' legislation had already released women from the requirement of a guardian's authorisation to encourage having a big family (three children for a freeborn and four for a freedwoman). Are we obliged to assume that every woman in Puteoli, acting without a guardian, must have had at least three (or four) children? This does not seem to me to be an elegant solution.[91]

As we have seen above, neither Domitia Lepida nor Lollia Saturnina appeared in person for business; only their freedmen and their slaves did so. In general, persons from the elite lent and borrowed money through their dependants as intermediaries. Without any doubt, it cannot be considered as a gender-specific phenomenon. However, acting through intermediaries seems to be useful for all the businesswomen, from each segment of population. It appears very likely that the widely accepted practice of contracting through slaves and freedmen released women (in fact) from a guardian's authorisation. A woman of some property, owning slaves or having freedmen, could take part in all business without any restriction – through her dependants, acting for her as intermediaries. There was no need to ask

[89] P.Tebt. III, 2 no. 890 (?, second century CE); see Jakab (2003), pp. 498–506.
[90] See Gröschler (1997), pp. 97–146, for a good survey.
[91] Camodeca (1999), p. 158 and Gardner (1999), p. 19 seem to tend to this solution.

her guardian or to be present at the bank at all. Using the advantages of a good fortune, women could participate in everyday business life on the same terms as male Romans. However, other women, who did not have the luxury of owning skilled slaves, were forced to appear personally at a bank in the company of a guardian.

There is one further question remaining: were the Sulpicii just money-lenders (*feneratores*) or rather *argentarii*, bankers with extended financial operations? Andreau argued that they were neither professional bankers nor wholesalers, therefore they must have specialised in moneylending: they must have been *faeneratores*.[92] Here is not the proper place for a detailed treatment of banking in the Roman Empire. With that said, a thorough examination of some writing tablets has demonstrated that a new definition might be possible. Considering the role of the Sulpicii in tablets which do not mention their names and in others with more than two parties I rather believe that they were occupied in several types of financial transactions, not only in moneylending.

BIBLIOGRAPHY

Andreau, J., *Banking and Business in the Roman World* (1999).

Berry, J., *The Complete Pompeii* (2007).

Bogaert, R., *Les origines antiques de la banque de dépôt* (1968).

Bove, L., *Documenti di operazioni finanziarie dall'archivio dei Sulpicii. Tabulae Pompeianae di Murécine* (1984).

Buckland, W. W., *A Manual of Roman Private Law* (1939).

Camodeca, G., 'Archivi privati e storia sociale delle città Campane: Puteoli ed Herculaneum, in W. Eck (ed.), *Prosopographie und Sozialgeschichte* (1993), p. 339.

Camodeca, G., *Tabulae Pompeianae Sulpiciorum. Edizione critica dell'archivio puteolano dei Sulpicii* (1999).

Camodeca, G., 'Per un primo aggiornamento all'edizione dell'archivio dei Sulpicii (TPSulp.)', CCG, 11 (2000), p. 173.

Cancik, H., and Schneider, H. (eds), *Der Neue Pauly. Enzyklopaedie der Antike* (1996).

Crook, J. A., *Law and Life of Rome: 90 B.C. – A.D. 212* (1967).

Crook, J. A., 'Working notes on some of the new Pompeii tablets', in *ZPE*, 29 (1978), p. 229.

Dernburg, H., *Pandecten I. Allgemeiner Teil und Sachenrecht*, 5th edn (1896).

Duncan-Jones, R., *The Economy of the Roman Empire: Quantitative Studies*, 2nd edn (1982).

Finkenauer, Th., *Vererblichkeit und Drittwirkung der Stipulation im klassischen römischen Recht* (2010).

Friedman, L. M., 'Some thoughts on comparative legal culture', in D. S. Clark (ed.), *Comparative Law and Private International Law* (1990), p. 53.

Gardner, J. F., *Women in Roman Law and Society* (1995).

---

[92] See Andreau (1999), p. 74 *passim*.

Gardner, J. F., 'Women in business life. Some evidence from Puteoli', in P. Setälä and L. Savunen (eds), *Female Networks and the Public Sphere in Roman Society, Acta Instituti Romani Finlandiae*, 22 (1999), p. 11.

Garnsey, P., 'Independent freedmen and the economy of Roman Italy under the principate', *Klio*, 63 (1981), p. 359.

Gröschler, P., *Die tabellae-Urkunden aus den pompeianischen und herkulanensischen Urkundenfunden* (1997).

Jakab É., 'Bankurkunden und Buchführung (TPSulp.60 und die graeco-ägyptischen Papyri)', in G. Thür and F. J. Nieto, *Symposion 1999* (Veröffentlichungen der Gesellschaft für Griechische und Hellenistische Rechtsgeschichte 14) (2003) p. 493.

Jakab É., 'Vectura pro mutua: Überlegungen zu Tab. Pomp. 13 und Ulp. D. 19.2.15.6', ZSS (rom. Abt.) 117 (2000), p. 244.

Jakab, É., *Risikomanagement beim Weinkauf. Periculum und Praxis im Imperium Romanum* (2009).

Jakab, É., 'Chirographie in Theorie und Praxis', in K. Muscheler (ed.), *Römische Jurisprudenz – Dogmatik, Überlieferung, Rezeption* (2011), p. 275.

Jhering, R. von, *Geist des römischen Rechts auf den verschiedenen Stufen seiner Entwicklung* II, 4th edn (1850).

Kaser, M., *Das römische Privatrecht* (1971).

Kaser, M., and Knütel, R., *Römisches Privatrecht*, 18th edn (2005).

Lemosse, M., 'La procédure contre l'esclave débiteur: une nouvelle révélation romanistique', *RHD*, 62 (1984), p. 225.

Legrand, P., *Fragments on Law-as-Culture* (1999).

Metzger, E., 'The Case of Petronia Iusta', *RIDA*, 47 (2000), p. 151.

Meyer, E. A., *Legitimacy and Law in the Roman World. Tabulae in Roman Belief and Practice* (2004).

Rowe, G., 'Trimalchio's world', *Scripta Classica Israelica*, 20 (2001), p. 225.

Wenger, L., *Die Quellen des römischen Rechts* (1953).

Wolf, J. G., *Neue Rechtsurkunden aus Puteoli. Tabulae Pompeianae Nuovae. Lateinisch und Deutsch* (2010).

Wolf J. G., and Crook J. A., *Rechtsurkunden in Vulgärlatein aus den Jahren 37–39 n. Chr.*, in Abh. Der Heidelberger Akademie der Wissenschaften, Phil.-hist. Kl. (1989).

Zweigert K., and Kötz H., *Einführung in die Rechtsvergleichung auf dem Gebiete des Privatrechts* (1996).

Chapter 8

Tapia's Banquet Hall and Eulogios' Cell: Transfer of Ownership as a Security in Some Late Byzantine Papyri*

Jakub Urbanik

1. INTRODUCTION: SECURING A LOAN IN THE LATE BYZANTINE PAPYRI

Modern scholarship has devoted much attention to *pignus* and *hypotheca* as forms of real security in classical Roman law.[1] The same could be said about the research on the practical application of these forms, or vice versa, the apparent practical origins of the later dogmatic forms: there has been an extensive study on real securities in Greek and Hellenistic traditions. Much attention has been also devoted to the documents constituting, revoking, and accepting a real security in the Demotic and Graeco-Roman legal traditions in Egypt. Thanks above all to the classical studies of Andreas Bertalan Schwartz, we understand much better the system of 'real' – in the civil law vocabulary – securities for debt in the law of papyri.[2] However, apart from Steinwenter's remarks in his *Recht der koptischen Urkunden*, the Byzantine practice and doctrine remains of much less scientific interest. Yet, my purpose in this chapter is not to provide an all-embracing general overview of Byzantine securities, even thought they merit particular attention in themselves, but to discuss their particularity. The deeds of legal practice bring about a few cases of guarantees of obligations in the form of transfer of ownership.

* This chapter started as a short presentation delivered in December 2006 in Vienna at a symposium to honour Peter E. Pieler's sixty-fifth birthday. I have developed the idea as a part of my research project on legal consciousness in late Antiquity financed by the Polish Ministry of Science and Higher Education. The draft has been read by José Luis Alonso (San Sebastian and Warsaw) and I thank him for the fruitful discussions and suggestions. I owe modern references and discussion to Kamil Zaradkiewicz and the practical modern examples of bank law to the kind advice of solicitor Elzbieta Krakowiak.

    The English translations of the papyri in Parts 1 and 2 have been taken from McGing (1990) and Porten and Farber (1996), respectively, and I have allowed myself minor alterations to keep the consistency of the texts. Other texts, unless otherwise specified, have been translated by me.

1 See, above a collection of studies devoted to pledges by Kaser (1982), *passim*.
2 Schwarz (1911); and see most recently on the subject, Alonso (2008) and (2010). See also a very general overview in Rupprecht (1995) and Alonso (2008).

Obviously, this type of collateral, called in the German doctrine *Sicherungsübereignung*,[3] which consists of a (conditional) surrender of the debtor's property to the creditor, is not limited to Byzantine Egypt. Any scholar of Roman law will recall the original form of the Roman real security, *fiducia*, still practised under classical Roman law – yet erased from the Codification.[4] There are also, quite naturally, Graeco-Egyptian counterparts of the same. The Ptolemaic and early Roman documents provide us with information about the so-called 'purchase on trust' (ὠνὴ ἐν πίστει).[5] In the deeds documenting these sales, nothing hints at their fiduciary character; they were, however, accompanied by a corresponding loan document, sometimes written in the second column of the sheet of the papyrus.[6] Had the latter not been preserved, we probably would not be able to detect the mock character of the sales. It has been argued that evolution of 'purchase on trust' was due to two distinctive but teleologically similar forms of sale upon redemption practised in mainland Greece[7] and the Demotic 'mortgage' (yet it is not certain whether the latter actually temporarily preceded the 'sale on trust').[8] Another interesting counterpart of *Sicherungsübereignung* were the Demotic conditional sales,[9] whereby the transfer of property was conditioned by the non-repayment of the loan on time (hence a form quite similar to the Roman *lex commissoria*).

The function of the examples that I will discuss here is identical to the above-mentioned cases. Yet, they differ from the 'sale on trust', demotic

---

[3] Throughout the article I shall from time to time refer to German legal terminology, for obvious reasons closer to the Roman notions. On the other hand – see below – the not-so-precise parlance of common law actually illustrates better the misty terminological situation of the Byzantine times (see further fn. 10).

[4] See, most recently, Noordraven (1999), *passim* with literature, specifically pp. 17–41 and ch. 4.

[5] On this security, see most recently Hermann (1989), *passim*; cf. as well Mitteis (1912), pp.135–41 and Taubenschlag (1955), pp. 270–4; the term itself does not appear in the actual sales, but only in the documents that refer to the original 'purchases on trust', cf., for example, MChr. 233 (= P .Heid. Inv. G 1278 Recto, Pathyris 13 September 111 BCE).

[6] Cf., for example, *PSI* VIII 908 (Tebtynis, 42–3 CE); *PSI* VIII 910 (dup. *P. Mich.* V 332, Tebtynis 48 CE); and see Pringsheim (1950), p. 119 and fn. 1.

[7] The so-called πρᾶσις ἐπὶ λύσει (Pringsheim (1950), pp. 117–18, noted the term was never present in the ancient sources). For an overview, see Pringsheim (1950) and more recently Thür in *Neue Pauly-Wissowa*, s.v., with literature.

[8] On this form, see most recently Markiewicz (2005), pp. 156–8 and Pestman (1985). For the pre-Roman genealogy of the 'Egyptian mortgage', cf. Pierce (1972), pp. 119–21, *contra*, very soundly, Markiewicz (2005), p. 158.

[9] Or *Kaufpfandverträge* in Spiegelberg's terminogy (Spiegelberg (1909), pp. 91–106); see also Markiewicz (2005), pp. 154–6. Still, for the transfer to take effect, it was probably necessary to draw a deed of cession in favour of the creditor; see Markiewicz (2005), p. 155 with the example of *P. Hauswald* 18B. We would then have a situation quite similar to the late Antique practice as presented by the Coptic loans and cessions of pledges: cf. Steinwenter (1954), p. 500 and O. *Medinet Habou* 69, 72, 73.

conditional sale, or Roman *fiducia*. Unlike them, they never expressively refer to any sum lent, there is nothing that suggests that any separate loan agreements have ever been made. In fact, the only reason to interpret them as guarantees rather than typical deeds of sale is the fact that they all constitute part of what modern papyrologists, following Alain Martin, describe as an *archive*, that is, they pertain to the same person or persons and were assembled together and selected already in Antiquity. It is therefore the context of each particular archive, which is not necessarily visible in these papyri, that reveals their true nature.

I will analyse three cases of such securities from two different archives. In order to present some conclusion, I will compare these with an instance of an actual pledge/mortgage[10] dated to late Antiquity as well.

2. EULOGIOS' CELL

The earlier set of documents consists of three deeds from the early sixth century CE: *P. Dubl.* 32, 33, and 34.[11] They all concern sales of a monastic dwelling in Labla, on the outskirts of Arsinoe.[12] According to the excavation

[10] The Byzantine legal practice does not distinguish between a conventional and possessory pledge (*Faustpfand* and *Hypotheke*): these terms are used synonymously and only the contexts allow us to reconstruct the actual legal situation. See, for instance, a loan deed with a mortgage: *P. Cairo Masp.* III 67309, ll. 21–2 (Antinoopolis, 569 CE):): ἐντεῦθεν ἤδη ὑποτίθημί σοι καὶ ὑπεθέμην, ἐν τάξει |²² ἐνεχύρου καὶ λόγῳ ὑποθήκης δικαίῳ ('and hence I am hypothecating to you and I have hypothecated as pledge and by the title of right of mortgage . . .'). Such confusion is by no means surprising, if we consider that some of the Justinianic legal sources could induce a careless reader to think of *pignus* and *hypotheca* as synonyms; cf. D.20.1.5.1 (Marcian. 1 ad Form. Hyp.) *inter pignus autem et hypothecam tantum nominis sonus differt* ('only the sound of the name makes a difference between a pledge and a mortgage'). Clearly, the classical jurist Marcian in his original work only wanted to state that one could avail oneself of *actio hypothecaria* no matter whether the pledge was conventional or possessory. Yet, the compilers putting this phrase in the general context of D.21.1 *De pignoribus et hypothecis et qualiter ea contrahantur et de pactis eorum* seem to have given it a practical, all-purpose meaning. This statement is further corroborated by Stephanos' reproach of the – apparently common – misidentification of *pignus* and *hypotheca*: scholion οὐ μόνον παραδόσει to B.25.1.1 (corresponding to D.13.7.1 (Ulpian. 40 ad Sab.) *pignus contrahitur non sola traditione, sed etiam nuda conventione, etsi non traditum est* ('pledge is contracted not only by conveyance by also by mere agreement, even if it is not conveyed'): ἐνέχυρον λέγεται καταχρηστικῶς ἡ ὑποθήκη. καὶ διὰ μὲν τοῦ εἰπεῖν, παραδόσει, ἐδήλωσε τὸ κυρίως ἐνέχυρον· διὰ δὲ τοῦ, ψιλῷ συμφώνῳ, τὴν ὑποθήκην ('pledge is wrongly called hypothec. And when it is said (through) conveyance, it properly means "pledge", instead (if it is contracted through) bare consent, (it signifies) hypothec').

[11] Two of the three documents were originally published by Sayce (1890), pp. 131–44, entered in the *Sammelbuch* under nos 5174 and 5175. A century later, Brian C. McGing identified the third piece of the dossier, and published and comprehensively commented on all three of them (McGing 1990). The texts were later incorporated in an abbreviated form in *P. Dubl.* by the same author. A new interpretation of the texts has been most recently offered by Ewa Wipszycka (2009).

[12] See Wipszycka (2009), pp. 240–1 for a tentative localisation of Labla, in the vicinity of the pyramid of Hawara. Unfortunately, Petrie does not describe the exact location of the find.

diary of Flinders Petrie, the find was of a very particular nature. The deeds
were found bound together, wrapped in linen and then woollen cloth, placed
in a jar and buried with it in the ground. It is hence without doubt that these
papyri belong together.

In the first document, P. *Dubl.* 32, dated 7 September 512 CE, a certain
monk, Eulogios son of Iosephos, who at the time lives in another monastic
community, that of Mikrou Psyon, sells his *monasterion* – not just a room,
but rather a small house, usually consisting of two or more chambers,
storage place, kitchen and sometimes even a workshop[13] – to another
monk, Pousis son of A [. . .], who already lives in Labla. The price, paid
on the spot in coins, was set to eight solidi and 1,200 myriads of denarii,
which for the beginning of the sixth century constitutes quite a remarkable
amount.

In the second document, P. *Dubl.* 33, less than a year later than its
counterpart (9 July 513 CE), the same monk Eulogios again sells his cell to
Paphnoutios, son of Isaac, and Ioulios, son of Aranthios, both living in
Labla. This time the price is set to ten solidi. I will not address here the very
interesting problem of the private assets owned by monks, a fact obviously
contrary to the canon and imperial legislation.[14] The reader may be referred
to authoritative recent studies on the subject.[15] Suffice to say that, notwithstanding the commandment of poverty, the monks kept command of their
mundane affairs, owned property, disposed of it, and borrowed and lent
money, a fact well attested by papyrological sources.[16] Another interesting
point, which cannot be discussed at length here, is the fact that Eulogios
declares himself to be an ex-Melitian monk, now orthodox, whereas his
purchasers are Melitian priests in the first case and monks of the same
denomination, in the second. Yet again we may observe that the picture of
highly troubled relations between various factions of Christianity, which we
usually extrapolate from the literary sources, risks being rather exaggerated
when compared with real life.

In both of the deeds, the customary clauses securing the rights of the purchasers are inserted, so at the very beginning of both the papyri we read that:

> Eulogios acknowledges that he has with free, independent and fixed will, sold and
> conveyed into complete ownership from the present for all succeeding time . . .
> the cell in the said monastery Labla which belongs to the vendor Eulogios, and

---

[13] On the terminology referring to monastic dwellings, see most recently Wipszycka (2009b),
pp. 281–91.
[14] Less than two decades later, Justinian forbade alienation and hypothecation of monasteries
to private individuals (Nov.7.11, 535 CE).
[15] There is obviously a vast body of literature on the subject; most importantly, see
Steinwenter (1930) and (1958); Barone Adesi (1988) and (1993); Wipszycka (1972), (2001),
(2009a), (2009b), pp. 471–566; and Markiewicz (2009) with further literature.
[16] See, most recently, Markiewicz (2009), *passim*.

which came down to him, as he has had confirmed and registered . . . [cf. lines 2–3 in both texts)]

And later, in *P. Dubl.* 32, we see:

> henceforth the purchaser Pousis possesses and owns the same cell he has purchased in its entirety, however many rooms it is, and the courtyard in front of the rooms, and with all its rights from the ground to the very top, as stated above; and have the authority to inhabit, manage, dispose of it, improve it, repair it, tear it down, rebuild it, redesign it, in whatever appearance and condition he wishes; hand it over to his heirs and successors, present it to the others or give it as a gift, in the manner he wishes and without hindrance. (lines 9–11)[17]

In *P. Dubl.* 33:

> henceforth the purchasers Papnouthios and Ioulios possess and own in equal half-shares the same cell they have purchased in its entirety, however many rooms it is, and they have authority to inhabit, manage, dispose of it, improve it, repair it, tear it down, rebuild it, redesign it, in whatever condition appearance and condition they wish hand it on to their heir and successors, present it to others, give it away as gift, in the manner they wish and without hindrance. (lines 10–13)[18]

In the final part of both documents, the vendor stipulates that he or his successors will take a stand against any possible claims of third parties *versus* the new owner and, should they fail to do so, they will be liable to pay as penalty double the price and costs incurred. The contracts were additionally secured by *hypotheca generalis* on Eulogios' present and future property, a typical feature of all late Byzantine documents (the commonness of the clause actually raises doubts as to its effectiveness). Finally, there is Eulogios' subscription (executed on his behalf as he declares himself to be illiterate) and the signatures of the witnesses (five and four, respectively), evidence that both documents are executed *lege artis* and thus fully effective. Also the payment of the price on the spot, attested to no less than thrice (in the documents, Eulogios' subscriptions and by each statement of the witnesses), inform us that the main condition for the transfer of property in Byzantine law has

---

[17] καὶ παντὶ δικαίῳ αὐτοῦ |¹⁰ ἀπ' ἐδάφους μέχρι παντὸς ὕψους, ὡς προγέγραπται, καὶ ἐξουσίαν ἔχειν διοικεῖν, οἰκονομεῖν, ἐπιτελεῖν περὶ αὐτοῦ, βελτιοῦν, φιλοκαλεῖν, καθελεῖν, ἀνοικοδομεῖν, μετασχηματίζειν, ἐν οἵᾳ βούλεται ὄψει καὶ διαθέσει, εἰς κληρονόμους καὶ διαδόχους παραπέμπειν, |¹¹ ἐκποιεῖν ἑτέροις καὶ ἀποχαρίζεσθαι καθ' ὃν βούλεται τρόπον, ἀνεπικωλύτως.

[18] πρὸς τω (l. τὸ) ἀπὸ τοῦ νῦν τοὺς πριαμένους Παπνούθιον καὶ Ἰούλιον κρατεῖν καὶ |¹¹ κυριεύειν ἐξ ἴσου μέρους ἡμίσεως τοῦ αὐτοῦ καὶ ἐώνηνται μοναστηρίου ἐξ ὁλοκλήρου, ὅσων δ' ἄν ἐστιν μενημάτων, καὶ παντὶ δικαίῳ αὐτοῦ ἀπ' ἐδάφους μέχρι παντὸς ὕψους, ὡς προγέγραπται, καὶ ἐξουσίαν ἔχειν |¹² διοικεῖν, οἰκονομεῖν, ἐπιτελεῖν περὶ αὐτοῦ, βελτιοῦν, φιλοκαλεῖν, καθελεῖν, ἀνοικοδομεῖν, μετασχηματίζειν, ἐν οἵᾳ βούλονται ὄψει καὶ διαθέσει, εἰς κληρονόμους καὶ διαδόχους παραπέμπειν, ἑτέροις ἐκποιεῖν |¹³ καὶ ἀποχαρίζεσθαι καθ' ὃν βούλονται τρόπον, ἀνεπικωλύτως.

been fulfilled.[19] All in all, two perfect deeds of sale and at the same time a transfer of property.

And yet there is a surprising feature: in both papyri the very same person sells exactly the same *monasterion* within the very same year. To prove it, we only need to compare the description of the dwelling found in both texts. In *P. Dubl.* 32 we have:

> the neighbours of the cell are: to the south, the desert and the cell of the late Andreas the priest; to the north, the cell of the priest Naaraos, to the east, the desert, to the west, the public road in front of the cell of Petros the deacon (lines 6–7),[20]

and in *P. Dubl.* 33, the description runs as follows:

> the neighbours of the cell are, as they (the parties) have cordially indicated, to the south, a deserted cell; to the north, the cell of the priest Naaraos, to the east, the desert and the entry and exit of the same cell; to the west, the public road in front of the cell of Peter the deacon. (lines 6–7)[21]

The only difference in these two reports is the fact the cell previously belonging to the late priest Andreas is now designated as deserted.[22] How was it possible that Eulogios sold the same estate twice to two different buyers within a year?

Before we attempt a plausible answer to this question, we still need to consider the third document from the *dossier*, *P. Dubl.* 34. It is a settlement of claims, *dialysis*, executed in poor Greek, rather difficult to understand, most probably on 24 August 511 CE,[23] so it predates both of the sales. Two monks living in the same hermitage at Labla settle their rights and claims to it. The owner of the *monasterion* (which unfortunately is not described further), Aioulios, son of Arantheios, writes to his brother, another Melitian monk, Eulogios, son of Pousi. Having declared as invalid any deed regarding the cell that he may have made with Isak, son of Sabinos, Aioulios stipulates that after his death the property of the cell, together with his other earthly goods as well as debts and assets, will pass to Eulogios. The same should happen,

---

[19] Cf. Kaser (1971–5), § 242 III and § 264 I.

[20] οὖ καί εἰσιν γίτονες, νότου τὸ ὅρος καὶ μοναστήριον τοῦ μακαρίου Ἀνδρέα πρεσβυτέρου, βορρᾶ μοναστήριον Νααραοῦ | [7] πρεσβυτέρου, ἀπηλιώτου τὸ ὅρος, λιβὸς ὁδὸς δημοσία, μεθ' ἣν μοναστήριον Πέτρου διακόνου.

[21] οὖ καί εἰσιν γίτονες, καθὼς ἐκ συμφώνου ὑπηγόρευσαν', νότου | [7] ἔρημον μοναστήριον, βορρᾶ μοναστήριον Νααραοῦ πρεσβυτέρου, ἀπηλιώτου ὅρος καὶ ἡ τοῦ αὐτοῦ μοναστηρίου εἴσοδος καὶ ἔξοδος, λιβὸς ὁδὸς δημοσία μεθ' ἣν μοναστήριον Πέτρου διακόνου.

[22] See also a schematic chart in Montevecchi (1941), p. 118. *Contra*, yet entirely solitary, is Barison (1938), pp. 69–72 but, as Montevecchi already showed, definitely wrongly. Barison also claimed, but with no actual textual proof, that Eulogios, having inherited 'both' estates, would sell them in 513 and 516.

[23] For dating see the very convincing argument of McGing (1995), p. 87.

should Aioulios decide to leave Eulogios and the cell or if he brings into the hermitage another monk or any man 'of the world' without Eulogios' consent.[24] Eulogios, in turn, promises not to expel Aioulios from the property. Both statements are followed by testimonies of the witnesses, two Melitian priests, one deacon and three orthodox priests.

It is quite likely that we deal in all the documents with the same people. Aioulios, son of Aranthieos, from *P. Dubl.* 34 could be quite securely identified with the Ioulios, son of Arantheios, who buys the *monasterion* in *P. Dubl.* 33. Aranthios is a very rare name, Aioulios is just a variant of Ioulios.[25] It is a bit more difficult to ascertain that Eulogios, son of Ioseph, the vendor in *P. Dubl.* 32 and 33, is the very same person as Eulogios, son of Pousi of *P. Dubl.* 34. The fact that the documents were found together, as well as the position of Eulogios, son of Ioseph, as the vendor and the rightful owner of the cell in the two latter documents may indicate that we have the same person in front of us, notwithstanding the difference in the father's name and the popularity of the name Eulogios. The scribe of *P. Dubl.* 34 might have made a mistake, or, more likely, Eulogios' father may have had a double name.[26]

Assuming that the above is true, the situation would be as follows: in 511 Aioulios practically cedes to Eulogios his rights to a *monasterion* in Labla. In 512 Eulogios sells the *monasterion* to Pousis, and one year later sells it again to Aioulios and Paphnoutios. Brian McGing, following the reasoning of Orsolina Montevecchi,[27] sees *P. Dubl.* 32 as a fictitious sale, aimed at securing a loan of eight solidi and 1,200 myriads of silver denarii. Ewa Wipszycka adopts this argument, assuming that the second sale was a real one. She reconstructs the story of Eulogios as follows: in 511 he gets a settlement with Ioulios, then acquires the ownership of the cell (the deed would be missing), afterwards he leaves Labla (perhaps after having converted to orthodoxy) for Mikrou Psyos, sells his cell to Pousi, presumably only as a guarantee for a loan of eight solidi and 1,200 myriads of silver denari; finally, in 513 he sells (back?) the cell to Ioulios and Paphnoutios, this time for real.

I suggest that the situation could have been more complex. As we well know from later land sales, the owner usually handed over to the buyer all the deeds that proved his right to the property sold. It is very surprising therefore not to find the missing link in the chain of the owners, that is the deed of sale between Aioulios/Ioulios and Eulogios. Who was, therefore, the original owner of the *monasterion* in Labla? I think the mysterious clauses in the settlement found in *P. Dubl.* 34 might give a clue to that matter.

---

[24] For this, doubtless correct, understanding of δίχα Εὐλογίω, see McGing (1990), commentary on line 7.

[25] See McGing (1990), p. 87.

[26] I have adopted here Ewa Wipszycka's argument (Wipszycka (2009), p. 241); differently McGing (1990), p. 87.

[27] Montevecchi (1941), pp. 105–16, 117–18.

Let me recapitulate: Aioulios occupies the cell but practically deprives
himself of his rights as the owner, being only guaranteed his title to live in his
own place; Eulogios' consent is a *sine qua non* for the introduction of any new
inhabitants into the hermitage. Yet there is nothing in the document that
may imply that Eulogios would actually share the dwelling with Aioulios;
less than a year later, he certainly lives elsewhere. I think therefore that the
first loan is granted by Eulogios to Aioulios. Being brethren of the same
denomination, they do not feel the need to secure it any further except by
creating a specific right of the creditor to the property of the debtor, under
a type of cession or gift *mortis causa*. Eulogios stipulates that the debtor will
remain in his home. Eulogios then 'sub-mortgages' the cell by means of a
fictitious sale to Pousi, getting eight solidi and 1200 myriad denarii as a loan.
This liberty should not surprise us in light of the late Antique documents
of real securities: the pledgee/hypothecary obtained virtually the full rights
over the thing pledged. Subsequently, Eulogios pays off the debt and is given
back the deed, and a year later disposes of the cell again. The lack of a re-sale
agreement between Pousi and Eulogios should not surprise us: the very fact
of handing back the deed has the same effect, the debt becoming equally
un-actionable in court. When in 513, Aioulios, the former owner of the cell,
gets it back by paying ten solidi to Eulogios, what he actually does may be
nothing less than repayment of the original loan taken in 511. This time the
deed is made, as (A)ioulios regains all his rights to the cell and will share them
with Papnoutios son of Isak.

If this – potentially dangerous – reconstruction is correct, I think I might
provide an answer to Wipszycka and McGing's question: who lived in the
monasterion in all that time? It was the original – 'true' if you like – owner,
Aioulios son of Aranthios. And it was indeed he, who having rolled the three
papyri, bound them with red string, wrapped them with linen and wool, and
packed them into a jar to be discovered 1,400 years later by Flinders Petrie.

This tiny archive of only three papyri seems to provide information of
no less than three loans secured with collaterals that are anything but the
standard pledge or mortgage: the possible first loan granted by Eulogios in
511, the second loan that Eulogios took in 512, and most probably another
transaction of the same kind between Aioulios and Isak (declared void by the
former in *P. Dubl.* 34).

3. TAPIA'S BANQUET HALL AND OTHER 'FICTITIOUS' SALES IN THE ARCHIVE OF KAKO AND PATERMOUTHIS

My second set of cases comes from the famous Archive of Patermouthis
and Kako.[28] They concern affairs of the main figures of the set of the papyri,

---

[28] The archive has been studied extensively since its publication in *P. Lond.* V and *P. Mon.* I.
For the latest update of the bibliography, see the *Leuven Trismegistos* database of the papyrus

Patermouthis and his quarrelsome mother-in-law Aurelia Tapia. The two transactions I shall present here reflect the troublesome financial situation of the Patermouthis' family members, their common entanglement in loans, disputes, settlements and inheritance divisions.[29]

A deed of sale executed in Syene on 30 May 585 CE (*P. Münch.* I 9 + *P. Lond.* V 1734 – protocol = *Pap. Eleph. Eng.* D40) informs us that Aurelia Tapia has sold five pieces of her property in Syene for ten gold solidi. The purchasers are her daughter Kako and her son-in-law Patermouthis:

> I, the aforesaid Tapia acknowledge by this my written security of purchase, willingly and convinced apart from any guile or fear or force or compulsion or deceit or flattery or contrivance or malice or maliciousness or any defect or any mean intention or any circumvention of the law, but of free will and self-chosen volition and sound understanding and pure purpose and fixed calculation and unchangeable design and clear conscience and at the same time swearing the dreadful and awesome oath by Almighty God and by the victory and permanence of our most pious masters, Flavi Tiberius Mauricius and Aelia Constantina, the eternal Augusti and Emperors and the greatest benefactors, that I have sold to you today, the aforesaid Patermouthis and Kako, his spouse, by the law of purchase and for eternal possession and total authority and every most complete right of ownership, and that I have transferred to you from now for all on-going time to come belonging to me [the list of pieces of property follows]. (lines 12–30)[30]

---

archives, and its description by Karolien Geens (2005). It is always useful, however, to get back to the original commentaries by Heisenberg/Wenger in *P. Mon.* and to Idris Bell's article (1913). See also the studies of Joel J. Farber and Bezalel Porten devoted to the Archive: Farber and Porten (1986); Farber (1990). Cf. also the same authors in *Pap. Eleph. Eng.*: pp. 395–9, with a detailed family tree. On the Coptic documents of the archive, see Clackson (1995). For an overview of various issues relating to house ownership and sales in the archive, cf. Husson (1990) and Dijkstra (2007) for the topographical observations on the houses in Syene.

[29] For an overview of the dispute resolution through arbitration, with the use of Patermouthis and Kako's Archive, see Urbanik (2007) with Palme (2007) and Kreuzsaler (2010), with resumés of the earlier literature.

[30] ὁμολογῶ ἐγὼ ἡ προγεγραμμένη Ταπία διὰ ταύτης | [13] μου τῆς ἐγγράφου ὠνιακῆς ἀσφαλείας ἑκοῦσα καὶ | [14] πεπεισμένοι (l. πεπεισμένη) δίχα παντὸς δόλου καὶ φόβου καὶ βίας | [15] καὶ ἀνάγκης καὶ συναρπαγῆς καὶ κολακίας (l. κολακείας) καὶ μηχανῆς | [16] καὶ κακονοίας καὶ κακοηθείας καὶ ἐλαττώματος παντὸς | [17] καί τινος φαύλου διανοήματος καὶ πάσης νομίμου | [18] περιγραφῆς, ἀλλ' ἑκουσίῳ γνώμῃ καὶ αὐθαιρέτῳ βουλήσει | [19] καὶ ὀρθῇ διανοίᾳ καὶ καθαρῷ σκοπῷ καὶ ἀμετατρέπτῳ λογισμῷ | [20] καὶ ἀμεταθέτῳ βουλήματι καὶ εἰλικρινεῖ συνειδήσει, ἅμα δὲ | [21] καὶ ὀμνύουσα τὸν φρικτὸν καὶ σεβάσμιον ὅρκον τοῦ | [22] παντοκράτορος θεοῦ καὶ τὴν (l. τῆς) νίκην (l. νίκης) καὶ διαμονὴν (l. διαμονῆς) τῶν | [23] εὐσεβεστάτων ἡμῶν δεσποτῶν Φλαυί(*)ων Τιβερίου Μαυρικίου | [24] καὶ Αἰλείας Κωνσταντίνης τῶν αἰωνίων Αὐγούστων | [25] καὶ Αὐτοκρατόρων καὶ μεγίστων εὐεργετῶν, πεπρακέναι | [26] ὑμῖν σήμερον τοῖς προγεγραμμένοις Πατερμουθείῳ καὶ | [27] Κακῶτι· συμβίῳ αὐτοῦ ὠνιακῷ νόμῳ καὶ αἰωνίᾳ κατοχῇ | [28] καὶ ἐξουσίᾳ πάσῃ καὶ παντὶ πληρεστάτῳ δεσποτείας | [29] δικαίῳ καὶ καταγεγραφέναι ἀπὸ τοῦ νῦν ἐπὶ τὸν ἑξῆς | [30] ἄπαντα διηνεκῆ χρόνον τὸ ὑπάρχον μοι, κτλ.

We know that Tapia had left Syene within the previous two years, in order to settle down in Antinoopolis, where her brother also resided,[31] possibly wishing for some fresh air after long hereditary disputes with her son Ioannes and daughter Aurelia Tsone, a nun, fathered by Tapia's (possibly divorced) first husband Menas. She seems therefore to be willing to close down her business in her native town. What should leave us a little suspicious about the nature of our sale is the fact that Tapia had not only already received the price for the immovables but had also used it partly for her living expenses in the capital, and partly for paying off a fine (ζημία) that had befallen her somehow in connection to her brother Ioannes:

> the price mutually agreed upon and approved being gold, ten solidi in the weight of Syenians, namely g(old) 10 so(lidi) in the w(eight) of the Syenians, which full price I have here received in full from you, the purchasers – part of it I have spent for my essential needs or upkeep in the city of the Antinoëans and part I have given towards the remaining incurred by me by reason of my brother Ioannes in the same city – on the present day, from your hand to my hand, from your cashbox, in number and weight complete. (lines 62–70)[32]

It seems therefore reasonable to believe that P. Münch. I 9 is not a regular deed of sale, but rather constitutes a datio in solutum: a sale of the buildings in lieu of the debt-repayment. This supposition seems to be corroborated by the wording of the 'price-clause'. Tapia declares she has received the money for her ἀνακαία χρεῖα – necessary needs, an expression typical for loans.[33]

The complications do not end here: as the first ones of the sold properties, there appear two shares in a house in Syene located in the southern part of the fortress: a part of the terrace and half of a banquet hall, or dining-room (symposion). Aurelia Tapia inherited a half-share of these spaces from her mother and the other half-share she bought from her brother Georgios:

> the half-share of the symposion belonging to me in the house of my mother, the other half of which belongs to Menas and Tselet, my siblings, facing north

---

[31] Cf. P. Münch. I 9, ll. 66–8. The assumption of Farber (1990), p. 117 that she had already lived there for two years may be true but does not find a solid textual evidence in the cited papyri: contrary to what he says, Tapia does not appear in P. Münch. I 7.

[32] τιμῆς τῆς πρὸς ἀλλήλους συμπεφωνημένης καὶ συναρεσάσης |63 χρυσοῦ νομισματίων δέκα ζυγῷ τῆς Συηνιτῶν |64 γί(νονται) χρ(υσοῦ) νο(μισμάτια) ι ζ(υγῷ) Συήν(ης), ἥνπερ τὴν τελείαν τιμὴν μὴν αὐτόθι |65 ἀπέσχον παρ' ὑμῶν τῶν ὠνουμένων μέρος μὲν ἀνήλωσα |66 εἰς τὴν ἀναγκαίαν χρεῖάν μου ἢ διατροφὴν ἐν τῇ Ἀντινοέων, |67 μέρος δὲ δέδωκα εἰς τὴν ὑπερβαίνουσάν μοι ζημίαν ἐν τῇ |68 αὐτῇ πόλει προφάσει Ἰωάννου τοῦ ἐμοῦ ἀδελφοῦ ἐν τῇ ἐνεστώσῃ |69 ἡμέρᾳ διὰ χειρὸς εἰς χεῖρά μου ἐξ οἴκου ὑμῶν ἀριθμῷ καὶ σταθμῷ |70 πλήρη.

[33] Cf., for example, some contemporary examples: P. Laur. III 75, l. 17 (Oxyrhynchos, 574 CE); BGU XII 2206, l. 11 (Hermoupolis, 591–602 CE); P. Köln. III 158, ll. 18–19 (Herakeopolis, 18 October 599 CE); likewise in some loan-deeds made in Syene: P. Lond. V 1723, l. 8 (Syene, 7 September 577 CE); P. Lond. V 1736, ll. 10–11 (Syene, 25 February 611 CE); P. Lond. V 1737, l. 8 (Syene, 9 February 613 CE).

towards the stair, on the second floor and also my share of the terrace on the fourth floor above the bedroom of Talephantis with my share of all the appurtenances. The house of which I have sold you half the living room is in Syene in the southern part of the fortress in the Quarter of the Oratory of the Holy and Triumphant Victor, having come around to me in this way: one quarter-share from a legacy from my mother, another quarter by purchase from Georgios, my brother. (lines 30–9)[34]

This very same half of the *symposion* and a quarter share of the terrace is again sold by Aurelia Tapia some nine years later, on 6 March 594 CE (*P. Lond.* V 1733 = *Pap. Eleph. Eng.* D49), to Flavius Apadios, son of Sourous, a soldier of the regiment of Syene:

the half share belonging to me and falling to me of the symposion on the second floor and the quarter share of the roof-terrace above the bedroom is above the symposion which belongs jointly to me and my siblings Menas and Tselet, and my share of appurtenances, (consisting) of the vestibule and gateway and stair and gallery and little oven, with entrance and exit and passage up and passage down, the same house lying in the same Syene in the southern part of the fortress and in the Quarter of Saint Apa Victor, triumphant martyr.[35] The same half-share of the symposion and the quarter-share of the terrace came to me in this way: one-quarter share of the symposion and the eighth-share (of the terrace) from the inheritance of my mother Mariam, and the other quarter-share and the eighth-share of the above-named places just as has been said above from a rightful purchase through a written document of purchase from Georgios my brother those that came to me and to my siblings Menas and Tselet, in common and undivided. And they came to the aforesaid Mariam herself though legitimate inheritance from her parents, Papnouthios and Thekla in force of their shares.[36]

[34] τὸ ὑπάρχον μοι ἥμισυ μέρος |³¹ τοῦ συμποσίου ἐν τῇ οἰκίᾳ τῆς μητρός, οὗ καὶ τὸ ἄλλο ἥμισυ μέρος |³² ἀνήκειν Μηνᾷ καὶ Τσελὲτ τοῖς ἀδελφοῖς μου, νεύοντος εἰς βορρᾷ(l. βορρᾶν) |³³ εἰς τὸν πεσσὸν ἐν τῇ δευτέρᾳ στέγῃ, καὶ τὸ μέρος μου ἀπὸ δώματος ἐν τῇ τετάρτῃ |³⁴ στέγῃ τοῦ ἐπάνωθεν τοῦ ἀκουβίτου Ταλιφάντις, σὺν τῷ μέρει μου |³⁵ τῶν ὅλων χρηστηρίων τῆς οἰκίας, ἀφ' ἧς πέπρακα ὑμῖν τὸ ἥμισυ |³⁶ <μέρος> τοῦ συμποσίου, οὔσης ἐν τῇ Συήνῃ περὶ τὸ νότινον μέρος το[ῦ] φρουρίου |³⁷ ἐπὶ λαύραν τοῦ εὐκτηρίου τοῦ ἁγίου καὶ ἀθλοφόρου Βίκτορος περιελθὸν |³⁸ εἰς ἐμὲ οὕτως· τέταρτον μὲν μέρος ἀπὸ κληρονομίας τῆς μητρός μου, |³⁹ ἕτερον δὲ τέταρτον ἀπὸ ἀγορασίας παρὰ Γεωργίου τοῦ ἀδελφοῦ μουο.
[35] For the location of the shrine, see Dijkstra (2007), pp. 194–5 and 208.
[36] τὸ ὑπάρχον μοι |¹⁸ καὶ ἐπιβάλλον ἥμισυ μέρος ἀπὸ τοῦ συμποσίου τοῦ ἐν τῇ δευτέρᾳ στέγῃ |¹⁹ καὶ τὸ τέταρτον μέρος ἀπὸ τοῦ ἀέρος ἐπάνω τοῦ ἀκουβίτου (l. ἀκκουβίτου) τοῦ ὄντος |²⁰ ἐπάνω τοῦ συμποσίου τοῦ καὶ ἀδιαιρέτου ὄντος μοι καὶ τῶν ἀδελφῶν |²¹ μου Μηνᾶ καὶ Τσελετ καὶ τὸ μέρος μου ἀπὸ πάντων τῶν χρηστηρίων |²² τοῦ τε προθύρου κ[αὶ] πυλόνος (l. πυλῶνος) καὶ πεσσοῦ παραδρομίδος καὶ |²³ κλιβανίου σὺν εἰσόδῳ καὶ ἐξόδῳ καὶ ἀνόδῳ καὶ καθόδῳ τῆς αὐτῆς οἰκίας |²⁴ διακειμένης ἐπὶ τῆς αὐτῆς Συήνης περὶ τὸ νότινον μέρος τοῦ Φρουρίου |²⁵ καὶ περὶ λαύραν τοῦ ἁγίου ἀθλοφόρου Ἄπα Βίκτορος μάρτυρος |²⁶ ἐλθὸν εἰς ἐμὲ τὸ αὐτὸ ἥμισυ μέρος συμποσίου καὶ τὸ τέταρτον μέρος |²⁷ ἀπὸ τοῦ δώματος οὕτως· τέταρτον μὲν μέρος ἀπὸ τοῦ συμποσίου |²⁸ καὶ τὸ ὄγδοον μέρος ἀπὸ κληρονομίας τῆς μητρὸς μου Μαρίας, |²⁹ τὸ δὲ ἄλλο τέταρτον μέρος καὶ τὸ ὄγδοον μέρος ἀπὸ τῶν προδεδηλουμέ(νων) |³⁰ τόπων

The price of the property was set at three solidi. How was it possible that Aurelia Tapia could sell the same piece of property twice within less than a decade? Porten and Farber suggest Tapia's daughter and her husband have at some point transferred the property back to their mother (-in-law).[37] There is no indication, however, that such a thing happened. I would rather follow Montevecchi's original idea that the first sale served only as a security for a loan.[38] In my opinion, also the second sale of the property to Apadios may have served the same purpose: otherwise we would not understand why both deeds found their place in Patermouthis and Kako's Archive. It is a clear indication, that it was they who eventually gained dominion over the quarter of the terrace and half of the banquet hall.

It seems likely – though it cannot be ascertained with complete certainty – that another piece of the five properties 'sold' (or transferred in lieu of repayment of the debt) by Tapia to her daughter and son-in-law is sold again by her only a year later. The asset in question is described in lines 49–57 of *P. Münch.* 9 (= D40) as

> the half share of a house that belongs to me, the one having come around to me by rightful purchase from Ioannes son of Paterchnoumios and its other half-share belonged to my late husband as a result of a purchase from the same Ioannes, the same house lying in Syene in the southern part of the fortress and in the Quarter of the Camp. The boundaries of the same house are: on the south the house of the heirs of Apadios; [. . .] of Abraam [blank line].[39]

The original acquisition-deed of the house by Tapia and her husband has not been preserved. Yet it is certain that this purchase is mentioned in *P. Lond.* V 1729 (= *FIRA* III 68, 12 March 584 CE), a curious deed by which Ioannes, son of Patechnoumios, 'the most humble monk', declares to have donated to Patermouthis a half share of another house as a token of gratitude for the

---

καθὼς ἀνωτέρω εἴρηται ἀπὸ δικαίας ἀγορασίας ἐξ ἐγγράφου |[31] ὠνιακῆς <ἀσφαλείας> παρὰ Γεωργίου τοῦ ἐμοῦ ἀδελφοῦ κοινῶν ὄντων |[32] καὶ ἀδιαιρέτων εἴς τε ἐμὲ καὶ τοὺς ἀδελφούς μου Μηνα (l. Μηνᾶν) καὶ Τσελετ |[33] καὶ εἰς αὐτὴν τὴν προγεγραμμένην Μαριὰμ · ἀπὸ δικαία[ς] κληρονομίας |[34] τῶν γονέων αὐτῆς Παπνουθίου καὶ Θέκλας πρὸς τὴν δύναμιν τοῦ |[35] κλήρου αὐτῶν. My translation of the last clause diverges from the one proposed in D49 and Bell's commentary, where *kleros* is understood as 'will'. Such a translation does not make sense. Mariam did not leave a will, her estate was passed over to her four children and then divided in equal *shares* between them. There is, therefore, no need either to read *kleros* as *Erbteilingsurkunde*, as Wenger did (cf. the translation of line 61 of *P. Münch.* I 9).

[37] Porter and Farber (1996), p. 540.

[38] Montevecchi (1941), p. 106.

[39] προσομολογῶ δὲ καὶ |[50] πεπρακέναι τὸ αἱροῦν μοι ἥμισυ μέρος · οἰκίας, τὸ περιελθὸν |[51] εἰς ἐμὲ ἐκ δικαίας ἀγορασίας παρὰ Ἰωάννου Πατεχνουμίου, οὐ (l. ἧς) καὶ |[52] τὸ ἄλλο ἥμισυ μέρος ἀνήκειν τῷ εὐμοίρῳ μου ἀνδρὶ ἐξ ἀγορασίας |[53] παρὰ τοῦ αὐτοῦ Ἰωάννου, τῆς αὐτῆς οἰκίας διακειμένης ἐν τῇ |[54] Συήνῃ περὶ τὸ νότινον μέρος τοῦ φρουρίου καὶ περὶ λαύραν τῆς |[55] παρεμβολῆς. εἰσὶ δὲ γείτονες τῆς αὐτῆς οἰκίας νότου οἰκία |[56] τῶν κληρονόμων Ἄπα Δίο(υ) . . . . Ἀβρ[ααμίο]υ | (vac.)

care and provisions that the latter had undertaken for him. Interestingly, the deed was originally most probably addressed to Tapia, and only later re-addressed to her son-in-law.[40] And so in lines 9–13, the monk originally acknowledges himself to

> have sold (erased: to you and) to your late (erasure: husband) Iakobos by a written deed of sale the parts of houses remaining to me and to have got their price from you in accordance with the power of the deed of sale done by me and to have spent (the price) for my essential needs) . . . [41]

I daresay it would not be too hazardous to assume that this sale of the monk's house was also originally intended to be a security one (we have again a mention –similar to Tapia's declaration in P. *Münch.* I 9; cf. above fn. 29 – that the price was used for the 'seller's' necessities), but as Ioannes did not recover financially before his death, it eventually turned out to be a definitive transfer.

A deed executed nineteen months later informs us that Tapia transfers to Flavius Kyriakos, son of Menas, soldier, *caballarius* of the regiment of Syene, the *dominium* over the half-share of a house which 'has come around to me through rightful purchase from Ioannes also called Paptsios and to him from the paternal inheritance'.[42] The woman mentions that the other half belongs[43] to her late husband Iakobos. The seller, from whom the couple had acquired the house, may very well be identified with the monk Ioannes, son of Patechnoumios.[44] It seems unlikely that Tapia and her husband could have bought an entire house from two different Ioannes. There is a problem, however, with the certain identification of the properties in P. *Münch.* I 9 and 11: their exact descriptions, *prima facie*, do not correspond. The property in P. *Münch.* 11 is

---

[40] See Bell's introduction to P. *Lond.* V 1729 and commentary *ad h. l.*

[41] ἐπράθην ⟦σοι καὶ⟧ τῷ μακαριωτάτῳ {σοῦ} ⟦ἀ[νδ]ρὶ⟧ Ἰακώβῳ τὰ |¹⁰ ὑπάρχοντά μοι μέρη οἰκημάτων ἐξ ἐγγράφο(υ) πράσεως καὶ τῆς |¹¹ τούτων τιμῆς ἔσχηκα παρ᾽ ὑμῶν πρὸς τὴν δύναμιν τῆς |¹² γεναμένης (vac.?) παρ᾽ ἐμο(ῦ) πράσεως τὴν τούτων τιμὴν καὶ |¹³ ἀνήλωσα εἰς τὰς ἀναγκαίας μου χρείας, κτλ.

[42] περιελθὸν εἰς ἐμὲ ἀπὸ δικαίας — |³⁷ ἀγορασίας παρὰ Ἰωάννου τοῦ καὶ Παπτσίου κἀκείνου (1. καὶ ἐκείνου) ἀπὸ γονικῆς διαδοχῆς |³⁸ πρὸς τὴν δύναμιν τῆς παλαιᾶς πράσεως,

[43] Still in present tense: ἀνήκει – J[ohn] S[helton] supposes that the house 'is still officially registered in his name', cf. *Pap. Eleph. Eng.* p. 523 fn. 5. This may be true as we do not find any mention of the house in the succession settlement made between Aurelia Tapia and her son Ioannes (P. *Münch.* I 6 + P. *Lond.* V 1849 = *Pap. Eleph. Eng.* D53, 7 June [?] 583 CE), in which Iakobos' estate was divided between them.

    Porten and Farber's idea (*Pap. Eleph. Eng.* p. 522) that Tapia in 585 sold her share and now is selling the share that once belonged to her husband cannot be accepted: in all three papyri, the object of sale is the share in the house in which the other half 'belongs to late Iakobos'.

[44] Cf. *Pap. Eleph. Eng.* p. 555, s.v. Ioannes, son of Paternoumios, as well as Bell's introduction to P. *Lond.* 1724, p. 174 and Heisenberger and Wenger's commentary in P. *Münch* (p. 11), who think it is the great-uncle of Tsone and Tsere, the vendors in P. *Lond.* V 1724.

lying in Syene in the southern part of the fortress and in the Quarter of the Public Camel Yard of the transfer from Philae and of the house of Abraamios son of Pachymios (lines 21–4)[45]

and its boundaries are

on the south the blind and narrow road and the house of Abraamios son of Pachymios; on the north the public road, on the east the house of Abraamios son of Pachymios; on the west the house of Allamon son of Paterchnoumios. (lines 31–3)[46]

Yet, I think the issue of the inexactitude in the topographical account may be overcome. The general location of the house, the southern part of the fortress, links to the one in P. Münch. I 9. The Quarter of the Public Camel Yard and Quarter of the Camp are definitely not the same, and the boundaries do not match, but let us notice that in the former document the scribe was by no means certain about them: he actually deleted the description he had made and left a blank space to fill the exact position later.[47] It seems as if the parties were not sure where the property really lay.[48] Finally, it looks unlikely that the monk Ioannes sold two of his estates to the couple Tapia-Iakobos, just days before the latter's death. Given all the above, I assume that we are dealing here with the same half-share of the same house.

The price in P. Münch. I 11 was set to five solidi. The fact that the amount is as much as 50% of the joint price of five estates sold by Tapia to Patermouthis and Kako in P. Münch. I 9 contributes once again to the assumption that the sale of 584 CE was indeed a fictitious one.

The half of the house originally belonging to Ioannes alias Paptsios is the object of sale again in P. Münch. I 12 (= Pap. Eleph. Eng. D46, 13 August 590 CE). Now it is Kyriakos who sells it back to Patermouthis and Kako (spelled in this document as 'Koko'), for the same price. The seller declares to have bought the property from Tapia and that the other part belongs to the late father of Kako.[49] It may be a true sale, this time, but it is also possible that

---

[45] διακειμένην |²² τὴν αὐτὴν οἰκίαν ἐπὶ τὴν Συήνην περὶ τὸ νότινον μέρος τοῦ φρουρίου καὶ |²³ περὶ λαύραν τοῦ δημοσίου καμηλῶνος τῆς βασταγῆς Φιλῶν καὶ τῆς οἰκίας |²⁴ Ἀβρααμίου Παχυμίου.

[46] νότου ἡ τυφλὴ καὶ στενὴ ῥύμη καὶ ἡ οἰκία Ἀβρααμίου Παχυμίου, |³² βορρᾶ ἡ ῥύμη δημοσία, ἀπηλιώτου ἡ οἰκία Ἀβρααμίου Παχυμίου, λιβὸς |³³ ἡ οἰκία Ἀλλάμονος Πατεχνουμίου.

[47] Cf. P. Münch., Tafel XVIII and Heisenberg/Wenger's commentary on lines 56–7 of P. Münch. I 9.

[48] Porten and Farber (1996), p. 511 fn. 21 suppose that Tapia simply did not remember the exact boundaries of her properties, and indeed all five estates sold in P. Münch. 9 are described with fewer details than was customary.

[49] Cf. ll. 13–15: τὸ ὑπάρχον μοι ἥμισυ μέρος ἀπὸ πάσης ὁλοκλήρου οἰκίας, οἵας ἐστὶν |¹⁴ διαθέσεως ἀπὸ ἐδάφους ἕως ἀέρος, οὐ (l. ἧς) καὶ τὸ ἄλλο ἥμισυ ἀνήκει Ἰακώβου ἀποιχομένου |¹⁵ πατρός σου Κοκὼ τῆς ὠνουμένης, 'the half-share belonging to me of a whole, entire house, in the condition it is in, from foundation to air, the other half of which belongs to Iakobos, the departed father of you, Koko, the purchaser' and ll. 29–30: περιελθὸν εἰς ἐμὲ ἀπὸ δικαίας ἀγορασίας |³⁰ παρὰ Ταπίας θυγατρὸς Τσίου κ(αὶ) εἰς αὐτὴν παρὰ Ἰωάννου τοῦ καὶ Παπ᾽τ᾽σίου

the son-in-law and daughter of Tapia simply paid back her original debt of 5 solidi and regained the ownership of the half-share of the house given originally by Tapia as security.

If my reconstruction is true, then we would have the same property used three times as a security for credit (Ioannes → Tapia and Iakobos, Tapia → Patermouthis and Kako, Tapia → Fl. Kyriakos)

Another example from the very same archive shows even better the mechanism of the mock-sales, and I think provides very convincing proof of how they actually functioned.

Some time between 578 and 582, two sisters, Aureliai Tsone and Tsere, daughters of Apadios and Rachel, sold[50] for ten solidi to Patermouthis and Kako, their relatives, their share consisting of three rooms in a house located between

> on the south: the house of Dios son of Kelol, on the north: the public street into which the main door opens; on the west: the house of Dios son of Takares on the east of the house of Pateröous. (Syene, *P. Lond.* V 1724 = *Pap. Eleph. Eng.* D32, ll. 35–7)[51]

The same property along with a share in a boat seems to be the subject of a controversy arising from division of the remaining parts of the estate of the late Iakobos, the father of Kako and Ioannes, and Tapia's husband.[52] The dispute found its solution in an arbitration, *P. Münch.* I 7 + *P. Lond.* V 1860 (23 June 583 CE, Antinoopolis = *Pap. Eleph. Eng.* D36). Ioannes, Kako's brother, contested the ownership of the house, which 'came around to him (Patermouthis) by right of purchase from Isakos and Tsone'.[53] Ioannes apparently had found a deed transferring its ownership to his late father. If Patermouthis and Kako had indeed sold the house to Iakobos, the property should have been part of the inheritance, and thus part of it should have been divided between the siblings after their father's death. Yet the parties finally decide, thanks to the help of some mediators (cf. l. 34), that Ioannes has no rights to the house formerly belonging to Tsone and Tsere, and shall therefore return the deed of sale to Patermouthis and Kako and recognise the validity of *P. Lond.* V 1724. What seems to have happened is as follows:

κακεινου (l. καὶ εἰς ἐκεῖνον) ἀπὸ γονικῆς δι[αδοχ]ῆς 'having come to me through rightful purchase from Tapia daughter of Tsios a(nd) to her from Ioannes *alias* Paptsios, and from him (read: to him) through inherited succession'.

50   On this sale and the history of the property, as well as its identification with the house–object of sale in the earliest document in the Patermouthis Archive, *P. Lond.* V 1722, see Porten and Farber (1985), pp. 87–90.

51   νότου ἡ οἰκία Δίου Κελώλ, βορρᾶ ἡ δημοσία |36 λαύρα εἰς ἣν ἠνέῳκται ἡ αὐθεντικὴ κύρα, λιβὸς ἡ οἰκία Δίου |37 Τακαρῆς, ἀπηλιώτου ἡ οἰκία Πατεροοῦτος

52   The rest was divided earlier between all of the parties, the widow and her two children in *P. Münch.* I 6 + *P. Lond.* V 1849 = *Pap. Eleph. Eng.* D53, 7 June [?] 583 CE).

53   περιελθόντος εἰς αὐτὸν |31 ἀπὸ ἀγοραστικοῦ δικαίου παρὰ Ἰσακίου καὶ Τσώνη.

Patermouthis and Kako who, as their archive clearly shows, were in constant need of ready money, fictitiously sold the recently acquired house of Tsore and Tsere to secure the loan that their father/father-in-law, a very wealthy man, had granted them. Later, the loan was repaid, but the deed never returned.[54] However, there must have been something not recorded in our documentation, that convinced the mediators that the sale was a fictitious one, and allowed them to award the contented house to the married couple and not to their brother(-in-law), Ioannes.

4. CONCLUSIONS: PURPLE-MERCHANT'S WIFE AND SISTER-IN-LAW

Why would Eulogios and his brethren, Tapia and other members of Patermouthis' clan choose for their financial affairs the form of a fictitious sale, rather than an ordinary loan secured by an ordinary pledge, a transaction still very well attested in the later Byzantine papyri (even in the same archive, we find examples of a typical mortgage)?[55]

We may of course only speculate as to their intentions. Obviously the creditor in our case is much better secured. My first guess was that when Constantine banned *lex commissoria*, obviously the lenders still wanted to have a strong security versus insolvent debtors, and thus they coined fictitious sales that dissimulated pledges. This may well have been so, but one has to observe that, notwithstanding the emperor's prohibition, later repeated in the Theodosian and then Justinian's Code (respectively, CTh.3.2.1 and C.8.34.3, 320 CE), the legal practice continued to include forfeiture clauses in the documents constituting pledges.[56] This usage is even more evident in some Coptic deeds, temporally closer to our documents.[57] In some other

---

[54] Cf. as well, the personal communication of John Shelton recorded in *Pap. Eleph. Eng.* pp. 496–7, fn. 9, and in Farber (1990) p. 112, fn. 32. Shelton thinks that the deed mentioned in *P. Münch.* I 7, ll. 52–4 was a fictitious deed of sale which was to secure a loan Patermouthis got from his father-in-law, Iakobos.

[55] *P. Lond.* V 1737 (= *Pap. Eleph. Eng.* D52, 9 February 613 CE): loan of three and one third solidi by Patermouthis secured with a pledge of articles of copper. For other examples, see above, footnote 33.

[56] Even if these are quite rare, cf., for example, *P. Lond.* III 870 (p. 235, fourth century CE), *P. Flor.* III 313 (449 CE), with Taubenschlag (1959), pp. 250–1 and (1955), pp. 279–80, cf. as well Kaser (1975), § 252, 2b.

[57] A good example of such practice is, for instance, *P. KRU* 30 (Thebes, mid-eighth century CE), in which most probably Demetrios mortgages to his ex-wife a house as a security of her still unreturned bridal gift. The woman, who receives the deed for her and her children's security, will have the right to live in the house and, if the gift should not be returned within a year, will become the full owner of the house. See also *O. Medinet Habou* 67, ll. 5–8: 'If it should happen that the appointed time passed without my having paid them to you it is you who are the owner of my pledges (ἐνέχυρον) so that I cannot seek them from you ever' (trans. M. Lichtheim); cf. as well Steinwenter (1954), p. 500 and (1955), pp. 29–30.

Coptic ostraka, the ownership of the pledged thing is openly transferred to the creditor and rests with him or her until the repayment.[58] So this may have not been a good enough reason to make the parties choose a fictitious sale over the conventional pledge.

Before an attempt at conclusion, let me have a look at just two instances, very late Greek and Coptic, of these 'conventional' pledges.

One of the first editions of papyri, *P. Paris*, offers under nos 20, 21, 21*bis* and 22*ter* and on the following pages seven documents related to the same person, a purple-merchant Aurelios Pachymios, son of Psates.[59] *P. Paris* 21*ter* is a deed of sale concluded in Panopolis on 13 July 599 between the protagonist of the archive, Pachymes and his wife Aurelia Maria, on one side, and his brother-in-law Arsenios, on the other.[60] The couple acquire from their brother (-in-law) a third share in the house, formerly belonging to Kallinikos and Eugenia, the late parents of Arsenios and Maria, for 2 solidi. Aurelia Maria already owns one third of the estate, and the remaining share rests with Aurelia Ioanna, the third sibling born to Kallinikos and Eugenia. Ioanna mortgages this share on 31 October 607 to her sister Maria, having received from her as a loan two thirds of a solidus, i.e. 15½ keratia (*SB* I 5285.ll. 22–7). The house is perfectly described, its boundaries are set by the great holy church, Panopolitan road and the estate of the heirs of the late Timotheos. Ioanna undertakes on her own and her future successors' behalf not to alienate, change anything within the house or further mortgage it.[61] Moreover, in lieu of interest, she allows her sister to use the house and to live in it.[62] So far, nothing strange: we have a typical antichretic loan in front of us.[63]

---

[58] See, for instance, *P. KSB* 937 (= *P. KRU*, p. 13, originally published in Crum (1922), p. 280; no 9; Thebes sixth/seventh century CE): 'Now I (Joseph, the debtor – JU) cede to you the above-named house, which is in the midmeadow. You are the lord of the above-named house, in return for your 2 *tremisia*. No man shall be able to dispute with you respecting it. You are its lord, until you shall be paid your 2 *tremissia*)' (lines 10–15, Crum's translation); cf. Steinwenter (1954), p. 500 and (1955), pp. 29–30.

[59] The only study particularly devoted to this small archive consisting of twelve documents, two of which are Coptic, is a brief description at the Trismegistos site, authored by Karolien Geens (2003); it contains as well a family tree. The compound of the papyri is a title-deed archive relating to Pachymes, a purple-dealer, his worker, who later became engaged to his master's daughter, and Pachymes' wife and her siblings, and possibly also their father.

[60] Geens (2003), pp. 1–2, fn. 5 argues rightly that *P. Jomard* published by W. Brunet de Presle in *P. Paris*, pp. 257–60 certainly belongs to this papyrus and they should be read together. Cf. as well the minor corrections to the original editions as listed in *Berichtigungsliste* X 159; XI 176.

[61] Lines 36–40: καὶ μὴ ἐξεῖναί |³⁷ μοι μήτε κληρονόμοις ἐμοῖς |³⁸ τὸ αὐτὸ μέρος τρίτον οἰκίας ἢ μέρος |³⁹ τούτου μεθυποθέσθαι ἢ διαπωλ(ῆσαι) |⁴⁰ ἢ ἄλλην τινὰ οἰκομίαν (l. οἰκ<νο>μίαν) θέσθαι κατ' αὐτοῦ ἄχρις ἀποδόσεως καὶ συμπληρώσεως τοῦ αὐτοῦ χρέου[ς] κινδύνῳ ἐμῷ, κτλ.

[62] Lines 33–6: πρὸς τῷ σε ἔχειν |³⁴ τὴν τούτου χρῆσίν τε καὶ |³⁵ οἴκησιν ἀντὶ τῆς παραμυθείας |³⁶ τοῦ αὐτοῦ χρέους, κτλ.

[63] See Kaser (1975), § 111. I; Kupiszewski (1974) and (1985); and Rupprecht (1992).

On the very next day Aurelia Maria rents the whole house to Theodoros, a purple-dyer, like her husband, for four gold keratia per year (*SB* I 5286). The object of rent is described as belonging to her: 'the whole house belonging to you with the upper and lower part and with its rightly befalling to it'.[64] Aurelia Maria behaves as if she were the real owner of the house; furthermore, the *antichresis* terms allow her to live and to use the house but do not specify the right to let it. Karolien Geens suggests that Ioanna's loan is a hidden sale.[65] I do not find this convincing. First of all, the price is way too low.[66] It is only the two thirds of a solidus as opposed to two solidi paid to their common brother seven years earlier for exactly same share of the house. Secondly, why would the parties want to hide a sale? In fact, in order to be able to sell the place further, Maria would have had to present the purchaser the deed confirming her property rights, and this she had not done. These two documents, I presume, prove something else: it seems that in these very late deeds the constitution of a pledge vested in the pledgee quasi owner-like rights, among them the right to dispose.[67]

Let us turn now to the practice of pledges in Coptic documents. A typical deed constituting a pledge would transfer detention of the thing pledged, and include sale and forfeiture clauses[68] as well as a penalty clause, often set at three holokottinoi, to be paid should the pledgor take the things away. Such is also the case of a document that is of particular interest in this instance. *P. KO* 28 (*Koptische Ostraka der Papyrussammlung*) *prima facie* seems to be a possessory pledge by which the debtor hands over to the creditor some arable land (*Besitzpfand*).[69] Yet, he also undertakes to do the field work and – which

---

[64] Lines 17–21: τὴν διαφέρουσ(άν) |[18] σοι οἰκίαν ὁλόκληρον |[19] σὺν ἀνωγείοις καὶ κατωγείῳ |[20] καὶ σὺν παντὶ αὐτῆς τῷ |[21] δικαίῳ κτλ.

[65] Geens (2003), p. 2.

[66] Cf. the list of prices assembled by Montevecchi (1941), pp. 122–6 and Husson (199), pp. 132–5, they vary from one solidus up to eighteen (for a very big house), most frequently they are set between one and a third and five nomismata.

[67] In many documented cases, the pledgor eventually ceded his or her rights to the pledge to the pledgee in lieu of payment: cf., for example, Coptic O. *Medinet Habou* 70; 72–3 and Greek *P. Lond.* V 1720 + *ST* 439 = *Pap. Eleph. Eng.* D24 (3 February 549 CE). In this document Aurelia Nonna acknowledges to have received from her creditor, Aurelia Maria, eight solidi for a pair (and not just one; cf. Porten and Farber (1996), p. 459 fn. 4, following Shelton's suggestion) of earrings which the latter had received in mortgage; the debtor renounces her claims to her former property.

[68] See, for example, P. KTM 42 'wenn der Termin versreicht, ohne daß ich dir die 6 Artaben und 1 Mnt Weizen (zurück)gegeben habe, hast du das Recht (ἐξουσία), die Pfänder die in deiner Hand sind, zu verkaufen (oder) dir zu behalten. Niemand wird gegen dich vorgehen können' (trans. W. C. Till (1954), p. 201); cf. as well Steinwenter (1955), pp. 29–30.

[69] Till's translation: *Ich Isak, der Sohn des [-- aus dem χω]ίον Patubastn im [Bezirk ---] ich schreibe an Patermuthis, den Sohn [des – aus dem Kas]tron Tschême.* Ἐπειδή *du bist zu [mir] gegangen [und hast] mir einen hablen holottinos zu meinem Bedarf* (χρεία) *[für meine Steuer] [gebracht]. Nun* δὲ, *so Gott will, bin ich bereit* (ἑτοίμος) *dir dafür ein Rerme Land zu bestellen . . . auf dem Rerme Land außerhalb des Weges .. Land des Pesnthios. Ich stehe dir dafür gut* (κινδυνεύειν)

was particularly important – to take care of the canal system of the plot.[70] Who actually had the land plot then? And to whom did the revenue of the crops go?[71] We clearly see that the borders between ownership and pledge had become very murky.

What does it all lead to? Firstly, we may have observed that the form of the pledge in late Antique times did not really follow the pure pattern of the classical Roman law forms of *pignus* and *hypotheca*. The boundaries between property rights and the rights vested with the pledgee became less and less visible, and they became more and more alike. Secondly, in our examples, the family relations of Aurelia Tapia, the special character of the monastic communities, made for an important factor of trust between the parties that possibly induced the debtors to agree to what would otherwise be considered harsh conditions of their loan securities. This trust foundation, moreover, seems to have worked fine, notwithstanding the tempestuous litigations between Tapia and her son. In these contexts, such securities must have safeguarded not just the repayment of the money but possibly the personal relationship between the parties involved. And thirdly, also given the above, the economic reality of money buying and lending led people to search for more forms of securing debts. In each particular case, the interest of the creditor and debtor was weighted, in order to tailor the form of real security that suited them best. Ordinary people do not follow the well established theoretical dogmatic legal patterns, they want to protect their transactions in the seemingly most secure way, and they sometimes tend to invent

---

    ohne Gottes Einfluß auf die Landarbeit (?), ich besorge dir ohne jedes Sträuben und ohne jeden Einwand (ἀμφιβολία) seine (d.h. Grundstückes) Bewässerungen. Ich, Ioseph, schreibe dir: wenn du zu mir kommst wegen irgend etwas, das dazu gehört, so werde ich es dir besorgen. Ich Isak schreibe dir: ich werde nichts weiter von dir dafür verlangen, da du mir seinen Preis (τιμή) gegeben hast. Ich, Isak, der schon erwähnte, stimme dieser Urkunde (ἀσφάλεια) zu (στοιχεῖν). Ich, Petros, der Sohn des Eustachios, bin Zeuge. Ich, Samu[el, der Sohn des –]ousios bin Zeuge. Ich, Athan[asios, der Sohn des] Ioannes aus Patubas[tn, bin gebeten worden und] habe diese Urkunde geschrieben.'

[70] Such an undertaking may have been quite risky: obviously it relieved the creditor from the burden of taking care of the pledge, but what if debtor could not pay the debt and decided to forsake his property? Elżbieta Krakowiak, manager of the legal department working for a large Polish bank, has told me about quite a few cases in which the bank has mistakenly, having obtained the ownership of the security, let the debtor take care of it. One of these cases ended up in a substantial financial and reputational loss as the debtor was not eager to look after a herd of cows he thought he was going to lose anyway: (http://gdynia.naszemiasto. pl/archiwum/499666,bankowy-los-krowy,id,t.html?akcja=przejdz_nastepny).

[71] Cf. also the analogous situation in *P. KRU 57* by which Mena, son of Psaja of Pmiles in the District of Koptos, hands over to Ioseph, son of Petros from Romou in Ermont, one aroura of land for one and one third nomisma of gold that the latter had lent him to pay taxes (*demosion*). The debtor promises and guarantees to also take care of the field work at his own risk, with *force majeure* excluded. There are two guarantors, Philotheos, son of Daniel, and Christophoros, son of Demetrios, who additionally provide security for Mena.

things that are not *dreamt of in* legal *philosophy* just to feel more protected.[72] Even today – in the time and realm of codified law of real securities – the parties would choose the *Sicherungsübereignung* as simply more secure than the traditional form of the pledge.[73] The security of credit comes before the dogmatic disgust towards this legal form (in the famous M. Salinger's dictum referring to *Sicherungsübereigung* as the bastard child of the legal practice),[74] until eventually the elegant legal dogmatic surrenders to the practicality of the institution. It is doubtful therefore if Paul Oertmann's prophecy, that 'Fiducia geht und nimmer kehrt sie wieder', will ever come true. Transfer of ownership as a security for credit seems to be and to have always been simply intrinsic to legal anthropology.[75]

POSTILLA

Only upon completion of this chapter did I receive a copy of the newly published volume of the Petra papyri, extremely rich in legal problems. One of the longest papyri written *transversa charta* preserved to this day, *P. Petra* IV 39, dated 8 August 574 CE, records a settlement of claims after an arbitration between Theodoros and Stephanos. One of the issues between the litigants was the question of the ownership of a courtyard and a refuse-pit located

---

[72] Cf., for instance, two ingenious creations found in the milieu of Dioskoros. The pair of documents, *P. Michael.* 42 a + b (30 December 566 CE, Aphrodites Kome, Antaiopolites), a mortgage and lease form together a very skilful marriage financial settlement securing at best the interest of the bride. In the first deed, the groom and his parents secure the bride's dowry by conveying to her ten arurae (even if the document nominally calls the act 'a mortgage', the clauses employed show that it produces effective transfer of ownership of the land), whereas in the second, the bride leases the land back to her in-laws for a rent equalling the tax due on the field. The second case , *P. Cairo Masp.* II 67158 (= *FIRA* III 158, Antinoopolis, 28 April [?] 568 CE) is a contract of partnership of fine-carpenters whose real purpose seems to be a marital financial settlement between one party thereof (parents-in-law) and the other (their son-in-law); on this document, see further Urbanik (2012).

[73] In Poland, transfer of ownership (either under suspensive or resolutive condition, whereas the latter is preferred) made its way into legal practice chiefly thanks to bank loans and hence is only regulated in the *Bank Law Act* (*Journal of Laws* 2002, no. 72, item 665). Art. 101 allows the transfer of ownership of chattels and bills of exchange as security. The case of estates, on the other hand, is not regulated and has resulted in contradictory case law. German legal dogma, even if with some reservation, decided not to legislate the issue and to follow customary practice. Still, because of the existence in practice of the transfer of ownership as a form of security, German law does not admit the institution of a register bank pledge. See further, for example, Baur and Stuerner (2009), pp. 784–5.

[74] Salinger (1912), p. 409 (cited after Kettler (2008), p. 309, fn. 1392). 'Die Sicherungsübeignung ist ein Kind des Verkerhrs. Aber rein illegitimes, den es kann sich auf die Vaterschaft des Gesetzes nicht berufen. Das hat ihr zum Nachtteil gereicht. Einmal schon aus dem äußeren Grunden, weil ihr der Makel unechter Geburt anklebt. Mehr aber noch deshalb, weil der Manger der gesetzlichen Regelung sie wild hat aufwachsen lassen'. See also Hromadka (1980), p. 89.

[75] For a general historical panorama, see Thiesen (2001).

between their houses. Unfortunately, the state of conservation of the deed does not allow a safe reconstruction of the facts, and both parties claimed that their fathers had bought the property a long time before the dispute. Surprisingly, Theodoros also claimed to have acquired the courtyard from Kassisaios and Gregoria, who, in turn seem to have mortgaged the property to Gregoria's brother, Stephanos. The editor suggests that Stephanos' family have secured the ownership of the contended yard through *longi temporis praescriptio*,[76] but there seems to be no ground for such an interpretation. I suggest the argument may have arisen because of the original fiduciary sale of the courtyard by Gregoria and Kassisaios first to her brother and then to the neighbour Theodoros. This would only prove that the problem I have described in this chapter may have been much more common than the examples I have collected might suggest. We have only not been lucky enough to know the exact context of all the late Antique deeds of sale.[77]

APPENDIX

A. The abridged family tree of Patermouthis and Kako (after Geens (2005))

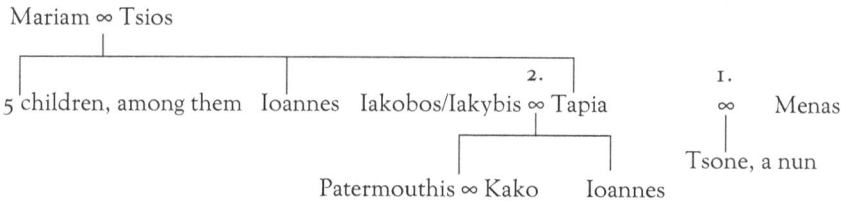

Mariam ∞ Tsios

5 children, among them Ioannes Iakobos/Iakybis ∞ Tapia   2.   1. ∞ Menas

Patermouthis ∞ Kako   Ioannes   Tsone, a nun

B. The abridged family tree of Aurelios Pachymios (after Geens (2003))

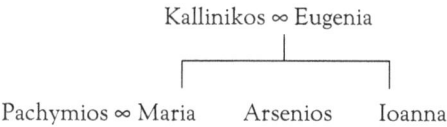

Kallinikos ∞ Eugenia

Pachymios ∞ Maria   Arsenios   Ioanna

---

[76] *P. Petra* IV, pp. 52–3.

[77] A thorough legal analysis of the papyrus is currently being prepared by Marzena Wojtczak (Warsaw) as part of her doctoral dissertation. Maria Nowak kindly informed me by email on 30 April 2012 that she has detected the same pattern of a 'mock' sale in *P. Lond.Copt.* 447 and 448 of unknown provenance published by Crum and in a Nubian deed from Qasr Ibrim she is presently studying (*Old Nubian Texts from Qaṣr Ibrīm* III 34).

BIBLIOGRAPHY

Alonso, J. L., 'The *Alpha* and *Omega* of *Hypallagma*', *JJP*, 38 (2008), p. 19.

Alonso, J. L., 'The *Bibliotheke Enkteseon* and the alienation of real securities in Roman Egypt', *JJP*, 40 (2010), p. 11.

Barison, P., 'Ricerche sui monasteri dell'Egitto bizantino ed Arabo', *Aegyptus*, 18 (1938), p. 29.

Barone Adesi, G., 'Il sistema giustinianeo delle proprietà eccesiastiche', in E. Cortese (ed.), *La proprietà e le proprietà* (1988), p. 75.

Barone Adesi, G., 'Dal dibattito cristiano sulla destinazione dei beni economici alla configurazione in termini di persona delle *venerabiles domus* destinate *piis causis*', in *Atti dell'Accademia Romanistica Costantiniana. IX Convegno Internazionale* (1993), p. 231.

Baur, J. F., and Stuerner, R., *Sachenrecht*, 18th edn (2009).

Bell, H. I., 'Syene papyri in the British Museum', *Klio*, 13 (1913), p. 160.

Clackson, S. J.,'Four Coptic papyri from the Pathermouthis Archive in the British Library', *Bulletin of the American Society of Papyrologists* 32 (1995), p. 97.

Dijkstra, J. H. F., 'New light on the Patermouthis Archive from excavations at Aswan. when archaeology and papyrology meet', *Bulletin of the American Society of Papyrologists*, 44 (2007), p. 179.

Farber, J. J., and Porten, B., 'The Pathermouthis Archive: a third look', *Bulletin of the American Society of Papyrologists*, 23 (1986), p. 81.

Farber, J. J., 'Family financial disputes in the Pathermouthis Archive', *Bulletin of the American Society of Papyrologists*, 27 (1990), p. 111.

Geens, K. 'Archive of Aurelius Pachymios, purple dealer', at *Leuven Homepage of Papyrus Collections* (2003), at http://www.trismegistos.org/arch/archives/pdf/36.pdf.

Geens, K., 'Archive of Flavius Patermouthis, son of Menas', at *Leuven Homepage of Papyrus Collections* (2005), at http://www.trismegistos.org/arch/archives/pdf/37.pdf.

Herrmann, J., 'Zur ὠνὴ ἐν πίστει des hellenistischen Rechts', in G. Thür (ed.), *Symposion 1985. Vorträge zur griechischen und hellenistischen Rechtsgeschichte* (1989), p. 317.

Hromadka, W., 'Sicherungsübereignung und Publizität', *Juristische Schulung* Heft 2 (1980), p. 89.

Husson, G., 'Houses in Syene in the Patermouthis Archive', *Bulletin of the American Society of Papyrologists*, 27 (1990), p. 123.

Kaser, M., *Das Römische Privatrecht*, vols I–II (*Handbuch der Altertumswissenschaft* X.3.3), 2nd edn (1971–5).

Kaser, M., *Studien zum römischen Pfandrecht* (*Antiqua* XVI) (1982).

Kettler, S. H., *Eigentumsvorbehalt und Sicherungsubereignung an beweglichen Sachen im Recht der russischen Föderation* (2008).

Kreuzsaler, C., 'Die Beurkundung außergerichtlicher Streitbeilegung in den ägyptischen Papyri', in C. Gastgeber (ed.), *Quellen zur byzantinischen Rechtspraxis. Aspekte der Textüberlieferung, Paläographie und Diplomatik Akten des internationalen Symposiums, Wien, 5.–7.11.2007* (2010), p. 17.

Kupiszewski, H., 'Quelques remarques sur les vocabula ἀντιχρήσις, ἄῤῥα, παραφήρνα dans le Digeste', *JJP* 18 (1974), p. 227 (= *Scritti Minori*, Napoli 2000), pp. 267–78).

Kupiszewski, H., 'Antichrese und Nutzpfand in den Papyri', in H.-P. Benöhr et al. (eds), *Iuris Professio. Festgabe M. Kaser zum 80. Geburtstag* (1986), p. 133 (= *Scritti minori*, Napoli (2000), p. 473).

Mitteis, J., and Wilcken, U., *Grundzüge und Chrestomathie der Papyruskunde*, 2 vols (1912).

Markiewicz, T., 'Security for debt in the Demotic papyri', *JJP*, 35 (2005), p. 141.

Markiewicz, T., 'The church, clerics, monks and credit in the papyri', in A. Boud'hors et al. (eds), *Monastic Estates in Late Antique and Early Islamic Egypt (P. Clackson) (American Studies in Papyrology* XLVI) (2009), p. 236.

McGing, B. C., 'The Melitian monks in Labla', *Tyche*, 5 (1990), p. 67.

Noordraven, B., *Die Fiduzia im römischen Recht* (1999).

Palme, P., 'Antwort auf Jakub Urbanik', in E. Cantarella, J. Mélèze Modrzejewski and G. Thür (eds), *Symposion 2005. Vorträge zur griechischen und hellenistischen Rechtsgeschichte* (2007), p. 401.

Pap. Eng. Eleph.: see Porten 1996

Pestman, P. W., 'Ventes provisoires de biens pour sûreté de dettes. ὠναὶ ἐν πίστει à Pathyris et à Krokodilopols', in P. W. Pestman (ed.), *Textes et études de papyrology grecque, démotique et copte* (P.L. Bat. XXIII) (1985), p. 45.

Pierce, R. H., *Three Demotic Papyri in the Brooklyn Museum* (1972).

Porten, B., and Farber, J. J., 'The Greek texts', in B. Porten et al. (eds), *The Elephantine Papyri in English* (1996), p. 386.

Porten, B., et al., *The Elephantine Papyri in English. Three Millennia of Cross-Cultural Continuity and Change* (1996).

Pringsheim, F., *The Greek Law of Sale* (1950).

Rupprecht, H.-A., 'Zur Antichrese in den griechischen Papyri bis Diokletian', in S. H. S. El-Mosalamy (ed.), *Proceedings of the XIXth International Congress of Papyrology* (1992), p. 271.

Rupprecht, H.-A., 'Die dinglichen Sicherungsrechte nach der Praxis der Papyri. Eine Übersicht über den urkundlichen Befund', in R. Feenstra et al. (eds), *Collatio iuris Romani. Études dédiées à Hans Ankum à l'occasion de son 65e anniversaire (= Studia Amstelodamensia ad epigraphicam, ius antiquum et papyrologicam pertinentia* XXXV) (1995), p. 425.

Salinger, M., 'Empfehlen sich gesetzliche Maßnahmen in Bezug auf die Sicherungsübereignung?,' in *Verhandlungen des 31. deutschen Juristentages*, vol. I (1912), p. x.

Sayce, A. H., 'Deux contrats grec du Fayoum', *Revue des Etudes Grecques*, 3 (1890), p. 131.

Schwarz, A. B., *Hypothek und Hypallagma, Beitrag zum Pfand-und Vollstreckungsrecht der griechischen Papyri* (1911).

Schwarz, A. B., 'Sicherungsübereignung und Zwangsvollstreckung in den Papyri (aus Anlass von *Stud. Ital.* XII)', *Aegyptus*, 17 (1937), p. 241.

Steinwenter, A. 'Die Rechtsstellung der Kirchen und Klöster nach den Papyri', ZSS (kan. Abt.), 19 (1930), p. 1.

Steinwenter, A., 'Review of *Coptic Ostraca from Medinet Habu*' ZSS (rom. Abt.), 71 (1954), p. 499.

Steinwenter, A., *Das Recht koptischen Urkunden* (1955) (HAW x.4.2).

Steinwenter, A., 'Aus dem kirchlichen Vermögensrechte der Papyri', ZSS (kan. Abt.), 44 (1958), p. 1.

Taubenschlag, R., *The Law of Greco-Roman Egypt in the Light of the Papyri 332 B.C.–640 A.D.*, 2nd edn (1955).

Taubenschlag, R., 'Die Geschichte der Rezeption des römischen Privatrechts in Ägypten', in *Opera minora*, vol. I (1959), p. 181 (originally published in *Studi in onore P. Bonfante*, I (1930).

Thiesen, F., 'Die Sicherungsübereignung und ihre römischrechtlichen Grundlagen in der Klassik. Betrachtungen des deutschen gemeinen Rechts des 19. Jahrhunderts', *TvR*, 67 (2001), p. 119.

Till, W. C., *Die koptischen Rechtsurkunden aus Theben* (1954).

Urbanik, J., 'Compromesso o processo? Alternativa risoluzione dei conflitti e tutela dei diritti nella prassi della tarda antichità' in E. Cantarella, J. Mélèze Modrzejewski and G. Thür (eds), *Symposion 2005. Vorträge zur griechischen und hellenistischen Rechtsgeschichte* (2007), p. 377.

Urbanik, J. 'Diligent carpenters in Dioscoros' papyri and the standard of diligence', in J. Urbanik (ed.), *Culpa, Acts of the Symposium* (2012).

Wipszycka, E., *Les resources et les activités économiques des églises en Égypte du IVe au VIIIe siècle* (1972).

Wipszycka, E., 'Le fonctionnement interne des monasteries et des laures en Égypte du point de vue économique', *JJP*, 31 (2001), p. 169.

Wipszycka, E., 'Monks and monastic dwellings. *P. Dubl.* 32–34, *P. KRU* 105 and BL Ms. Or. 6201–6206 revisited', in A. Boud'hors et al. (eds), *Monastic Estates in Late Antique and Early Islamic Egypt (P. Clackson) (American Studies in Papyrology XLVI)* (2009a), p. 178.

Wipszycka, E., *Moines et communautés monastique en Égypte (IVe–VIIIe siècles)*, (*The Journal of Juristic Papyrology. Supplement XI*) (2009b).

Part III

Economic Realities and Law

Chapter 9

Law, Agency and Growth in the Roman Economy

Dennis P. Kehoe

1. INTRODUCTION

In recent years, scholars have increasingly recognised the significant role that law and legal institutions could play in the Roman economy. Although population and technology, as in all pre-industrial economies, posed basic constraints on the possibilities for growth, law and legal institutions could play a decisive role in the organisation of economic activity and the distribution of wealth across society.[1] In several recent studies, I have sought to analyse how Roman law and legal policies affected the Roman Empire's rural economy.[2] I argued that, in formulating policies affecting various aspects of land tenure, the Roman legal authorities, including the classical jurists and the Roman chancery when it responded to petitions, were concerned with the economic consequences of the rules they formulated for land tenure. Above all, they recognised the importance of the long-term occupation of the land to the economic interests of both large landowners and the state. The rules they formulated tended to foster this, as they endeavoured to curb the worst effects of opportunistic behaviour, especially on the part of large landowners, who might take advantage of the precarious position of small farmers and tenants. The concern that the legal authorities government demonstrated in the rural economy raises the question whether they exhibited similar concerns in other key areas of the law affecting private property.

One area of the law that is likely to have had widespread economic consequences is agency, in the sense of people carrying out financial functions on behalf of others.[3] The most obvious form of agency in the Roman world involved business agents, such as freedmen managing businesses or commercial ventures on behalf of wealthy property owners, and it seems clear that the social and legal institutions surrounding this form of agency had important implications for the organisation of commerce in the Roman Empire, and,

---

[1] The importance of population and technology in setting the parameters for economic development is emphasised in many chapters in the new *Cambridge Economic History of the Greco-Roman World* (2007).

[2] Kehoe (2007); Kehoe (forthcoming).

[3] On agency issues, see in general Furubotn and Richter (2005), pp. 162–70.

by extension, for the possibilities for economic development.[4] I will focus, however, on another form of agency important for the Roman economy, namely, the role that guardians, or tutors, played in managing the property of fatherless children, wards, or pupils.[5] Tutorship was certainly an institution that affected a significant portion of the property in the Roman Empire. In his model of the demographic structure of Roman society, Richard Saller posits that about one third of Roman children would have lost their fathers by the age of fourteen.[6] In addition, many of the same rules that Roman law developed for tutors who managed the property for underage orphans also applied to minors (males under the age of twenty-five), who were commonly represented in their business dealings by curators. In Saller's reconstruction, another third of the children would have lost their fathers by the age of twenty-five. In view of this situation, an analysis of agency relationships connected with tutorship had potentially important economic consequences, since the rules surrounding this institution affected the disposition of a considerable portion of the Empire's property. In formulating rules for tutorship, as I will argue, the Roman legal authorities faced an immediate challenge, but the rules they developed to respond to it had wider implications for society. On the one hand, pupils required protection against any threat to their property. The problem was that, as agents, tutors operated largely autonomously. So the Roman legal authorities had to develop rules, and sanctions for violating them, that aligned the tutor's incentives with the interests of the pupil. On the other hand, these rules could be too stringent if they gave the tutor a positive disincentive to invest the pupil's property in potentially lucrative economic activities. The result would be that the pupil's property would be used 'inefficiently' (as defined below), at a loss to society. The rules for tutorship, then, could have a very real effect on the ways in which property in the Roman world was used, and so would represent part of the broad institutional constraints to which the Roman economy was subject.

The difficulty, of course, is to develop a methodology to analyse the economic ramifications of Roman agency law. In what follows, I will examine the likely economic consequences of the Roman legal rules surrounding agency by drawing from the contemporary debate on the relationship between law and the economy in the fields of law and economics and the New Institutional Economics (NIE). One particular advantage to this debate is that it presents a useful methodology for understanding the economic incentives arising from various definitions of property rights, as well as the

---

[4] Agency in business relationships is addressed in Frier and Kehoe (2007), pp. 122–34, and in Kehoe (forthcoming).

[5] An analysis of agency relationships can be extended to cover many other activities, including lease relationships, the contract of mandate, and even dowry; see Frier and Kehoe (2007), pp. 122–6.

[6] Saller (1994), pp. 189–90.

difficulties involved in changing such definitions to more productive ones. An analysis of the Roman legal institutions surrounding agency suggests the difficulties that the Roman legal authorities faced in adapting long-standing social institutions to the changing needs of Roman society. As I will argue, to protect the interests of orphans and minors, the Roman legal authorities imposed restrictions on tutors' scope for action as well as devastating penalties when they failed in their duties. These policies were designed to overcome the difficulties involved in monitoring agents, but at the same time the restrictions they imposed on the management of pupils' property diminished the possibilities for aggressive investment in entrepreneurial activities that could enhance economic growth.

It will be useful at the outset to sketch out some important theoretical perspectives offered by the fields of law and economics and NIE. These provide a starting point to analyse the likely effects on the Roman economy of 'institutional arrangements', which include laws and property rights, court systems, and the like, as well as informal institutions, such as social norms and customs, that establish the 'rules of the game' under which individuals engage in economic activity.[7] NIE takes into account basic constraints that affect economic activity and decision-making. These constraints include 'transaction costs', a concept that encompasses all the costs associated with creating and maintaining property rights, such as the costs of obtaining information, negotiating and enforcing contracts. A second constraint can be understood as 'bounded rationality', a term denoting constraints on our knowledge that limit our ability to make optimising decisions. In other words, knowledge is costly, so any analysis of the development and performance of economic institutions has to take into account the costs of acquiring information and the difficulty of evaluating, say, one approach to investing wealth against another.[8] Economic institutions are considered 'efficient' when they allow resources to be put to their highest valued use.[9] In theory, institutions that are inefficient, in that they prevent people from making more remunerative use of available resources, eventually fail, to be replaced by more efficient ones. In the case of tutorship, the evolution of institutions is not likely to be so straightforward, since it was an institution that was not primarily oriented towards profit. Instead, the institutions imposed restrictions on tutors as managers of private property to which other Roman property owners were not subject. Since the purpose of these restrictions was to protect the financial interests of a key social group, they would remain in effect as long as society valued this protection.

[7] For an introduction to NIE, see Mercuro and Medema (1997), pp. 130–56, and Klein (2000); for further discussion, see Frier and Kehoe (2007); Kehoe (2007), pp. 29–39, and Kehoe (forthcoming). For 'the rules of the game', see North (1990).
[8] For 'bounded rationality', see Simon (1983) and Simon (1986); as well as Williamson (1985).
[9] For this concept of efficiency, see Coase (1960).

2. TUTORSHIP AND AGENCY

Tutors can be usefully analysed as agents working on behalf of pupils, since they were responsible for managing pupils' property in such a way as to protect their long-term interests, and enforcing their obligations as agents was a thorny problem for the Roman legal authorities. The tutorship of orphans was an institution basic to Roman society.[10] In Roman law, fatherless children, up to the age of fourteen for boys and twelve for girls, were subject to the supervision of tutors, *tutores*. Tutors might be named by the father in his will (*tutores testmentarii*), gain this position because of their agnatic relationship with the child (tutors by law, or *tutores legitimi*), or, in the event that no candidates for these two categories were available, be appointed by a magistrate (*tutores dativi*). The tutor was responsible for managing the property of the ward, or pupil, as well as for providing for the pupil's support including education, food, clothing, and housing, and other expenses associated with the pupil's social class and resources, such as slaves and, for a female pupil, a dowry. For understanding agency relationships in the Roman economy, the most important duty for the tutor was his management of the pupil's finances. In this area of the law, the overriding concern of the legal authorities was to protect the resources of a vital and vulnerable social class against any threat to the loss of their property, and so they imposed stringent rules on the tutors who were responsible for administering the pupils' property. Surely one motivation for these rules was to protect the resources of a class of people who in the future would be called upon to hold municipal offices and perform liturgical duties for their home towns. Many of the same rules imposed on the property belonging to pupils also affected the property of minors, fatherless men under the age of twenty-five, who were also considered vulnerable to ill-considered financial decisions, in particular, the restrictions on alienating land, to be discussed below.[11]

The major problem that exists in all agency relationships, the asymmetries of information between principal and agent, was especially acute in tutorship. In agency relationships, the agent commonly has greater knowledge of the business he is conducting than the principal, and so is in a position to engage in opportunistic behaviour at the principal's expense. In theory, the tutor as agent had complete power over the pupil's property. The tutor purchased property for the pupil, managed his or her income, lent the pupil's

---

[10] For basic discussion of the duties of tutors and curators, see Saller (1994), pp. 181–203, as well as Kehoe (1997), pp. 22–76, and Kaser (1971), pp. 85–91, 352–72.

[11] Although a curator's authority was not strictly required for a minor to complete a significant financial transaction, a transaction was subject to being rescinded, that is, a *restitutio in integrum*, if the minor could show that it was to his financial disadvantage. For this reason, it was easier to transact business with a minor when he was aided by a *curator*. See Lenel (1914), pp. 132–5.

money out at interest, and spent money on the pupil's behalf. An unscrupulous tutor was in the position to take advantage of his responsibilities and use the pupil's property for his own purposes, or, in the worst-case scenario, steal from it. The question is whether Roman law developed adequate oversight mechanisms to protect the interests of the pupil.

Monitoring agents was a basic problem in commercial relationships in the Roman world, and in this sector of the economy, Roman society developed a combination of formal legal institutions and social values to maintain a workable system of agency. The greater integration of Roman commercial markets in the Mediterranean world would not have been possible without adequate means of enforcing contracts between trading partners, as well as mechanisms by which Roman property owners could exercise reasonable oversight over their employees or agents in far-flung locations.[12] Any solution to this problem involved aligning the interests of business agents with those of the property owner by providing the former group with incentives to work productively for their principals, while also reserving for the principal the means to sanction an unsatisfactory agent. The Romans approached this problem by relying on social dependants, slaves or freedmen, as agents. The use of social dependants as agents finds its origin, to a large extent, in the institutions of a society largely dependent on the ownership and employment of slaves.[13] The *familia* provided a ready-made structure around which to organise business activities, just as it did in the Empire to organise the bureaucracy of the Roman government, as represented by the *familia Caesaris*.[14] A slave operating with a *peculium* became an independent businessman in his own right. As a kind of 'residual claimant', the slave had many of the same incentives as an owner of the business, so it would be in his interest to operate the business properly, since, unless there was some catastrophic falling out with his owner, he could be confident of retaining the profits that he generated. The agent also would take on much of the responsibility of running the business, including the monitoring of employees, many of whom were also slaves, and in many circumstances it seems clear that agents could act quite independently of their employers. This pattern of organising business was common in many areas of the Roman economy, not just in the business affairs of the wealthiest Romans, but also in much more modest levels of production and commerce, and its advantages are well known. By using slaves operating with a *peculium* as business managers, Roman property owners were in a position to provide specialised training to certain highly skilled individuals while

---

[12] For this section I have drawn on some of the conclusions from Frier and Kehoe (2007), pp. 126–34, which discusses some additional examples. I address the subject more briefly in Kehoe (2011).

[13] For Rome as a slave society, see Bradley (1994), pp. 10–30. For an overview of slavery in the Roman Empire, see now Bradley (2011).

[14] Weaver (1972).

also being more assured of reaping the benefit of their investment in human capital. Such a pattern of training and employing social dependants was an essential feature in many types of commercial activity in the Roman world; Gunnar Fülle's detailed analysis of the Arretine ceramic industry indicates how this system worked in the training of highly skilled artisans producing products of considerable commercial importance.[15]

To the extent that this system of employing social dependants as agents solved problems of monitoring, it did so by making the agent as independent from the principal as possible, and limiting the involvement of the principal in the slave (or freed) agent's activities. This limitation finds an expression in the remedies that Roman law created to allow people doing business with slave agents to sue their owners to enforce obligations. Originally in Roman law, a property owner would assume no liability for obligations assumed by third parties. In the third or second centuries BCE, however, a series of six remedies was introduced, later called the *actiones adiecticiae qualitatis*.[16] These remedies afforded some protection to people engaging in contracts with agents representing principals, such as sons in power or slaves who disposed over *peculia* with which they operated their businesses. Through these actions, the praetor granted people who were owed money by agents or who had otherwise entered into contractual relationships a way to recover their losses by suing the principal, the *pater familias* or the slave-owner. In many cases, the liability of the principal was limited to a slave agent's *peculium*, or the agent, functioning as an *institor*, had to have the principal's permission to obligate the latter party (although it seems that this permission was commonly assumed). Certainly it would be an oversimplification to see these legal remedies as directly serving the needs of a society in which commercial life was highly decentralised, with agents working mostly independently with funds provided by a principal, whose chief interest in the activities of his agent was simply to be paid some return on the money he invested in him. In complex commercial undertakings, no matter what the strict requirements of the law were, property owners would have every incentive to make good on the obligations entered into by their agents, since failing to do so would impede their ability to do business in the future.

The control that the property owner exercised over a slave or freedman working as an agent would give him considerable leverage to protect against the agent's opportunistic behaviour, but the sanctions that the owner could impose, such as revoking a promise of freedom, removing financial support from a freedman, or even returning a freedman to slavery, would probably only work as a last resort. They would not allow the property owner to recover losses, and they would effectively tend to end any cooperation

---

[15] Fülle (1997).

[16] On the *actiones adiecticiae qualitiatis*, see de Ligt (1999); Aubert (1994), pp. 46–91; Plescia (1984).

between the principal and agent. Crucially important for enforcement, as Henrik Mouritsen argues, in his recent study of the role that freedmen played in Roman society, was an ideology that praised slaves and freedman for virtues such as *probitas* and *fides*.[17] This ideology emphasised the freedman's continuing loyalty. The freedman lived in accordance with a substantially different code of virtue from that of a freeborn citizen. The ideology that Mouritsen analyses seems designed to enforce trust precisely in those situations in which it was very difficult for a patron or principal to exercise any kind of meaningful control over an agent, because of the asymmetries of information involved.

Monitoring tutors

Tutorship as a system of agency posed perhaps even more complicated problems of enforcement, because the relationship between the tutor and pupil represented an extreme in the asymmetries of information between an agent and a principal. Certainly avenues existed to enforce the removal of a tutor who was suspected of malfeasance while managing the affairs of a pupil. The *actio suspecti tutoris* provided a procedure for sanctioning a tutor appointed in the will. This action, which could be brought by anyone, was a criminal procedure.[18] A testamentary tutor who was found to have acted in a fraudulent manner would be removed from his post and replaced by another, and at the same time would be declared *infamis* (see below). Tutors by law were subject to the *actio rationibus distrahendis*; if they were found to have acted fraudulently, they were subject to a double penalty of the property taken. This measure was apparently available only after the end of the tutorship, however. A further protection consisted in the requirement that tutors provide a stipulation that the property of the pupil would be secure, as well as offering sureties to support this undertaking. The provision of sureties was demanded of tutors by law and those appointed by magistrates, but not of tutors appointed in the will or by high-ranking magistrates such as the consuls, since in these circumstances the reputation of the tutor was deemed to be beyond reproach. Notwithstanding the occasional legal intervention when a tutor was suspected of malfeasance, the pupil's main opportunity to recover from a tutor for mismanagement was to sue him in the *actio tutelae*, a remedy that was only available after the tutor's service was over. Bringing this action against the tutor after the fact, however, might be cold comfort for the pupil whose property had been raided, if the tutor had become insolvent. To protect against this possibility, Roman law made co-tutors all liable in full for whatever losses the pupil suffered. Certainly the vigilance of close connections of orphaned children, especially the mother,

---

[17] Mouritsen (2011), pp. 206–47.
[18] On these procedures, see Kaser (1971), pp. 363–7; Saller (1994), pp. 185–7.

could be crucial in monitoring the actions of tutors, but the asymmetries of information remained.

The Roman legal authorities seem to have been well aware of the vulnerable position of pupils, and accordingly they developed rules that sought to protect the pupil's interests by carefully defining the tutor's responsibilities in managing the property and also circumscribing the tutor's freedom of action. Tutors had a positive responsibility to invest the pupil's money appropriately so as to provide a stable income. They could not allow the pupil's money to lie idle, and they could be required to pay interest for the period in which they failed to invest the pupil's funds. Whenever possible, the tutor was to use these funds to purchase land. Previously, I have argued that the responsibilities that the Roman legal authorities imposed on tutors in administering the property of pupils stemmed from a cautious approach to financial decision-making characteristic of upper-class Romans.[19] From this perspective, land was privileged over all other forms of investment, and the tutor could be interpreted as fulfilling his responsibilities by purchasing land and leasing it out. In the understanding of the Roman jurists, it would not be difficult to determine whether the tutor had acted prudently in managing the pupil's property when he took this step, since the price of the land was a function of the rent that it provided. Tutors of course could be liable when they purchased unsuitable land through fraud, but otherwise they were liable only for broad negligence in purchasing land (D.26.7.7 2–3) (Ulpian. 35 ad Ed.). Only when it was not possible to purchase land – say, when insufficient funds were available – was the tutor expected to lend the pupil's money out at interest; such loans could presumably cover a wide range of purposes, from consumer loans to investment in businesses. In enforcing such loans, the tutor was expected to display the same care and energy with the pupil's money as he would with his own.

The important point is that the law imposed restrictions on the tutor that in some cases could have sacrificed income for the pupil, but these restrictions provided clear guidelines for the tutor, and also mitigated the effects on the finances of pupils as a class that might be caused by incompetent or unenergetic management on the part of the tutor. Thus the tutor was discouraged from alienating any land that the pupil might own. One could imagine circumstances in which this might be financially advantageous for the pupil, say, when selling property in an inconvenient location to purchase something more easily managed might actually reduce costs for the pupil. In some circumstances, mortgaging land to undertake a potentially lucrative business venture might provide profits to the pupil unavailable through his or her landed property. None of this was legally permissible, and the Roman legal authorities' preference for caution reached its fullest expression with legislation enacted by the emperor Septimius Severus in 195, the so-called

---

[19] Kehoe (1997).

Oratio Severi (D.27.9.1) (Ulpian. 35 ad Ed.). This law made it unlawful for the tutor to sell, mortgage, or otherwise alienate the pupil's land, except to pay off debts; its provisions were also applied to curators managing the property of minors.[20] Even to sell property to pay off a debt, tutors had to gain permission from the provincial governor. The basic premise behind this legislation is that land represented the best assurance of long-term financial security, and so protecting pupils against any possible threat to their continued ownership of land was the best means to look after their interests.

The Roman government would apply this conception of land as a form of economic security in other areas of the law, especially in late Antiquity. Thus the late imperial government was concerned to maintain the resources of a group vital for local office holding and the performance of liturgies, and so it discouraged the alienation of land by members of town councils across the empire.[21] To ensure the continued provision of ships to serve the *annona* at Rome and Constantinople, it linked the ownership of land with the duty to invest in cargo ships. In effect, the government designated the lands belonging to the shipowners as security for their continued investment in shipping.[22] As the ownership of ships serving the *annona*, like other key professions, became hereditary, the duty to invest in ships came to be imposed as a kind of lien on certain lands.

Penalties for tutors

Tutors served as agents responsible for managing a considerable portion of the private property in the Roman Empire. To understand the economic implications of this service, it will be helpful to consider it from the perspective of a contractual relationship with their pupils, although Roman law did not define tutorship in this way. There are two significant aspects of contract law that are important for understanding the role of the tutor as agent, the notion of 'default rules' in a contract, and the penalties imposed for breach of contract.

In any system of contract law, a key element in defining the property rights of the parties involved the enforcement of default rules. Default rules serve to fill in 'gaps' in the contract, that is, contingencies that the parties could not take the time to negotiate at the outset of their relationship, either because they were unforeseen or because it would simply be too costly to negotiate

---

[20] For full discussion of the *Oratio Severi*, see Kehoe (1997), pp. 54–67.

[21] See, for example, the decree of the emperors Valentinian, Theodosius and Arcadius making it unlawful for a decurion to sell rural or urban properties without the intervention of a judge (C.10.34.1, CTh.12.3.1, 386 CE). The emperors Honorius and Theodosius II required that the approval be gained from the provincial governor rather than simply from a judge (CTh.12.3.2, 423 CE).

[22] See, for example, C.11.3.1 (CTh.13.6.5, 367 CE), 11.3.2 (CTh.13.6.7, 375 CE), 11.3.3 (CTh.13.6.8, 399 CE).

all possible ones.[23] Modern courts, at least in the US, tend to impose default rules that are termed 'majoritarian' or 'market-mimicking', in that they would represent the preference of what most contracting parties would have negotiated had they taken the time to do so, and not what the individual people in the contract might have preferred. The other type of default rule would be 'tailored' toward the preferences of the parties involved in the contract under dispute. As we will see, the Roman legal authorities tended to follow majoritarian default rules, which offer the advantage that the courts are spared the often difficult task of figuring out the intentions of the parties. At the same time, the treatment of contracts in courts will be predictable, so parties will have a baseline against which to negotiate before a dispute ever ends in court. In the Roman consensual contract, sale, lease, partnership, and mandate, the default rules depended on the good faith of both parties, which in turn revolved around the common meaning of the terms that might be part of a contract.[24]

From the perspective of tutorship as an agency contract, Roman law ruled out any deviation from a 'majoritarian' default rule, imposing the same stringent set of rules on all tutors. Before the promulgation of the Severan legislation that imposed severe restrictions on tutors, the legal validity of transactions involving the property of pupils would have been subject to a great deal of uncertainty. The law protected the pupil against the tutor's mismanagement of his or her property, but the relief often came only after the completion of the tutorship, when the former pupil could sue the tutor to recover any losses that his faulty management of the pupil's property might have caused. With the promulgation of the Severan legislation that imposed severe restrictions on tutors in managing pupils' property, the rules became more clear-cut for both people entering into financial relationships with tutors, and for the tutors themselves. To address the interests of the former group, for someone seeking to purchase property belonging to a pupil or to lend money against the security of the pupil's property, the rules surrounding such a transaction became transparent and predictable. The requirement to obtain the approval of the provincial governor before entering into a contract involving the pupil's real property would provide a strong disincentive for people to make unauthorised purchases of pupil's property, since such contracts could not be enforced in court and would be subject to being rescinded. Likewise, the same rule would deter tutors from entering into such contracts. At the same time, the strict rules imposed on tutors would provide them with some protection, since they could follow a prescribed set of norms in managing their pupils' property and avoid civil

---

[23] For default rules, see Craswell (2000), as well as Schwartz (1992), and Ayres and Gertner (1989), and Katz (1990), p. 217, among a great deal of literature.

[24] I plan to address this issue further in a paper called 'Contracts, agency, and transactions costs in the Roman economy'.

and criminal liability. Thus a tutor would be interpreted as having fulfilled his duty if he maintained his pupil's agricultural property and leased it out for a conventional rent, one that represented a commonly accepted return on the property's nominal value (see above).[25] When the tutor loaned the pupil's money at interest, he would be protected from liability if he showed that he demonstrated the same diligence in enforcing these loans as he did with loans of his own money.[26] The tutor would not be liable simply because the loan turned out badly. The carefully crafted and stringent 'default' rules limited the tutor's discretion in managing the pupil's property and so helped to overcome some of the disadvantages arising from the asymmetries of information inherent in the tutor's service.

From the perspective of an agency contract, another important issue concerns the penalties that might be imposed on the tutor if he failed in his fiduciary obligations toward the pupil. The restrictions on the tutor's scope of action provided one means of protecting the pupil's interests, but the difficulty of monitoring the tutor remained, since generally the full scope of the tutor's actions could only be known after his service was over, at the *actio tutelae* (see above). In this type of lawsuit, Roman law did require the tutor to compensate the pupil for any losses from his property resulting from negligence. In so doing, Roman law made the tutor liable to something akin to 'expectation damages' in modern contract law.[27] Expectation damages provide greater compensation to a party to a contract that has been breeched than 'reliance' or 'restitution' damages. Restitution damages compensate the party suffering a breach for only what he has provided to the party who has breached the contract. With reliance damages, the party suffering the breach is better protected, since he is owed any investment that he has made in connection with the contract whereas expectation damages restore lost profits.[28] This degree of liability corresponds to that of the tutor toward the pupil, since the tutor was not only required to restore any property lost to the pupil through his negligence, but also to pay interest if he failed to enforce loans of the pupil's money or otherwise failed to collect money owed to the pupil. The tutor was generally expected to display the same standard of care with the pupil's property as with his own. But this degree of liability could only provide the pupil with meaningful protection if the tutor had sufficient property. As we have seen, Roman law addressed this issue by requiring certain tutors to provide sureties for their performance, and magistrates who appointed insolvent tutors could themselves be held liable for losses resulting from the tutor's failure.[29]

---

[25] For the tutor's purchasing land on behalf of the pupil, see Kehoe (1997), pp. 38–42.

[26] For discussion of the relevant legal texts on lending the pupil's money, see Kehoe (1997), pp. 49–54.

[27] Craswell (2000), p. 3; Mahoney (2000); De Geest and Wuyts (2000), p. 143.

[28] Mahoney (2000), p. 121.

[29] Kaser (1971), p. 364.

Perhaps the penalty resulting from an unfavourable judgment in the *actio tutelae* that provided the strongest deterrence against the tutor's malfeasance was *infamia*. Since tutorship was one of several legal relationships involving *bona fides*, or good faith, an adverse judgment involved *infamia*, which meant that the tutor, as *infamis*, was removed from Rome's 'community of honor', or 'meritocracy of virtue', to use the formulation of Thomas McGinn. Being *infamis* barred a person from many aspects of Roman social and political life involving honour. At first, the tutor would incur *infamia* only for deliberate misconduct, or *dolus*, but this sanction was extended to cover broad negligence on the part of the tutor.[30] The penalty of *infamia*, which did nothing to restore the pupil's property, functioned to some degree like the penalties that could be imposed on freedmen who failed in their role as agents for Roman property owners, such as being forced back into slavery, or even being cut off from the patron's financial and social support. *Infamia* was a severe penalty that in theory induced tutors, as members of Rome's elite classes, to act in accordance with norms essential to the orderly functioning of society, but not fully enforceable by the courts. From another perspective, the severe penalty of *infamia* could be viewed as comparable to penalty clauses in contracts. These clauses tend to overcompensate one side for breach of contract, but they are included to induce both parties' compliance with the agreement. In the law of tutorship, the issue was not compliance with a contract, but deterring fraud (and negligence), which can be hard to detect until it is too late. From a theoretical perspective, when violations are difficult to detect, severe penalties, imposed in rare cases, can be an effective means of enforcement.[31]

The expectations about the tutor's duties as an agent for the pupil and the penalties for his failing to meet them imposed considerable costs on society. As mentioned previously, given likely ancient life expectancies, a very substantial portion of the empire's private property was under the management of tutors or curators. The restrictions on alienating pupils' land, like the late imperial restrictions on land belonging to decurions and ship owners, certainly must have imposed significant limits on the market for agricultural land. To the extent that pupils or minors could not alienate land, even when it was in their interest to do so, this must have discouraged potentially profitable commercial ventures, while also distorting the market for agricultural land by creating an artificial scarcity.[32] But to protect themselves against liability in an *actio tutelae*, it seems logical that many tutors would have exercised extreme caution in managing the pupil's property, say, by purchasing land but taking no steps to invest the pupil's money in improving it to gain

---

[30] For the penalty of *infamia* in the *actio tutelae*, see Kaser (1971), p. 510. For the notion of Rome's 'community of honor', see McGinn (1998), pp. 21–69, 213.

[31] See De Geest and Wuyts (2000), pp. 152–3.

[32] Saller (1994), pp. 181–203; Crook (1976).

a larger return, or avoiding risk at all costs when lending the pupil's money out at interest.

3. CONCLUSION

In this chapter, I have sought to show how an economic analysis of agency in an area of the law of undeniable importance to Roman society can help us come to a better understanding of the complex relationship between law and the economy of the Roman Empire. The institution of tutorship arose out of a basic concern to protect the property of underage orphans. But the legal regulations shaping the institution of tutorship seem designed to protect pupils in a relationship characterised by substantial asymmetries of information between principal and agent. Viewed in this way, the legal institutions surrounding these forms of agency, like the institutions surrounding agents serving as business managers for wealthy property owners, can be regarded as 'instrumental,' in the sense that they were established or developed by policy-makers to achieve particular goals, in these two cases to protect the interests of important constituencies in the Roman world.[33] The forms of agency that I have discussed in this chapter were the products, then, of both the basic structures of Roman society and upper-class economic interests. They fulfilled basic goals, and so can be seen, from the perspective of bounded rationality, as 'satisficing' solutions, even if they were not 'efficient', in the sense of promoting the most valued use of resources and fostering economic growth.

The development and maintenance of legal institutions designed to protect the interests of pupils had broader implications for the Roman economy. In developing rules for this type of agency, the Roman legal authorities were guided by a basic understanding of the Roman economy that they shared with other members of their class, and so to this extent it can be argued that they were aware of the economic implications of their policies. But the law of tutorship was not developed to serve an economic policy, but to achieve a social goal, with costs imposed on the economy as a whole.[34] To the extent that the law of tutorship had consequences for the distribution of wealth in Roman society, it supported efforts to maintain the economic viability of a broad class of property owners in the Roman Empire, not simply the wealthiest members of the elite, but property owners who would eventually serve on town councils around the Empire. The law of tutorship, then, represented an institution that promoted stability and thus the efforts of the Roman government to maintain the broad social structure essential to its policies in ruling the empire.

---

[33] For this concept of 'instrumental' institutions, see Greif (2006), pp. 40–1.
[34] For discussion of this problem, see Ogilvie (2007), and earlier Rutherford (1994).

BIBLIOGRAPHY

Aubert, J.-J., *Business Managers in Ancient Rome: A Social and Economic Study of Institores, 200 B.C.–A.D. 250* (1994).

Ayres, I., and Gertner, R., 'Filling gaps in incomplete contracts: an economic theory of default rules', *Yale Law J.*, 99 (1989), p. 87.

Bouckaert, B., and de Geest, G. (eds), *Encyclopedia of Law and Economics*. 5 vols (2000). Online edition (1999): http://users.ugent.be/~gdegeest/.

Bradley, K., *Slavery and Society at Rome* (1994).

Bradley, K., 'Slavery under the Principate', in K. Bradley and P. Cartledge (eds), *The Cambridge World History of Slavery*, vol. 1: *The Ancient Mediterranean World* (2011), p. 265.

Coase, R. H., 'The problem of social cost', *J. Law Econ* (1960), p. 1, reprinted in R. H. Coase, *The Firm, the Market, and the Law* (1990).

Craswell, R., 'Contract law: general theories', in B. Bouckaert and G. de Geest (eds), *Encyclopedia of Law and Economics*, vol. III (2000), p. 1.

Crook, J., 'Classical Roman law and the sale of land', in M. I. Finley (ed.), *Studies in Roman Property* (1976), p. 71.

De Geest, G., and F. Wuyts, F., 'Penalty clauses and liquidated damages', in B. Bouckaert and G. de Geest (eds), *Encyclopedia of Law and Economics*, vol. III (2000), p. 141.

De Ligt, L., 'Legal history and economic history: the case of the *actiones adiecticiae qualitatis*', *TvR*, 47 (1999), p. 205.

Frier, B. W., and Kehoe, D. P., 'Law and economic institutions', in W. Scheidel, I. Morris, and R. P. Saller (eds), *Cambridge Economic History of the Greco-Roman World* (2007), p. 113.

Fülle, G., 'The internal organization of the Arretine *terra sigillata* industry: problems of evidence and interpretation', *JRS*, 87 (1997), p. 111.

Furubotn, E. G. and Richter, R., *Institutions and Economic Theory: The Contribution of New Institutional Economics* (2005).

Greif, A., *Institutions and the Path to the Modern Economy: Lessons from Medieval Trade* (2006).

Kaser, M., *Das römische Privatrecht. Erster Abschnitt, Das altrömische, das vorklassische und klassische Recht. Handbuch der Altertumswissenschaft*, 2nd edn (1971).

Katz, A. W. (ed.), *Foundations of the Economic Approach to Law* (1998).

Kehoe, D. P., *Investment, Profit, and Tenancy: The Jurists and the Roman Agrarian Economy* (1997).

Kehoe, D. P., *Law and the Rural Economy in the Roman Empire* (2007).

Kehoe, D. P., 'Law and Social Formation in the Roman Empire', in M. Peachin (ed.), *The Oxford Social History of the Roman Empire* (2011), p. 144.

Kehoe, D. P., 'Roman Economic Policy and the Law of Contracts', in T. A. J. McGinn (ed.), *The Future of Obligations* (forthcoming).

Klein, P. G., 'New Institutional Economics', in B. Bouckaert and G. de Geest (eds), *Encyclopedia of Law and Economics*, vol. I (2000), p. 456.

Lenel, O., Die *cura minorum* in der klassischen Zeit', *ZSS* (rom. Abt.) 35 (1914), p. 129.

Mahoney, P. G., 'Contract remedies: general', in B. Bouckaert and G. de Geest (eds), *Encyclopedia of Law and Economics*, vol. III (2000), p. 117.

Mercuro, N., and Medema, S. G., *Economics and the Law: From Posner to Post-Modernism* (1997).

McGinn, T. A. J., *Prostitution, Sexuality, and the Law in Ancient Rome* (1998).

Mouritsen, H., *The Freedman in the Roman World* (2011).

North, D. C., *Institutions, Institutional Change and Economic Performance* (1990, repr. 2002).

Plescia, J., 'The development of agency in Roman law', *Labeo*, 30 (1984), p. 171.

Rutherford, M., *Institutions in Economics: The Old and the New Institutionalism* (1994).

Saller, R. P., *Patriarchy, Property and Death in the Roman Family* (1994).

Scheidel, W., Morris, I., and Saller, R. P. (eds), *The Cambridge Economic History of the Greco-Roman World* (2007).

Schwartz, A., 'Relational contracts in the courts: an analysis of incomplete agreements and judicial strategies', *JLS*, 21 (1992), p. 271.

Simon, H., *Reason in Human Affairs* (1983).

Simon, H., 'Rationality in psychology and economics', *J. Bus.*, 59 (1986), p. 209, excerpted in Katz (1998), p. 288–303.

Weaver, P. R. C., *Familia Caesaris: A Social Study of the Emperor's Freedmen and Slaves* (1972).

Williamson, O. E., *The Economic Institutions of Capitalism: Firms, Markets, Relational Contracting* (1985).

Chapter 10

Dumtaxat de peculio: *What's in a* Peculium, *or Establishing the Extent of the Principal's Liability*

Jean-Jacques Aubert

1. INTRODUCTION

In contrast with modern slave systems, the Graeco-Roman world used slaves in all kinds of ways and functions. Besides what we consider liberal trades, such as medicine or banking, there is plenty of evidence for slaves being involved in business activities, producing and distributing goods and services, or in public administration at all levels of government. Roman law regards slaves as things (*res*), which implies that they could avail themselves of no legal rights, no juristic personality and no patrimonial capacity. Their condition was, however, no obstacle to their participating in management, as shown by the case of one Midas in charge of a perfumery in late fourth-century BCE Athens, recorded by the speechwriter Hyperides. We will return to this case shortly.[1]

Craftsmen, traders and businessmen (and businesswomen) of servile status had many an opportunity to enter into contractual relationships with others, be they citizens, resident aliens and foreign travellers, freedmen, or slaves. In Athenian law, just like in archaic Roman law, contracts made by slaves apparently entailed no legal sanctions, social or religious pressure being presumably sufficient to enforce their provisions through fulfilment of obligations by both parties, whatever their respective social, economic and legal status.[2] In pre-classical Roman law, all acquisitions by a slave benefit-ted the master's patrimony exclusively, while conveyances were considered legally void, according to the twofold principle that slaves were entitled to better, meaning increase, their master's patrimony, though not to worsen, meaning decrease, it. Such an imbalance was detrimental to those who wanted, needed, or were compelled to do business with slaves, while lowering the latter's practical efficiency and therefore economic value. Consequently, Roman praetors devised ways of correcting this situation during the mid or late Republican period (at some point between the late third and early first centuries BCE) by granting business people a set of legal remedies (*actiones*)

---

[1] Hyperid., *c. Athenog.* Cf. Aubert (2007), pp. 215–30.

[2] For religious sanctions against patrons convicted of deceiving their clients, cf. XII Tables 8.10 (Crawford 1996) = 8.21 (*FIRA* I², p. 62): 'Si patronus clienti fraudem fecerit, sacer esto'.

establishing, under specific conditions, various levels of contractual liability for the principal with regards to his dependant's transactions.[3]

In the ninth book of his commentary on the provincial edict, Gaius notes that

> a proconsul does everything in order that anyone who enters into a contract with a person in power (*alieni iuris, in potestate*) gets his due in so far as circumstances allow it, based upon fairness, even though previously mentioned remedies, namely the *actiones exercitoria, institoria*, and *tributoria*, do not apply.[4]

Gaius goes on, mentioning three separate remedies, one calling for total liability (*in solidum*), equivalent to the amount of the debt incurred through the contract, on the part of the principal on the ground of an invitation (*iussum*) pre-emptively addressed to potential contracting parties to deal with the dependant.[5] The other two remedies call for the principal's limited liability, up to the amount of the principal's enrichment (*versum*) from his dependant's transaction, or up to the amount of the dependant's *peculium*, even in the absence of invitation or enrichment on the part of the principal.

Those six remedies were created by one or more praetors by the late Republican period. Later commentators labelled them *actiones adiecticiae qualitatis*, to reflect a change of names within the formula. All of these remedies apply to obligations arising from contracts made by dependants in the context of economic activities carried out with various levels of autonomy that were instrumental in defining the extent of the principal's liability. Unlike contracts, delicts called for total liability.[6]

Not much will be said here about those three remedies calling for the principal's total liability. The *actio quod iussu* implies the awareness (*scientia*) and will (*voluntas*) of the principal to let third contracting parties deal with his dependant(s). Will and awareness are also implicit in the appointment (*praepositio*) by the principal of an agent as business manager or shipmaster, whose legal transactions carried out in connection with this specific activity (*negotiatio*) give rise, respectively, to an *actio institoria* or *exercitoria*. In all three cases, the principal unambiguously retains control over his

---

[3] Inst.Gai.4.69–74a. For an overview, cf. Aubert (1994), ch. 2, pp. 40–116; Wacke (1994), pp. 280–362; and Miceli (2001).

[4] D.14.5.1 (Gaius 9 ad Ed. Prov.): 'Omnia proconsul agit ut qui contraxit cum eo qui in aliena potestate sit, etiamsi deficient superiores actiones id est exercitoria institoria tributoriave, nihilo minus tamen in quantum ex bono et aequo res patitur suum consequatur. Sive enim iussu eius, cuius in potestate sit, negotium gestum fuerit, in solidum eo nomine iudicium pollicetur: sive non iussu, sed tamen in rem eius versum fuerit, eatenus introducit actionem quatenus in rem eius versum fuerit: sive neutrum eorum sit, de peculio actionem constituit'.

[5] Cf. D.14.5.7 (Scaev. 1 Resp.), on a similar case involving a son in power (*filius familias*) and an alternative juristic response owing to particular circumstances (the father's death).

[6] D.14.5.4.2 (Ulpian. 29 ad Ed.): 'Quamquam autem ex contractu in id quod facere potest actio in eum datur, tamen ex delictis in solidum convenietur'.

dependant's activity, the nature of which is clearly defined at the outset. In exchange, he stands surety for all debts arising from the dependant's transactions. Litigation bears on simple, binary questions: is the slave indebted or not? Does the transaction fit the principal's intention, expressed through *iussum* or implied in the *praepositio*, or not? If the answer to any of these questions is negative, the principal is not liable.

With regard to the other three remedies, namely the *actiones de peculio, tributoria* or *de in rem verso*, things are not so clear-cut, because the principal's liability must not only be established, but also quantitatively estimated, on the basis of a sophisticated analysis of the assets and liabilities of the principal's and/or agent's property. Such an estimate requires the examination of account books and inventories, provided that they exist and are reliably kept. The purpose of this chapter is to identify and list the main obstacles a creditor could and undoubtedly would meet in figuring out what is in a slave's *peculium*, and to ponder the consequences of this.

2. ACTIO DE PECULIO

Unfortunately, the chapters dealing with the *actio de peculio* in Gaius' Institutes (4.72–72a) are partly lost or badly damaged, both in the Verona palimpsest and in the Oxyrhynchite papyrus (*P.Oxy.* XVII 2103) that miraculously supplements it in this part of book 4. On the other hand, thanks to the compilers' diligence, a large collection of juristic opinions from the classical period of Roman law is preserved in title 15.1 of Justinian's Digest. Ulpian reports that the *actio de peculio* had been created after – meaning, possibly but not necessarily much later than – the above-mentioned remedies calling for the principal's total liability (*in solidum*).[7] The *actio de peculio* is available if the *peculium* has seen an increase due to the transaction under litigation,[8] thus benefitting the principal, whatever his legal relationship (ownership, possession, usufruct, and so on) with the slave.[9] The question is how would such an increase be traced? What evidence would a creditor resort to in order to establish and quantify it? Pomponius regards the *peculium* as a sub-account, created by the slave's master and likely to grow or shrink, to be

---

[7] D.15.1.1pr (Ulpian. 29 ad Ed.): 'Ordinarium praetor arbitratus est prius eos contractus exponere eorum qui alienae potestati subiecti sunt, qui in solidum tribuunt actionem, sic deinde ad hunc pervenire, ubi de peculio datur actio'. The standard work on the *peculium* is Micolier (1932). Cf. also Buti (1976); and Pesaresi (2008). More recently, in an historical perspective, Roth (2005), pp. 278–92; Grotkamp (2005), pp. 125–45; Aubert (2009), pp. 167–85; Rosafio (2009), pp. 287–302.

[8] D.15.1.1.4 (Ulpian. 29 ad Ed.): 'Si cum impubere filio familias vel servo contractum sit, ita dabitur in dominum vel patrem de peculio, si locupletius eorum peculium factum est'.

[9] D.15.1.2 (Pompon. 5 ad Sab.): 'Ex ea causa ex qua soleret servus fructuarius vel usuarius adquirere, in eum cuius usus fructus vel usus sit actio dumtaxat de peculio ceteraeque honorariae dantur, ex reliquis in dominum proprietatis'.

eventually cancelled at the master's will. In legal terms, a *peculium* requires the master's initial permission.[10] Thus Q. Aelius Tubero, a late Republican jurist quoted by Ulpian through P. Iuventius Celsus of Hadrianic time, defines the *peculium* as 'what a slave keeps separate from the master's accounts with the latter's permission, after deduction of what the slave owes his master'.[11] The master's permission rests less on his will (*volente domino*) than on his acceptance (*patientia*) with regard to his awareness (*scientia*) of the very existence of the *peculium*. To have a *peculium* does not imply the right to dispose of it, by transfer of some or all of its parts, because it would worsen the economic position of the principal. Consequently, more is required to do so, such as the *concessio liberae administrationis*,[12] a special permission whereby the slave is enabled to do on a regular basis what should have been allowed only on a case-by-case basis, according to Paul who implicitly refers to some kind of *iussum*.[13] In so far as the *peculium* can be shown to exist, the principal becomes liable for his dependant's transactions in spite of specific restrictions or prohibitions to deal with the latter. The same Paul refers to a shop employee whose status has been clarified by a written sign (*proscriptio*) – he is not to be considered a business manager[14] – but whose transactions nevertheless give rise to an *actio de peculio*: the standard of liability is admittedly restricted with regard to the *actio institoria*, but nonetheless potentially significant.[15]

3. ACCOUNTING AND BOOK-KEEPING

The *peculium* cannot exist without the master's knowledge and agreement. He, however, may be unclear about its content and components, both

---

[10] D.15.1.4pr (Pompon. 7 ad Sab.): 'Peculii est non id cuius servus seorsum a domino rationem habuerit, sed quod dominus ipse separaverit suam a servi rationem discernens: nam cum servi peculium totum adimere vel augere vel minuere dominus possit, animadvertendum est non quid servus, sed quid dominus constituendi servilis peculii gratia fecerit'.

[11] D.15.1.5.4 (Ulpian. 29 ad Ed.): 'Peculium autem Tubero quidem sic definit, ut Celsus libro sexto digestorum refert, quod servus domini permissu separatum a rationibus dominicis habet, deducto inde si quid domino debetur'.

[12] Marcellus, according to Iulianus, quoted by Ulpian (D.15.1.7.1 (Ulpian. 29 ad Ed.): '[. . .] si (ut quidam, inquit, putant) peculium servus habere non potest nisi concedente domino. Ego autem puto non esse opus concedi peculium a domino servum habere, sed non adimi, ut habeat. Alia causa est peculii liberae administrationis: nam haec specialiter concedenda est'.

[13] D.15.1.46 (Paul. 60 ad Ed.): 'Qui peculii administrationem concedit videtur permittere generaliter quod et specialiter permissurus est'.

[14] D.14.3.11.2–4 (Ulpian. 28 ad Ed.) on the practical aspects of *proscriptio*.

[15] D.15.1.47pr (Paul. 4 ad Plaut.): 'Quotiens in taberna ita scriptum fuisset "cum ianuario servo meo geri negotium veto", hoc solum consecutum esse dominum constat, ne institoria teneatur, non etiam de peculio'. This is already attested in Gaius D.15.1.29.1 (Gaius 9 ad Ed. Prov.): 'Etiamsi prohibuerit contrahi cum servo dominus, erit in eum de peculio actio'.

in terms of nature (or quality) and quantity.[16] Ulpian approvingly cites Pomponius who considers that the principal is not bound to know in detail what the *peculium* is made of: a rough idea (*pachymeresteron*) would suffice.[17] In addition, the late second-century CE jurist Papirius Fronto compares the *peculium* with a human being, a statement explained by Marcian, possibly in reference to Polybius' thought (*Hist.* 6.5) about the natural cycle of political regimes: a *peculium* is born, grows, declines, and dies. This evolution is not straightforward, since a *peculium* can be totally empty without losing its legal status and existence.[18]

Concerning the 'birth' or establishment of the *peculium*, it can be ascribed to various causes and origins. Florentinus lists the slave's personal savings out of his daily rations, and all incomes and rewards that his master allows him to keep for himself.[19] To be added are whatever the slave is about to acquire: returns from pending litigation, inheritance, legacies, damages, refunds and other payments.

Just as the *peculium* arises from the master's will, it is cancelled in the same way.[20] The praetor's edict provides that the *peculium* ceases to exist at the time of the slave's death, manumission, or conveyance, through sale, gift, or legacy. However, creditors can bring an action on the *peculium* for a whole year after that, because, according to Pomponius, the *peculium* may still change over that period of time, through increase (gains) or decrease (losses).[21] By contrast, the slave's escape or kidnapping brings the autono-

---

[16] D.15.1.4.1–6 (Pompon. 7 ad Sab.): 'Sed hoc ita verum puto, si debito servum liberare voluit dominus, ut, etiamsi nuda voluntate remiserit dominus quod debuerit, desinat servus debitor esse: si vero nomina ita fecerit dominus, ut quasi debitorem se servo faceret, cum re vera debitor non esset, contra puto: re enim, non verbis peculium augendum est. 2. Ex his apparet non quid servus ignorante domino habuerit peculii esse, sed quid volente: alioquin et quod subripuit servus domino, fiet peculii, quod non est verum. 3. Sed saepe fit, ut ignorante domino incipiat minui servi peculium, veluti cum damnum domino dat servus aut furtum facit. 4. Si opem ferente servo meo furtum mihi feceris, id ex peculio deducendum est, quo minus ob rem subreptam consequi possim. 5. Si aere alieno dominico exhauriatur peculium servi, res tamen in causa peculiaria manent: nam si aut servo donasset debitum dominus aut nomine servi alius domino intulisset, peculium suppletur nec est nova concessione domini opus. 6. Non solum id in peculio vicariorum ponendum est, cuius rei a domino, sed etiam id cuius ab eo cuius in peculio sint seorsum rationem habeant'.

[17] D.15.1.7.2 (Ulpian. 29 ad Ed.): 'Scire autem non utique singulas res debet, sed *pachymeresteron [id est: magis in universum]*, et in hanc sententiam Pomponius inclinat'.

[18] D.15.1.40pr (Marcian. 5 Reg.): 'Peculium nascitur crescit decrescit moritur, et ideo eleganter Papirius Fronto dicebat peculium simile esse homini'.

[19] D.15.1.39 (Florent. 11 Inst.): 'Peculium et ex eo consistit, quod parsimonia sua quis paravit vel officio meruerit a quolibet sibi donari idque velut proprium patrimonium servum suum habere quis voluerit'.

[20] D.15.1.8 (Paul. 4 ad Sab.): 'Contra autem simul atque noluit, peculium servi desinit peculium esse'.

[21] D.15.2.1pr -1 (Ulpian. 29 ad Ed.): 'Praetor ait: "Post mortem eius qui in alterius potestate fuerit, posteave quam is emancipatus manumissus alienatusve fuerit, dumtaxat de peculio et si quid dolo malo eius in cuius potestate est factum erit, quo minus peculii esset, in anno,

mous management of the *peculium* to an end. So does any doubt about the slave's survival.[22]

I would like to suggest here that no one except the slave in charge of the *peculium* may actually know with precision and accuracy what it is made of. The slave's master – not to say third contracting parties – is, at best, able to acknowledge the existence of a *peculium*, the content of which is revealed in inventories and account books. Provided that such documents exist, that they are kept diligently up-to-date, and that they can be produced, consulted, deciphered and understood, it is possible to get an idea – however impressionistic – of the nature of the *peculium*, therefore of its value and volatility.

4. THE MAKE-UP OF THE *PECULIUM*

Classical Roman jurists surmise that the *peculium* was originally a small and simple entity. Ulpian provides an etymological definition of the word *peculium*: 'quasi pusilla pecunia sive patrimonium pusillum'.[23] Elsewhere, the same author and others specify that a *peculium* can contain all sorts of goods and commodities:

- movables, such as clothes, as long as they are kept for regular and personal use:[24]
- real estate, be it agricultural land and buildings, or urban property;[25]
- living beings, such as slaves' slaves (*vicarii*) or animals;

---

quo primum de ea re experiundi potestas erit, iudicium dabo". 1. Quamdiu servus vel filius in potestate est, de peculio actio perpetua est: post mortem autem eius vel postquam emancipatus manumissus alienatusve fuerit, temporaria esse incipit, id est annalis'. Pomponius D. 15.2.3 (Pompon. 4 ad Quint. Muc.): 'Definitione peculii interdum utendum est etiam, si servus in rerum natura esse desiit et actionem praetor de peculio intra annum dat: nam et tunc et accessionem et decessionem quasi peculii recipiendam (quamquam iam desiit morte servi vel manumissione esse peculium), ut possit ei accedere ut peculio fructibus vel pecorum fetu ancillarumque partubus et decedere, veluti si mortuum sit animal vel alio quolibet modo perierit'.

[22] D.15.1.48pr (Paul. 17 ad Plaut.): 'Libera peculii administratio non permanet neque in fugitivo neque in subrepto neque in eo, de quo nesciat quis vivat an mortuus sit'.

[23] D.15.1.5.3 (Ulpian. 29 ad Ed.): 'Peculium dictum est quasi pusilla pecunia sive patrimonium pusillum'.

[24] D.15.1.25 (Pompon. 23 ad Sab.): 'Id vestimentum peculii esse incipit, quod ita dederit dominus, ut eo vestitu servum perpetuo uti vellet eoque nomine ei traderet, ne quis alius eo uteretur idque ab eo eius usus gratia custodiretur. Sed quod vestimentum servo dominus ita dedit utendum, ut non semper, sed ad certum usum certis temporibus eo uteretur, veluti cum sequeretur eum sive cenanti ministravit, id vestimentum non esse peculii'.

[25] D.15.1.22 (Pompon. 7 ad Sab.): 'Si damni infecti aedium peculiarium nomine promiserit dominus, ratio eius haberi debet et ideo ab eo qui de peculio agit domino cavendum est'. *Idem* D.15.1.23 (Pompon. 9 ad Sab.): 'Aedium autem peculiarium nomine in solidum damni infecti promitti debet, sicut vicarii nomine noxale iudicium in solidum pati, quia pro pignore ea, si non defendantur, actor abducit vel possidet'.

- assets (credit, damages to be collected as a result of litigation, inheritance and legacies to come, *peculia* entrusted to *vicarii*) and liabilities (mostly debts = *nomina*).[26]

The *peculium* can be empty of any or all of the above[27] or consist exclusively of debts owed by the slave to his master.[28] In the books, it also contains whatever the latter has deceivingly withdrawn from it.[29] Last, it includes everything the slave has acquired and kept hidden from his master, insofar as it can be assumed that the latter would have let him have it, had he known about it.[30]

5. LITIGATION WITH SEVERAL CREDITORS: FIRST COME, FIRST SERVED

A slave in business entrusted with a *peculium* may owe money to several creditors. When one of them wants to sue the master, he introduces an action on the *peculium* and can expect to be compensated up to the amount of the *peculium*. His position is obviously advantageous with regard to other creditors who would sue later, provided that a decision is made about his case first. Consequently, the timing of the judicial decision matters more than the chronological order of litigation, as Gaius clearly states in his commentary to the provincial edict.[31] A pending decision, which may drastically change the content of the *peculium*, is irrelevant.

---

[26] D.15.1.7.4 (Ulpian. 29 ad Ed.): 'In peculio autem res esse possunt omnes et mobiles et soli: vicarios quoque in peculium potest habere et vicariorum peculium: hoc amplius et nomina debitorum'. Cf. also D.15.1.17 (Ulpian. 29 ad Ed.).

[27] D.15.1.30pr (Ulpian. 29 ad Ed.): 'Quaesitum est, an teneat actio de peculio, etiamsi nihil sit in peculio cum ageretur, si modo sit rei iudicatae tempore. Proculus et Pegasus nihilo minus teneri aiunt: intenditur enim recte, etiamsi nihil sit in peculio. Idem et circa ad exhibendum et in rem actionem placuit, quae sententia et a nobis probanda est'.

[28] D.15.1.16 (Iulian. 12 Dig.): 'Marcellus notat: est etiam ille casus, si alter ademerit: vel si omni quidem modo concesserit dominus sed in nominibus erit concessio'.

[29] D.15.1.21pr (Ulpian. 29 ad Ed.): 'Summa cum ratione etiam hoc peculio praetor imputavit, quod dolo malo domini factum est, quo minus in peculio esset. Sed dolum malum accipere debemus, si ei ademit peculium: sed et si eum intricare peculium in necem creditorum passus est, Mela scribit dolo malo eius factum. Sed et si quis, cum suspicaretur alium secum acturum, alio peculium avertat, dolo non caret. Sed si alii solvit, non dubito de hoc, quin non teneatur, quoniam creditori solvitur et licet creditori vigilare ad suum consequendum'.

[30] D.15.1.49pr (Pompon. 4 ad Quint. Muc.): 'Non solum id peculium est, quod dominus servo concessit, verum id quoque, quod ignorante quidem eo adquisitum sit, tamen, si rescisset, passurus erat esse in peculio'.

[31] D.15.1.10 (Gaius 9 ad Ed. Prov.): 'Si vero adhuc in suspenso est prius iudicium de peculio et ex posteriore iudicio res iudicaretur, nullo modo debet prioris iudicii ratio haberi in posteriore condemnatione, quia in actione de peculio occupantis melior est condicio, occupare autem videtur non qui prior litem contestatus est, sed qui prior ad sententiam iudicis pervenit'.

6. TIME OF ESTIMATE

Like modern financial portfolios, *peculia* may fluctuate widely and quickly. In case of litigation on the *peculium*, it is vital for the plaintiff(s) to establish when the *peculium* must be taken into consideration, because the time is instrumental in defining the level of the master's liability. Whether the *peculium* incurs major losses after the estimate is irrelevant, because the master's other assets – outside the *peculium* – can be called upon for compensation. Theoretically, various moments can be envisaged:

- the initial establishment of the *peculium* (= *concessio peculii*), or any time the *peculium* has been re-evaluated or recapitalised, assuming that the master has then a precise and accurate knowledge of its content;
- the time of the transaction, assuming that the contracting party would check the state of the *peculium* standing as a kind of surety;
- the time when the plaintiff introduces his claim *in iure*, thus starting litigation;
- the time when the joinder of issue (*litis contestatio*) is pronounced, before sending the case to a judge (*apud iudicem*);
- the time when the judge makes his decision (*iudicium*);
- outside of the proceedings, whenever the *peculium* is cancelled because of the slave's death, manumission or conveyance, or at any given moment within one year of the event, while the *actio de peculio* is still available.

Classical jurists are rather discreet about this fundamental issue, and occasionally make ambiguous and somewhat contradictory statements. Following Proculus and Pegasus, Ulpian considers that a *peculium* may be empty at the start of litigation, but rebuilt later on by the time of the judicial decision, thus making the *actio de peculio* valid.[32] Along the same lines, if the *peculium* is insufficient to repay a debt at the time of judgment, complementary proceedings can start anew for the balance if the state of the *peculium* subsequently improves.[33] Whoever makes a contract with a slave is bound to pay attention to changes in the value of the *peculium*, which does not preclude a certain amount of speculation.[34] Paul denies any guarantee (*cautio*) bearing

---

[32] D.15.1.30pr (Ulpian. 29 ad Ed.): 'Quaesitum est an teneat actio de peculio, etiamsi nihil sit in peculio cum ageretur, si modo sit rei iudicatae tempore. Proculus et Pegasus nihilo minus teneri aiunt: intenditur enim recte, etiamsi nihil sit in peculio. Idem et circa ad exhibendum et in rem actionem placuit, quae sententia et a nobis probanda est'.

[33] D.15.1.30.4 (Ulpian. 29 ad Ed.): 'Is, qui semel de peculio egit, rursus aucto peculio de residuo debiti agere potest'.

[34] D.15.1.32pr – 1 (Ulpian. 2 Disp.): 'Sed licet hoc iure contingat, tamen aequitas dictat iudicium in eos dari, qui occasione iuris liberantur, ut magis eos perceptio quam intentio liberet: nam qui cum servo contrahit, universum peculium eius quod ubicumque est veluti patrimonium intuetur. 1. In hoc autem iudicio licet restauretur praecedens, tamen et augmenti

on a possible, though hypothetical, increase of the *peculium*, no matter how insufficient it was at the time of judgment.[35] In some – admittedly far-fetched – cases, the estimate must take place at a given moment, for instance when the principal becomes the heir of a creditor of the *peculium*[36] or is kidnapped:[37] an estimate is made at the very moment when the principal's status is altered. The same opportunity occurs when the slave dies during litigation on his *peculium*, or when the late principal's estate includes a legacy of the *peculium*, either to the slave to be manumitted by will or to an outsider.[38]

Because any *peculium* is potentially volatile, depending on its components and its management, it is difficult for would-be contracting parties to foresee future developments in the value of the *peculium*.

7. DEDUCTIONS FROM THE *PECULIUM*

Title 15.1 of Justinian's Digest displays several excerpts dealing with deductions from the *peculium* on behalf of the principal prior to its estimate. Aelius Tubero's definition discussed above specifies that the *peculium* does not include what the slave owes his master.[39] Ulpian, who cites Tubero through Celsus, specifies elsewhere that those deductions are based on the assumption that the master was the first creditor to sue on the *peculium* and that his claim is valid, thus forestalling all others. This principle goes back a long way, as Ulpian also cites Cicero's contemporary, Servius Sulpicius Rufus,

---

et decessionis rationem haberi oportet, et ideo sive hodie nihil sit in peculio sive accesserit aliquid, praesens status peculii spectandus est. Quare circa venditorem quoque et emptorem hoc nobis videtur verius, quod accessit peculio posse nos ab emptore consequi, nec retrorsus velut in uno iudicio ad id tempus conventionem reducere emptoris, quo venditor conventus sit'.

[35] D.15.1.47.2 (Paul. 4 ad Plaut.): 'Si semel actum sit de peculio, quamvis minus inveniatur rei iudicandae tempore in peculio quam debet, tamen cautionibus locum esse non placuit de futuro incremento peculii: hoc enim in pro socio actione locum habet, quia socius universum debet'.

[36] D.15.1.50.1 (Papinian. 9 Quaest.): 'Si creditor patrem, qui de peculio tenebatur, heredem instituerit, quia mortis tempus in Falcidiae ratione spectatur, illius temporis peculium considerabitur'.

[37] D.15.1.55 (Nerat. 1 Resp.): 'Is cum quo de peculio agebam a te vi exemptus est: quod tunc cum vi eximeres in peculio fuerit, spectari'.

[38] D.15.1.57 (Tryphonin. 8 Disp.): 'Si filius vel servus, cuius nomine dumtaxat de peculio actum est, ante finitum iudicium decesserit, id peculium respicietur, quod aliquis eorum cum moriebatur habuit. 1. Sed eum, qui servum testamento liberum esse iubet et ei peculium legat, eius temporis peculium legare intellegi Iulianus scribit, quo libertas competit: ideoque omnia incrementa peculii quoquo modo ante aditam hereditatem adquisita ad manumissum pertinere. 2. At si quis extraneo peculium servi legaverit, in coniectura voluntatis testatoris quaestionem esse, et verosimilius esse id legatum quod mortis tempore in peculio fuerit ita, ut quae ex rebus peculiaribus ante aditam hereditatem accesserint debeantur, veluti partus ancillarum et fetus pecudum, quae autem servo donata fuerint sive quid ex operis suis adquisierit, ad legatarium non pertinere'.

[39] D.15.1.5.4 (Ulpian. 29 ad Ed.): '[. . .] deducto inde si quid domino debetur'.

who includes all debts owed by the slaves not only to the master, but also to all dependants attached to his household (*familia*).[40] This is not the place to inventory and discuss at length the many types of deductions retained by classical jurists. Let us note, however, that no less than fourteen passages, out of all fifty-eight included in the title *De peculio*, deal with this issue.[41] The ratio underlines the advantageous position enjoyed by the principal by comparison with all other creditors, who are left with the difficult task of figuring out to what extent the *peculium* is burdened with internal debts, either when the contract is concluded or when litigation starts or ends.

8. *ACTIO TRIBUTORIA*

A comparison of the respective modalities of application and effects of the three remedies *in solidum* (*actiones quod iussu*, *institoria* and *exercitoria*) with those of the *actio de peculio* suggests that the set of three remedies aims at protecting third contracting parties while the latter is more advantageous to the principal while limiting his liability for his dependant's transaction. Since the explicitly acknowledged purpose of all these remedies is to promote those economic activities carried out by dependants in order to maximise their principal's profit (*quaestus*), it is obvious that the *actio de peculio* is lacking in this respect because of its bias toward the latter. The Roman praetor obviously ended up noticing this shortcoming and came up with an analogous remedy, maintaining both the dependent's autonomy in his economic activities and the principal's limited liability for his dependant's transaction, but cancelling, in specific conditions, the preferential treatment of the latter, now to be set on an equal footing with all other creditors with regard to the *peculium*, provided that he was aware of his dependant's dealing with his *peculium*, or *merx peculiaris*, as surety.[42] This additional remedy is the so-called *actio tributoria*, with which D.14.4 (a total of twelve *excerpta*, from Labeo to Ulpian) is concerned.[43]

Ulpian rightly underlines that this remedy is of significant usefulness ('edicti non minima utilitas'), because it stands halfway between the *actiones*

---

[40] D.15.1.9.2–3 (Ulpian. 29 ad Ed.): 'Peculium autem deducto quod domino debetur computandum esse, quia praevenisse dominus et cum servo suo egisse creditur. 3. Huic definitioni Servius adiecit et si quid his debeatur qui sunt in eius potestate, quoniam hoc quoque domino deberi nemo ambigit. 4. Praeterea id etiam deducetur, quod his personis debetur, quae sunt in tutela vel cura domini vel patris vel quorum negotia administrant, dummodo dolo careant [. . .]'

[41] D.15.1.9, 11, 13, 14, 15, 17, 19, 27, 30, 37, 38, 47, 52 et 56, based on a search for 'deduc'.

[42] D.14.4.1pr (Ulpian. 29 ad Ed.): 'Huius quoque edicti non minima utilitas est, ut dominus, qui alioquin in servi contractibus privilegium habet (quippe cum de peculio dumtaxat teneatur, cuius peculii aestimatio deducto quod domino debetur fit), tamen, si scierit servum peculiari merce negotiari, velut extraneus creditor ex hoc edicto in tributum vocatur'.

[43] The standard study is now Chiusi (1993). Cf. also Chiusi (2007), pp. 94–112.

in solidum and the *actio de peculio*, in that it increases all creditors' (other than the principal) protection, as they are no longer topped by the principal with regard to distribution of the *peculium* in case of bankruptcy. Both required conditions are fairly easy to meet: the principal's knowledge (*scientia*) is passive, and calls not for an explicit show of willingness (*voluntas*) typical of the *actiones quod iussu*, *institoria*, and *exercitoria* – through *iussum* or *praepositio* – but for acceptance (*patientia*) on his part of his dependant's creativity and dynamism, possibly, but not necessarily, within the context of a business (*negotiatio*) to which the *merx peculiaris* may be attached.

The very concept of *merx peculiaris* is controversial. Whether it represents some kind of capital investment attached to the dependant or a fictitious patrimony akin to the *peculium* after deductions, it bestows on the *actio tributoria* its commercial relevance.[44] Like the *peculium*, the *merx peculiaris* must be estimated. Consequently, all difficulties described in connection with the practical application of the *actio de peculio* remain well alive with the *actio tributoria*. Worse, the third contracting party acting as plaintiff on the *actio tributoria* must prove the principal's awareness (*scientia*) – less traceable than his willingness expressed through *iussum* or *praepositio* – and establish a connection between the *merx peculiaris* and the transaction at the origin of litigation. In addition, the asset to be distributed needs clarification. Ulpian unambiguously states that only what belongs to the *merx peculiaris* – as opposed to the *peculium* as a whole – is taken into account ('sed id dumtaxat quod ex ea merce est').[45] The same author acknowledges that the principal may be in doubt of what belongs to it.[46] Gaius suggests in his commentary of the provincial edict that the difference may be substantial enough for a plaintiff to choose the *actio de peculio* over the *actio tributoria*, since the *merx peculiaris* may consist at times of a small part only of the whole *peculium* or since the deductions to which the principal would have been entitled in connection with the *actio de peculio* happen to be insignificant.[47] The plaintiff's choice of one or the other remedy will in any case extinguish his claim.[48]

---

[44] Földi (2001), pp. 65–90.
[45] D.14.4.5.11 (Ulpian. 29 ad Ed.): 'Non autem totum peculium venit in tributum, sed id dumtaxat, quod ex ea merce est, sive merces manent sive pretium earum receptum conversumve est in peculium'.
[46] D.14.4.7.2 (Ulpian. 2 ad Ed.): 'Si tamen ignorans in merce servum habere minus tribuit, non videtur dolo minus tribuisse, sed re comperta si non tribuat, dolo nunc non caret'.
[47] D.14.4.11 (Gaius 9 ad Ed. Prov.): 'aliquando etiam agentibus expedit potius de peculio agere quam tributoria: nam in hac actione de qua loquimur hoc solum in divisionem venit, quod in mercibus est quibus negotiatur quodque eo nomine receptum est: at in actione de peculio totius peculii quantitas spectatur, in quo et merces continentur. Et fieri potest, ut dimidia forte parte peculii aut tertia vel etiam minore negotietur: fieri praeterea potest, ut patri dominove nihil debeat'.
[48] D.14.4.9.1 (Ulpian. 29 ad Ed.): 'Eligere quis debet, qua actione experiatur, utrum de peculio an tributoria, cum scit sibi regressum ad aliam non futurum'.

9. *ACTIO DE IN REM VERSO*

For the sake of comprehensiveness, we should at this point have a look at the last remedy (*actio de in rem verso*)[49] and examine how the principal's enrichment (*versum*) as a result of his dependant's activity shows in his own accounts (*rationes dominicae*), namely in his *codex accepti et expensi*[50]. However, this would bring us outside the context of the *peculium*.

There is undoubtedly a connection between the principal's main account and his slaves' sub-accounts (including *peculia* of *vicarii*). The jurists are mute about it, and there is no documentary evidence in spite of the wealth of surviving accounts in papyri and wooden tablets. We may assume that such documents did exist, and will be identified as such in a nearby future.[51] The production, use and conservation of such documents require a rather high level of literacy and numeracy, and specific skills in financial administration and business management. Whether such competencies are likely to be found among those slaves, aliens and have-nots who were involved in crafts and trade is debatable.[52]

10. CONCLUSION

What are the consequences of these observations? Those remedies calling for a limited liability on the part of the principal for his dependant's transactions are difficult, if not impossible, to apply without a sophisticated system of book-keeping and accounting to be used at both levels on a day-to-day basis. Provided that accounts were indeed kept on either side – nothing suggests that it was a legal obligation – there is no guarantee that traders knew how to consult them.

People who were dealing with slaves in business were vulnerable at best. The situation alluded to by Hyperides in his speech *Against Athenogenes*, written in Athens between 330 and 324 BCE, must have been standard in the classical world. Short of being able to consult the accounts of the perfume shop managed by Midas, Epikrates, blinded by his love, was sold a bunch of slaves and a business crippled with debts. It took only a few weeks for the new owner to measure, from the inside, the extent of his disastrous purchase.

---

[49] The standard work is Chiusi (2001).
[50] D.15.3.3.5 (Ulpian. 29 ad Ed.): 'Idem Labeo ait, si servus mutuatus nummos a me alii eos crediderit, de in rem verso dominum teneri, quod nomen ei adquisitum est: quam sententiam Pomponius ita probat, si non peculiare nomen fecit, sed quasi dominicae rationis. Ex qua causa hactenus erit dominus obligatus, ut, si non putat sibi expedire nomen debitoris habere, cedat creditori actionibus procuratoremque eum faciat'.
[51] Cf. Bresson and Aubert, in a forthcoming chapter on accounting in the *Oxford Handbook of Economies in the Classical World* (2012). The standard book on Roman accounting is Minaud (2005).
[52] Cf. Aubert (2004), pp. 127–47.

In the Roman world, praetorian law, explained and enlarged by abundant juristic opinions, allowed economic actors, including slaves and other dependants, to minimise the risks attached to contractual transactions by granting them legal remedies easy to use because they are resting on a simple question, to be answered by yes or no. These remedies called for total liability on the part of the principal if his willingness to let his dependant enter into contracts with third parties could be established. The practical usefulness and commercial feature of the *actiones institoria* and *exercitoria*, accessorily of the *actio tributoria* conceived as a lesser evil, may explain the label of *superiores actiones* adopted by Gaius,[53] and underlines the lesser importance of those remedies included in *triplex hoc edictum*: possibly marginal in practice, the *actiones de peculio, de in rem verso*, or *quod iussu* retained all along their major legal interest.[54]

The very existence of legal remedies such as the *actiones adiecticiae qualitatis* does not imply that business people resorted to them on an equal, or even regular, basis. Like so many other legal institutions of praetorian law, the *actiones adiecticiae qualitatis* are products of the Republican period. Among them, the *actio de peculio* and, to a lesser extent, the *actiones tributoria* and *quod iussu* seem better adapted to a situation of relative proximity among economic actors, in the context of local or regional trade. On the other hand, the *actiones institoria* and, a fortiori, *exercitoria* are suited for a wider commercial space, on an interprovincial, Mediterranean or even global scale.

The impracticality of the *actio de peculio* for reasons stated above and the trend toward simplification, however tentative, started by the – necessarily – later creation of the *actio tributoria* may have led to the development of the commercial features of the *actiones adiecticiae qualitatis*, thus bolstering the case for the posteriority of the *actiones institoria* and *exercitoria*, a *communis opinio* which I have been trying to disrupt for many years.[55] However, both Gaius and Ulpian unambiguously speak against it.

The main commercial feature of the *actiones tributoria, institoria* and *exercitoria* (the so-called *actiones superiores*) lies in the reduction and cancellation of the privileges of the *dominus/paterfamilias*, who eventually stands on an equal footing with other creditors of the *peculium* and must accept liability *in tributum* or *in solidum* for the debts contracted by his dependants/agents. To echo another Paul, the apostle and author of the Epistle to the Galatians

---

[53] D.14.5.1 (Gaius 9 ad Ed. Prov.): 'Omnia proconsul agit, ut qui contraxit cum eo, qui in aliena potestate sit, etiamsi deficient superiores actiones, id est exercitoria institoria tributoriave, nihilo minus tamen in quantum ex bono et aequo res patitur suum consequatur. Sive enim iussu eius, cuius in potestate sit, negotium gestum fuerit, in solidum eo nomine iudicium pollicetur: sive non iussu, sed tamen in rem eius versum fuerit, eatenus introducit actionem, quatenus in rem eius versum fuerit: sive neutrum eorum sit, de peculio actionem constituit'.

[54] D.15.1.1.1 (Ulpian. 29 ad Ed.): 'Est autem triplex hoc edictum: aut enim de peculio aut de in rem verso aut quod iussu hinc oritur actio'.

[55] Best represented lately by De Ligt (1999), pp. 205–26.

(3:28), it could be said that a 'world' economy cannot afford to make a distinction between freeborn and slaves, citizens and foreigners, men and women, adults and minors, Latin and non-Latin speakers.[56] The *actiones institoria* and *exercitoria* celebrate the priority of businesses over individuals.

Lastly, let us stress that the picture we get about the history of the *actiones adiecticiae qualitatis*, from their creation in the mid or late Republic through the classical period until the time of the compilers, is based less on the reconstruction of the praetorian edict than on the classical jurists' opinions, mostly in the second and third centuries CE. The chronological distance between the time of their conception and that of the legal controversies surrounding them up to half a millennium later reflects the perennial adequacy of the solutions offered by the Republican praetors to no less perennial problems raised by the organisation of trade. Obviously, both were still relevant enough in the sixth century to find their way into Justinian's Digest.

BIBLIOGRAPHY

Aubert, J.-J., *Business Managers in Ancient Rome. A Social and Economic Study of Institores, 200 BC – AD 250* (1994).

Aubert, J.-J., 'De l'usage de l'écriture dans la gestion d'entreprise à l'époque romaine', in J. Andreau, J. France and S. Pittia (eds), *Mentalités et choix économiques des Romains* (2004), p. 127.

Aubert, J.-J., 'L'économie romaine et le droit de la représentation indirecte sous la République,' in C. Cascione and C. Masi Doria (eds), *Fides, Humanitas, Ius: Studi in onore del prof. L. Labruna* I (2007), p. 215.

Aubert, J.-J., 'Productive investments in agriculture: *Instrumentum fundi* and *peculium* in the later Roman Republic', in J. Carlsen and E. Lo Cascio (eds), *Agricoltura e scambi nell'Italia tardo-repubblicana* (2009), p. 167.

Bresson A., and Aubert J.-J., 'Accounting', in A. Bresson, E. Lo Cascio and F. Velde (eds), *The Oxford Handbook of Economies in the Classical World* (2012) (forthcoming).

Buti, I., *Studi sulla capacità patrimoniale dei 'servi'* (1976).

Chiusi, T. J., *Contributo allo studio dell'editto 'de tributoria actione'* (1993).

Chiusi, T. J., 'Zum Zusammenspiel von Haftung und Organisation im römischen

---

[56] D.14.1.1.4 (Ulpian. 28 ad Ed.): 'Cuius autem condicionis sit magister iste, nihil interest, utrum liber an servus, et utrum exercitoris an alienus: sed nec cuius aetatis sit, intererit, sibi imputaturo qui praeposuit'. Ibid. 16: 'Parvi autem refert, qui exercet masculus sit an mulier, pater familias an filius familias vel servus: pupillus autem si navem exerceat, exigemus tutoris auctoritatem'. D.14.3.7.1 Ibid.:'Parvi autem refert, quis sit institor, masculus an femina, liber an servus proprius vel alienus. Item quisquis praeposuit: nam et si mulier praeposuit, competet institoria exemplo exercitoriae actionis et si mulier sit praeposita, tenebitur etiam ipsa. Sed et si filia familias sit vel ancilla praeposita, competit institoria actio'. D.14.3.8 (Gaius 9 ad Ed. Prov.): 'Nam et plerique pueros puellasque tabernis praeponunt'. D.15.1.3.2 (Ulpian. 29 ad Ed.): 'Parvi autem refert, servus quis masculi an mulieris fuerit: nam de peculio et mulier convenietur'.

Handelsverkehr: "scientia", "voluntas" und "peculium" in D. 14,1,1,19–20', ZSS (rom. Abt.), 124 (2007), p. 94.

De Ligt L., 'Legal history and economic history: the case of the *actiones adiecticiae qualitatis*', *TvR*, 67.3–4 (1999), p. 205.

Földi, A., 'Eine alternative Annäherungsweise: Gedanken zum Problem des Handelsrechts in der römischen Welt', *RIDA*, 48 (2001), p. 65.

Grotkamp, N., 'Missbrauch und Gebrauch des peculium', *MBAH*, 24.2 (2005), p. 125.

Miceli, M., *Sulla struttura formulare delle actiones adiecticiae qualitatis* (2001).

Micolier, G., *Pécule et capacité patrimoniale. Etude sur le pécule, dit profectice, depuis l'édit 'de peculio' jusqu'à la fin de l'époque classique* (1932).

Minaud, G., *La comptabilité à Rome: essai d'histoire économique sur la pensée comptable commerciale et privée dans le monde antique romain* (2005).

Pesaresi, R., *Ricerche sul peculium imprenditoriale* (2008).

Rosafio, P., 'Il peculio dei coloni nella tarda antichità', in J.-J. Aubert and P. Blanchard (eds), *Droit, religion et société dans le Code Théodosien* (2009), p. 287.

Roth, U., 'Food, status, and the *peculium* of agricultural slaves', *JRA*, 18 (2005), p. 278.

Wacke, A., 'Die adjektizischen Klagen im Überblick I. Von der Reeder- und der Betriebsleiterklage zur direkten Stellvertretung', *ZSS* (rom. Abt.), 111 (1994), p. 280.

Chapter 11

Pipes and Property in the Sale of Real Estate
(D.19.1.38.2)

Cynthia J. Bannon

1. INTRODUCTION

Ancient Romans, like their modern counterparts, considered several factors when buying property. Amenities, productivity and, of course, location affected the decision.[1] Cato urged potential buyers to visit the land more than once, inspecting it carefully, to determine whether its cultivation would repay the investment (*On Agriculture*, 1). Charm also mattered. Cicero, for example, exclaimed more over the elegant porticos than the meadows on Quintus' recently purchased estate (*Q. Fr.* 3.1.3).[2] Both agricultural productivity and enjoyment of amenities, however, depended on the property's having appropriate equipment or accessories. How could the landowner enjoy a garden fountain if there were no pipes bringing water?[3] Domestic tasks as well as farm work depended on a water supply. In general, productivity depended on equipment and materials and was increased when they were included with the property, eliminating the cost of procuring them. Pipes and plumbing were a key feature and could be costly to install.[4]

Although Roman landowners had good reason to pay close attention to movable property or accessories connected with real estate, they may not always have done so; indeed there is some truth to the stereotype of

---

[1] Rawson (1976), p. 85, and on rural land, de Neeve (1985).

[2] To paraphrase Varro, no one pays more for unattractive land than for a charming estate with the same productivity (*On Agriculture*, 1.4.2; cf. Pliny, *H.N.* 14.51, 17.3–6).

[3] See, for example, Pliny's loving descriptions of fountains at his villa, *Ep.* 5.6.23, 36–37, 40, and more generally on the importance of water supply for the villa, *Ep.* 2.17.25–26. Compare also Seneca, *Ep.* 86.4–13 where baths are the focus of Seneca's reflections on the luxurious renovations to Scipio's villa by its new owner.

[4] Though materials for pipes (i.e., lead) might be inexpensive, construction was neither cheap nor easy: Hodge (1991), pp. 156–7. Cost varied depending on the type and extent of the work: for examples, though none with pipes specifically, see Duncan Jones (1982), pp. 160–1, for example no. 469 (HS 380,000, total rebuilding), no. 474 (HS 50,000, gilding the roof, marble pavement, new cement), no. 476 (HS 20,000 pavement); and for other repairs to baths, see nos 468, 469a, 470, 478, 479, 480. Cicero, *Q. Fr.*, 3.1.3 describes a contract for building an aqueduct with a price per foot of three sesterces. For the slow pace of construction work, see Martin (1989), p. 57.

the absentee landlord.[5] The jurist Celsus worked on similar assumptions, writing about the sale of land from the eighth book of his *Digest*. Celsus reported an earlier opinion by the jurist Proculus in which he replied to a question from a certain Firmus about underground pipes on a property.[6] Though Firmus cannot be identified with certainty, the specificity of the question suggests a real situation, rather than a hypothetical case.[7] Celsus at any rate approached the problem with the realities of the real estate market in mind:

> Firmus a Proculo quaesiit, si de plumbeo castello fistulae sub terram missae aquam ducerent in aenum lateribus circumstructum, an hae aedium essent, ut vincta fixaque, an ut ruta caesa, quae aedium non essent. ille rescripsit referre, quid acti esset. quid ergo si nihil de ea re neque emptor neque venditor cogitaverunt, ut plerumque in eiusmodi rebus evenisse solet, nonne propius est, ut inserta et inclusa aedificio partem eius esse existimemus? (D.19.1.38.2 (Cels. 8 Dig.))[8]

Firmus inquired of Proculus whether pipes, leading underground from a lead cistern and bringing water into a basin built in around the sides, belonged to the buildings (*aedium*), like things bound and fixed, or whether they were like things dug [or] cut (*ruta caesa*) that did not belong to the buildings. He wrote back that it depended on what was agreed. But really then, if neither the buyer nor the seller

---

[5] De Neeve (1985), p. 91; Kehoe (1997), pp. 17–18, 146.

[6] Celsus' *Digest* was his own collection of comments, letters and questions; on the nature of Celsus' *Digest*, see Hausmaninger (1991), p. 384; Scarano-Ussani (1989), pp. 90–1. The older part of the case, Firmus' question and Proculus' reply, may have been included in Proculus' letters, though its original source is not known; see Stella Maranca (1915), p. 59 fn. 17.

[7] Firmus may have been one of the parties to the sale, or a magistrate or *iudex* involved in resolving the dispute. It is tempting to connect him with M. Obellius Firmus who was both *aedile* and *duovir* at Pompeii before 54 CE: see Jongman (1978–9), pp. 63–4. An A. Vettius Firmus also stood for the aedileship in Pompeii: see Franklin (1979), p. 406. It would make sense if Firmus was a Pompeian magistrate with jurisdiction over civil law. The plumbing arrangements are also consistent with archaeological evidence from Pompeii (see below).

[8] The Latin text of Firmus' question here differs from Mommsen's edition. Mommsen prints: 'an hae aedium essent, an ut ruta caesa vincta fixaque quae aedium non essent'. The text above adopts corrections printed in two early editions that I have not been able to inspect: Gebauer and Spangeberg (1776), cited by Marrone, 1971, p. 216 fn. 10, and Gregorium Haloandrum Meltzer (1529), cited by Stella Maranca (1915), p. 59 fn. 20. Mommsen's text is confusing because the second pair of participles (*vincta fixaque*) illustrates the first alternative (*an hae aedium essent*), while the first pair of participles (*ruta caesa*) illustrates the second alternative (*quae aedium non essent*). In these early editions, the order of the pairs is reversed and an '*ut*' is added to restore a parallel, chiastic arrangement of the alternatives and the illustrative phrases. In addition, Celsus' comment, the last part of the case from '*quid ergo si nihil . . .*' to the end of the case was labelled an interpolation by Riccobono (1922), p. 286 fn. 2, and Levy and Rabel (1929–35), I, p. 351. It is now accepted as genuine by Marrone (1971), p. 216 fn. 10, and Hausmaninger (1991), pp. 59–60. The tone and style match Celsus' in other fragments, especially where he rejects Proculus' opinions: see Hausmaninger (1991), pp. 59–61; see also Hausmaninger (1976), pp. 394–5; Scarano-Ussani (1989), pp. 96–8.

thought about his matter, as is often accustomed to happen in dealings of this sort, it is more appropriate that we consider things inserted and built into a building to be part of it (*partem eius*), isn't it?

Firmus asked whether the pipes should be treated as part of the property and thus belong to the buyer, or whether they should be classified as *ruta caesa*, an old term for property that belonged to the seller after the sale. According to Proculus, the problem should be resolved on the basis of contracts between the parties (*quid acti est*) which, he assumes, specified how the pipes were to be treated. This is all well and good if the parties have paid attention to underground plumbing and added appropriate agreements to their sale contract. But, Celsus remarks, underground pipes should belong to the buyer because they are built into the structure for, after all, buyers and sellers often disregarded such details, *ut plerumque in eiusmodi rebus evenisse solet, nonne propius est.*

Despite the apparent ease of Celsus' conclusion, there was no overall rule about accessories in the law of sale.[9] In the early form of sale by *mancipatio*, real property was sold with everything that was connected with it, though there was no specific treatment of accessories.[10] The buyer could expect vacant possession and continued enjoyment of the property, but otherwise only limited protection. In general, buyers were expected to look out for their own interests, quite literally, as the assumption was that the buyer could see any defects or problems before he agreed to the sale.[11] But even a buyer who followed Cato's advice might make a mistake with unhappy consequences. Starting in the late Republic, protections of the buyer were expanded with the development of consensual sale (*emptio venditio*) under the influence of the Curule Aediles' edict, which regulated market sales.[12] From the beginning, the seller was liable for outright fraud, deliberate misrepresentation of the sale property, if not for real estate hype.[13] Over time, the jurists expanded liability, though at the time when Celsus gave

---

[9] Meincke (1971), pp. 175–7. The problem is recognised but not explored by Crook (1976), p. 77; and briefly mentioned in Watson (1965), pp. 91–2. There are two common law terms for such things, as defined in *Black's Law Dictionary* (2009) and *Ballentine's Law Dictionary* (2010). Appurtenances, the older and broader term, refers to corporeal or incorporeal things that belong to the land. Fixtures are attached to land or building and are generally regarded as immovable. Because the Roman categories do not align with those in modern common law, I will use 'accessories' to refer generally to things that go with property and the Roman legal terms *ruta caesa* and 'part of the property' (*aedium* or *pars aedium*) as the jurists do in order to investigate the development and application of their ideas.

[10] Marrone (1971), p. 221.

[11] *Caveat emptor* was the rule, though the Romans did not use the phrase: see Zimmermann (1990), p. 307, cf. pp. 606–7 on *mancipatio*, warranty for title was a separate matter: see Zimmermann (1990), pp. 278–96.

[12] Zimmermann (1990), pp. 311–19, cf. Jakab (1997), pp. 131–5.

[13] D.21.1.19pr (Ulpian. 1 ad Ed. Cur. Aed.), D.18.1.43pr (Florian. 8 Inst.), with Zimmermann (1990), pp. 241–3, 308–9; Watson (1965), p. 89, on Cic. *Off.* 3.55.

his opinion in D.19.1.38.2, protection of the buyer was 'still somewhat patchy'.[14]

The buyer's interest in accessories was addressed in Roman law in the same way as latent defects, that is, deficiencies that were not apparent before the sale. Typically, contracts were used as express warranties to extend the seller's liability for latent defects and they were also used to assign accessories to one party or the other.[15] In D.19.1.38.2, Proculus assumes that the parties have done so when he writes that they should settle the question on the basis of what they agreed. He may have in mind one of the standard contract clauses that sellers used to reserve *ruta caesa* after the sale, or an individual agreement reflecting the specific circumstances of this case.[16] Even without a specific contract, the seller could in some cases be liable, and this is the underlying issue in D.19.1.38.2. If the pipes are classified as *ruta caesa*, they belong to the seller after the sale, and he is liable to deliver them to the buyer only if there is a contract to this effect. Alternatively, if the pipes are part of the property, the buyer acquires them through purchase and the seller is liable for their delivery without a contract. Of course, the parties would need to know whether the pipes were *ruta caesa* or part of the property in order to frame an effective contract. It could, however, be difficult for buyers and sellers to know which items belonged in each category. Jurists disagreed about the definition of *ruta caesa*, and laymen might be confused; it was just the kind of legal language an orator could manipulate to his advantage, according to Cicero (*Part. Or.* 107).[17] The category 'part of the property' was not much easier to apply, as reflected in the jurists' discussions of the topic.[18] Both categories were defined in terms of physical attachment, but this criterion was less clear-cut than it might at first appear. The question in D.19.1.38.2 reflects uncertainty about these categories, specifically their

[14] Zimmermann (1990), p. 319, cf. 319–21: when Celsus commented on D.19.1.38.2 around 100 CE, the seller of land was liable only for outright fraud or overstating the acreage, and the buyer's interests could be protected only by express warranties, as Proculus' opinion assumes.

[15] Zimmermann (1990), p. 309; Kaser (1971), I, pp. 557–8

[16] The standard clause reserving *ruta caesa* was probably used first in connection with *mancipatio*; see Marrone (1971), p. 215 fn. 9, and Olde Kalter (1963), pp. 24–5 (thank you to M. Kramer-Hajos for translating the Dutch). This clause may have been used less frequently with *emptio venditio* because this form of consensual sale typically included contracts adapted to the specifics of individual transactions: see Marrone (1971), p. 222, cf. pp. 218–20.

[17] *Ruta caesa* relates only to sale, and it occurs in two forms with no difference in meaning, according to Marrone (1971), p. 213. *Ruta caesa* in D.19.1.38.2; and also in Var., *L.L.* 9.104; Cic. *Part. Or.* 107; Cic. *Top.* 100; Fest. p. 320 L; D.50.16.241 (Quint. Muc. 1 ὅρων); D.18.1.66.2 (Pompon. 31 ad Quint. Muc.); D.10.4.5.2 (Ulp. 24 ad Ed.). *Ruta et caesa* in Cic., *de Or.* 2.226; D.19.1.18 (Iavolen. 7 ex Cass.); D.19.1.17.6 (Ulpian. 32 ad Ed.). Cicero's use of the term also assumes the economic value of accessories so designated: see *Top.* 100 and *de Or.* 2.226.

[18] The category 'part of the property' operates in various legal contexts, for example, sale, inheritance: see, generally, Meincke (1971).

application to underground pipes. The situation illustrates the incomplete correspondence between legal knowledge and commercial practice as well as the jurists' attempts to address the problem. Celsus' opinion and, even more, his rationale, recognised the problem and attempted to solve it.

This chapter traces the legal discussion of *ruta caesa* and part of the property in cases about sale, in order to contextualise Celsus' opinion in D.19.1.38.2. Investigating these categories offers insight into the way the jurists changed law, both by responding to social need and by working within existing legal frameworks to systematise their approach to accessories.[19] The analysis sheds light on the social adequacy of these legal responses: specifically, to what extent did they facilitate the use of law that supported the economic interests of buyers and sellers? The jurists' discussion of accessories is part of an overall response in the law of sale to the increasing complexity of economic transactions.[20] In D.19.1.38.2, Celsus recognised that contracts gave insufficient protection because buyers and sellers often did not even think to use them. While his opinion may at first seem extreme, perhaps because of its rhetorical flourish, it represents, in fact, an emerging consensus about the treatment of pipes that is ultimately integrated into Ulpian's rules about accessories.[21] As the jurists addressed the realities of the real estate market, the legal categories became less analytically consistent, and yet, paradoxically, they provided more clarity and certainty to buyers and sellers as they contemplated the accessories to property.

2. RUTA CAESA (SELLER'S PROPERTY)

The category of *ruta caesa* was used in sale by *mancipatio* to designate accessories that belonged to the seller after the sale.[22] The jurists explained *ruta caesa* in terms of physical attachment, and this criterion appears in two definitions of the term ascribed to the early jurist Q. Mucius (cos. 105 BCE). First, in his book of definitions:

> in, rutis caesis, ea sunt, quae terra non tenentur quaeque opere structili tectoriove non continentur. (D.50.16.241 (Quint. Muc. 1 ὅρων))

> Among things dug and cut are those which are not held in position by the earth and those which are not secured by concrete or plaster work.

---

[19] Typically, new legal rules are modelled on existing institutions, while the impetus for change comes from outside the legal system itself: Frier (1986), pp. 888–9. For the primacy of legal tradition, see Watson (2007), p. 9, and on contracts, pp. 31–5.

[20] Zimmermann (1990), p. 604: 'gradual development from a strictly objective, declaration oriented approach towards a more flexible and individualistic one'.

[21] Protection of the buyer was developed by Celsus' near contemporaries, Julian and Pomponius during the reigns of Hadrian, Antoninus Pius, and Marcus Aurelius: Zimmermann (1990), pp. 320–1; von Lübtow (1955) pp. 493–4.

[22] See references above at n. 16.

Mucius gives a similar definition in what was probably a response to a question from a litigant or magistrate:

> Quintus Mucius scribit, qui scribsit 'ruta caesa quaeque aedium fundive non sunt,' bis idem scriptum: nam ruta caesa ea sunt quae neque aedium neque fundi sunt D.18.1.66.2 (Pompon. 31 ad Quint. Muc.) .

> Quintus Mucius writes, the one who wrote '*ruta caesa quaeque aedium fundive non sunt,*' wrote the same thing twice: for things dug or cut are those which belong neither to the buildings nor to an estate.

In this passage, there are two layers of reporting, Pomponius quotes Mucius' interpretation of a sentence from another source (*qui scribsit . . .*)[23] Mucius' opinion that the same thing was written twice (*bis scriptum*) endorses the definition of *ruta caesa* as *quae aedium fundive non sunt* that may have appeared in a sale contract or legal opinion. In both passages, Mucius defines *ruta caesa* by what they are not, namely, not attached to or not part of land or buildings. The first definition specifies the type of attachment that limited the category of *ruta caesa*: accessories that were attached to the land itself (*quae terra continentur*) or joined to the building by cement or plaster were excluded from *ruta caesa*, (*opere structili tectoriove*). His definitions depend on what could be observed in an inspection of the property, and they thus fit the early legal approaches to the buyer's responsibility, even though there is no mention of sale.

The term *ruta caesa* is connected with sale by the late Republican jurist Aquilius Gallus in a case that, like D.19.1.38.2, also involves agreements added to the sale contract. Though Aquilius' opinion survives only in fragments (reported at third hand, first by Mela and then Ulpian), the outlines of the situation can be reconstructed. The case begins with Ulpian's definition of *ruta caesa* which is illustrated by Aquilius' opinion about a sale of land.[24] Before the sale, the seller used an additional agreement (*in lege venditionis*) to reserve for himself some accessories to the property, possibly earth materials or lumber, the examples in the definition of *ruta caesa*:

> Si ruta et caesa excipiantur in venditione, ea placuit esse ruta, quae eruta sunt, ut harena creta et similia: caesa ea esse, ut arbores caesas et carbones et his similia. Gallus autem Aquilius, cuius Mela refert opinionem, recte ait frustra in lege venditionis de rutis et caesis contineri, quia, si non specialiter venierunt, ad exhibendum de his agi potest neque enim magis de materia caesa aut de caementis aut de harena cavendum est venditori quam de ceteris quae sunt pretiosiora. (D.19.1.17.6 (Ulpian. 32 ad Ed.))

---

[23] The repetition of *scribit* has been taken as a sign of interpolation, but it is better taken as part of Mucius' discussion, see Marrone (1971), p. 215 n. 9. On the authenticity of Mucius' opinion in D.50.16.241, see Marrone (1971), p. 214 fn. 8.

[24] Lenel (1889), I, p. 55.

If *ruta* and *caesa* are reserved in a sale, it is understood that *ruta* are those things which are dug out, such as sand, clay, and the like; *caesa* are those things, such as cut trees and charcoal and things similar to these. But Aquilius Gallus, whose opinion Mela reports, rightly said that it was useless for a clause about *ruta* and *caesa* to be included in a sale [contract] because, if these things are not sold individually, it is possible to bring a claim for them with the an *actio ad exhibendum*, for the seller need not give a promise about cut materials, either gravel or sand, any more than about other things that are more valuable.

After the sale, the seller apparently wanted to compel the buyer to deliver the accessories, making a claim on the agreement reserving property. Aquilius determined that this was not possible because the contract was invalid, *frustra in lege venditione de rutis et caesis contineri*. There could be no contract for the buyer to deliver *ruta caesa* because by definition they already belonged to the seller. This point is made indirectly by Aquilius when he explains that the seller can use the *actio ad exhibendum* to claim them, *ad exhibendum de his agi potest*.[25]

Aquilius' opinion contextualises the problem in D.19.1.38.2. In Aquilius' case, the seller added a contract to the sale agreement, just as Proculus expects in D.19.1.38.2. The seller's contract is, however, of no use because it specified accessories that fell into the category of *ruta caesa*. In D.19.1.38.2, if the seller had made a contract about underground pipes and was trying to use it to claim them, he would need to know whether or not the pipes counted as *ruta caesa*, and this is just what Firmus asked. Proculus, as reported, disregards this category; his emphasis on contracts may seek to change the practices described by Aquilius, who explains that sellers rarely make contracts about stone and sand or even about more valuable things, *potest neque enim magis de materia caesa aut de caementis aut de harena cavendum est venditori quam de ceteris quae sunt pretiosiora*. The examples – both Ulpian's (timber, charcoal) and Aquilius' (gravel, sand) – are all natural materials that are classified as *ruta caesa* or not, based on their connection to the land, one of the criteria in Mucius' definition (*quae terra continentur*). Because of the nature of these examples, it appears that connection to the land was interpreted to mean natural materials and not manmade structures that were attached to the land.[26] For this reason, the classification of underground pipes could seem ambiguous to buyers and sellers who were unfamiliar with the legal distinctions. Their location under the ground might seem to exclude them from

---

[25] Marrone (1971), p. 217; cf. Watson (1965), p. 95. *Vindicatio* was the standard mechanism for establishing ownership and the *actio ad exhibendum* was a special type of *vindicatio* used for movable property: see D.10.4.5.2 with Kaser (1971), I, p. 434, and Lemosse (1983), pp. 68–9.

[26] Cassius takes a similar approach to reeds and willows in the legacy of a farm with equipment (*fundus cum instrumento*): they were part of the property before they were cut, but once cut they were *instrumenta*, D.33.7.12.11 (Ulpian. 20 ad Sab.), with Meincke (1971), pp. 137–8. Similarly Inst.Gai.2.73–75, with Maddalena (1971) p. 179.

ruta caesa. Yet, because they were not natural materials, they would have to be *ruta caesa* unless they were connected by masonry or plaster. Such uncertainty may have motivated Firmus' question in D.19.1.38.2, though it is hard to know exactly what type of installation was involved or how the jurists understood it. Archaeological sources for pipes and plumbing installation, especially in the houses from Pompeii, offer some guidance about how legal categories might have been applied in this case.

3. FOUNTAINS AND UNDERGROUND PIPES

When water was delivered to a Roman house from a public supply in Italy, typically it arrived through underground lead pipes that were connected to a lead distribution box near the door. From there, lead pipes carried the water to other parts of the house, usually to the *impluvium* and fountains in the peristyle, where there might be a second distribution box.[27] The *castellum plumbeum* in D.19.1.38.2 could fit into this arrangement in several ways. It could, for example, represent part of the municipal water distribution system, one of the neighbourhood reservoirs used in Pompeii to regulate pressure.[28] Alternatively the lead basin could be a distribution box or a cistern on the property, possibly fed by roof run-off like the ones commonly found in Pompeian gardens.[29] The bronze basin is likely to have been part of fountain or *impluvium*, a common feature of Roman houses, or possibly a tank for a bath. Pliny, *Letters*, 5.6.40, describes a courtyard with fountains running underground and emerging here and there to charming effect (*Letters*, 5.6.40),[30] whilst in a rural setting, the lead cistern could be a catch basin for a developed spring that supplied the house.[31]

---

[27] Jansen (2000), pp. 115–19 for the typical arrangements, based on Ostia and Pompeii.

[28] On neighbourhood reservoirs, see Hodge (1991), pp. 300–1; Bruun (1991), p. 125. According to Capogrossi Colognesi (1966), p. 37 fn. 61 and p. 43 fn. 77, the *castellum* in this case was in an urban settting, but may have been public or private; in either case, the pipes were owned by the landowner because they were located on the property.

[29] For a *castellum* as reservoir: D 8.2.19pr (Paul. 6 ad Sab.); D.8.4.2 (Ulpian. 17 ad Ed.); D.18.1.78pr (Lab. 4 Post. a Iavolen. Epit.); D.19.1.7.8 (Ulpian. 32 ad Ed.); D.30.41.10 (Ulpian. 21 ad Sab.); D.43.20.1.38–41 (Ulpian. 70 ad Ed.). Garden cisterns with lead pipes (*fistulae*) are described by Vitr. 6.3.2, but it is all ceramic *dolia* at Pompeii, in Jashemski (1996), pp. 51–2, 54, 56. For lead tanks inside houses, see Hodge (1991), p. 301.

[30] See Glaser (2000), pp. 432–6, for a description of domestic fountains with open basins, sometimes made of stone, for example Plin. *Ep.* 5.6.36–37. Jansen (2000), p. 111, thinks the evidence for fountains in houses under-represents their actual occurrence. For *aenea* for bronze tanks in a bath: Vitr. 5.10.1. More commonly in both literary sources and the Digest, *aeneum* (also spelled *aenum* and *ahenum*) refers to a portable cooking kettle; see, for example, Cato, *On Agriculture*, 13, 79; Varro, *On Agriculture*, 1.22; D.19.2.19.2 (Ulpian. 32 ad Ed.); D. 33.7.18.3 (Paul. 2 ad Vitel.). Built-in bath tubs are masonry, portable ones bronze, in de Haan (1996), pp. 59–61.

[31] Bronze or lead basins for developing a spring: Vitr., 8.1.4, with Hodge (1991), p. 27 (examples from the Greek world, no metal reservoirs); Oleson (2000), p. 259 (spring house at Cosa

While the archaeological evidence helps to reconstruct the configuration of the plumbing in D.19.1.38.2, it is not dispositive. The material that the pipes were made of – ceramic or lead –was key to applying Mucius' definition of *ruta caesa* because it determined how they would be attached to the basin and its surrounding masonry. Either ceramic or lead pipes could have been used in all three possible configurations. If the pipes were ceramic, they would not be *ruta caesa* but part of the property, because this kind of pipe was usually attached by masonry.[32] But the use of the term *fistula* probably indicates that the pipes were made of lead and joined to the basin by soldering not masonry.[33] According to Mucius' definition, then, the pipes in D.19.1.38.2 were *ruta caesa*, and if the buyer wanted to buy them with the property, he would need to use a contract, as Proculus expected. The possibility that pipes could be excluded from the purchase of property seems counter-intuitive, considering that lead pipes were the usual technology, and also considering the desirability of running water. This mismatch between legal categories and social practices could have led to Firmus' question in D.19.1.38.2 and may also have motivated the continued legal discussion of *ruta caesa* and its application to different situations at the time when Celsus considered underground pipes.

4. IAVOLENUS ON UNDERGROUND PIPES

In two legal cases, Celsus' contemporary Iavolenus discusses building materials or accessories that are comparable to underground pipes. Though the term *ruta caesa* occurs in only one of these cases, both are important for reconstructing the debate that Celsus answered in D.19.1.38. The first case posed a question about pipes and a reservoir, *castellum*, to which the pipes were attached: should the *castellum* be included with the pipes even though it was not mentioned in the contract (*licet scriptura non continetur?* D.18.1.78pr (Iavolen. 4 Post. a Labeo. Epit.)).[34] The answer was 'yes', because the reservoir was attached to the pipes. The use of a contract to specify the pipes is consistent with Proculus' view in D.19.1.38.2, and assumes that pipes

---

with a masonry cistern); Glaser (2000), pp. 416–31 (more Greek examples). Stone cisterns may be preserved in greater numbers because metal ones were melted down for re-use.

[32] Vitr. 8.6.8 on joining ceramic pipes with quick lime, and 8.6.14 on construction of masonry reservoirs, with Hodge (1991), pp. 114–15.

[33] Vitr. 8.6.1 with Hodge (1991), p. 420 fn. 47, and Bruun (1991), pp. 124–7. For lead pipes joined by soldering: Hodge (1991), pp. 156, 314–15, 466 fn. 15; and Jansen (2000), p. 119.

[34] D.18.1.78pr (Lab. 4 Iavolen. Epit.): 'fistulas emptori accessuras in lege dictum erat: quaerebatur, an castellum, ex quo fistulis aqua duceretur, accederet. respondi apparere id actum esse, ut id quoque accederet, licet scriptura non continetur'. (It was stated in a contract that pipes belonged to the buyer: it was asked whether the buyer also got the reservoir, from which water was conducted by pipes. I answered that it seems to have been agreed that it also belonged [to the buyer] even though it was not included in the written document.) This is Iavolenus' opinion not Labeo's, according to Lenel (1889), I, p. 299 n. 4.

were *ruta caesa*. But once the pipes are included with the property, anything attached to them is also included, viz. the *castellum*. Pipes may have been a special case when they were connected with a servitude for channelling water because they were necessary for exercising the right.[35] Iavolenus folds functionality into the criterion of attachment to extend the meaning of the contract in a way that makes it possible for the landowner to use the water supply on the property.[36]

In the second case, Iavolenus contemplates two examples, grain bins and roof tiles, that each suggest a partial analogy with pipes. Grain bins were classified as *ruta caesa* when they stood on the ground, but if they had underground foundations they should be included with the property (D.19.1.18pr (Iavolen. 7 ex Cass.)). Iavolenus' approach here recalls Aquilius' opinion about earth materials, which excluded from *ruta caesa* things connected with the land itself. Because Iavolenus explicitly applies the rule to buildings, his opinion provides a clear analogy for the pipes in D.19.1.38.2. Iavolenus would include them with the property.[37] His opinion on roof tiles complicates the picture because it essentially rejects the criterion of physical attachment. The case concerns roof tiles that are not installed on the roof but are piled up elsewhere on the property. If they had been removed and will be re-installed, they are 'part of the property', but if they were delivered and not yet installed, they are *ruta caesa*, though this term is not used (D.19.1.18.1 (Iavolen. 7 ex Cass.)). Iavolenus' discussion of roof tiles suggests an alternative rationale for excluding pipes from *ruta caesa*, namely, that they are permanent and functional parts of the property, an idea that was already in discussion in cases involving pipes and servitudes.[38] The criterion of permanence does not originate with Iavolenus, as we will see shortly, in the discussion of 'part of the property'.

For the present discussion of *ruta caesa*, Iavolenus' approach adapts the law to the expectations of buyers and sellers while working within the legal tradition. Iavolenus improves on Mucius' definition, adding to the types of physical attachment that served as criteria. He also draws on the insights of Aquilius and Cassius about connection to the land, transferring this idea

---

[35] Meincke (1971), p. 168, assumes that the pipes were used to exercise a servitude to channel water; see also Maddalena (1971), p. 174, on functionality without mention of servitudes. In general when land was sold, servitudes were transferred automatically because they were considered to be permanent assets of the land: D.8.4.12 (Paul. 15 ad Sab.), with Grosso (1969), pp. 94–5. Pipes were necessary for exercising the right: D.18.1.47 (Ulpian. 29 ad Sab.), cf. Solazzi (1948), p. 48.

[36] *Scriptura* shows there was a *lex venditionis* in this case: Capogrossi Colognesi (1966), p. 72 fn. 140.

[37] For underground structures as part of the property in general without reference to this case: Meincke (1971), p. 144.

[38] For permanence or continuity as a requirement, see Meincke (1971), p. 145.

from natural materials to building components such as pipes and foundations, suitably enough because Iavolenus' opinion about grain bins comes from his commentary on Cassius. When it comes to roof tiles, Iavolenus invokes physical attachment but, paradoxically, his opinion undermines the traditional function of this criterion. Traditionally, roof tiles that are no longer attached to the building should be *ruta caesa*, regardless of whether they were once attached or not. Iavolenus, however, looks beyond strict physical attachment, arguing from a concept of the building that is at once more abstract and more practical: it is abstract in the sense that it requires a shared understanding of what parts or accessories belong to a building, and practical to the extent that the abstract idea conforms to expectations among laymen and landowners. His narrower definition of *ruta caesa* recognises variety in materials and methods of construction. In addition, his approach depends on more than a snapshot of the building at the moment of sale; rather, it envisions the property existing over time. In narrowing the category of *ruta caesa*, Iavolenus limits its usefulness, and also implicitly privileges its counterpart 'part of the property'.

5. CELSUS ON UNDERGROUND PIPES

Where *ruta caesa* concerned property that the seller retained after the sale, the buyer acquired ownership of accessories that were classified as part of the property, *aedium* or *pars aedium*. These categories were recognised as alternatives in Firmus' question about pipes in D.19.1.38.2, *an hae aedium essent, an ut ruta . . . quae aedium non essent.* While Proculus' response ignores the categories, Celsus addresses them directly when he states that the pipes should belong to the buyer on the grounds that they were attached to the building, *ut inserta et inclusa aedificio partem eius esse.* His opinion is part of a larger juristic discussion of what belonged with a property, not just among contemporary jurists (for example, Iavolenus on grain bins, discussed previously) but also in the Republican era and later in the writings of Ulpian. In these discussions, the jurists broaden the category of part of the property, working with the traditional criteria of physical attachment to address the complexities of the real estate market, for example, by making the categories flexible enough to cover the sale of an estate with many working parts and not just a building with part attached by masonry or plaster. Celsus' opinion in D.19.1.38.2 both recognises these social needs and connects them with the legal dialogue about parts of the property.

Celsus urged that the pipes should be classified as part of the property because they were built in and connected to the building, *inserta et inclusa*, though the two parts of this expression probably should not be taken together. The first term, *inserta*, seems out of place because it is used of buildings and real property only in this passage of the Digest. *Inserere* usually applies to writing, that is, inserting a phrase or clause into a legal document.[39] It seems likely, then, that the text was disrupted in compilation and that *inserta* was not originally part of Celsus' description of the pipes. Instead, *inserta* shows that Celsus discussed contracts in a now lost part of his commentary on this case. On this reconstruction, Celsus directly addressed Proculus, reconciling their views by recommending that the pipes be treated as if they had been specified in a contract. In this reconstruction, Celsus adopts a similar strategy to Iavolenus in the case about the pipes and *castellum*, where the *castellum* is included as part of the property even though it is not in the written contract.

The other part of Celsus' description of the pipes, *inclusa*, resonates with the juristic discussion of 'part of the property', specifically with the issue of physical attachment that involves joining metal, like the pipes in D.19.1.38.2. The verb *inclusa* connects Celsus' rationale to a case that tested the limits of part of the property, first in relation to real estate and then movables (D.41.3.30.1 (Pompon. 30 ad Sab.)). This case was not about sale but more generally claims for ownership when different people owned different parts of an object that, when joined, were considered a unified whole, a situation analogous to the division of accessories between buyer and seller. The first part of the case involves columns and roof tiles owned by someone other than the landowner: could he claim them after they were built into someone else's building? In general, the answer was 'no', not while the building was standing, but he could claim them back if at some point it was demolished.[40] In the second part of the case, the rule was generalised from buildings to movable property through the example of a gemstone and its gold setting. Though the comparison between buildings and jewellery is made by Pomponius, a younger contemporary of Celsus, it may have already been in discussion at the time of D.19.1.38.2. Indeed, Celsus' use of the term *inclusa* invokes the analogy because this verb is the usual word describing gems set in gold and silver in the Digest.[41]

---

[39] *Vocabularium, s.v. insero* = 'to put in', most often figuratively of inserting names/dates/clauses into legal documents.

[40] Meincke (1971), p. 146; Riccobono (1915–17), pp. 468–9. This rule was explicitly set out in a *senatus consultum* of 139–140 that prohibited legacies that could be fulfilled only by demolishing a building: see Riccobono (1915–17), pp. 476–7.

[41] For *includo* in descriptions of building materials: D.19.1.17.3 (Ulpian. 32 ad Ed.: wall paintings and marble architectural details); D.24.1.63 (Paul. 3 ad Nerat.: wife's property joined to husband's structure); and possibly D.47.3.1.2 (Ulpian. 37 ad Ed.) where it is an emendation. For gems with *includo* to illustrate component parts: D.10.4.6 (Paul. 14 ad Sab.); D.19.2.13.5 (Ulpian. 32 ad Ed.); D.33.10.9.1 (Papinian. 7 Resp.); D.34.2.19.13 (Ulpian. 20 ad Sab.); D.34.2.19.16 (Ulpian. 20 ad Sab.); D.34.2.20 (Paul. 3 ad Sab.); D.34.2.32.1 (Paul. 2 ad Vitell.). *Includo* is used most often in the Digest in the sense of shutting something or someone in, for example people in jail or animals in pens (for *inclusos* and *vinctorum* of prisoners in the quarries: D.4.6.9 (Callist. 2 Ed. Monit.)). Its use in the figurative sense for documents is least common.

Soldering pipes may seem far from delicate welding in gold, and indeed the two processes are distinguished by jurists and laymen alike.[42] But for Celsus, any kind of metal joining has the same legal outcome and, as a result, he classifies the lead pipes as part of the building. Celsus may not have been the first to take this approach to 'part of the property'. Cassius considered an arm welded onto a metal statue as part of it, even if it originally belonged somewhere else because it seems the join was not visible, in contrast to lead soldering which leaves a seam.[43] The same principle may have been applied to buildings as early as Labeo, whose opinion Iavolenus cites in a case about plant pots. Whether the pots were ceramic or lead, they were part of the property if they were permanently attached to it, 'if they were bound to the buildings in such a way that that they were permanently installed, (*si ita illigata sint aedibus, ut ibi perpetuo posita sint*, D 33.7.26pr (Iavolen. 5 Post. Labeo.)).[44] The type of attachment is vague – *illigata* can include tying with straps or soldering – and perhaps this is the point.[45] By diversifying the type of attachment, the category 'part of the property' could take into account construction techniques and typical building features neglected by the early definitions of *ruta caesa*, just as in Iavolenus' opinions on grain bins and roof tiles.[46] Celsus takes a similarly expansive view of part of the property

[42] For *ferruminare* or *ferruminatio* for welding metals or fusing with heat or glue: for example Plin. *N.H.* 34.116 (gold), 34.136 (stones in a furnace), 36.176 (cement), 36.199 (glass and sulphur), 37.28 (crystals); D.6.1.23.5 (Paul. 21 ad Ed.) (no material specified); D.41.27pr (Pompon. 30 ad Sab.) (silver to silver). For *plumbare* for soldering with lead only: Cato, *On Agriculture*, 21.5 (parts of the olive press); Tac. *Ann.* 2.69 (lead tablets); Plin., *N.H.* 34.161 (silver is not joined with lead because of different melting points); Front. *Aq.* 124; D.41.27pr. (Pompon. 30 ad Sab.) (lead to lead); D.19.1.17.8 (Ulpian. 32 ad Ed.) (*adplumbare*, faucets onto pipes). There is some slippage in D. 34.2.32.1 (Paul. 2 ad Vitell.), where joins of gems and fine metals are described with all three verbs: *includo*, *illigo*, and *replumbo*.
[43] D.6.1.23.5 (Paul. 21 ad Ed.): 'Non idem in eo quod plumbatum sit, quia ferruminatio per eandem materiam facit confusionem, plumbatura non idem efficit'. (It is not the same for something that has been soldered because welding makes a join with the same material, soldering does not do the same.) Even if the arm is removed, it does not revert to its prior owner. See Maddalena (1971) pp. 184–5.
[44] D.33.7.26pr (Iavolen. 5 Post. Labeo.): 'Dolia fictilia, item plumbea, quibus terra adgesta est, et in his viridiaria posita aedium esse Labeo Trebatius putant. ita id verum puto, si ita illigata sint aedibus, ut ibi perpetuo posita sint'. (Labeo [and] Trebatius think that ceramic jars, and likewise those made of lead, that are filled with dirt, in which plants are planted, are part of the property. I think that this is true also if they are attached to the buildings in such a way that they are installed permanently). Though the case concerns accessories in legacy rather than sale, the jurists compared these two legal contexts and attempted to apply the same rules in both: for example, for an explicit comparison, D.19.1.17.2 (Ulpian. 32 ad Ed.) (citing Trebatius).
[45] Labeo may have soldering lead in mind if D.50.16.242.2 (Iavolen. 2 Post. Labeo.) (lead on roof tiles) comes from the same context and, as assumed by Riccobono (1915–17), p. 482, was the opinion of Labeo not Iavolenus'.
[46] As noted in Meincke (1971), p. 143, the superficies rule applied to materials and construction of all types.

in D.19.1.38.2, and, if the analogy implied by *inclusa* was part of his original opinion, he also addresses the traditional legal categories in his rationale.[47] Yet his attitude towards these categories and the distinctions on which they depend seems decidedly untechnical, for example, when he treats jewellery and plumbing in the same way. In his rationale, Celsus explicitly recognises the inadequacy of a legal category that protected buyers only when they carefully inspected the property and knew how to apply the relevant legal categories. Some buyers and sellers might rise to the occasion, but Celsus is concerned to make the law more broadly effective by adapting it to the needs of typical Roman landowners, who were not often closely engaged in the management of their estates or well versed in the law.[48]

6. ULPIAN'S RETROSPECTIVE AND SOME CONCLUSIONS

Celsus' opinion in D.19.1.38.2 prefigures Ulpian's treatment of pipes as 'part of the property' in the sale of real estate. According to Ulpian, pipes were to be transferred with land even if there was no servitude because, he explains, they are comparable to part of the property, *quasi pars aedium ad emptorem perveniunt* (D.18.1.47 (Ulpian. 29 ad Sab.)). Though he equivocates here, in other cases he emphasises their permanent functionality, and maintains that pipes are part of the property even if they run far from the building or are laid underground.[49] Furthermore, Ulpian's category 'part of the building' understands accessories as part of the permanent fabric of a building even if not permanently attached, for example window panes or roof tiles (D.19.1.17.10 (Ulpian. 32 ad Ed.); D.33.1.12.25 (Ulpian. 20 ad Sab.)). Like roof tiles, pipes might be removed for repair or replacement, but they served a permanent function in providing water or drainage to the property and thus they should be included in 'part of the property'. Ulpian's opinions on pipes represent a move to treat at least plumbing

---

[47] Celsus may even respond to Proculus' impractical solution of how to assign ownership of things welded together reported by Pomponius in D.41.1.27.2 (Pompon. 30 ad Sab.). When the welding (*ferruminatio*) obliterates the distinction between the two things, Cassius allows for monetary compensation, but Proculus, along with Pegasus, insists that each part belongs to its original owner.

[48] For typical landowners' expertise in farm management: Kehoe (1997), pp. 144–6, 156–7; and their expertise in the law: Zimmermann (1990), p. 605. Expansion of protections for the buyer are based more on practical need than legal consistency: see Zimmermann (1990), p. 243.

[49] D.19.1.13.31 (Ulpian. 32 ad Ed.) (well covers); D.19.1.15 (Ulpian. 32 ad Ed.) (pipes, basins, fountains, evn fr the building); D.19.1.17.7 (Ulpian. 32 ad Ed.) (Permanent function, *uae perpetui usus*); D.19.1.17.8 (Ulpian. 32 ad Ed.) (reservoirs, well-covers, decorative fountain spouts attached by soldering, *adplumbata*, underground even not attached); cf. D.18.1.47 (Ulpian. 29 ad Sab.) (pipes and a servitude); and in legacy: D.30.41.10 (Ulpian. 21 ad Sab.) (pipes, reservoirs); D.33.7.12.24 (Ulpian. 20 ad Sab.) (pipes, channels, basins, fixtures for fountains).

accessories systematically as 'part of the property', yielding a flexible category that accounted for various methods of construction as well as the behaviour of buyers and sellers.

Looking back to the situation in D.19.1.38.2, Ulpian's approach accommodates the practices in the real estate market described by Celsus.[50] His flexible definition of 'part of the property' expands protection for buyers who did not inspect the property carefully or were not able to use contracts to pursue their interests, as Proculus expected. The two solutions to the problem in D.19.1.38.2 represent two perspectives on the relationship between law and society. Proculus takes an idealising view because his solution protects buyers' and sellers' interests only when they are well informed, honest, and proactive in using the legal system. Celsus, like Ulpian, recognises that the real estate market rarely lives up to this ideal, and he explicitly aims to adapt law to these realities.[51] Accessories like pipes were important to Roman landowners. Some Romans even bought property because of its valuable accessories, as Labeo recognised (D 18.1.34pr) (Paul. 33 ad Ed.)). Though Labeo's opinion concerns a slave, probably the most valuable accessory, the cases discussed in this chapter show that even humble items like gravel and pipes could be worth a trip to court.[52] The law did not always provide clear guidance about accessories, and buyers and sellers might be ill informed and inexperienced. Such difficulties could be interpreted as evidence that the jurists were out of touch with the real estate market, and that Celsus' rationale is exceptional. The cases on accessories, however, show that the Romans tried to make the legal system work for them and that jurists addressed actual problems as they adapted legal traditions to the real estate market.

BIBLIOGRAPHY

Ballentine's Law Dictionary, 3rd edn (2010).

Black's Law Dictionary, 9th edn (2009).

Bruun, C., *The water supply of Ancient Rome: a study of Roman Imperial administration: Commentationes Humanarum Litterarum*, vol. 93 (1991).

---

[50] In fact, Ulpian uses the same verb, *includo*, to describe wall paintings that he classifies as part of the property (D.19.1.17.3 (Ulp. 32 ad Ed.)): 'quae tabulae pictae pro tectorio includuntur itemque crustae marmoreae aedium sunt' (those pictures painted in wall frescoes and likewise marble panels are part of the property). The phrase *pro tectorio* may also connect this case with Mucius' definition *of ruta caesa* which specified attachment by plaster.

[51] A similar characterisation of Celsus' approach in contrast to Proculus' approach is in Frier (1994), pp. 136–7, and Hausmaninger (1991), p. 60. Celsus' limited expectations of buyers is also in D.6.1.38 (Cels. 3 Dig.), where a buyer unknowingly (*imprudens*) purchased land and built on it without discovering that he had not bought it from the real owner, with de Neeve (1985), p. 90. More generally on Celsus' awareness of the diversity among individuals, see Scarano-Ussani (1989), pp. 108–9.

[52] Accessories to land were often more valuable: Maddalena (1971) pp. 179–80.

Capogrossi Colognesi, L., *Ricerche sulla struttura delle servitù d'acqua in diritto romano* (1966).

Crook, J. A., 'Classical Roman law and the sale of land', in M. I. Finley (ed.), *Studies in Roman Property* (1976), p. 71.

De Haan, N., 'Die Wasserversorgung der Privatbäder in Pompeji', in N. de Haan and G. C. M. Jansen (eds), *Cura Aquarum in Campania* (1996), p. 59.

De Neeve, P. W., 'The price of agricultural land in Roman Italy and the problem of rationalism', *Opus*, 4 (1985), p. 77.

Duncan-Jones, R. P., *The Economy of the Roman Empire: Quantitative Studies*, 2nd edn (1982).

Franklin, J. L., 'Notes on Pompeian Prosopography', *PP*, 34 (1979), p. 405.

Frier, B. W., 'Why did the jurists change Roman law? Bees and lawyers revisited', *Index*, 22 (1994), p. 135.

Frier, B. W., 'Why law changes. Review of A. Watson, *The Evolution of Law*', *Columbia LJ*, 86 (1986), p. 888.

Glaser, F., 'Fountains and *nymphaea*', in Ö. Wikander (ed.), *Handbook of Ancient Water Technology* (2000), p. 413.

Grosso, G., *Le servitù prediale nel diritto romano* (1969).

Hausmaninger, H., 'Celsus gegen Proculus', in *Tradition und Fortentwicklung im Recht, Festschrift zum 90. Geburtstag von Ulrich von Lübtow am 21. August 1990* (1991), p. 53.

Hausmaniger, H., 'Publius Iuventius Celsus: Persönalichkeit und juristische Argumentation', *ANRW*, 15.2 (1976), p. 384.

Hodge, A. T., *Roman Aqueducts and Water Supply* (1991).

Jakab, É., *Praedicere und cavere beim Marktkauf: Sachmängel im griechischen und römischen Recht. Münchener Beiträge zur Papyrusforschung und antiken Rechtsgeschichte*, vol. 87 (1997).

Jansen, G. C. M., 'Urban water transport and distribution', in Ö. Wikander (ed.), *Handbook of Ancient Water Technology* (2000), p. 103.

Jashemski, W., 'The use of water in Pompeian gardens', in N. de Haan and G. C. M. Jansen (eds), *Cura Aquarum in Campania* (1996), p. 51.

Jongman, W. M., 'M. Obellius M. F. Firmus, Pompeian *Duovir*', *Talanta*, 10–11 (1978–9), p. 62.

Kaser, M., *Das Römische Privatrecht*, 2nd edn, 2 vols (1971).

Kehoe, D. P., *Investment, Profit, and Tenancy: The Jurists and the Roman Agrarian Economy* (1997).

Lemosse, M., 'Ad exhibendum', *Iura*, 34 (1983), p. 67.

Lenel, O., *Palingenesia Iuris Civilis*. 2 vols (1889; reprint 2000).

Levy, E., and Rabel, E., *Index Interpolationum quae in Iustiniani Digestis inesse dicuntur*, 3 vols (1929–35).

Maddalena, P., '*Accedere* e *cedere* nelle fonti classiche', *Labeo*, 17 (1871), p. 169.

Marrone, M., 'Considerazioni sui "ruta (et) caesa"', in G. Falcone (ed.), *Studi in onore di Edoardo Volterra*, vol. I (1971), p. 213; reprinted in *Scritti Giuridica* (2003), p. 167.

Martin, S. D., *The Roman Jurists and the Organization of Private Building in the Late Republic and Early Empire* (1989).

Meincke, J. P., 'Superficies solo cedit', ZSS (rom. Abt.) 88 (1971), p. 136.

Olde Kalter, A. L., *Dicta et promissa de Aansprakelijkheid van der Verkoper wegens gedane toezeggingen betreffende de hoedanigheid van de verkochte zaak in het klassieke romeinse recht* (Ph. D. dissertation, Utrecht) (1963).

Oleson, J. P., 'Water-lifting', in Ö. Wikander (ed.), *Handbook of Ancient Water Technology* (2000), p. 217.

Rawson, E., 'The Ciceronian aristocracy and its properties', in M. I. Finley (ed.), *Studies in Roman Property* (1976), p. 85.

Riccobono, S., 'Dal diritto romano classico al diritto moderno', in *Annali del seminario giuridico della R. università di Palermo* 3 & 4 (1915–17), p. 165, available at: http://openlibrary.org/works/OL7564319W/Dal_diritto_romano_classico_al_diritto_moderno.

Riccobono, S., '*Stipulatio* ed *instrumentum* nel diritto giustinianeo', ZSS (rom. Abt.) 43 (1922), p. 262.

Scarano-Ussani, V., *Empiria e dogmi. La scuola proculiana fra Nerva e Adriano* (1989).

Solazzi, S., *Specie ed estinzione delle servitù prediali* (1948).

Steinwenter, A., *Fundus cum instrumento: Eine agrar- und rechtsgeschichtliche Studie. Akademie der Wissenschaften in Wien. Philosopisch-historische Klasse, Sitzungsberichte,* 221, vol. 1. Abhandlung (1942).

Stella Maranca, F., *Intorno ai frammenti di Celso* (1915).

Vocabularium Iurisprudentiae Romanae (1903–87).

Von Lübtow, U., 'Zur Frage der Sachmängelhaftung im römischen Recht', in *Studi in onore di Ugo Enrico Paoli* (1955), p. 489.

Watson, A., 'Law and society', in J. W. Cairns and P. J. du Plessis (eds), *Beyond Dogmatics: Law and Society in the Roman World* (2007), p. 9.

Watson, A., *The Law of Obligations in the Later Roman Republic* (1965).

Zimmermann, R., *The Law of Obligations: Roman Foundations of the Civilian Tradition* (1990).

Part IV

Concluding Thoughts

Chapter 12

The Standpoint Determines the View: Jacques Barzun's Theory of Aspect

Philip Thomas

1. INTRODUCTION

In E. M. Forster's novel *A Room with a View*,[1] the management of Pensione Bertolini does not provide the rooms with the promised views on the river to Lucy Honeychurch and her chaperone Charlotte Bartlett. Mr Emerson, another guest, interrupts the altercation, saying 'I have a view, I have a view . . . This is my son . . . He has a view, too'. It can be argued that the text has a double meaning and that the novel deals with the philosophical view of life of the Emersons.[2] Projected onto Roman law, the metaphor of the ivory tower[3] is by now flogged to death, but the question may be asked whether this tower had windows and what views did the occupants have? Romanists and legal historians may have been unaware of Thomas Kuhn,[4] but his theory would hardly have come as a revelation to their ranks, as it has been common cause that since the days of the glossators the second life of Roman law has been characterised by a variety of paradigms, succeeding one another or co-existing.[5] The common denominator of the majority of these 'schools' has been that Roman law played handmaiden to legal theory.

---

[1] E. M. Forster (1908). In 1958 the author published *A View without a Room* in the *Observer*, which is included in some Penguin editions.

[2] R. Doll, www.emforster.info/pages/roomview.html (last accessed 3 January 2012).

[3] Song of Solomon, 7:4. French critic Charles Augustin Sainte-Beuve (1804–69) was the first to use the expression in the figurative sense of a place or state of privileged seclusion, disconnected from practical matters and harsh realities of life: at wordsmith.org/words/ivory_tower.html (last accessed 3 January 2012).

[4] Thomas S. Kuhn (1922–96), American historian and philosopher of science. *The Structure of Scientific Revolutions* (1962) popularised the concept 'paradigm' and the idea that different paradigms competed for hegemony. Kuhn holds that a paradigm does not only relate to theory, methods, techniques and methodology, but also to assumptions, hypotheses and values.

[5] The Glossators, Commentators, School of Orléans, Humanists, Antiquarians, Usus Modernus Pandectarum and the Historical School are discussed in textbooks on legal history. The Interpolationalists and the various directions Romanist studies have taken during the twentieth century are less clearly defined in the general literature and vary from country to country, and a discussion thereof falls outside the scope of this essay. Interesting is Wubbe (2003), pp. 512–16.

This entailed that all rooms faced the same direction in the hope of lucre, appointments, relevance and utility. In consequence, the immediate purpose of Roman law from the late Middle Ages onwards has been to develop a coherent and logical legal system as well as the harmonisation of local law within this system. Achievement of this objective was possible on account of the dominant position of Roman law in academic legal education. The result-ing development of Western-European legal science achieved *communes opin-iones* on most essential points, which became codified in the European and derivative codes. Internal contradictions had been argued away by finesses of the glossators or manipulation of texts. Much valuable research was labelled antiquarian by ruling dogma.

2. VOICES IN THE WILDERNESS: NEW PARADIGMS

At present the removal of Latin from the law curriculum and the con-sequent disappearance of the classics from school curricula have made expertise in Roman law an elitist pastime, which in a culture of materialism and instant gratification is no longer considered 'relevant'. The voices of Romanists who have argued in favour of the essential role of Roman law in European legal studies[6] have not convinced the marketplace, and I limit my references to the *oratio pro domo* of Paul du Plessis,[7] whose well researched[8] and well argued thoughts on the topic deserve to be heard outside the choir. National and academic policymakers adhere to the belief that legal educa-tion, legal science and harmonisation can be successful without Roman law,[9] in spite of arguments against reinvention of the wheel. The pragmatic arguments relative to the development of a European legal system have been widely and excellently canvassed by Reinhard Zimmermann[10] and it is obvious that the same arguments apply in respect of globalisation. More esoteric beliefs strive for wider following and the philosophical argument of this essay is that the genius of the Roman jurists has been widely acclaimed, but remains often misunderstood as the texts have been interpreted within a doctrinal perspective.[11] Generations of dogmatists have

---

[6] Too many to mention as since codification virtually every professor of Roman law has at some stage voiced his opinion. Some random examples: J. C. Naber (1858–1950), professor of Roman law at the University of Utrecht, whose inaugural lecture was titled *De vormende kracht van het Romeinse recht* (1885); Wubbe (2003), pp. 556–60; van Rhee and Winkel (2010), pp. 163–5. See also Hoffmeier (1995), pp. 19–22.

[7] Du Plessis (2010), pp. 64–72.

[8] The literature on the topic is copious and the main contributions are found in the footnotes of du Plessis' article.

[9] Du Plessis (2010), *passim*; Heirbaut (2005), pp. 136–53; van Rhee and Winkel (2010), p. 167; Martyn and Coppens (2008), pp. 19–24.

[10] Heirbaut (2005), *passim*; du Plessis (2010), *passim*. In n. 9, du Plessis lists the books and articles by Zimmermann on the subject.

[11] Thomas (1997), pp. 202–13.

carefully selected texts from the sources in order to argue their cases with the Roman jurists as their media. Enlightened positivists have used vague references to social, economic and political factors such as class struggle,[12] inflation,[13] Christianity[14] and absolutism. However, the over-riding ideas have been that the classical jurists reasoned within an established doctrine subject to steady development and always reached the correct legal solution.[15] This chapter proffers the argument that, literally and figuratively, where one stands determines the view, which in turn brings the idea of the correct legal solution under discussion.[16] This also entails placing the individual texts into new perspectives. Authority for this relativism can be found in the work of the historian Barzun,[17] who floated a theory of aspect. Thus, Barzun's ideas will be briefly set out and then illustrated on the basis of recent research on the Twelve Tables, and thereafter applied to several related texts from the *Corpus Iuris Civilis*. The contemporary doctrinal *communis opinio* concerning these texts will be discussed, followed by a view from another room.

3. JACQUES BARZUN'S THEORY OF ASPECT

In his work *From Dawn to Decadence. 500 Years of Western Cultural Life*, the historian Jacques Barzun proffers the thesis that during the last 500 years, four main upheavals shook the West: the sixteenth-century religious, the seventeenth-century monarchical, the eighteenth-century liberal individualistic French, and the twentieth-century Russian social and collectivist revolution. In the same book Barzun introduces his ideas of a theory of aspect, which is a recurring subtext.[18] He proposes that no person, object or event is ever viewed in his/her totality.[19] All present a variety of faces, and observers only take in one or a few of these faces or aspects and consider this to be the whole or at least the essence. Barzun accepts this partiality as a fact of life, namely the rule of spontaneous choice. In this rule, he finds the explanation for the surprising differences in value placed on the same thinker and for the

---

[12] Most descriptions of the Twelve Tables employ the existence of different orders and Livy's narrative as such. Random examples: Sohm, Mitteis and Wenger (1926), p. 52; Jolowicz (1952), pp. 5–13; van Oven (1948), pp. 4–7; Söllner (1971), pp. 25, 39, 41; Hermesdorf (1972), pp. 123–31, also 49–50; Lokin and Zwalve (2006), pp. 58–60.

[13] As an explanation for *laesio enormis*, Becker (1993), p. 13 fns 22 and 23 provide the literature.

[14] Random references include: van Oven (1948), pp. 31–2, literature in fn. 62; Jolowicz (1952), pp. 521, 524, 535, on p. 584 a reference to further literature is found; Buckland and Stein (1963), pp. 32, 320, 338.

[15] Thomas (1998), pp. 647–57; Thomas (1997), pp. 202–13.

[16] Thomas (1998), pp. 649–51, 655–7; Thomas (1997), pp. 205, 207, 213.

[17] Jacques Barzun (1907–), Franco-American historian. His last major work *From Dawn to Decadence. 500 Years of Western Cultural Life 1500 to the Present* was published in 2000.

[18] Barzun (2000), pp. 46–7, 174, 246–7, 250, 253, 430–1, 435–7, 568–74, 652–6, 759–63, 768–9.

[19] Barzun uses the simile of a mountain at p. 47.

different pasts depicted by different historians.[20] These ideas may fruitfully be applied to the *fons et origo* of Roman law, the codification of the Twelve Tables, as the interest in and studies of this code were resuscitated by the humanists and thus coincide with the time frame of Barzun's work.

The various interpretations of the events during the first half of the fifth century BCE show a number of recurring themes, such as secularisation of the law as the priests were forced into revelation of the law, the democratisation of the oligarchic rule of the aristocracy, equal rights, land reform and debt reform. It is not difficult to link these issues to points in the programmes of the four above-mentioned revolutions, which supports the hypothesis that the aspects that shine out of a particular historical event and grab the attention of researchers are to a large extent reflections of their own *Zeitgeist*.

4. CEDANT[21] AND THE TWELVE TABLES

The University of Pavia has facilitated access to new research with the launch of the *Collegio di Diritto Romano*, a series of seminars giving Romanists and classicists the opportunity to interact with the leading researchers in their disciplines. The topic in 2003 was the Twelve Tables and the contributions published in a volume offered new faces of the code.[22] Michel Humbert reviewed the old, more fanciful theories, such as a complete law reform based on a Greek model, the revelation of religious secrets, and equality in law as the result of the threats of the proletarian masses.[23] He concludes that textual authority is lacking for the underlying hypotheses, and offers an alternative objective of the statute, namely placing the administration of justice on an exhaustive legislative basis in order to eliminate the discretion of the holders of *imperium* in this field.[24] In his analysis of the political events, he redefined the concepts *plebs* and *patres* from about 450 BCE and the nature of their conflict. The traditional description of the plebeians as the marginalised, poor masses without political rights clamouring for equality and economic benefits is replaced by the view of the *plebs* as a political movement of rich citizens opposed to the ruling oligarchy.[25] He views the struggle between *plebs* and *patres* as not for power, nor for equality of law, but for equality before the law, to be effected by controlling the administration of

---

[20] A harbinger of this credo is found in the theoretical work of Hoetink and in the scientific work of Ankum, namely that every generation has a different Roman law, because they approach the texts with different scientific equipment and luggage: Hoetink (1982); van Rhee and Winkel (2010), p. 163.

[21] *Centro di studi e ricerche sui Diritti Antichi.*

[22] Humbert (2005).

[23] Humbert (2005), pp. 4–25.

[24] Humbert (2005), pp. 26–41.

[25] Humbert (2005), pp. 7–11.

justice or, in other words, the *imperium* of the consuls.[26] In this interpretation, the collaboration by the priests was an absolute necessity and Humbert
considers the priests the intellectual fathers of the codification.[27] He argues
that an analysis of the text of the Twelve Tables shows that the code does
not provide the general public with access to the law, but necessitates learned
assistance by an expert.[28]

The text of the Twelve Tables,[29] or in particular the order thereof, is questioned by Diliberto,[30] whose argument that it is highly improbable that the
decemviri would have applied a system, which was developed centuries afterwards, is rather suggestive. The paucity of solid beacons indicating the place
of various fragments[31] gives the argument a smack of deconstruction in spite
of Diliberto's argument that the fourth book of Gaius holds the key.[32] He
proposes an alternative non-dogmatic arrangement of the texts on the basis
of the interests protected. Diliberto applied the methodology first suggested
and tried by Bona[33] to the *Noctes Attici*,[34] but the development of a theory
for an alternative sequence of the verses is fraught with disappointments, as
was illustrated by the attempt of Agnati[35] to test the application of the law of
Lindsay against the rhetorical tradition in the form of Cicero, *De inventione*
and the *Rhetorica ad Herennium* in respect of the position of the *furiosus* text
in Table 5.[36]

---

[26] Humbert (2005), pp. 49–50.

[27] Humbert (2005), p. 22.

[28] Humbert (2005), pp. 24–5. Thus, the Twelve Tables bear resemblance to the edict of the
praetor, namely a catalogue of legal remedies. See also Talamanca (2005), pp. 331–75.

[29] For the reconstructions since 1515 and a critical analysis thereof: Ferrary (2005), pp. 503–56.

[30] Diliberto (2005), pp. 217–38.

[31] Cic. *Leg.* 2.23.59 and 2.25.64 (*in ius vocatio* and funerals); Fest. *s.v. reus* (*dies diffusus*); Dion.
Hal. 2.27.3 (*si pater*); Ulpian. D.38.6.1pr (testamentary succession before intestate); and fragments of the commentaries of Labeo and Gaius on the Twelve Tables. The first are found
in Gell. *N.A.* 1.12.18 (the vestals), 6.15.1 (*furtum*), 20.1.12–13 (*iniuria*), and the second in the
Digest: see Lenel (1889), pp. 242–6.

[32] Namely, the protection of land, the most important means of production in the economy of
Antiquity. Diliberto (2005), pp. 225–9.

[33] Bona (1990), p. 392, where he proposed application of the so-called law of Lindsay: Lindsay
(1901), *passim*; Marcellus cited passages from earlier authors in the order of the original
work. The application followed in Bona (1992), pp. 211–28.

[34] Diliberto, 'Contributo' (1992), pp. 229–77; Diliberto, *Materiali* (1992); Diliberto (2005),
pp. 229–35. In these publications, Diliberto illustrates how a number of texts could be re-
assigned to different tables.

[35] Agnati (2005), pp. 239–64.

[36] No indications were found that the authors in question adhered to a fixed system in respect
of their citations. The author explains this on the basis of the nature of the works and the use
of the texts for the purpose of examples in forensic argumentation rather than lexicography
or similar enterprises. More success was achieved by de Francesco (2005), pp. 415–40. In this
contribution, fragments from Hor. (*Sat.* 1.9.74–78), Plaut. (*Cur.* 5.2.620–625) and Ter. (*Phor.*
980–996) are analysed with the objective to relate the *actio iniuriarum* and the *in ius vocatio*.
In terms of this analysis, *iniuria* and *furtum* are repositioned into the beginning of the code as

The theory of aspect which holds that the perspective from which an event is approached to a large degree determines its importance and meaning is cor‑ roborated by the different socio‑economic interpretations. Several authors have described how the picture of Roman society during the fifth century BCE has been blurred by later sources, starting with Polybius' *Historiae* and Cicero's *De re publica*, which projected the problems of their own time – for example, land reform – or political theories back into reconstructions of the events revolving around the codification.[37] Thus the desire to illustrate an evolutionary model coupled with the desire to actualise the past as well as the unavoidability of anachronisms all play a role in the theory of aspect.

Dieter Nörr[38] delved into his encyclopaedic knowledge to depict another view, which replaces the traditional description of Rome of the Twelve Tables as the market town of an isolated group of primitive agrarians, with an inter‑ pretation integrating pre‑Twelve‑Tables Rome into a Mediterranean world of shipping and commerce. The first treaty between Carthage and Rome[39] indicates that the Romans also participated in international relations.[40] Nörr analyses this treaty and proposes that Rome of the Twelve Tables was already a maritime power and opts for a Rome with ships and international traders, a commercial centre, placed by him in a wide historical context.

Such a socio‑economic landscape inevitably leads to new interpretations of the Twelve Tables. David Kremer[41] argues that the *foedus Cassianum*[42] granted reciprocal *commercium*[43] to citizens of the signatories. This would permit foreigners to participate in *negotia per aes et libram*, to acquire owner‑ ship *ex iure Quiritium*, and access to the *legis actiones*.[44] In terms of the *foedus Cassianum*, contractual litigation was to be conducted, and concluded within ten days, in the city where the contract had been entered into.[45] Thus, the *decemviri* were obliged to take this provision of the treaty into account, which resulted in the redaction of verses 2.2 and 6.4. Litigation with a *hostis*[46] received priority in terms of verse 2.2, which introduced an *excusatio* for a Roman party and/or judge.[47] Verse 6.4 is another consequence of the *foedus*

---

the communal criterion is self‑help and the application of the *actio iniuriarum* in cases where such self‑help exceeded the boundaries of what was allowed.

[37] Gabba (2005), pp. 117–24; Garrasco Garcia (2005), p. 125–45.

[38] Nörr (2005), pp. 147–89.

[39] Dated by Polybius in the first year of the republic: Polyb. *Hist.* 3. 21–7; Nörr (2005), *passim*.

[40] Ziegler (2002), pp. 55–67.

[41] Kremer (2005), pp. 191–207.

[42] The treaty concluded in 493 between Rome and the twenty‑nine cities of the Latin league; Kremer (2005), p. 192.

[43] Liv. *Hist.* 8.14.10; Kremer (2005), pp. 193–6.

[44] Kremer (2005), p. 193.

[45] Dion. Hal. 6.95.2. Kremer (2005), pp. 196–7.

[46] A foreigner *pari iure cum populo romano*. Cic. *Off.* 1.37 and Fest. *s. v. status dies*; Kremer (2005), pp. 191, 205.

[47] Kremer (2005), pp. 197–203.

Cassianum, namely the granting of the duty of legal assistance for a period without defined limit.[48] This matter is also addressed by Michel Humbert in his discussion of the homogeneity of *usus* in the codification.[49] He offers a coherent and convincing hypothesis[50] restricting the meaning of *usus* in the code to the exercise of the right of ownership or *patria potestas* and to be distinguished from *usucapio*.[51] Humbert argues that *usus* and *auctoritas*, the obligation placed by the *mancipatio* on the transferor to assist the recipient against a *reivindicatio*, are inextricably linked.[52] Thus *aeterna auctoritas* is a non-defined period during which the obligation to provide assistance rests on the *mancipio dans* where the transferee had been a foreigner with *commercium*.[53] Selling by *mancipatio* to a foreigner incurred the duty to provide legal assistance for an unknown period, whether in Tibur, Rome or Praeneste, or wherever the buyer is threatened with eviction. This is the logical consequence of international trade and the treaties accommodating the same by extension of *commercium*. However, the reciprocity provided for in the *foedus Cassianum* gave the Roman citizen who had bought a slave in Tibur *dominium ex iure Quiritium* in Rome.[54]

Although our present knowledge is built upon the results of our predecessors, the theory of aspect encourages revisiting old sights from a different angle and explains why the demise of religion, the fall of communism and the advent of globalisation may change our views on Rome anno 450 BCE. The second application of the theory of aspect relates to some well known texts

---

[48] Kremer suggests that the Roman legislator was unaware whether *usus* would exist in the foreigner's legal system and if so, what the duration thereof would be. Verse 6.4 serves the interests of the foreign buyer with *commercium*, who acquires a *res mancipi* object in Rome and has taken his purchase home, in other words outside Roman territory. Whenever this object is brought back into Roman territory, the possibility of a *rei vindicatio* must be taken into consideration. In terms of the *foedus Cassianum*, the Roman judge will have jurisdiction and the seller will have to provide his assistance in the proceedings irrespective of the question of how much time has expired since the *mancipatio*. Kremer (2005), pp. 203–6.

[49] M Humbert, 'Il valore semantico' (2005), pp. 377–400. *Usus* appears in XII Tab. 6.3, 6.4, 8.17, 7.4, 10.10, and 6.5.

[50] Other theories can be found in the text and notes of Humbert's article.

[51] *Usucapio* was developed from *usus* at a much later stage by way of an audacious interpretation by the old jurists. Humbert (2005), p. 387.

[52] Humbert (2005), pp. 378–88.

[53] Humbert proposes that *commercium* implied that the Roman judge had to take foreign law into account. He compares *commercium* to *conubium* and gives the example of a citizen of Tibur who marries a Roman woman. This union is subject to the law of Tibur and recognised by Roman law. On Roman soil, a Roman judge will apply the law of Tibur to the offspring of this union, which law may well be different from Roman law. Humbert (2005), pp. 394–7.

[54] Humbert's theory in respect of *mancipatio*, *usus* and *auctoritas* falls outside the scope of this essay, but it suffices to mention that Humbert's interpretation of verses 6.3, 7.4, 10.10, 6.5 and 8.17 are clear and logical, follow the text and appear to fit into the new context better than most alternative interpretations.

from the *Corpus Iuris Civilis*. Included for dogmatic reasons and interpreted as such, an interpretation from a different perspective – namely, the world of usury – is proposed.

5. SAINT AMBROSE AND THE THEORY OF ASPECT

The texts to be discussed are D.12.1.11pr,[55] D.19.5.19pr,[56] D.17.1.34pr,[57]

---

[55] 'Ulpianus libro vicensimo sexto ad edictum. Rogasti me, ut tibi pecuniam crederem: ego cum non haberem, lancem tibi dedi vel massam auri, ut eam venderes et nummis utereris. Si vendideris, puto mutuam pecuniam factam. Quod si lancem vel massam sine tua culpa perdideris prius quam venderes, utrum mihi an tibi perierit, quaestionis est. mihi videtur Nervae distinctio verissima existimantis multum interesse, venalem habui hanc lancem vel massam nec ne, ut, si venalem habui, mihi perierit, quemadmodum si alii dedissem vendendam: quod si non fui proposito hoc ut venderem, sed haec causa fuit vendendi, ut tu utereris, tibi eam perisse, et maxime si sine usuris credidi' (Ulpian in his twenty-sixth book of his commentary on the Edict. You asked me to lend you money; because I had no money I gave you a dish or a piece of gold so you could sell this and use the money. If you sold it, I think that the money made is owed as a loan. What is the position if the dish or the lump of gold was lost without your fault before you sold it, does the loss fall upon me or upon you. It is my opinion that the distinction made by Nerva is perfectly correct, namely that the point of importance is whether I had the dish or the lump of gold for sale or not. If I had had it for sale, the loss is mine in the same manner as if I had given it to someone else to sell; but if it has not been my intention to sell it, but the only reason of the sale was that you might use the proceeds, you must carry the loss, especially if I lent the money to you interest free).

[56] 'Ulpianus libro trigesimo primo ad edictum. Rogasti me ut tibi nummos mutuos darem: ego cum non haberem, dedi tibi rem vendendam, ut pretio utereris. Si non vendidisti aut vendidisti quidem, pecuniam autem non accepisti, tutius est ita agere, ut Labeo ait, praescriptis verbis, quasi negotio quodam inter nos gesto proprii contractus' (Ulpian in the thirty-first book of his commentary on the Edict. You asked me to lend you money: because I did not have any, I gave you a thing to sell so that you could use the price. If you did not sell it or sold it but did not accept the money as a loan, it is safer to proceed, as Labeo held, with the *actio praescriptis verbis* as if whatever transaction performed between us had been a special contract).

[57] 'Africanus libro octavo quaestionum. Qui negotia Lucii Titii procurabat, is, cum a debitoribus eius pecuniam exegisset, epistulam ad eum emisit, qua significaret certam summam ex administratione apud se esse eamque creditam sibi se debiturum eum usuris semissibus: quaesitum est, an ex ea causa credita pecunia peti possit et an usurae peti possint. respondit non esse creditam: alioquin dicendum ex omni contractu nuda pactione creditam creditam fieri posse. nec huic simile esse, quod, si pecuniam apud te depositam convenerit ut creditam habeas, credita fiat, quia tunc nummi, qui mei erant, tui fiunt: item quod, si a debitore meo iussero te accipere pecuniam, credita fiat, id enim benigne receptum est. his argumentum esse eum, qui, cum mutuam pecuniam dare vellet, argentum vendendum dedisset, nihilomagis pecuniam creditam recte petiturum: et tamen pecuniam ex argento redactam periculo eius fore, qui accepisset argentum' (Africanus in the eighth book of his Questions. When the procurator of Lucius Titius had collected money from the debtors, he sent him a letter informing him that he held a certain sum in terms of his administration and that if this was lent to him he would pay six percent interest. It was asked whether from such cause the money could be claimed as lent and whether the interest could be claimed. He (Julianus) opined that the money was not lent, because otherwise it could be said that money from any contract could be made into a loan by mere agreement. And this was not similar to the case

C.4.2.8,[58] and C.4.32.25.[59] The last two texts lead[60] to Saint Ambrose's *De Tobia*, sermons on the story of Tobia, directed against usury.[61]

The facts in the Digest texts are briefly that A asked B for a loan of money, but B had no money. Instead, B gave A a valuable object to sell so he could use the money from the sale. The legal questions under discussion revolved

---

where money was lent if it had been agreed that you could borrow the money deposited with you, because in that instance the coins which were mine, became yours. The same applies in the case where money was lent, if I instruct you to receive money from my debtor, because that has been accepted benevolently. For these the argument is that he, who has given silver to sell when he wanted to lend money, would neither be correct in claiming for money owed; although the money realised from the sale of the silver will be at the risk of him who accepted the silver). The words *his argumentum esse* are rather inconclusive and therefore confusing. The Watson translation reads '[He went on to say that] from these [remarks] it could be argued that a man who, wishing to give money as a loan for consumption, had given silver to be sold would not, for all that, be right to claim the money as lent'. Compare the German translation (by C. Krampe): 'Dafür diene als Argument, dass ebenso wenig derjenige zu Recht die Darlehensklage erhebe, der ein Gelddarlehen gewähren wollte und dem Empfänger Silber zum Verkauf gegeben hat'.

58 'Impp. Diocletianus et Maximianus AA. et CC. Proculo. Si pro mutua pecunia, quam a creditore poscebas, argentum vel iumenta vel alias species utriusque consensu aestimatas accepisti, dato auro pignori, licet ultra unam centesimam usuras stipulanti spopondisti, tamen sors, quae aestimatione partium placito definita est, et usurarum titulo legitima tantum recte petitur. Nec quicquam tibi prodesse potest, quod minoris esse pretii pignus quod dedisti proponis, quominus huius quantitatis solutioni pareas' (Emperors Diocletianus and Maximianus to Proculus. If instead of the loan of money, which you asked from the creditor, you did accept silver or beasts of burden or other specific things the estimated value of which had been agreed upon by both of you, gold having been given in pledge, even though you promised the stipulator interest exceeding twelve per cent, nonetheless only the principal which was determined by the agreement of the parties, and as interest only the interest allowed by law can be claimed. And the fact that you declare that the pledge you gave was of lower value, cannot help you at all to avoid obeying the demand for payment of this amount).

59 'Imp Constantinus A ad populum. Pro auro et argento et veste facto chirographo licitas solvi vel promitti usuras iussimus' (Emperor Constantine to the people. We have decreed that lawful interest be paid or promised on gold and silver and cloth owed in terms of a debt contained in a document).

60 Via the intercession of Noodt (1735), p. 178.

61 'Caput III. *Ambrosius feneratorum inhumanitatem in pauperes, et eorum artes quibus illos sibi addicunt, oculia subjicit; ac demum in eosdem invehitur.* 10. At ubi usurarum mentio facta fuerit, aut pignoris, tunc dejecto supercilio fenerator arridet, et quem ante sibi cognitum denegebat, eundem tanquam paternam amicitiam recordatus osculo excipit, haereditariae pignus charitatis appellat, flere prohibet. Quaeremus, inquit, domi si quid nobis pecuniae est, frangam propter te argentum paternum quod fabrefactum est, plurimum damni erit: quae usurae compensabunt emblematum? Sed pro amico dispendium non reformidabo, cum reddideris, reficiam. Itaque antequam det, recipere festinat et qui in summa subvenire se dicit, usuras exigit. Kalendis, inquit, usuras dabis: fenus interim, si non habueris unde restituas, non requiro. Ita semet det, frequenter exagitat, et semper sibi debere efficit. Hac arte tractat virum. Itaque prius eum chirographis ligat, et astringit vocis suae nexibus. Numeratur pecunia, addicitur libertas, absolvitur miser minore debito, majore ligatur' (But when interest was mentioned, or pledge, the moneylender smiles with down-cast eye-brows, and with

around risk, in respect of the object prior to the sale, or the risk of the money after the sale, or how to get the object or the money back when A did not sell or use the money. The answer depends on the question of which contract or contracts the parties had concluded, but since this was never directly asked, the texts are silent on this point. The questions addressed to the imperial chancery in C.4.2.8 were different,[62] and indicate the context and purpose of such transactions. At last, a room with a view is offered by Saint Ambrose. His text clearly illustrates that moneylenders were in actual fact delivering goods rather than cash to their clients. It may be argued that his words are not completely logical, since the obvious translation of 'Sed pro amico dispendium non reformidabo, cum reddideris, reficiam' is 'But for a friend, I shall not shirk the loss, when you return it, I shall repair it', which is not congruent with the fact that the debtor is to sell the object. However, the translation 'For a friend I will shun the loss, when you pay me back, I will make it back' may be open to philological debate, but is supported by the legal texts and reveals a stratagem to avoid the limits on lawful interest.[63]

6. HELPING A FRIEND?

At first glance the facts relate to two friends, and it is indeed this benevolent interpretation that has prevailed. It does not surprise that during the Middle Ages Vivianus sidestepped explanations on usury,[64] but it is a show of strength of the legal tradition that friendship continues to be mentioned in the interpretations of Koschaker,[65] Kaser[66] and Zimmermann.[67] This raises

---

a kiss welcomes the same man, whom he previously denied knowing, as if remembering a family friendship and invokes the pledge of hereditary affection, and tells him not to weep. We shall see, he says, whether we have any money at home; for you I shall break the beautifully made family silver: the loss will be very great. What interest will compensate the value of the ornaments? But for a friend, I shall not shun the loss, when you pay me back, I shall have it repaired. Thus before he gives, he hastens to take back: and he who says that he is helping in the matter of a sum of money, demands interest. On the first of the month, he says, you shall pay interest: in the meantime I do not seek the principal, if you do not have the means to pay back. Thus he gives once, but demands frequently, and always manages that he is owed money. In this way he plays the man. Thus before he binds him with IOUs, he ties him down with his voice. Money is paid, liberty is enslaved, the wretch is released of a small debt and bound for a bigger one).

[62] The questions posed revolved around the quantum of both principal and interest, which becomes clear from the opinion 'tamen sors, quae aestimatione partium placito definita est, et usurarum titulo legitima tantum recte petitur'.

[63] Thomas (2012), pp. 101–12.

[64] Vivianus, *Casus* on *Rogasti me* (D.12.1.11pr) Eram amicus tuus. Gloss *Si quis nec causam* ad D.12.1.4pr Vel amicitia eum esse motum ad mutuandum. For usury during the Middle Ages: Piron (2005), p. 73–101.

[65] Koschaker (1923), p. X.

[66] Kaser (1964), pp. 77–8.

[67] Zimmermann (1990), p. 162.

the question why the case of two 'friends', who do not have cash but are engaged in moneylending, keeps making the law reports.[68]

7. RISK AND TRANSFORMATION OF CONTRACT

The question concerning the risk and transformation of a contract had been addressed by Ulpian in D.12.1.4pr.[69] In this case money was given in deposit with the arrangement that it could be used and the effect of this arrangement on the allocation of risk was discussed.[70] Even prior to use, the deposit was held to be at the risk of the receiver, which deviation from the normal risk rule Ulpian motivated with the analogy that he who has received a thing to sell in order to use the money, holds the object at his own risk. However, in D.12.1.9.9[71] and D.12.1.10,[72] similar situations were addressed along different lines. In the first text, a straightforward deposit is transformed in what

---

[68] 'Law reports' is used tongue in cheek. However, from the days of Labeo (ob. c. 10 CE; referred to by Ulpian in D.19.5.19pr), Nerva (either father (ob. 33 CE) or son (*praetor* designate 65 CE); referred to by Ulpian in D.12.1.11pr until Ulpian (c 170–223 CE; D.12.11.1pr and D.19.5.19pr) these 'friends' were consulting jurists, whose opinions were in writing and saved. C.4.2.8 dates from 293 CE.

[69] 'Ulpianus libro trigensimo quarto ad Sabinum. Si quis nec causam nec propositum faenerandi habuerit et tu empturus praedia desideraveris mutuam pecuniam nec volueris creditae nomine antequam emisses suscipere atque ita creditor, quia necessitate forte proficiscendi habebat, deposuerit apud te hanc eandem pecuniam, ut, si emisses, crediti nomine obligatus esses, hoc depositum periculo est eius qui suscepit. Nam et qui rem vendendam acceperit, ut pretio uteretur, periculo suo rem habebit' (Ulpian in his thirty-fourth book of his commentary on Sabinus. In the case of a person who has no reason or made no proposal to lend out money at interest, and you who are on the point of buying land and are desirous to borrow money; but you do not want to owe this money before you have bought the property; in consequence, the creditor, who may have an urgent reason to leave, has deposited that money with you, with the arrangement that, if you should buy, you will be liable for the credit. This deposit is at the risk of the party who received it. Because anyone who has received an object in order to sell it so he can use the purchase price, holds that object at his own risk).

[70] Thomas (2012) (forthcoming).

[71] D.12.1.9 Ulpianus libro vicensimo sexto ad edictum: 'Deposui apud te decem, postea permisi tibi uti: Nerva Proculus etiam antequam moveantur, condicere quasi mutua tibi haec posse aiunt, et est verum, ut et Marcello videtur: animo enim coepit possidere. Ergo transit periculum ad eum, qui mutuam rogavit et poterit ei condici' (Ulpian in the twenty-sixth book of his commentary on the edict. I deposited ten with you, and later I allowed you to use the money; Nerva and Proculus hold that I can claim the money with a *condictio* from you, even before it was used, as if it had been lent. And this is correct and Marcellus is of the same opinion; because you had already become the possessor with your intention, in your mind. Therefore the risk passes on him, who asked for the loan, and the *condictio* lays against him).

[72] D.12.1.10 Ulpianus libro secundo ad edictum: 'Quod si ab initio, cum deponerem, uti tibi si voles permisero, creditam non esse antequam mota sit, quoniam debitu iri non est certum' (Ulpian in his second book of his commentary on the edict 10. If I allowed you from the beginning when I deposited the money with you to use it, if you wanted to, the money is not owed before the money is used, because it is not certain that anything will be owed).

later would become known as a *depositum irregulare*.[73] Ulpian follows Nerva
and Proculus who held that the *condictio*[74] became available as soon as the
parties agreed that the deposited money could be used. Thus, before usage
the contractual relationship between the parties changed from *depositum*
into *mutuum*. Marcellus held the same opinion and motivated this with the
argument that he who held the money had already become possessor *animo*.
In the following text, Ulpian holds that if the depositor had allowed use of
the money from the beginning, the money only becomes owed in terms of
mutuum, once it has been used, arguing that it is not certain whether it will
be owed. Why this argument was not applied in the previous text and in
D.12.1.4pr is not made clear. Furthermore, in D.12.11.1pr, Ulpian on the
authority of Nerva introduced the distinction whether the object had been
for sale or not.[75] Another inconsistency is found where his opinion that
if the object is sold, the money made is owed as a loan[76] was changed in
D.19.5.19pr.

8. TWENTIETH-CENTURY ROMAN LAW

Sohm-Mitteis-Wenger[77] considered the so-called *contractus mohatrae*[78]
another relaxation of the direct transfer requirement.[79] Kaser[80] confined
himself in his textbook to stating that D.12.1.11pr shows that since Nerva
these facts[81] were considered to be *mutuum*. In *Synteleia Vicenzo Arangio-
Ruiz*,[82] he analysed an essay by Koschaker[83] and rejected the earlier interpretation as well as the older secondary sources on this topic on account
of the interpolation method employed. In his essay, Kaser suggests that the
recognition of *mutuum* in the circumstances described in D.12.1.11pr was

---

[73] Recognised by Justinian; named by Jason de Mayno. Zimmermann (1990), pp. 218–19.
[74] The action from *mutuum*.
[75] '(V)enalem habui hanc lancem vel massam nec ne, ut, si venalem habui, mihi perierit,
      quemadmodum si alii dedissem vendendam: quod si non fui proposito hoc ut venderem, sed
      haec causa fuit vendendi, ut tu utereris, tibi eam perisse, et maxime si sine usuris credidi'.
[76] Si vendideris, puto mutuam pecuniam factam.
[77] Sohm, Mitteis and Wenger (1926), p. 392.
[78] A misnomer, this term was coined during the fourteenth century, derived from the Arabic
      mohatra, and involved a sale with immediate delivery and resale at a future higher price
      with concomitant delivery, in order to evade the prohibition of usury. Kaser (1964), p. 75;
      Zimmermann (1990), p. 163; al-Mujahid (2008).
[79] Comparable to D.12.1.15. In the same vein: van Oven (1948), p. 229; Spruit (2003), p. 322–3.
      The authors do not indicate at what moment *mutuum* is concluded, and remain silent on the
      quantum of the amount due.
[80] Kaser (1971), p. 531.
[81] A asked B for a loan of money. B had no money, but gave him a valuable object to sell and
      use the money from the sale. Ulpian was of the opinion that if the object was sold, the money
      was owed on the basis of a loan of consumption.
[82] Kaser (1964), pp. 74–83.
[83] Koschaker (1923), IX-XI.

not unanimous,[84] and considers Nerva's solution of the risk-allocation representative of the proper classical interest theory.[85] He considered C.4.2.8 a step forward because an action[86] became immediately available, which represented an extension of recognition of indirect provision of money in *mutuum*.[87] Zimmermann[88] follows Kaser and discusses D.12.1.11pr and C.4.2.8 as steps within the evolution towards a consensual loan for consumption. Without derogating the value of this approach, this essay argues in favour of viewing these texts from another perspective, *in casu* the world of usurious moneylending.

9. COMMON PRACTICE

The first striking fact is that the practice of giving a thing to sell when asked for a loan of money was well known among jurists. D.19.5.19pr dates from the early Empire and Labeo is not surprised at the facts, but could not place a label on the legal construct. He accepted that some type of contract had been entered into and presumably advised to proceed with an *actio in factum*.[89] Ulpian concurred with this argument and neither jurist distinguished whether the object had been sold or not.[90] In D.17.1.34pr, Africanus relies on his mentor Julianus[91] to confirm that a loan of money cannot be concluded by mere agreement.[92] In the motivation, a distinction is made between this case and other instances in which the requirement of delivery had been relaxed, such as the agreement that deposited money could be borrowed,[93] or the instruction to receive money from another's debtor.[94]

---

[84] Kaser (1964), pp. 75 fn. 4 and 80 fn. 25.

[85] Kaser (1964), p. 81: 'Und Nerva fand dieses (ein Kriterium) darin, ob der Verkauf im Interesse auch des Gebers lag, weil er die Sache ohnehin verkaufen wollte, oder ausschliesslich in dem des kredit-suchenden Nehmers. [. . .] Diese Unterscheidung [. . .] beruht auf gut klassischer Interessenabwägung'.

[86] Kaser (1964), p. 82, holds that the principal determined by the valuation by the parties can be claimed 'mit der Klage aus dem Darlehen'; in fn. 33 he adds 'Allenfalls aus Stipulation'. Zimmermann (1990), p. 162.

[87] Kaser (1964), p. 82.

[88] Zimmermann (1990), pp. 160–3. D.12.1.15 and 12.1.11pr are viewed as precursors to C.4.2.8.

[89] Kaser (1964), p. 79; Kaser (1971), pp. 486, 580–3. There is controversy whether the *actio praescriptis verbis* was available in classical law. Van Oven (1948), pp. 296–302; Zimmermann (1990), p. 534.

[90] The borrower had either not sold the object 'lent' to him or had not, after selling the thing, accepted the money realised by the sale as a loan. The legal question was thus how to get back the object or the price thereof.

[91] In c 110–c 170 CE.

[92] A procurator asked his principal in a letter whether he could borrow the money collected for the latter.

[93] Cf. D.12.1.9.9.

[94] Cf. D.12.1.15 and D.24.1.3.12 and 13.

The moneylender who gave silver instead of money was also mentioned and neither jurist considered the possibility of *mutuum* even after the sale, but agreed that the risk was on the 'borrower'.

10. C.4.2.8: ESTIMATED VALUE

This rescript imparts important information: prior to delivery of the object the parties had agreed upon its value, the borrower had delivered gold in pledge, and the lender had stipulated interest of more than 12 per cent. The imperial chancery was of the opinion that the debtor owed the estimated value of the objects as principal and 12 per cent interest on this amount.

The salient fact that the parties had placed an estimated value on the object, which amount would be claimable, has been hailed as an important step within legal development. It is submitted that it is difficult to visualise the transaction under discussion without such valuation, because in that case the lender would be at the mercy of the borrower. The latter would be in the position to sell below the value and would only be liable for the realised price.[95] In reality, the borrower is at the mercy of the lender, and the text indicates that the petitioner objected to both the amount of the principal[96] and the rate of interest. The petitioner's argument that the pledged gold was worth less than the estimated value of the delivered object may be an indication that the estimate exceeded the proceeds. The construct reeks of usury, as the borrower is indebted for much more than he actually received and pays 12 per cent on this fictitious amount. Viewed from this perspective, a meaningful interpretation of C.4.32.25 becomes possible.[97]

---

[95] To believe that valuation of the object represents a later development is naive. Omission to place an estimated value on the object from the start would leave the lender at the mercy of the borrower. The latter could and would offer the object at a bargain price to realise a quick sale and get his hands on some money. Moreover, he would only be liable to repay the amount realised by the sale.

[96] There is no indication how much the borrower actually received as price for the borrowed objects.

[97] C.4.32.25 Imp. Constantinus A. ad populum: 'Pro auro et argento et veste facto chirographo licitas solvi vel promitti usuras iussimus' (Emperor Constantine to the people: 'We have decreed that lawful interest be paid or promised on gold and silver and cloth owed in terms of a debt contained in a document'). This constitution addresses two points of law. First, whether interest only applies to money, and then the amount of interest payable when instead of money, objects have been given to the debtor. The emperor decreed that lawful interest, that is 12 per cent per year, may be paid or promised on the basis of the valuation of the goods. The constitution requires that a document is drawn up and it is obvious that the valuation had to be made before or when the IOU was drafted. The widespread belief that interest relates only to money was also addressed in C. 4.32.23 and 4.32.11.(12). Also Saint Hieronymus (c 340–420 CE) *Ezekiel*, 6.8.206; Noodt (1735), pp. 177–80.

11. CONCLUSION

It is probable that the texts under discussion were included in the Digest for dogmatic reasons, for example the relationship between the utility principle and the allocation of risk, and drawing the boundaries for *traditio ficta*.[98] It is, however, remarkable that the classical Roman jurists did not address the doctrinal question whether the handing over of the object established a contract and if so, which contract or contracts. There appears to be a wide variety of choice, such as a conditional or unconditional *mutuum*,[99] or *precarium*[100] or *mandatum*[101] or *aestimatum*[102] or *do ut facias*,[103] which was changed into *mutuum*, if and when the dish was sold. The Codex texts indicate that in post-classical law, the described relationship between the usurer and his client was classified under *mutuum*, but the *responsa* show the wide variety of Roman casuistry. It is submitted that a change of perspective gives insight into the original function of the opinions, in other words law in action as opposed to law in the books. These texts dealt with an age-old practice of avoidance of interest limits. When the client approached the moneylender, the latter pretended not to have cash available. Instead of money, one or more objects were offered with the arrangement that the debtor should sell the goods and use the price realised as a loan. Before delivery of the object, an estimated value was agreed upon. Thus, from the beginning, valuation of the object was an integral part of the transaction and the 'borrower' was liable to repay the amount agreed upon and not the price he received as the result of the sale. In this manner usurious interest could be realised. If an object was valued at one 100, the principal was 100. Twelve per cent interest was calculated. The object was sold for seventy-five. After one year, the debtor owed 112, of which in reality thirty-seven was interest, which is nearly 50 per cent of the seventy-five he had received.

In this essay, Barzun's theory was applied to widely diverging topics. The essence of his idea that the topic of research appears like a mountain in front of the researcher is an *a posteriori*. His assertion that the researcher takes a few of the faces for the whole is hard to contest, but the explanation of such partiality as spontaneous choice exaggerates freedom of the individual. This theory promotes diversity of opinion and stimulates a new look at many texts, and an excellent example is found in the project of Nikolaus Benke at the University of Vienna, which approaches texts from

---

[98] See, for example, the interpretation by Voet (1731), 12.1.4, 5 and 6.

[99] A loan for consumption subject to the suspensive condition that the object is sold (within a certain time); an unconditional loan for consumption would be a possibility if the handing over of the object were to be accepted as a *datio in solutum*.

[100] D.43.26.2.2; D.43.26.14; and D.43.26.19.2.

[101] Inst.Gai.3.155–6; D 17.1.2 *passim*; Inst 3.26.pr.–6. Kaser (1964), pp. 77 and 79.

[102] Kaser (1964), pp. 79–80, in particular p. 80 fn. 22.

[103] Accursius in gloss *Si vendideris* ad D.12.1.11pr.

the perspective of gender. However, in spite of the promise 'In my Father's house are many rooms',[104] the study of law herds most students into the same room,[105] while anonymous peer review discourages coming out of this room. Furthermore, every person remains a product of his upbringing, education and time. However, the argument that it will be difficult if not impossible to ascertain from which perspective a Roman law text or texts should be approached can be rebutted with the *replicatio* that although these texts have been exclusively studied from a dogmatic point of view, it is common ground that they were never written for that purpose. Thus, a third life of Roman law as a methodological and philosophical instrument in legal education could promote independent and nuanced thought. This may be considered irrelevant in today's age, but to paraphrase the doyen of Romanists, Hans Ankum: you never know what will be considered useful in a 100 years.[106] The final words of this essay come from the same *maestro*, whose answer to the question concerning the relevance of Roman law is: to learn to think.[107]

BIBLIOGRAPHY

Agnati, U., 'Sequenze decemvirali. Analisi di Cicerone *De Inventione* 2. 148 e *Rhetorica ad Herrenium* 1. 23', in M. Humbert (ed.), *Le Dodici Tavole: Dai Decemviri agli Umanisti* (2005), p. 239.

Barzun, J., *From Dawn to Decadence. 500 Years of Western Cultural Life 1500 to the Present* (2000).

Becker, C., *Die Lehre von der laesio enormis in der Sicht der heutigen Wucherproblematik* (1993).

Bona, F., 'Intervento', *Index*, 18 (1990), p. 392.

Bona, F., 'Il "de verborum significatu" di Festo e le XII Tavole. I. Gli "auctores" di Verrio Flacco', *Index*, 20 (1992), p. 211.

Buckland, W. W., and Stein, P., *A Textbook of Roman law from Augustus to Justinian*, 3rd edn (1963).

de Francesco, A., 'Autodifesa privata e iniuria nelle Dodici Tavole', in M. Humbert (ed.), *Le Dodici Tavole: Dai Decemviri agli Umanisti* (2005), p. 415.

Diliberto, O., 'Contributo alla palingenesi delle XII Tavole. Le "sequenze" nei testi gelliani', *Index*, 20 (1992), p. 229.

Diliberto, O., *Materiali per la palingenesi delle XII Tavole*, vol. I (1992).

Diliberto, O., 'Una palingenesi "aperta"', in M. Humbert (ed.), *Le Dodici Tavole: Dai Decemviri agli Umanisti* (2005), p. 217.

---

[104] John, 14:2.
[105] Kennedy (1982), pp. 38–58.
[106] Van Rhee and Winkel (2010), p. 167: 'Je weet nooit wat er over honderd jaar nuttig wordt gevonden. Dat vind ik ook zo gevaarlijk met dat nut'.
[107] Van Rhee and Winkel (2010), p. 164: 'Als je mij vraagt wat de relevantie is van het Romeinse recht, dan zou ik zeggen: leren denken'.

Doll, R., *An Interpretation of E. M. Forster's A Room with a View*, at www.emforster. info/pages/roomview.html (last accessed 3 January 2012).

Du Plessis, P., 'Legal history and method(s)', in R. Van den Bergh and G. van Niekerk (eds), *Libellus ad Thomasium: Essays in Roman Law, Roman-Dutch Law and Legal History in honour of Philip J. Thomas* (2010), p. 64.

Ferrary, J.-L., 'Saggio di storia della palingenesi della Dodici Tavole', in M. Humbert (ed.), *Le Dodici Tavole: Dai Decemviri agli Umanisti* (2005), p. 503.

Forster E. M., *A Room with a View*, 1st edn (1908).

Gabba, E., 'Proposta per un quadro storico di Roma nel V sec. a. C.', in M. Humbert (ed.), *Le Dodici Tavole: Dai Decemviri agli Umanisti* (2005), p. 117.

Garrasco Garcia, C., 'Res publica come costituzione mista e decemvirati; Polibio e Cicerone', in M. Humbert (ed.), *Le Dodici Tavole: Dai Decemviri agli Umanisti* (2005), p. 125.

Heirbaut, D., 'Comparative law and Zimmermann's new ius commune: a life line or death sentence for legal history? Some reflections on the use of legal history for comparative law and vice versa', in R. van den Bergh et al. (eds), *Ex Iusta Causa Traditum: Essays in Honour of Eric H. Pool* (2005), p. 136.

Hermesdorf, B. H. D., *Schets der uitwendige geschiedenis van het Romeins recht*, 7th edn (1972).

Hoetink, H. R., *Rechtsgeleerde Opstellen* (1982).

Hoffmeier, M. H., *Eduard Gans and the Hegelian Philosophy of Law* (1995).

Humbert, M. (ed.), *Le Dodici Tavole: Dai Decemviri agli Umanisti* (2005).

Humbert, M., 'Il valore semantico e giuridico di *usus* nelle Dodici Tavole', in M. Humbert (ed.), *Le Dodici Tavole: Dai Decemviri agli Umanisti* (2005), p. 377.

Humbert, M., 'La codificazione decemvirale tentativo d'interpretazione', in M. Humbert (ed.), *Le Dodici Tavole: Dai Decemviri agli Umanisti* (2005), p. 4.

Jolowicz, H. F., *Historical Introduction to the Study of Roman Law*, 2nd edn (1952).

Kaser, M., 'Die Verteilung der Gefahr beim sogenannten "Contractus mohatrae"', in A. Guarino and L. Labruna (eds), *Synteleia Vincenzo Arangio-Ruiz* (1964), p. 77.

Kaser, M., *Das römische Privatrecht* (1971).

Kennedy, D., 'Legal education as training for hierarchy', in D. Kairys (ed.), *The Politics of Law. A Progressive Critique* (1982), p. 54.

Koschaker, P., 'Die Verteilung der Gefahr beim sogenannten "contractus mohatrae"', *Gerichts-Zeitung, Sondernummer J. Schey* (1923).

Kremer, D., 'Trattato internazionale e legge delle Dodici Tavole', in M. Humbert (ed.), *Le Dodici Tavole: Dai Decemviri agli Umanisti* (2005), p. 191.

Kuhn, T. S., *The Structure of Scientific Revolutions* (1962).

Lenel, O., *Palingenesia Iuris Civilis*, vol. I (1889), p. 242.

Lindsay, W. M., *Nonius Marcellus' Dictionary of Republican Latin* (1901).

Lokin, J. A. H., and Zwalve, W. J., *Hoofdstukken uit de Europese Codificatie-geschiedenis*, 3rd edn (2006), p. 58–60.

Martyn, G., and Coppens, E. C., 'Het geschiedt zoals het geschiedt: Rechtshistorici uit de Lage Landen (10): Interview met Paul Nève', *Pro Memorie: Bijdragen tot de rechtsgeschiedenis der Nederlanden*, 10 (2008), Aflevering 1, p. 19.

al-Mujahid, M., 'In the shadows of Deuteronomy: approaches to interest and usury in Judaism and Christianity' (2008), at http:/www.ikhwanweb.com/article. php?id=15717 (accessed 7 February 2012).

Noodt, G., 'De foenore et usuris libri tres', in *Opera Omnia*, vol. I (1735).

Nörr, D., 'Osservazioni in tema di terminologia predecemvirale e di ius mercatorum mediterraneo: il primo trattato cartaginese-romano', in M. Humbert (ed.), *Le Dodici Tavole: Dai Decemviri agli Umanisti* (2005), p. 147.

Piron, S., 'Le devoir de gratitude: Émergence et vogue de la notion d'antidora au xiii siècle', in D. Quaglione et al. (eds), *Credito e usura fra teologia, diritto e amministrazione. Linguaggi a confronto (sec. XII–XVI). Convegno internazionale di Trento, 3–5 settembre 2001* (2005), p. 73.

Sohm, R., Mitteis, L., and Wenger, L., *Institutionen: Geschichte und System des römischen Privatrechts*, 17th edn (1926).

Söllner, A., *Römische Rechtsgeschichte, Eine Einführung* (1971).

Spruit, J. E., *Cunabula iuris: Elementen van het Romeinse privaatrecht* (2003).

Talamanca, M., 'Le Dodici Tavole ed i negozi obbligatori', in M. Humbert (ed.), *Le Dodici Tavole: Dai Decemviri agli Umanisti* (2005), p. 331.

Thomas, P. J., 'Fin de siècle of funksionele Romeinse reg?', *THRHR*, 60.2 (1997), p. 202.

Thomas, P. J., 'Alternative paradigm for Roman law', *RIDA*, 45 (1998), p. 647.

Thomas, P. J., 'A stratagem to avoid the limit on interest', *THRHR*, 75.1 (2012), p. 101.

Wubbe, F. B. J., 'Bei Max Kaser in Münster', in *Ius vigilantibus scriptum, Ausgewählte Schriften* (2003), p. 512.

Wubbe, F. B. J., 'Wozu römisches Recht?', in P. Pichonnaz (ed.), *Ius vigilantibus scriptum* (2003), p. 556.

van Oven, J. C., *Leerboek van Romeinsch Privaatrecht*, 3rd edn (1948).

van Rhee, C. H., and Winkel, L. C., 'Een Romeinsrechtelijke Coryfee, Rechtshistorici uit de Lage Landen (11): Interview met Hans Ankum', *Pro Memorie: Bijdragen tot de rechtsgeschiedenis der Nederlanden*, Jaargang 12 (2010), Aflevering 2, p. 163.

Voet, J., *Commentarius ad Pandectas*, vol. I (1731).

Ziegler, K.-H., 'Regeln für Handelsverkehr in Staatsverträgern des Altertums', *TvR*, 70 (2002), p. 55.

Zimmermann, R., *The Law of Obligations: Roman Foundations of the Civilian Tradition* (1990).

Index

EU representative:
Easy Access System Europe
Mustamäe tee 50, 10621 Tallinn, Estonia
Gpsr.requests@easproject.com

www.ingramcontent.com/pod-product-compliance
Lightning Source LLC
Chambersburg PA
CBHW061151220326
41599CB00025B/4439